Effective Financial Management in Public and Nonprofit Agencies, 2nd Edition

Effective Financial Management in Public and Nonprofit Agencies, 2nd Edition

A Practical and Integrative Approach

Jerome B. McKinney

Q

QUORUM BOOKS
Westport, Connecticut • London

Library of Congress Cataloging-in-Publication Data

McKinney, Jerome B.
    Effective financial management in public and nonprofit agencies :
a practical and integrative approach / Jerome B. McKinney.—2nd
ed.
      p.   cm.
    Includes bibliographical references (p.   ) and index.
    ISBN 0–89930–925–9 (alk. paper)
    1. Finance, Public.   2. Nonprofit organizations—Finance.
I. Title.
HJ197.M35   1995
658.15—dc20   94–16994

British Library Cataloguing in Publication Data is available.

Library of Congress Catalog Card Number: 94–16994
ISBN: 0–89930–925–9

First Published in 1995

Quorum Books, 88 Post Road West, Westport, CT 06881
An imprint of Greenwood Publishing Group, Inc.

Printed in the United States of America

The paper used in this book complies with the
Permanent Paper Standard issued by the National
Information Standards Organization (Z39.48–1984).

10 9 8 7 6 5 4 3 2

Contents

Illustrations

FIGURES

TABLES

Preface

Public and other not-for-profit financial management has been going through profound change during the past decade. We are passing through a period in which the public is demanding more and better services while demonstrating an unwillingness to pay higher taxes or fees. Accordingly, there is a strongly held view that public and other not-for-profit agencies can and must find new ways to cut costs while improving efficiency, effectiveness, and accountability.

Even more so than in the past, effective management of financial resources will be critical to the success and survival of public and other not-for-profit agencies. While the non-financial manager will not be expected to be an accountant/bookkeeper or an auditor, any lack of familiarity with the concepts of accounting and other financial processes will limit the manager's ability to ask the critical questions, and to monitor and evaluate fiscal activities. This text is written to be understandable to those who are not "experts" but those who are or may become managers.

A major shortcoming in the financial management field has been the lack of integrated financial management systems that tie together the fiscal side (budgeting, financing and controlling) and the substantive management side (planning, programming and evaluating) so as to facilitate the unimpeded flow of required information to the appropriate responsibility centers decision points. This book is written to fill that vacuum, providing integration and practicality.

Among the benefits that this volume provides are the following: (1) it combines budgeting and financial management in one volume; (2) it permits easy adaptation to both public and not-for-profit agencies; (3) it balances theory with practice; (4) it includes understandable descriptions of technical subjects; (5) it shows how to think about resource needs and translate them into effective budgets; (6) it shows how to develop, implement, and maintain control over expenditures; (7) it provides a step-by-step approach for the development and use of critical measurement indicators for important function; (8) it discusses such infrequently examined topics as cash, risk, internal control, fiscal health and fraud, waste and abuse management, and the very popular topic of TQM; (9) it shows how to obtain and use financial advisory services; and (10) its simplicity of style makes it a useful book for the novice as well as the experienced reader.

The author thanks Professor Aman Khan of Texas A & M University for his early critical review of the project, and students and practitioner who exchanged ideas and examples. Thanks go to Mary McKinney and Professor Lawrence Howard for their continued encouragement. I also owe thanks to Margaret Lisjak for editing and the Graduate School of Public and International Affairs of the University of Pittsburgh, especially Sheila Kelly and Willadean Bailey for secretarial support.

1

Understanding Financial Management

The pursuit of virtually every collective public purpose has financial implications. Undertakings that have no cost seldom have many benefits. Financial management plays an indispensable role in the achievement of an organization's objective. It is the fuel that gives life and substance to the engine of public administration. Financial management is the only activity that touches every employee in an organization. The continuing upward spiral of inflation, the rising cost of governmental programs, and citizens' demands for a better and more cost-effective delivery of goods and services are forcing public managers and others in not-for-profit organizations to make creative use of their scarce financial resources. This is happening at a time when taxpayers are not only showing an unwillingness to support more services but are making an unmistakable demand to prune or cut back existing services.

This chapter gives the reader a broad overview of the components and processes involved in financial administration. The discussion is presented in five sections. The first presents a definition of financial management showing how it is emerging as a critical force in everyday operations. The second and third examine the federal financial management system and the role of the federal chief financial officer. The fourth compares public and private financial management indicating the similarities and differences and the ways in which articulated objectives are pursued. The fifth discusses the organizational framework in which financial administration takes place.[1] Next, the duties of financial managers are briefly examined and the important role of accountability and improved financial management are introduced, along with an overview. The final section of the chapter contains an overview of the rest of the book.

DEFINING FINANCIAL MANAGEMENT

Public financial management is the process wherein a governmental unit or agency (1) employs the means to obtain and allocate resources and/or money, based on implied or articulated priorities; and (2) utilizes methods and controls to effectively achieve publicly determined ends. Two important elements are emphasized: efficient raising of resources and the wise and accountable usage of funds to achieve end products of the highest possible quality. Though the definition does not stress time and uncertainty (and the literature seldom articulates these concepts), both have particular importance to the field of applied public financial management. So defined, financial management is viewed, not as a staff specialty concerned only with controlling the government or agency funds, but as an integral part of management.

In general terms, financial management comprises three main activities. (1) It determines the scope and content of fiscal policies. This is a process in which agency, community, or relevant political leaders set forth programs and provide the appropriation or resources required to accomplish them. (Issues such as employment, inflation, borrowing, taxation and revenue raising are considered and resolved.) (2) It establishes general guidelines and standards to ensure that funds are spent honestly and wisely to achieve publicly determined purposes. (3) It provides organizational structures and controls to effectively carry out fiscal duties and responsibilities.[2] Traditionally, the main financial management components include budgeting, taxation (revenue raising), accounting, treasury management, purchasing, and auditing.

In Figure 1.1 the integrated approach to financial management incorporates an additional set of components, including planning, programming, and evaluating functions. The key to Figure 1.1 clarifies what is meant by each of these six processes.

Integrative Role

The critical and integrative role that financial management plays in the operation of everyday management can be seen in Figure 1.1. For simplicity, the combination of the two processes may be seen as a set of sequential steps: planning, programming, budgeting, financing, controlling, and evaluating.

The first of the basic management processes depicted in Figure 1.1 involves the articulation of the goals and objectives to be pursued (planning). Their feasibility for implementation is determined and the selection of appropriate activities to realize the planned goals is made (programming).

The first action on the "financial process side" is completion of the budget (or expenditure plan), which allocates available resources based on these programmed activities and priorities. Once the expenditure plan has been

Figure 1.1
The Integrative Role of Financial Management

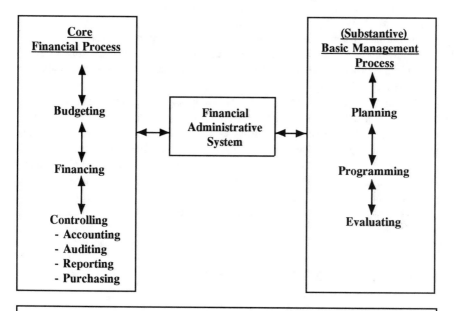

Integrated Financial Management

Defining Its Components

1. *Planning* defines the goals, objectives, and priorities to be pursued.

2. *Programming* selects the best available activities to achieve stated goals and priorities, usually within a specific time period.

3. *Budgeting* develops a specific, detailed work plan to achieve stated goals and priorities, usually within a specific time period.

4. *Financing* provides the necessary financial resources to carry out the planned and programmed objectives.

5. *Controlling* assures that the planned and programmed activities are carried out according to the detailed, preestablished work plan.

6. *Evaluating* assesses the utility, appropriateness, and congruence between stated goals and objectives and achieved results.

developed, financial resources are sought to execute the plan (financing). In order to monitor the progress of activities through the execution stages, and thereby to ensure that the planned, programmed, and financial objectives are being carried out according to targets and expectations, a system of control is created. Whenever it is determined that progress is not meeting expectations, interventions can be made to redirect the activity toward its target.

Returning to the management side, it can be seen that evaluation is the final action in the process. This activity determines whether the articulated goals and objectives have been achieved.

Traditionally, financial management has given little attention to the basic management processes of planning, programming and evaluation. Instead, it has dwelled on the core financial functions, especially the budgeting and controlling activities. However, because of continuing competition for declining financial resources, the basic management processes are beginning to receive more attention as evidenced by two recent books. Planning, programming, and evaluating require policy makers to observe, understand, and reflect before they enact potentially unwise policies. This changing emphasis will be discussed later in this volume.

FRAGMENTATED FEDERAL FINANCIAL MANAGEMENT SYSTEM

The federal government provides an excellent example of a system that needs greater linkage and integration between the financial and management processes (as shown in Figure 1.2). There are gaps in six principal areas:

- "poor quality of financial management information;
- poor linkage between the phases of the financial management process;
- inadequate attention to monitoring and comparing budgeted activity with results;
- primary emphasis on fund control;
- inadequate disclosure of assets, cost and liabilities; [and]
- antiquated and fragmented financial management systems."[3]

THE FEDERAL CHIEF FINANCIAL OFFICER (CFO): TOWARD INTEGRATED MANAGEMENT

In 1990, in the Chief Financial Officers Act, the federal government enacted legislation to achieve an integrated system of financial management paralleling the approach depicted in Figure 1.1.[4] The CFO Act strengthened the management side of the Office of Management and Budget (OMB) by creating

Figure 1.2
Observations on Governmentwide Financial Management Processes and Systems

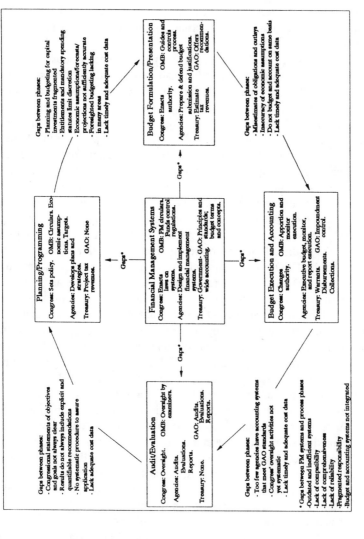

Source: U.S. Government Accounting Office (GAO), *Managing the Cost of Government*, Vol. 2, GAO AFMD 85 35 A (Washington, D.C.: U.S. GAO, 1985).

a deputy director of management at executive pay level 3 who reports directly to the OMB director. The new deputy now has equal status with the powerful budget side at OMB. This is a significant upgrading and improvement of the management responsibilities at OMB. Because of the vacuum that had existed on the management side, administrative functions delegated to the Office of Federal Procurement Policy (OFPP) and the Office of Information and Regulatory Affairs (OIRA) overseeing federal paperwork clearance and information resource management activities could not be effectively coordinated and implemented.[5]

In the agencies, the 23 CFOs occupy, in name or substance, positions coterminous with that of the principle management official (assistant secretary for management), plus a purely financial management role or portfolio duties. This organization placement and design provides for optimum integration between the naturally interrelated functions of management and finance. The broad responsibilities of each agency's CFO purposely parallels the duties of the U.S. chief financial officer, the OMB deputy director for management and finance who has been given charge of the functions that include management systems, procurement, human resources, and regulatory affairs.[6]

Because of the decentralized nature of many agencies whose activities are carried out by bureaus or units that are geographically remote from the direct access and supervision of the central agency, the CFO Act permits the personnel of these units to directly report to the subunit head, with a broken line type of reporting to the CFO. This approach "recognizes financial management as an integral component of any overall administrative structure and must remain imbedded in that infrastructure for both to be effective."[7] The broken-line model permits the subunit to exercise a chain-of-command over the financial managers while allowing the CFO authority to be maintained throughout the agency by means of an integrated financial management system.

The CFO Act requires that the 23 departments and agencies be given CFOs, who must develop financial management plans and provide annual progress reports to the agency head and Congress. Based on CFO reports; Inspectors General (IGs), Treasury Department, and GAO, program manager; and private sector inputs, OMB is required to annually produce a governmentwide financial management status report and a projected five-year plan. Clearly defined strategy for generating audited financial statements is prepared and submitted to Congress, identifying agency vulnerabilities and proposed actions for correcting them. Additionally, CFOs must maintain permanently audited financial statements for revolving funds, trust funds, and funds substantially related to commercial activities.[8]

Dual monitoring responsibility for budget execution is given to OMB's deputy director for management and the agency CFOs. The latter is also directed to maintain systems that facilitate the integration of accounting and budgeting information aimed at improving policy-making, decision making, and enhancing program efficiency. The responsibility is given to the CFO to recruit, select, and train all personnel who carry out the financial functions; this includes "all financial management, personnel activities and operations, including . . . the implementation of agency assets, [as well as] management systems, including systems for cash management, credit management, debt collection and property and inventory management and control."[9]

In summary, the CFO Act is based on three main premises: (1) continual improvement in the quality of government financial management systems is possible by effectively linking management programs, budgeting, and accounting into an efficiently operating financial management system (see Figure 1.1); (2) audited financial statements can be valuable inputs to decision makers; and (3) the production of timely audit reports in accordance with audit recommendations can be facilitated. Thus, the CFO structure is viewed as the best means that could be developed and implemented to appropriately achieve these objectives.[10] In reflecting on the role of the CFOs, one member of Congress stated: [A] "strong, independent statutory CFO who keeps tract of how much is being spent will be able to let Congress know what the program is really costing, not keep it hidden until it is too late. The CFO should play a key role in reviewing contracts, determining how much and when to pay. [The] CFO should [be] someone without pet projects."[11]

The effectiveness of the CFO will greatly depend on the relationship that develops between the office and the head of the agency to which it is attached. Unless the agency head involves the CFO in key agency decisions and activities and the CFO is given an equivalent place with counterpart officers in the making of important decisions, the maximum efficacy and potential of the CFO are not likely to be reached.

The intent of the CFO Act is not to have the CFO replace the inspectors general but to complement and parallel their functions. The act explicitly requires that the CFO provide federal agencies with systems capability to develop "internal controls adequate to . . . deter fraud, waste and abuse of government resources."[12] Prior to the CFO Act, the charge to reduce fraud, waste, and abuse was viewed as being in the province of the IGs. Currently, however, the broad oversight authority given to the CFOs does blur the line between the agency's traditional operational role and the oversight functions of the IGs.

Changing Orientation in Financial Management

The financial crises experienced by cities such as New York and Cleveland have increased the interest in financial management at all levels of government, and particularly at the local levels. While the traditional emphases on control and compliance (making sure activities conform to laws, rules, and procedures laid down by the purchasing, accounting, auditing, and budget systems) are still important, new, critical concerns have emerged. These can be stated as a series of questions, including the following:

1. What indicators would permit us to assess the fiscal health of a governmental unit?

2. What is the most effective approach for forecasting revenue and expenditures?

3. What are the best methods for meeting the needs and demands of the community?

4. What methods are used to evaluate the adequacy of financial management systems in: (a) permitting managers to anticipate financial problems and (b) allowing managers to solve these problems before they   reach critical limits?

5. What are the best systems, methods, and techniques that must be created to enhance performance, to minimize fraud, waste, and abuse, and promote maximum accountability?

PUBLIC VERSUS PRIVATE FINANCIAL MANAGEMENT

As in the public sector, virtually every key decision made in a firm has financial implications. Managers ask questions such as the following: In an attempt to make the best financial decision how can risk and the potential return on an investment be balanced? Is sufficient cash or access to funds available to meet daily needs and maturing obligations? What should be the firm's credit policy toward its customers and what privileges should particular customers be granted? What are the potential sources of funds that may be used to finance investments?

Many of the concepts, objectives and techniques employed in one sector are also utilized in the other (as shown in Table 1.1). First of all, both public and private sectors are concerned with financing ongoing operations and effectively managing the flow of funds. Second, in seeking debt funds, both sectors must go to the same financial markets. Third, large purchases require competitive bidding in the public sector, though to a lesser extent than in the private sector. Fourth, both sectors have systems of employee pension plans. Finally, both have unions that require contract negotiations and wage/salary administration, although unionization is a greater factor in the private sector.

Major differences between the private and public sectors relate to the end objectives and how resources are raised. Ideally, the ultimate objective of the public financial decision makers is to maximize the production and delivery of goods and services. The emphasis is on the provision of socially beneficial services to the community, a large portion of which are distributed on the basis of need. Business decision makers seek to maximize profit and/or wealth for their stockholders.

The private sector depends on the contribution of investors in order to obtain funds to conduct business. The public sector imposes taxes to meet its objectives. These tax resources are typically extracted based on some measure of ability to pay. There are no equity shares that can be traded or sold.

In pure public or nonprofit agencies where the provision of government services is based entirely on need, no individual charges or costs are paid by recipients of the services. Pure public or nonprofit agencies produce collective or indivisible services and/or goods, such as defense, that cannot be excluded from the simultaneous enjoyment of the service - hence the impossibility of pricing.

In between the conceptual poles of purely public and purely private lie a host of quasi-public agencies and organizations. Services provided by such quasi-public or nonprofit agencies are provided on a break-even or partial cost recovery basis (e.g., school lunches, parking facilities, and sewage). However, there are cases where public policy requires that individuals with incomes below a particular cutoff point be exempted from paying for the provision of services.

Finally, nongovernment/nonprofit agencies experiencing heavy deficits will suffer the same fate as any business unless the leadership of these organizations can find sympathetic ears among the corporate managers and/or publicly elected officials.

ORGANIZING FOR FINANCIAL ADMINISTRATION

Particularly at the state and local levels of government, checks and balances and separation of powers (functions) have dominated the way in which financial administration is conducted in the United States. The view that honesty can be promoted by dividing powers among independently elected officers has led to the election of many fiscal officials. Though this value is widely held and the practice is still prevalent, there is little evidence to show that it produces competent and creative officials. On the contrary, it has led at times to fragmented, decentralized, uncoordinated, and ineffective financial systems. This has generated a number of problems including the following: (1) inability to act quickly; (2) competition over policy space and responsibility for financial activities; and (3) multiple clearances and conflicting advice from financial decision makers.

While the particular form of a *decentralized financial decision-making model* may vary, financial activities are typically administered by separate officers who are appointed or elected. In each case, a board or individual other than the chief executive is given some powers over the officials, who have insufficient supervisory authority to bring about an integration of the financial management system.

The complexity of modern government and the need to respond quickly to citizens' demands has led to the movement away from the decentralized financial model to the *centralized one* (see Figure 1.3). This model is closely allied with the hierarchical decision-making approach and the integrated model of decision making. Both models locate power at the top of the hierarchy, from which authority flows downward and responsibility and accountability flow upward. In this centralized organization, supervisory powers to direct financial officials reside in one individual, who is typically appointed by the chief executive of the governmental unit. This arrangement promotes policy integration, minimizing divided responsibility and making it more likely that plans will be executed according to planned policy intentions.

Three major guidelines have been suggested by Moak and Hillhouse to use in organizing for financial administration: (1) standards for effective leadership, (2) guidelines for the efficient and effective use of resources, and (3) ways for ensuring accountability to citizens.[13]

The first of these guidelines, the pursuit of effective leadership, requires that the chief executive be judicious in the delegation of responsibility. This will aid in achieving an appropriate span of control in the administration of financial activities. To facilitate this objective, staff with the capacity to develop alternative financial plans must be available or be trained; a system of controls to assure that articulated policies are executed as planned and programmed must be developed as well. To promote honesty and integrity, due cognizance should be given to the segregation of duties to minimize the occurrence of errors and make collusion among employees difficult. Additionally, efforts should be made to provide technical assistance to operating managers.

The efficient and effective application of financial resources requires, first, that provision be made for the specialization and division of labor regarding the main financial functions. There is also a strong need for coordination, namely, through the grouping of related financial activities. This facilitates the establishment of "responsibility centers" to permit a comparison of standards with achieved results. To ensure that resources are used as planned, monetary and nonmonetary control systems are developed to monitor the expenditures and amount of goods or services produced from one time period to the next.

Table 1.1

Comparing Objectives: Public/Nonprofit and Private Organizations

ACTIVITY	OBJECTIVE	
	Public Nonprofit Organization	Private Organization
Resource allocation	Budget and political process.	Market and pricing system.
Resource application	Optimal use-provision of goods and services to meet stated objectives.	Optimal use in terms of higher return on investment.
Expenditure/ Expense	Wise usage of funds to achieve policy objectives.	Wise usage of funds to maximize return on investment.
Finance	Less integrated with management.	Usually integral part of top management.
Managing and determining source of funds	From taxation and borrowing; political officials with financial manager's advice; raising additional funds at least cost; ensuring liquidity position to enable entity to meet current maturing obligations and to deliver appropriate goods and services.	From earnings, equity, and borrowing according to financial plans; ensuring liquidity position to meet current and maturing obligations to achieve profit and wealth maximization.
Determining organizational structures	Provision normally is made by legislative or by funding sources; lesser functions determined by practice, convention and financial necessity to better provide goods and services.	Usually by practice, industry, rationality, or pragmatic necessity, to achieve greater profits.
Production of goods and services reporting	Dollar accountability (fiscal-stewardship) and operational accountability of managers.	Operational accountability of managers.

Because of the demand for responsiveness and the need to fix blame or approbation for job performance in governments, concern for accountability (the Moak and Hillhouse third guideline) has particular significance in financial management. This requires that clear lines of authority be set up to identify the duties of executing officers. It is important to establish a system of financial controls leading directly to the chief executive. The identification of financial duties and institutionalization of executive controls sets in place the structure needed to obtain an integrated financial-reporting system for the organization.

In addition to the internal control system, responsiveness to public concerns typically requires that a system be established that permits citizens to appeal arbitrary financial rules and regulations. Perhaps the means most widely employed to promote accountability of financial activities is the use of the independent postauditor.

DUTIES OF FINANCIAL MANAGERS

The financial management duties and roles have traditionally been looked upon as mainly a staff specialty function that provides support and advice to line managers.[14] This compartmentalized approach, though still present in some organizations, has given way to the integrated practice, in which the financial manager acts as an integral part of the management decision-making team.

The major functions of financial managers include the following:

1. *Financial planning:* (a) participation in short- and long-range planning and evaluation of various courses of action; (b) interpretation of the financial implications of legislation and regulations; (c) preparation of procedural manuals and instructions to facilitate compliance with such regulations; and (d) definition of programs and activities.

2. *Budget preparation and expenditure control,* in which the manager provides: (a) guidance and assistance in the preparation and submission of budgets; (b) establishment of expenditure classification control; and (c) management of cash requirements.

3. *Accounting system and procedures,* for which the manager: (a) develops the accounting system to permit an incorporation of budgeting and internal controls in order to meet agency and other mandated needs; (b) develops appropriate cost-accounting systems to accommodate agency needs and undertakes special cost and

work measurement studies, when necessary, to assist in alternative decision making; (c) advises operating heads on how best to use the accounting system; and (d) periodically reviews agency accounting, budgeting, financial, and statistical reporting systems and procedures, making improvements where required.

4. *Reporting for financial management control* by developing agency information systems for reporting financial and other relevant data to operating and supervisory management. This information should indicate variances between the budget and actual performance.

5. *Maintenance of asset control system* by establishing a control procedure for the safekeeping of assets such as inventories, cash, materials, and equipment.

6. *Financial liaison* by developing and maintaining an effective liaison with officials (e.g., state auditors general) as well as other agencies whose regulations may require changes in agency financial regulations.

7. *Staff training* by advising and participating in the development of staff training.

8. *Analysis of fiscal health* through the analysis of fiscal conditions. The manager must constantly be able to answer questions such as: Can the unit of government or agency pay its own way? Can the unit pay for services and avoid large tax or fee increases? Proper attention to these questions requires an evaluation of the community's fiscal condition. This requires having reliable information on local infra-structure such as roads, bridges and sewers, as well as on the extent of unfunded obligations for pension liabilities.

The financial manager is expected to sort out key factors affecting the fiscal condition of the community. For example, can it maintain an economic base to meet expenditure demands and revenue expectations? Can the community maintain existing service levels? In addition, the manager must be able to determine the causes of fiscal distress and be able to measure its extent.

It can be seen that the financial manager is a key player in maintaining the viability of an agency. The manager is expected to assist in developing plans and options for keeping and attracting businesses. In the case of an agency, managers must develop, maintain, and/or expand revenue sources. They act as negotiator in union contracts and with community groups seeking goods and services that involve the use of monetary resources. Finally, the manager acts as a controller in all financial activities.

ACCOUNTABILITY AND IMPROVED FINANCIAL MANAGEMENT

The close of the twentieth century finds clients and constituents demanding improved goods and services while resources decline at all levels of government. Taxpayers resist tax increases, while donors demand results for their contribution. Demands are made that public managers and other not-for-profit organizations utilize available resources wisely. Additionally, there is a growing concern that systems be devised to facilitate greater accountability for the expenditure of public money.

Accountability will require that managers at all organizational levels know specifically to whom and for what they are accountable. This will necessitate that objectives be clearly articulated. Performance operations must be planned and programmed, indicating explicitly what is to be done, what are the (allowable) resources, what methods will be employed, what the required performance is, and how the results will be measured and evaluated. All this requires that an increased emphasis be given to program planning.

In program planning, each manager has the responsibility to allocate resources in such a way as to achieve the organization's objective with maximum efficiency and effectiveness. Program planning involves prioritizing both the objectives sought and the tasks to achieve them. If fewer resources are allocated to the manager than were anticipated, the manager will need to decide what operations will be pruned or dropped and what combination of resources will be required to achieve the organizational objective.

To improve the utilization of resources and avoid a hit-or-miss approach to decision making, participants concerned with financial management are expected to assist, engage in, and provide guidance for both short- and long-range financial planning. Elements such as the following must be set forth: (a) clear identification of objectives; (b) proposed plans of action to achieve the objectives; (c) expected results for each unit of time in the plan; (d) alternative plans of action; and (e) measures to judge the efficiency and effectiveness in meeting the objectives.

Accountability requires that there be a constant matching of stated or implied (desired) goals and objectives with achieved results. The difference between the achieved and the desired results is the accountability gap. The aim is to minimize, and ultimately eliminate, the gap. The integrative role of financial management provides a strategic means in facilitating the achievement of accountability.

ORGANIZATION OF THE TEXT

The first three chapters of this volume provide the reader with an understanding of the scope, nature, and function of modern financial management, stressing the changing focus and important role of accounting and the critical role of internal controls.

Resource management functions are examined in chapters 3 through 8. Nationally successful practices and techniques in revenue administration, purchasing, cash management, and debt and risk management are evaluated. While some attention is given to theory, the major focus is on how the systems work, indicating their potentials and possible restraints.

Chapters 9 through 19 discuss the management control process as a means of achieving accountability. The reader is shown how linkage may effectively be achieved among the accounting, auditing, reporting, and monitoring systems in financial management. This section also shows how indicators can be developed and used to control day-to-day operations and permit a close watch on community fiscal health.

Chapters 20 and 21 explore special concerns such as fraud, waste and abuse (FWA), along with the advising functions that are important to the modern financial manager.

APPENDIX: THE FINANCIAL MANAGER: SOME USEFUL CONCEPTS TO READ THE ECONOMY

The economic terms and acronyms appearing in the popular media have been growing in number yet few definitions or primers are provided to aid the reader. The following discussion attempts to briefly describe the terms.

Gross National Product (GNP)

This is the broadest indicator or measure of economic output and growth in the U.S. economy. It comprises goods and services produced and consumed in the private, public, and international sectors. GNP measures the market value of all goods produced, including those produced outside the United States.

Gross Domestic Product (GDP)

This indicator contrasts with GNP in that it measures the market value of only those goods that have been solely produced in the United States. GNP and GDP emphasize two components: (1) the demand, identifying the market

Figure 1.3

Suggested Division of Large Non-Profit Organizations

Board of Directors *
Chairman of the Finance Committee
Approval of budget

Secretary of Board

Legal Matters

President or Executive Director

Budget Recommendations;
Internal Control

Vice President or
Director, Development

Fund Raising, financial
and tax advice to potential
contributors

Vice-President or Director,
Finance

Internal control;
budget preparation

Vice-president or Director,
Program Activities

New and existing programs

Chief Accountant or
Controller

Accounting and financial
reporting;
complying with federal, state,
local as well as grant and
organizational reporting
requirements; bookkeeping

Purchasing
Agent

Purchasing

Director of
Physical
Plant

Physical
Plant and
construction

Treasurer

Disbursement of
cash; receipt and
custody of funds,
including
investments

Personnel
Director

Personnel
actions and
records

* All activities are ultimately the responsibility of the board of directors

Source: John H. Engstrom and Timothy O'Keefe, *"Staffing: The Financial Function"*, in Tracy D. Connors and
Christopher T. Callaghan eds., *Financial Management for Non-profit Organizations*, New York:
AMACOM , division of American Management Association, 1982), p.184, (with permission of the publisher).

for goods and services, and (2) the supply, identifying the costs required to produce the goods and services. The U.S. Department of Commerce Division of the Bureau of Economic Research (BER) publishes GNP/GDP data on a quarterly basis in its monthly magazine, *Survey of Current Business*.

Gross State Product (GSP)

This is a new concept that is the state counterpart to GDP. The GSP is the gross market value of goods and services relating to labor and property located in a given state. Unlike the national GNP and GDP, the BER produces the state GSP figures annually. Estimates of the GSP are prepared for 61 industries. Four components are included for each industry: (1) employee compensation, (2) business income with adjustment for inventory and capital consumption allowances, (3) indirect business taxes and nontax liability, and (4) other charges related mainly to capital.

Consumer Price Index (CPI)

This is an indicator that measures the changes in prices taking place for a fixed basket of consumer goods and services with constant quantity and quality as purchased by average urban consumers. This indicator is a representative reflection of the prices of the goods and services that consumers use for everyday living. The CPI is made up of seven major components: apparel, medical care, housing, food and beverages, transportation, entertainment, and "other goods and services." Eighty five locations are averaged and weighed, representing the different population groups and comparisons of the monthly indexes are made. Two CPIs are calculated and published: (1) for all urban consumers (CPI-U), covering 80 percent of the population, and (2) for urban wage earners and clerical workers (CPI-W), covering 32 percent of the population.

The index value of current prices is compared to average prices in an assigned base period with a value of 100. Hence, a CPI of 141 would mean that what cost $100 in the base period has now risen to $141. (The U.S. Department of Labor's Bureau of Labor Statistics [BLS] provides the data monthly following the month to which they relate.)

The CPI is widely used as a barometer to chart the direction of the national economy, and also as an indicator of inflation in decisions relating to the future production and consumption. The CPI is widely used in "escalator" clauses in the determination of income payment agreements. This practice is commonly referred to as *indexing*. For this reason the CPI has figured prominently in collective bargaining agreements for millions of workers. Presently, approximately 50 million social security beneficiaries, retired military personnel, civil service employees, food stamp recipients, and others use the CPI to monitor potential changes in their income.

While many people think of the CPI as the cost-of-living index, the Bureau of Labor Statistics has often attempted to debunk this interpretation. The CPI is simply a measure of prices, reflecting changes in the purchasing power of the average family. The view is expressed that there is an inherent upward bias notion about the CPI that results in overstating inflation, thus giving rise to demands for wage, benefit, and other increases. Additionally, the CPI does not give recognition to substitution effects of the fixed basket of goods because of the way in which it treats home ownership.

Predicting the Direction of the Economy: Trend Indicators

Economic trend indicators are classified as leading, coincident, and lagging, describing the result of activities or processes, such as employment and unemployment, production, income, consumption, and trade, that provide us with clues or insights about present and future economic trends, particularly as they relate to recessions (contractions) and cyclical expansions. Key indicators are grouped and categorized according to their tendency or sensitivity to "change direction before, during, or after the general economy turns from an expansion to a recession or from recession to expansion."[15]

The system of economic indicators is premised on the basis that capitalistic economies are subject to recurring business cycles that depend on the profit outlook. When the profit outlook is favorable, businesses expand. The reverse (contraction) occurs when the profit outlook is negative. Positive advances in the average manufacturing workweek, production, and the financial markets are *leading indicators* and reflect business commitments and expectations. *Coincident indicators* show the existing level of sales and production, while *lagging indicators* give a view of what has happened in the economy. These indicators are all retrospective because they are used to assess and confirm prior economic activities.

Some General Guidelines for Interpreting Economic Indicators

The indicators have varying economic impacts, especially on federal spending and revenue results, as follows:

- A change in the economy typically affects federal revenue more than federal spending. Relatedly, a decline in the inflation rate may sometimes have a negative impact on the deficit, as may a rise in unemployment.
- A rise of one percentage point in unemployment reduces revenue by $12 billion, while the reverse (i.e., a one percentage point rise in employment) generates an increase of $5 billion in revenue.
- An increase of one percentage point in the inflation rate subsequent to the budget preparation generates an additional $5 billion in revenue and adds $1 billion to the spending side.
- A rise of one percentage point in the interest rate adds $2 billion to the spending side while it generates $1 in additional revenues.
- A decrease in unemployment by one percentage point reduces state and local revenues by $6 billion.
- A reduction of one percentage point creates an additional 1.25 million jobs.

NOTES

1. Jerome B. McKinney and Lawrence C. Howard, *Public Administration: Balancing Power and Accountability* (Oak Park, Ill: Moore Publishing Co.; 1979), pp. 345-47.

2. U.S. General Accounting Office, *GAO Managing the Cost of Government: Building an Effective Financial Management Structure*, AFMD 83 35A (Washington, D.C.: GAO, February 1985), p. 11.

3. Ibid., p. 12.

4. Frank Horton, "Insights into the Chief Financial Officers Act of 1990," *Governments Accountant Journal*, 40, no. 5 (Spring 1991): 9.

5. Jill E. Kent, "Organization of the Agency Chief Financial Officers," *Government Accountants Journal*, 40, no. 5 (Spring 1991): 27.

6. Ibid., p. 28.

7. Ibid.

8. See CFO Act, Section 205(a) (Codified at 31 U.S.C 902(a).

9. Frank Hodsoll, "Office of Management and Budget's Plans for Implementation of Chief Financial Officers Act," *Government Accounts Journal*, 40, no. 5 (Spring 1991): 17.

10. John Conyers Jr., "Vigilance in Government," *Government Accountant's Journal*, 40, no. 5 (Spring 1991): 24.

11. CFO Act, Section 102(b)(2).

12. Ibid.

13. Lennox L. Moak and Albert M. Hillhouse, *Local Government Finance* (Chicago: Municipal Finance Officers Association, 1979), pp. 345-347.

14. Line managers are the individuals responsible for the direct delivery of goods and services to the clients and constituents that the agency was created to serve these persons are known as doers, as opposed to staff people, who are known as advisors.

15. David Levitan, "How to Read the Economy: A Primer", *Government Finance Review*, 9, no. 2 (April 1993): 25.

2

Accounting: Its Important Role in Financial Management

In both public and private organizations, accounting has served as a major mechanism of management control. It is important to note that the structure of financial analysis is dependent predominantly on accounting information, which is the means by which the consequences of the various options available to management are revealed. Management can use accounting information as a control and monitoring tool to assess performance and take corrective action. In public and not-for-profit agencies, decision makers should, therefore, have an understanding of the accounting process as well as its strengths and weaknesses. While it is not required that decision makers be accountants, an understanding of the function and structure of accounting systems is necessary for effective fiscal planning and management. To be of maximum use, the accounting system should have a flexible account structure that provides data, not only for appropriated expenditures, but also for (1) program elements or activities to aid in budget analysis and presentation, (2) special project details, (3) major organizational and geographical divisions, (4) a common data base to facilitate performance measurement, and (5) determination of the full cost of the intended programs and activities.

The purpose of this chapter is to give the reader who is unfamiliar with accounting a general overview of the accounting process and its practice. Those who desire a more extensive and detailed introduction to this subject are directed to any of the standard introductory texts.[1]

DEFINING ACCOUNTING

Accounting translates economic activities of a business into quantitative terms or dollars as the common unit of measure. Accounting is an instrument of the controlling process directed at collecting, summarizing, recording, ordering, reporting, and analyzing the financial resources and transactions of an organization. Accounting keeps track of the activities of an organization (e.g., a governmental unit, hospital, club, or family) and facilitates its standardizing, monitoring, and use of data. Accounting reduces all transactions into common denominator money terms, allowing for comparison of two or more activities that otherwise would be difficult to compare (the proverbial "apples and oranges"). Accounting is thus a common language that keeps track of transactions that occur within an organization and with other organizations. The accounting system is retrospective in that it records information relating mainly to an organization's past fiscal condition.

There are a number of fundamental objectives that an effective accounting system should seek to satisfy. They include the following:

1. *Control*: As the basic element of the financial control structure, accounting is the most important means for ensuring that public expenditures are limited to the purposes and amounts that were legally authorized.

2. *Accountability*: The accounting system maintains a set of procedures to ensure that officers and employees are held responsible and accountable for the safeguarding of money and property entrusted or assigned to them. A system of internal controls must be maintained to permit the continual review of commitments in an effort to promote confidence and integrity in the system.

3. *Responsibility Accounting*: This plays an integral role in achieving accountability. Responsibility accounting is organized to permit the accumulation of actual budgeting data and accounting records to show the expense or expenditure responsibilities of each manager. This allows top management to hold each manager accountable for the efficient and effective use of resources.

4. *Internal and external reporting*: (a) Internal reporting relates to the use of accounting information in the planning and control of routine operations in the organization, while (b) external reporting relays the state and condition of the organization to other administrative officers, government regulatory agencies, various constituencies or client groups, creditors, and the general public.

5. *Information*: The accounting system facilitates the provision of information to appropriate officials, bond raters, and creditors in the form, frequency, and timeliness desired. Information is the single most important product, especially in local governments, where accounting is the only system that provides comprehensive,

detailed, and comparable information on the activities of all agencies. The accounting system also provides information to assist management in the formulation of long-range policy plans and strategies. Unfortunately, this latter aspect is at present more a hope than a reality in most governments and not-for-profit agencies.

Financial Accounting

The major objective of financial accounting is the preparation of a financial statement, which offers a measurement of past and current financial status mainly to external users (bond holders, taxpayers, the press, creditors, bond raters, the general public, and other interested groups) in conformance with generally accepted accounting principles (GAAP) as they apply to government and not-for-profit organizations.[2] Financial accounting focuses on the recording of financial transactions. By means of a predetermined code or chart of accounts, financial transactions are systematically recorded in accounting ledgers (books containing the summary of account). The data from these ledgers are used periodically to produce required fiscal statements, which provide monetary information and are used for budget preparation, internal control, and adherence to legal and other external reporting requirements. In the private sector, four major reports are typically presented to external users: (1) statement of financial position, or balance sheet, (2) statement of earnings, (3) statement of earnings or equity, and (4) statement of cash flows. In the governmental entity, under the *comprehensive annual financial report* (CAFR) system, there are five required financial statements: (1) combined balance sheet - involving all types of funds and account groups, (2) combined statement of revenues, expenditures, and changes in fund balances - used in all governmental fund types, (3) combined statement of revenues, expenditures, and changes in fund balances - both budgeted and actual - involving both general and special revenues types (and similar governmental fund types for which annual budgets have been legally adopted), (4) combined statement of revenues, expenses, and changes in fund balances (or equity) - involving all propriety fund types, and (5) combined statement of changes in financial position, again in all proprietary fund types.

Managerial Accounting

The provision of information to aid internal management in improving the effectiveness of programming, decision making, and control is the concern of managerial accounting, which uses both financial (historical) and estimated data. Attention is focused on the organization of information to enable and to enhance decision making related to daily operations, activities, programs, or responsibility centers, and also to the planning of future operations. Distinguishing features of managerial accounting include the following:

- It is future oriented.
- It provides data for internal use, management decision making, and internal reporting.
- It is eclectic in that it is not bound by generally accepted accounting principles but emphasizes the relevance and flexibility of data selection, including data from other disciplines.
- It is driven by the decision makers' requests.
- It places emphasis on nonmonetary data, unlike financial accounting, and it provides information that is very useful in preparing short- and long-range budget preparation.
- It uses variance reports to analyze deviations from planned performance.
- It encourages cost consciousness with its emphasis on performance standards and unit costs as they relate to responsibility centers. A responsibility center is a section or division of an organization (for example, purchasing and maintenance) for which an individual is assigned responsibility and given control over resources to achieve one or more purposes (objectives) as part of the overall goals of an organization.
- It is audited, if at all, by internal auditors.
- It promotes, through its cost approach, linkage between management control and program, along with performance and zero-base budgeting.
- It acts as a motivating mechanism, holding officials accountable to attain planned results and reward accomplishments.
- It uses an understanding of the past to plan, shape, and redirect the future.[3]

Cost Accounting

The assemblage and recording of all cost elements related to a project or unit of work is the responsibility of cost accounting. Expressed in another way, "it is an art of determining the cost of a product, service or activity."[4] Cost accounting is the connecting link between financial and managerial accounting. Financial accounting provides historical data which may be used in

Figure 2.1
The Costing Matrix

	Direct Cost	Marginal Cost	Fixed Cost	Unit Cost	Variable Cost	Avoidable Cost	Life-Cycle Cost	Total Cost
Eliminate Service			x		x	x		
Reassign Personnel					x	x		
Reduce Service	x	x			x	x		
Improve Productivity		x		x				
Contract Out						x		
Civilianize the Delivery	x					x		
Substitute Equipment			x	x		x	x	
Charge for Service		x						x
Status Quo	x							x

Source: Joseph T. Kelley, Costing Government Services: A Guide to Decision Making (Washington, D.C.: Government Research Center, 1984), p. 36.

costing out options for management decision making. Figure 2.1 shows how a cost accounting system may be used strategically to aid management decision making. Cost information can be used to enhance planning, budgeting, controlling, evaluating, pricing, and reporting. There are a number of important uses for governmental cost information, including the following:

- *Budgeting* provides the basic costing data for preparing the budget, planning, and making decisions regarding resource allocation.
- *Cost efficiency analysis* provides information to assess the efficiency of programs and activities.
- *Life-cycle costing* furnishes the total cost associated with a long-lived asset, including acquisition, operation, and maintenance costs over the life of the equipment, less any resale value.
- *Avoidable cost* accounts for the amount of expense that would not occur if a given decision were implemented.
- The *contracting-out decision* provides a basis to determine if an activity should be completed in-house or contracted out.
- *Fee determination* facilitates the development of a fee schedule and reimbursement costs.
- *Reporting* adds greater cost consciousness to financial statements, as fund accounting does not permit cost and performance analysis.
- *Opportunity cost* shows the maximum value of benefits foregone by selecting one option over another. Opportunity cost is useful when choices must be made between alternative courses of action. For example, if a governmental unit wishes to contract out its garbage collection rather than continue to do it in-house, opportunity cost is considered.
- *Differential costs* present the amount of increase or decrease in revenue or expenses that is expected to result from a particular course of action as compared to an alternative.
  It may also be viewed as the difference between incremental costs at two different levels of activity.
- *Diagnostically-related group (DRG)* is the flat price the U.S. government pays hospitals for medicare patients, requiring hospitals to modify their accounting system from an actual, process-measuring system to one that adopts standard costs per product in DRG.
- *Full cost* offers another way of presenting total or absorption "cost."
- A *process costing system* produces an average per unit cost by aggregating all relevant costs of a process and dividing it by the units of output produced. For example, in a hospital all costs

related to inpatient care are divided by the total number of days of care, resulting in an average cost per patient day, as in the following example:

Activity or Process	Costs (A)	Output (B)
Inpatient Care	$50,000	400 patient days

Average cost (A) ÷ (B) = $1,250 per patient day.

- *Activity-based costing* links the cost of each specific activity to its related program, output and the revenues or benefits it generates. The emphasis on linking activity to cost allows management to take specific action to increase benefits or reduce resource consumption. When activities are reduced to a final output without costing individual components, it becomes impossible to tell what contribution each specific activity is making. For example, a department may report the average cost of each course taught at a given figure indicating that some classes have as many as 200 students while one-fourth have fewer than 15 students.[5]

Cost Behavior

It is important to be able to discern the behavior of various kinds of costs as they relate to managerial decisions. Costs may be categorized according to their behavior patterns at different levels of activity. Based on the changes of total cost generated by a change in activity level, there are four basic cost relationships, as shown in Figure 2.2.

- *Fixed cost* is one that remains constant regardless of the variation in volume of activity. Since the expense does not change as the number of units or products increases, the cost per unit decreases. Yearly rent and insurance premiums are good examples of fixed costs.
- *Semifixed cost* is also known as "step cost". It is fixed for a given level of activity, but it increases to higher plateaus as activity increases. Supervision is a good example. An additional supervisor is expected to be taken on when the volume of work reaches a specific level of activity.
- *Variable cost* is one that tends to fluctuate according to the variation in the volume of the activity. Variable cost increases or decreases directly in proportion to a change in the level of activity.

Figure 2.2
Patterns of Cost Behavior

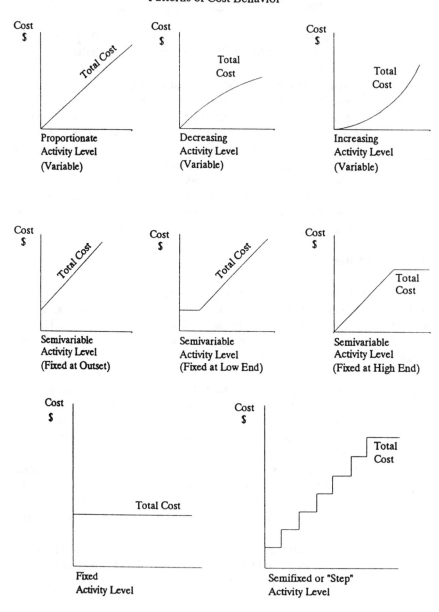

For example, the materials cost for making license plates increases or decreases depending on the number of units produced.

- *Semivariable cost* is a cost that has both fixed and semivariable characteristics. The predominant element of the cost is variable, but it has some element of fixed costs at either the lower or higher range of activity. The guaranteed minimum wage is a good example of fixed cost at the lower end of activity, while Social Security, unemployment taxes, maintenance, and salary plus commission represent examples of fixed cost at the higher level of activity.[6]

Responsibility Centers/Accounting

These two concepts are intertwined in theory and in practice. Responsibility accounting is the mechanism used to provide performance information to the individual directly responsible for a particular activity or function (when viewed in this context, the unit, section, department, and division are all considered responsibility centers). The reporting of results is made possible, permitting the identification and fixing of responsibility for significant variances from planned performance. It permits management to take timely and corrective action. It is particularly noteworthy that responsibility accounting assigns responsibility to those individuals who have influence over day-to-day costs, minimizing the potential for passing the buck. In a county health department, for example, the costs of sanitation, inspection, communicable disease control, environmental control, and community mental health may be reported separately. The county health director, then, could hold each unit accountable for the results in its respective responsibility area.

In responsibility accounting, appropriated funds are made available to specific organizational units within an agency. Each unit is responsible for the resources entrusted to it. The responsible unit official may authorize a commitment of expenditure and is ultimately accountable for the actions taken and the results achieved. The resources made available are stipulated in the budget and must be recorded in the accounts, wherein each commitment, payment, or refund must be recorded. Thus, at any given time, the amount allocated less the recorded transaction provides the balance available for use. Responsibility costs in monetary terms are costs incurred by, and on behalf of, a responsibility center over a period of time.

Anthony and Young suggested the following procedures in determining and allocating costs:

- Determine the object or unit of goods or services for which cost is being sought. For example, a cost object for a hospital may be a patient day, and for a university, a student year. A university may choose to use different cost objects, such as the cost for a classroom or laboratory hour.
- Determine the responsibility cost center (an area over which management is held accountable for inputs and outputs and over which a reasonable degree of control is exercised) from which the cost is to be collected.
- Determine the direct costs (traceable to a specific cost object or cost center) and indirect costs (applicable to more than one cost object or responsibility cost center).
- Allocate service support center costs to the mission (the main purpose for which an agency exists), as shown in Table 2.1. The basis or technique for allocating or apportioning those service center costs is the one that is most appropriate, in relation to the experience of the particular agency or individual. It may be the square footage occupied by the mission cost center or the hours of service rendered by the service cost center.[7]

Table 2.1
Responsibility Centers and Programs

Responsibility Center	Alcohol Detoxification	Drug Rehabilitation	Trauma Center	Renal Dialysis
Mission Centers				
Routine exam	No. days	No. days	No. days	No. days
Surgery	--	--	No. procedures	
Laboratory	No. tests	No. tests	No. tests	No. tests
Radiology	No. procedures	No. procedures	No. procedures	No.procedures
Outpatient care	No. visits	No. visits	No. visits	No. visits
Service Centers				
	Cost distributed to mission centers and programs to determine their full costs.			
Housekeeping				
Dieting				
Laundry				
Administration				
Social Services				

Four types of responsibility centers are common, especially in the private sector. (1) The *cost center* (also known as an *expense center*) is the smallest area of responsibility for which costs or expenses are collected; it does not measure the monetary value of the responsibility center's output. (2) A *revenue center* is charged with the responsibility of achieving some predetermined output as expressed in monetary terms or revenue. (3) A *profit center* measures the monetary value of the input (expenses) incurred and the output (revenue) produced. The difference between expense and revenue equals profit. (4) The *investment center* measures, not only the profit generated, but also the amount of capital employed, providing the basis for determining the return on investment (ROI). Of the four types of centers, the cost/expense center is the most widely used in public and not-for-profit organizations.

BASIC ACCOUNTING CONCEPTS AND PRINCIPLES

Accounting principles are built on a number of important concepts. Accountants habitually apply these concepts in their day-to-day accounting activities (recording, classifying, summarizing, and interpreting data), seldom making specific reference to them. The following are the major concepts and principles of accounting:

- *Money as a measure:* Accounting recognizes only those activities that can be quantitatively expressed in monetary terms; this gives accounting the power to express heterogenous activities in a common language. It permits items owned by an agency, such as receivables, equipment, and inventories, to be aggregated as one total. A possible shortcoming is that it cannot measure quality improvement in the service delivery or morale of an organization.
- *The entity concept:* Accounting reports are required for each economic or legal organization that uses a body of resources to achieve a common operating goal. A useful distinction is that the accounting system recognizes transactions only as they affect the business, not the individuals who manage the organization.
- *The going concern concept and periodicity:* The assumption is made that a business will continue in existence for an indefinite period. Assets are thus valued according to what is expected to happen to them in the normal course of operations. An implicit assumption is that accounting is a means whereby an organization's value is enhanced over an indefinite time horizon. To determine how well managers are performing their resource-enhancing objective, an arbitrary time period such as a calendar year or a 12-

month fiscal period is identified as the required time to present reports on the organization's accomplishment.

- *Consistency:* The ability to make comparisons is an important requirement in the analysis and use of financial data. In the accumulation and presentation of financial data, the principle of consistency requires that an enterprise follow the same generally accepted accounting practices in the recording and reporting of financial data in succeeding periods. When an independent auditor finds exceptions to these practices, such inconsistencies must be reported.

- *Conservatism and the cost concept:* Given two equally acceptable alternatives, the accountant will typically accept the option that tends to portray an entity in the least optimistic financial position. If given the choice between two or more equally acceptable asset values to record, the one with the least value will be accepted, and similarly, the larger of two acceptable liability options will be chosen. The guiding principles relating to the recognition of expense and income suggest that when in doubt, it is better to overstate expense and understate revenue. The operating view is to anticipate losses but not gains. It is particularly noteworthy that this does not justify the deliberate misinterpretation of the operating results of an enterprise unit.

- *Matching:* Under this principle, accountants attempt to match all expenses or expenditures incurred with the revenues generated in the achievement of objectives for a specific period of time. The main aim is to permit an evaluation of the effort-achievement relationship. The matching of effort (expenses) with achievement (revenue) in determining operating profit or loss is difficult in the not-for-profit sector because of problems in assigning value to service achievements.

- *Duality concept:* This is a central guiding norm and strength of the accounting system. The principle requires the identification of the source from which the available resources of an organization are received. The concept generates the following equation: assets equal liabilities plus equity (or funds). It matches assets with liabilities and funds, providing the system with internal checks by relating each inflow to an outflow entity.

Generally Accepted Accounting Principles

Until 1984 there were two primary authoritative sources of generally accepted accounting principles (GAAP) that were applicable to state and local government: (1) American Institute of Certified Public Accountants (AICPA), *Audit of State and Local Governmental Units* (and related interpretations); and (2) Government Finance Officers Association (GFOA), *Governmental Accounting, Auditing, and Financial Reporting* (1980), and National Committee on Governmental Accounting (NCGA), *Statement #1, Governmental Accounting and Financial Reporting Principles* (1979). As of 1984, accounting and financial reporting standards for state and local governments were set by the Governmental Accounting Standards Board (GASB), which was established by the Financial Accounting Foundation. The GASB consults with, and is advised by, the Governmental Accounting Advisory Council (GAAC). This group is made up of organizations such as the National Association of Counties, U.S. Conference of Mayors, U.S. General Accounting Office, Governmental Finance Officers Association, Health Care Financial Management Association, National Association of College and University Business Office Officers, American Accounting Association, bond raters, municipal underwriters, and representatives of the Financial Accounting Standards Advisory Council (FASAC), the advisory group to the Financial Accounting Standards Board (FASB).

In the private sector, this is paralleled by FASB, which has the responsibility for setting standards for business organizations. GAAP is applicable to the general purpose financial statements of entities or activities in the public sector, such as hospitals, colleges, universities, utilities, and pension plans. Organizations in the public sector are subject to FASB standards except in those instances where GASB has issued pronouncements applicable to such entities or activities. Existing standards established by AICPA and NCGA will remain in effect until amended or superseded by GASB. Other authoritative sources that guide governmental entities include two federal bodies, the General Accounting Office (GAO) and Office of Management and Budget (OMB).

Nongovernmental not-for-profit agencies rely on AICPA pronouncements and a variety of authoritative bodies such as the Internal Revenue Service (IRS) and the federal Securities and Exchange Commission (SEC), from which they obtain guidelines for accounting. In the hospital field, the American Hospital Association sets accounting standards, while similarly, in the not-for-profit human service organizations, United Way acts as an authoritative body (see its *Accounting and Financial Reporting Manual*).

BASIS OF ACCOUNTING

Basis of accounting identifies when revenues, expenditures, expenses, transfers, and liabilities are to be recognized. Stated another way, a basis of accounting is the procedure used for indicating specific points in the transaction cycle when resource inflows and outflows are to be recognized. Basis of accounting indicates when to record the measurement of income, expenditure, commitment, liability, or transfer. There are three bases that are generally found in practice: the cash basis, the accrual basis, and the modified cash accrual basis.

Cash Basis

This approach measures and records changes in an entity's books only when cash is paid out or received. Because many nonprofit enterprises predominantly provide socially desirable services, they typically measure only inflows (revenue) and outflows (expenditures) of spendable resources. Likewise, profit-oriented entities that provide services in exchange for fees often use the cash basis of accounting, emphasizing the points of cash receipt and disbursement as opposed to the points where resources are earned and used (accrual basis). Most individuals maintain their finances on the cash basis.

The cash basis is highly desirable because of its simplicity and the low cost to maintain it. A checkbook is the only accounting record that is needed, as the entity needs only to summarize its check stubs to generate financial statements. For entities that transact most operations on a cash basis, this approach can be useful.

Accrual Basis

The accrual basis presents, for a given period, the recognition and recording of all revenues earned, all expenses or expenditures incurred or consumed, all assets purchased, and all liabilities owed or incurred. Stated another way, to accrue means to record an amount in the accounting records in anticipation of future receipt or payment (i.e., cash flow). The accrual basis is required by GAAP in the private sector because it is accepted as a better measure of assessing enterprise performance than the cash basis. The accrual basis permits a direct matching between expense outflow and revenue inflow in a responsibility center. The General Accounting Office (GAO) has noted the following requirements for accrual accounting:

1. Expenditures accrue when charges are incurred (i.e., when services are performed, property is received, amounts become owed for which no performance is required), irrespective of the time when payment is made and invoice and/or property are received.
2. Revenues due are recorded when earned; money received in advance of government's performance is recorded as a liability.
3. Expired costs or resources consumed constitute the measure of performance of an activity or unit of work and should be accumulated by major organizational segments, budget activities, programs, or responsibility centers.[8]

The accrual concept places emphasis on earning and on that point at which resources are consumed, rather than on inflow and outflow, as in the cash basis. Accrual accounting is an example of the matching principle-revenues are matched with expenses for a specific period of time.

Though accrual accounting is widely practiced in the private sector and in proprietary operations in the not-for-profit sector, difficulties are encountered when attempts are made to apply it to most governmental and not-for-profit agencies. Some revenues, such as property taxes, can be accrued (with reasonable allowance for uncollectible revenues) in those cases where taxpayers are obligated to pay given amounts when the tax is levied. There are, however, revenues, such as permits and fees, that are not measurable until the cash is actually collected because there is no reliable way to determine how much will be collected. The same can be said about the collectability of fees in public and not-for-profit agencies when goods and services are distributed to clients on a need basis. Liability for long-term debt is an example. While a liability exists on long-term debt at the time of issuance, the liability is not recognized until the period when payment is due because only then are resources required to meet the liability.

Modified Accrual Basis

Under this basis are presented expenditures other than accrued interest on general long-term debt, inventory, and disbursements, which may be recorded at the time of purchase or when used, and prepaid expenses, which are normally recorded or recognized on the accrual basis at the time the liability is incurred. Revenues are recorded when received, and those that are measurable and available for expenditure are accrued to properly reflect the taxes levied and the revenues earned.

Because revenue and expenditure measurements are subject to unique constraints, legal and otherwise, in the not-for-profit sector, and especially in governmental units, the modified cash accrual basis of accounting is used. The modified cash accrual basis also accords with the principle of conservatism, which is relevant to not-for-profit organizations. The system permits expenditures to be fully stated, or perhaps, overstated, while the reverse is true for revenue. This procedure enhances the possibility of creating a surplus and reduces the chances of generating a deficit.

Accounting Basis: Advantages and Disadvantages

Before an agency chooses a basis of accounting, it should evaluate the advantages and disadvantages of each type. The cash basis is the simplest method to implement and is widely used in small businesses, small governmental units, and other not-for-profit organizations. The cash basis is also the least expensive to operate. In addition, it requires the least accounting knowledge and experience to operate the system. On the negative side, the cash basis provides the least accurate information. For example, revenues and expenses for which cash has not been received or paid are not recognized. Also, it is more difficult for a certified public accountant to express an opinion about the accounting statements.

The accrual basis provides the most accurate picture of the financial position of an agency because the method requires the recording of all transactions affecting the agency, whether or not cash changes hands. The accrual basis gives an accurate picture of the organization at any point in time, assuming that accurate and up-to-date records are kept. A disadvantage of the accrual basis is its added cost, because of the extra knowledge, experience, and training needed to implement it. A decision to use the accrual basis should weigh the accuracy to be gained against the cost of implementing it.

The modified cash accrual basis is a compromise between these two extremes. It increases the accuracy of accounts without all the additional costs associated with the accrual system. The modified basis does, however, require additional personnel because bookkeeping is slightly more complicated than under the cash basis.

In determining which basis of accounting is best for an organization, recognition should be given to the following factors:

- technical knowledge of the available personnel;
- sophistication of information required to ensure efficient and effective operation;
- comparative cost of the basis;
- external reporting requirements; and
- internal reporting requirements.

In Tables 2.2 and 2.3, the cash and accrual accounting bases are compared in the acquisition and use of an asset.

CONTRASTING PUBLIC AND PRIVATE ACCOUNTING

Not-for-profit organizations, especially government agencies, operate in a different political and economic environment than do business enterprises. Thus, governmental accounting standards have developed differently than have business enterprise standards. Despite this, there are many common practices that make governmental and business accounting standards more alike than different. Many of the principles and concepts (e.g., controlling, reporting, concern for relevance, comparability, consistency, and understandability) enumerated earlier in this volume have applicability in both the not-for-profit and the private sectors. The basic differences between the two sectors can be stated as follows:

1. Not-for-profit agencies, especially those in the public sector, require strict adherence to legal and administrative directives.
2. In the private sector, the income statement (the principal inflow and outflow statement) emphasizes earning and using resources. This inflow and outflow statement shows the extent to which operating objectives have been met, focusing on how resource outflows benefit future periods as well as the current reporting period.
3. Not-for-profit agencies have inflow (revenue) and outflow (expenditure) statements. However, they are concerned with raising and expending resources according to specific budget plans.
4. Not-for-profit agencies are expenditure- rather than expense-oriented. (Expenditure measures the monetary value of resources used in the acquisition of goods and or services.)
5. Emphasis is put on the source of revenues and ways in which they are used. Therefore, not-for-profit organizations are dollar accountability-oriented. Typical is the expression, "Where got, where gone."
6. GAAP takes precedence in private sector accounting. In a public organization, when GAAP and legal requirements conflict, GAAP gives way.

Table 2.2
Cash Basis versus Accrual Basis:
Asset Acquisition and Use

Period/Description	1	2	3
Transaction	Asset purchased but not paid for (on credit or account)	Asset consumed or used	Asset purchased (on credit) paid in cash
Accrual Basis	Asset and liability recognized	The use and decrease in asset value recognized	Decrease in liability and cash recognized
Cash Basis	No entry	No entry	Decrease in cash and asset recognized

Table 2.3
Cash Basis versus Accrual Basis:
Revenue Recognition

Period/Description	1	2	3
Transaction	Service delivered	Bill sent	Bill paid in cash
Accrual Basis	Revenue and accounts receivable recognized	No entry	Accounts receivable decreased and cash increased
Cash Basis	No entry	No entry	Cash increased and revenue recognized

7. Public sector accounting transactions are guided by an inflexible budget plan, while the private sector employs a flexible budget which changes as the volume of output changes.

8. Private sector accounting records are maintained to show the owner's equity in one consolidated account, whereas in the not-for-profit sector, there is no equity accounting and funds are based on legal requirements.

9. Not-for-profit accounting emphasizes current funds, with no recognition of capital or fixed assets.

10. Private accounting uses the accrual basis, while not-for-profit accounting typically uses either the cash basis or the modified cash accrual basis.

11. Ideally, private sector accounting, reflects the results of economic activities or *operational accountability*, expressing the efficiency with which the profit objective has been achieved. This is made possible by the direct matching of revenues with expenses for a given period and a specific responsibility center. Thus, management can be held operationally accountable to owners, creditors, and other interests.

12. The public and other not-for-profit sectors do not typically have operational accountability or the matching principle as a central objective. Typically, these organizations, do not set prices for their goods and services. Most often, little or no revenue is collected from the beneficiaries to whom their activities are mainly directed. Even in hospitals whose major source of revenues are derived from the sale of health care, services are not totally market determined. (Hospitals structure their prices to take care of indigent and other non-paying patients.) Thus, operational accountability is not reflected in the accounting statement. Because of this reality, the major emphasis in not-for-profit organizations is put on stewardship or the fiduciary role of administrators. This requires that management be able to account for inflow of funds and their expenditure in the pursuit of basic objectives. As noted throughout this volume, it results in financial statements that typically show dollar accountability.

13. Dollar accountability systems emphasize cash inflows (revenues or receipts and outflow expenditures).

PRINCIPAL ACCOUNTING STATEMENTS

All accounting transactions are summarized in three principal statements: the balance sheet, the income statement, and the statement of changes in financial position.

The *balance sheet* is one of the basic accounting reports indicating the resources controlled by an organization and the ways in which they are financed. The main purpose of the balance sheet is to show the financial position of an agency at a specific point in time. The financial position shows the available resources (assets) as compared with outstanding obligations (liabilities and fund equity) on a particular date. The balance sheet may be compared to a snapshot; in every moment following the snapshot, the picture is likely to change. The balance sheet for Bright Hospital is shown in Table 2.4. An examination of the format and categories provides a general idea.

Two broad categories contained in a balance sheet are assets and liabilities. Assets are things of value that can be owned. They constitute the resources of an organization measured in monetary terms on a specific date (for example, resources of Bright Hospital on December 31, 1996). Liabilities are the debts owed by an organization to others outside the organization (for example, claims that outsiders have against the hospital that must be paid at certain known times in the future). When total liabilities are subtracted from total assets, the difference represents the funds or equity invested by contributors or shareholders. Inspection of the asset and liability categories reveals that they are subdivided into current and fixed assets and current and long-term liabilities.

Current assets refers to cash or other assets that may reasonably be expected to be converted or realized in cash, sold, or consumed, usually within a year or less, through the normal operation of a business. This balance sheet was simplified for ease in understanding nonprofit institutions typically consisting of several separate divisions, such as current funds unrestricted and restricted, and fund categories such as construction, building, land, endowment, or other funds, depending on the original source and disposition of capital funds. Each fund has a set of self-balancing accounts.

There is no set number of current assets. Rather, they vary according to the type and needs of an individual organization. Table 2.4 provides a list of the items frequently found in the current asset subdivision of a balance sheet.

- Cash consists of money, in the form of currency, coin, checks, money orders, banker's drafts on hand or on deposit with an official, and bank deposits, that is free for disbursement at any time.
- Accounts receivable are claims against customers for amounts owed on open accounts or on credit from private persons, firms,

Table 2.4
Bright Hospital-Simplified Consolidated Balance
Sheet as of December 31, 1996, and December 31, 1997

ASSETS	1996		1997	
Current Assets				
Cash		305,000		$225,000
Accounts receivable-patients	$1,200,000		$ 840,000	
less uncollectible accounts	21,000	1,179,000	15,000	825,600
Marketable securities (market value)		20,000		75,000
Inventories		134,400		115,000
Prepaid expenses		23,000		23,000
Total current assets		1,661,400		1,263,600
Fixed Assets				
Land ($200,000 in 1996)		250,000		250,000
Buildings and equipment	6,500,000		$6,826,400	
less accumulated depreciation	860,000		905,000	
Total net fixed assets		5,640,000		5,921,400
Total assets		$7,571,400		$7,435,000

Table 2.4 cont'd.

LIABILITIES

Current Liabilities

Accounts payable	$ 170,000	$ 120,000
Taxes payable	6,000	7,000
Salaries payable	150,000	145,000
Current loans	400,000	350,000
Advance payments-third-party contracts	130,000	140,000
Total current liabilities	856,000	762,000

Long-Term Liabilities

Long-term loans ($400,000 in 1996)	1,397,400	1,300,000
Bonds ($1,000,000 in 1996)	2,000,000	2,000,000
Mortgages	350,000	330,000
Total long-term liabilities	3,747,400	3,630,000
Fund balance	2,968,000	3,043,000
Total liabilities and fund balances	$7,571,400	$7,435,000

Note: This balance sheet was simplified for ease in understanding nonprofit institutions typically consisting of several separate divisions, such as current funds unrestricted and restricted, and fund categories such as construction, building, land, endowment, or other funds depending on the original source and disposition of capital funds. Each fund would have a set of self-balancing accounts.

or corporations for the delivery of goods and services. In Table 2.4, *accounts receivable* refers to services rendered to patients. In government organizations, *accounts receivable* does not usually include amounts due from other funds of the same governmental unit. Note that although taxes and assessments receivable are included in the term *receivable*, they are reported separately as taxes receivable and special assessments receivable. In accounts receivable, a provision is made for the uncollectible amount that is likely to prove worthless. This amount is subtracted from the accounts receivable, showing the net amount.

- *Inventory* refers to items or merchandise for sale in the normal course of business. In not-for-profit organizations, *inventory* has at least two different meanings: (l) supplies not for sale but for use in the delivery of goods or services; and (2) a detailed list showing quantities, descriptions, and values of owned property (e.g., desks, cabinets).

Fixed assets represent assets such as land, buildings, machinery, furniture, and other equipment having a nominal life of more than one year. The purchase price of most fixed assets is reduced by a depreciation charge each year. Fixed assets less accumulated depreciation represents the remaining economic and potential productive value of the assets. During each fiscal period, the amount allowed for depreciation is included in the income statement as part of the cost of doing business. The depreciation expense may be viewed as an allowance for capital recovery that may be managed to generate sufficient funds to replace the asset at the end of its useful life.

Current liabilities comprise those obligations that can be objectively determined and will come due in a short period of time (usually a year or less) and will have to be paid out of current assets. Table 2.4 shows the categories that are classified as current liabilities:

- Accounts payable constitutes the claims of vendors or suppliers to the organization.
- Taxes payable is the amount owed but not yet paid.
- Salaries payable represents the salaries that employees have earned but are still owed by the organization.
- Advance payments on third-party (insurance company) contracts are payments that have been received for which no services were rendered.
- *Current loan* refers to the short-term loans that have been obtained from banks and other financial institutions.

Long-term liabilities comprise the obligations that are not required to be met for at least a year or more. The following are key examples that are usually classified as long-term liabilities:

- Long-term loans are funds borrowed from banks and other financial institutions.
- Bonds are a form of interest-bearing note employed by organizations to borrow money on a long-term basis. They are like long-term loans but have more formal requirements. Typically, they are secured by specific assets, except in the case of governmental units and large corporations, which may float some bonds on their general credit. In addition, bonds may be traded on exchanges, while long-term loans may not.
- Mortgages are long-term loans that are usually secured by some identified fixed assets.

Funds in not-for-profit organizations are resources that are available to obtain goods and services. Examples of funds in not-for-profit organizations are unspent resources from taxes, charges, donations, and endowments, which may be restricted or unrestricted. The presence of restricted funds means that the donor or authorizing body (legislature or board) stipulates the conditions regarding the use of the funds; no such conditions apply on the use of unrestricted funds.

Income statement is a summary of revenues and expenses or expenditures for a specific period of time. In profit-oriented companies, profits are measured by comparing revenues generated in a given period with expenses incurred to produce those revenues in the same time period (this is known as the matching principle). Revenues represent the inflow of assets from the sale of products or the delivery of services to customers or clients. Expenses are the sacrifices made or the costs incurred to produce those revenues. When revenue exceeds expense, net income results. If the reverse is true, the organization or business is said to be operating at a loss. Table 2.5 presents the income statement of Bright Hospital for January 1, 1996 to December 31, 1996 and 1997.

The income statement typically contains three parts, showing revenues, expenses, and net profit or loss. The revenues in Bright Hospital were generated mainly from inpatient, ambulatory, and auxiliary services.

Not-for-profit organizations that operate on the cash basis simply compare the total fund's inflow and outflow and accept the result as an adequate measure of the organization's performance. The use of this approach violates the matching principle if some revenues are earned in one period but are not

Table 2.5
Bright Hospital-Income Statement for the Period
January 1, 1996 as of December 31, 1996 and 1997

Revenues*	1996		1997	
Income from				
Inpatient services	$4,800,000		$4,625,000	
Ambulatory services	400,000		425,000	
Auxiliary income	1,100,000		1,220,000	
Total deductions including				
free service	300,000		320,000	
Other revenue: Sale of				
radiology equipment	180,000		-0-	
Total revenues (net)		$6,780,000		$6,690,000

EXPENSES**

Salaries and wages	$4,925,000		$4,625,000	
Supplies	80,000		40,000	
Depreciation	290,000		340,000	
Administrative and general expenses	890,200		1,205,200	
Interest	129,800		60,800	
Miscellaneous and other expenses ($50,000 rate payable)	390,000		297,000	
Total Expenses		$6,705,000		$6,568,000

Net Profit (Excess of Revenues over Expenses)	$ 75,000		$ 123,000	
Fund balance at beginning of year	2,968,000		3,043,000	
Fund balance at end of year	3,043,000		3,166,000	

* Total operating revenues ($6,780,000 less $120,000) from radiology equipment sale.

** While interest expense is not excluded in this calculation of ratios, some analysts do exclude them.

recognized until the next, when they are physically received. This is true for expenses as well. When the matching of revenues and expenses does not occur, it may distort the performance assessment. This is the main reason why many not-for-profit organizations are moving toward a greater use of the accrual concept for measuring income. The accrual concept effectively overcomes the distortion of net income because it matches revenues with expenses for each given period. Bright Hospital is on the accrual basis. Thus, the $75,000 shown in net income or surplus may not be equated with cash. Net income and cash will be exactly the same only when all expenses incurred are actually paid and when all revenues earned are received in the period for which the income statement is prepared.

The *funds flow statement* or *statement of changes in financial position* is devoted exclusively to reporting changes in fiscal position for a specified period of time. This statement identifies the sources from which additional investable funds or cash were derived and the uses to which these funds were put. For this reason, the statement is known variously as a statement of funds provided and applied, sources and uses of funds, or changes in financial position.

The funds flow statement has come into general use because of the need to provide information to decision makers relating to finance and investment activities. Information on sources and uses of funds may be obtained from an analysis of the income statement and the balance sheet. The principal sources (inflow) and uses (outflow) may be summarized as follows:

Sources
> Net cash revenue from operations for the period;
> Additional investment (e.g., donations and endowment); and
> Increase in bonds or long-term loans.

Uses
> Additions to plant and equipment;
> Reduction of expenses during period; and
> Distribution of income.

A statement of changes in financial position for Bright Hospital is shown in Table 2.6.

ACCOUNTING AND INTERNAL CONTROLS

Internal controls are commonly classified as either administrative controls or accounting controls. Internal administrative controls are comprised

Table 2.6
Bright Hospital-Statement of Changes
in Financial Position for Year Ending
December 31, 1996

From operations:		
Cash revenue	$ 5,200,000	
Less cash expenses	5,150,000	50,000
From other sources:		
Sale of operating equipment	300,000	
Long-term loans	400,000	
Bonds	1,000,000	1,700,000
Total cash generated		1,750,000
Uses (cash):		
Purchase of land	200,000	
Purchase of equipment	1,500,000	1,700,000
Increase in cash during the year		$ 50,000

of procedures and records that assist management in achieving an organization's goals. For example, when poor-quality work occurs in a particular responsibility center, the use of internal controls permits management to better evaluate personnel performance and attempt to improve the quality of the output. Internal accounting controls refer to procedures, records, and reports that have been designed to safeguard assets and promote the reliability of financial records and reports. For example, guidelines and specific procedures developed to ensure the recording of transactions in accordance with generally accepted accounting principles aid in assuring the reliability of financial records. An important means for safeguarding assets is to limit access to authorized personnel.

The internal control system varies, depending on the size of the not-for-profit organization. In organizations where there are few employees and the manager of the organization provides direct supervision and oversight, few controls are needed. The situation changes as the complexity and size of the organization increase. This requires that management delegate greater authority, making it necessary to put more reliance on the accounting system.

THE FUND-ACCOUNTING SYSTEM

The universe of not-for-profit organizations using the fund-accounting system may be classified as follows: (1) voluntary health and welfare organizations, (2) hospitals, (3) colleges and universities, (4) federal state and local governments, and (5) others, including, church associations, political parties, museums, and cemeteries.

The fund is the basic accounting entity for the public sector and, to a lesser extent, for other not-for-profit organizations. An important objective is to ensure that donated and restricted resources are applied in accordance with the authorizing body or donor's wishes. While the private organization focuses on profitability, the not-for-profit entity focuses on resources-the relationship between inflows and outflows (balance budget or surplus). In private sector accounting, the entire business or firm is the basic accounting and reporting unit; in government, the fund is the basic unit. Unlike the not-for-profit sector, there are no restricted funds in the private sector. The fund is referred to as:

- a fiscal and accounting entity;
- a system with a self-balancing set of accounts.

It is characterized by:

- recording of cash and all other financial resources, related liabilities, and residual balances and charges therein;
- segregation for the purpose of carrying out specific activities or attaining particular objectives, special regulations, restrictions, and limitations; and
- a fund-accounting equation of: Assets + Expenditures = Liabilities + Receipts + Fund Balance.

Fund Balance Requirement

Each fund contains a set of self-balancing accounts. When total revenue exceeds total expenditure, the fund has a surplus balance. Especially in local government, each fund is typically required to be balanced. In a number of governmental jurisdictions, a negative fund balance may have to be erased by increasing revenues during the succeeding periods. The fund balance (net or residual assets) represents the net amount of resources of the fund. It is equivalent to, or a counterpart of, the for-profit organization's retained earnings.

Types of Funds

There are three main categories of funds: governmental funds, proprietary funds, and fiduciary funds, funds may be restricted or non-restricted. The nature of the activity accounted for determines the category. The following are brief definitions of the funds used in governmental units:

- The *general fund* accounts for all financial resources except those required to be accounted for in another fund. Most revenues are accounted for in the general fund. This is usually the largest fund and is created to carry out the basic purposes (services) for which the governmental unit was established. For example, fire, sanitation, and health would be in the general fund, but the construction of a firehouse typically would be accounted for in another fund. Normally, a bond is floated to finance building costs, subject to certain laws and legal requirements.
- *Special revenue funds* account for proceeds or specific revenue sources (often earmarked) that are restricted to expenditure for specific purposes. Typically, special revenues exclude special assessments, expendable trusts, and major capital projects.
- *Capital project funds* account for financial resources to be used for the acquisition or construction of capital facilities unless the transactions are handled by special assessment, enterprise, or trust funds.
- *Debt service funds* account for monies accumulated for the payment of general long-term debt principal and interest.
- *Special assessment funds* account for funds utilized for projects financed from special assessments levied against property owners.
- *Enterprise funds* measure income. They are like commercial or nonexpendable funds used to account for activities that parallel those of a profit-oriented organization. For example, a publicly owned water or electric utility applying user charges according to services received is similar to a privately operated water utility. The earnings from the enterprise fund may be used for general purposes or other uses when it has been determined that such uses are justified.
- *Internal service funds* account for the financing of goods and services provided by one department or agency to other departments or agencies of a governmental unit on a cost recovery or reimbursement basis. A motor pool for which each department makes a contribution would be an example.

- *Plant, property and equipment funds* maintain records on resources invested in the plant, property, and equipment, and accounts for the payment of debt used to finance these activities.
- *Endowment funds* account for donors' gifts that are to be maintained in perpetuity to produce income that may be expended or be used for either restricted or nonrestricted purposes. Sometimes, quasi-endowments may be restricted by a governing board instead of the owner.
- *Fiduciary funds* account for assets (trust and agency funds) held by a governmental unit in a trustee or agency capacity. A bequest left to a city to maintain a park would be an example. Both expendable and nonexpendable funds are included in this category. Expendable trust funds account for monies being held that may be totally expended. In the case of nonexpendable funds, only the interest earned may be expended; such funds are accounted in a manner similar to proprietary funds. Since agency funds are purely custodial, they do not require a measurement of results of the operation. Thus, there is no fund balance, only assets and liabilities.
- *Expendable funds* are usable in current operations and consumption, while funds that are dedicated to the maintenance of capital and self-sustaining are nonexpendable. The expendable fund puts emphasis on the flow of resources, focusing on current assets and liabilities and modified accrual on the operating statement. Four funds (general fund, special revenue funds, capital projects, and debt service funds) are viewed as expendable funds (they are sometimes referred to as source and disposition funds). These funds are created to offer services to the public, often without charge or with only a nominal fee. Since all the resources raised are to be expended within a reasonable time period, the accountability system is organized to control cash or dollar accountability. The expendable funds focus only on resources raised to be expended. The nonexpendable funds put emphasis on the preservation or maintenance of capital such as property or self-sustaining funds, including enterprise, internal, and trust funds, and permanent funds such as endowment.
- *Restricted funds* and *nonrestricted funds* are categorized based on the restraint or control that governs their use or application. The unrestricted funds typically include all expendable resources that are not constrained by a specific stipulation about their use. Generally, this means that any resources that are unrestricted are available for general operations of the entity, governmental unit,

TABLE 2.7

City of A-Balance Sheet as of December 31, 1997

Assets		Liabilities, Reserves, and Fund Balance	
Cash	$ 10,000	Vouchers Payable	$ 90,000
Taxes Receivable	100,000	Due to Working Capital Fund	10,000
		Reserve for Encumbrances	50,000
		Fund Balance	(40,000)
Total Assets	$110,000	Total Liabilities, Reserves, and Fund	$110,000

TABLE 2.8

**City of A--General Fund Analysis of Changes in Fund Balance
For Year Ended December 31, 1997**

Beginning fund balance, January 1, 1997	$ -0-
Deduct excess of expenditures and encumbrances over revenues for period ended January 31, 1996	
Expenditures	940,000
Revenues	900,000
	(40,000)
Fund Balance	$(40,000)

or organization. Restricted funds include those that can be expended only as the law, regulation, authorizing body or donor require, consistent with public policy.

Fund-Accounting Cycle

The major objective of fund accounting, especially governmental fund accounting, is to show that resources (unrestricted and restricted funds) have been used in accordance with authorized purposes. Accounting records are expected to show data from budgetary authority and transactions relating thereto. Accounting for funds begins as soon as authority has been granted to obtain and expend resources for specified purposes. The boxes below show entries that might be typical of a fund-accounting cycle. Tables 2.7 and 2.8 show the ending balance for the hypothetical city as of the end of 1997.

DOUBLE ENTRY BOOKKEEPING: SOME BASIC MECHANICS

The convention of debit and credit was designed to show increases and decreases affecting a financial entity. For every debit there must be an equal credit, and vice versa, in order to maintain an absolute balance or equality at all times. Before an entry can be made, all the possible accounts that can be debited or credited for the entity or organization must be known. The following must also be determined: all the asset accounts (things owned by the organization), such as cash, accounts receivable, inventory, and supplies; all the liabilities (claims or obligations others have against the organization), such as accounts payable and loans payable; all the revenue or income accounts, such as taxes, donations, and endowments; all the expenses/expenditures (expired costs, things to be acquired, or obligations against the organization), such as rent, postage, salaries, insurance, and travel.

An Illustration of Governmental Fund Accounting

A simplified example of the fund accounting journalizing and closing of the City of Bright is presented. The illustration includes the general fund, the internal service fund, and the debt service fund. Assume the following balances:

City of Bright General Fund
Statement as of December 31, 1996

Assets	Liabilities and Fund Balance	
Cash	Payables	$ 6,000
$20,000	Unrestricted fund balance	20,000
		$20,000
$20,000		

The following transactions took place during the 1996 fiscal year:

1. Budgeted revenues by source:

Property taxes	$ 600,000
Court fines	100,000
Other taxes	300,000
	$1,000,000

Budgeted expenditures by function:

Administration	$ 200,000
Fire/Police	300,000
Sanitation	100,000
	$ 600,000

Payments to:

Motor pool fund	$ 40,000
Debt service fund	60,000
Utility fund	90,000
Special assessment fund	100,000
Working capital fund	10,000
	$ 900,000
Budgeted fund balance	$ 100,000

2. The tax assessor's office mailed property tax statements to taxpayers amounting to $600,000.
3. Other revenues in the amount of $400,000, including $100,000 of court fines, were collected.
4. Property taxes in the amount of $500,000 were collected.
5. Expenditures for the period are as follows:

Administration	$ 102,000
Fire/Police	198,000

Sanitation	100,000
Payments:	
Motor pool fund	$ 40,000
Debt Service fund	60,000
Utility fund	90,000
Special assessment fund	100,000
Working capital fund	$ 10,000
	$ 700,000

6. A contract in the amount of $250,000 was placed for equipment and supplies.
7. A truck originally costing $10,000 was no longer needed and was sold for $2,000.
8. Receipts of goods and supplies in the amount of $190,000 were delivered relating to encumbrances of $200,000.
9. Vouchers of $790,000 were approved for payment including $90,000 to the utility fund, $100,000 to the assessment fund, $40,000 to the motor pool fund and $60,000 to the debt service fund.
10. Payables in the amount of $5,000 were paid.
11. Close the revenue and expenditure accounts.

General Fund Books' Journal

Transaction	Entry	Debit	Credit
1. Adoption of budget for fiscal year ending Dec. 31, 1996, indicating estimated revenues of $1,000,000 and appropriations of $900,000.	Estimated Revenues Appropriations Unrestricted Fund Balance	$1,000,000	$900,000 100,000
2. Accrual of income from tax levy.	Taxes Receivable Revenues	600,000	600,000
3. To record the receipt or realization of other taxes.	Cash Revenues	400,000	400,000
4. Collection of taxes previously levied.	Cash Taxes Receivable	500,000	500,000

5. Expenditures made in accordance with appropriations.	Expenditures	800,000	
	Vouchers Payable		500,000
	Due to Utility Fund		90,000
	Due to Special Assessment Fund		100,000
	Due to Working Capital		10,000
	Due to Motor Pool Fund		40,000
	Due to Debt Service Fund		60,000
6. Estimates of expenditures for orders placed for supplies and equipment.	Encumbrances	250,000	
	Reserve for Encumbrances		250,000
7. Sold truck at auction	Cash	2,000	
	Revenues		2,000
8. Liquidation of encumbrances ($200,000) upon receipt of invoices and determination of actual expenditures ($190,000) to record the obligation ($190,000) and approve vouchers to bepaid.	Reserve for Encumbrances	250,000	
	Encumbrances		250,000
	Expenditures	190,000	
	Vouchers Payable		190,000
9. Payment of vouchers and billing.	Vouchers Payable	500,000	
	Due to Utility Fund	90,000	
	Due to Assessment Fund	100,000	
	Due to Motor Pool Fund	40,000	
	Due to Debt Service Fund	60,000	
	Cash		790,000
10. Paid payables in the amount of $5,000.	Payables	5,000	
	Cash		5,000
11. Closing the Accounts	Revenues	1,002,000	
	Estimated Revenues		1,000,000
C1. To close revenues and estimated revenue accounts at end of fiscal year.	Fund Balance		2,000

C2. To close appropriations,	Appropriations	900,000	
expenditures, and	Fund Balance	40,000	
encumbrances at end of	Expenditures		890,000
fiscal year. To restrict	Encumbrances		50,000
fund balance due to			
outstanding encumbrances.			

Transactions 1-10 in the General Fund Books' Journal must be posted into a set of books called the ledgers (the place where the summaries of all accounts are recorded on a regular basis, for example, weekly or monthly). The ledgers represent "T" accounts having a debit and a credit side. The "T" accounts for transactions 1-10 are as follows:

A. Balance Sheet "T" Accounts

Cash

*B. Bal.	$ 20,000	(8)	$790,000
(3)	400,000		
(4)	500,000		
(7)	2,000		
E. Bal.	132,000		

Taxes Receivable

| (2) | $600,000 | (4) $500,000 |
| E. Bal. 100,000 | | |

Due to Working Capital Fund

| **E. Bal. | (5) $10,000 |

Payables

| | B. Bal. $6,000 |

Due to Utility Fund

| (8) | 90,000 | (5) 90,000 |

Reserve Encumbrances

(7)	$200,000	(6)	$250,000
E. Bal.		50,000.00	

Vouchers Payable

(6)	$600,000	(5)	$500,000
		(7)	190,000
	600,000	690,000.00	
	90,000		
E. Bal.		90,000.00	

Fund Balance

B. Bal. $ 14,000	(1)	$100,000
(9) 100,000		
(10) 40,000		
140,000.00		
	100,000	
	40,000	
E. Bal. 40,000		

Due to Special Assessment Fund

(8)	$100,000	(5)	$100,000

Due to Motor Pool

E. Bal.		(5) $40,000

Due to Debt Service Fund

E. Bal.		(5) $60,000

*B. Bal. means beginning balance.
**E. Bal. means ending balance.

B. Expenditure/Expense and Revenue "T" Accounts

Expenditures

(5)	$800,000	(10)	$890,000
(7)	190,000		
	890,000		
		890,000	

Encumbrances

(6) $250,000	(7)	$200,000
	(10)	50,000
250,000		
	250,000	

Estimated Revenues		Appropriations	
(1) $1,000,000	(9) $1,000,000	(9) $900,000	(1) $900,000

Revenues	
(10) $900,000	(2) $600,000
	(3) 400,000
1,002,000	1,002,000

Treatment of Encumbrances on the Books

The transactions just shown do not use the restricted and unrestricted fund balance. The alternate way for reflecting the outstanding reserve for encumbrances at the end of the period is as follows: treat the reserve for encumbrance accounts as a nominal account and close it out as a regular income statement transaction. Thus, at the end of the period, the outstanding reserve for the encumbrance amount is closed. For example, in our case, we have a $50,000 encumbrance balance. This amount would be closed on the expenditure side and set up on the balance sheet as follows: (a) debit reserve for encumbrance for $50,000 and credit encumbrance $50,000; (b) debit unrestricted fund balance for $50,000 and credit restricted fund balance for $50,000, earmarking and reducing the amount available to be spent and showing the amount outstanding and obligated.

Lapsing Assumptions A and B: Legal Provisions

These assumptions are the most frequently used assumptions in public and not-for-profit agencies. This is an important concern that determines how unspent or unused appropriated resources will be reflected in closing entries and how much discretion and trust is given to the administrators in settling outstanding obligations. Under Assumption A, encumbered appropriations do not lapse. The reserve for encumbrance accounts remains on the books as a continuing authorization to spend until the objective of the authorization has been fulfilled. The closing entries recognize whatever the outstanding obligations (amounts) are as expenditure, as follows:

> Expenditure   xxx (debited);
> Encumbrance   xxx (credited).

Under Assumption B, unexpended appropriations lapse and the unspent resources are returned to the authorizing body. All outstanding unfilled orders relating to appropriations are closed as follows:

> Reserve for Encumbrance   xxx (debited);
> Encumbrance   xxx (credited).

Unlike Assumption A, Assumption B does not delegate discretion to administrators to liquidate outstanding obligations. Thus, authority to expend funds for past unfilled orders will lapse and must be reauthorized or reappropriated during the following year.

It is important that administrators and vendors dealing with public and other not-for-profit agencies know the assumption under which they are operating when transacting business. Not knowing the operating assumption may create unnecessary problems.

Disclosing and Controlling Supplies Inventories

The balance sheet is designed to reflect the value of appropriable (spendable) resources and identifiable claims against such resources. The present system applies the acquisition approach. Expenditure is charged at the time purchase is made as follows:

> Expenditure (debited);
> Vouchers payable or cash (credited).

Since this approach treats inventory supplies on hand as a nonapproachable resource, they are excluded from the balance sheet or the general fund assets. The principle of full disclosure suggests that the cost of significant supplies on hand should be shown on the balance sheet. This can be done by using a memo entry:

> Inventory supplies (debited);
> Reserve for inventory supplies (credited).

When this system is used, the memo account is adjusted periodically to account for increases and decreases in the balance of supplies on hand. If a reduction in the supplies on hand occurs, a reversing memo entry is made. An increase is recorded by another memo.

Important reasons for reflecting the inventory on hand at the end of the period may relate to management's need to increase control over the efficient use of supplies and to minimize waste and abuse. By reflecting the inventory in the account, it draws management attention to the need for a prudent use of supplies. This recognition is likely to make employees more sensitive about misusing or casually removing supplies from the organization. Responsibility managers are not permitted to incrementally increase their budget for supplies without considering what is on hand when this practice is used.

Controlling Subsidiary Entries

This is a means of maintaining a check between what is entered in the subsidiary ledger accounts and the individual details that support the summary totals entered in the controlling ledger account. To record the adoption of the City of Bright budget the subsidiary account can be reflected as follows:

Estimated Revenues	$1,000,000	
Debit Revenue Subsidiary Ledger:		
Property taxes	600,000	
Court fines	100,000	
Other taxes	300,000	
	$1,000,000	
Appropriations		$ 900,000
Fund Balance		$ 100,000
Credit Expenditure Subsidiary Ledger:		
Administration		$200,000
Fire/Police		300,000
Sanitation		100,000
Motor pool fund		40,000
Debt service fund		60,000
Utility fund		90,000
Special assessment fund		100,000
Working Capital fund		10,000
		$ 900,000

In order to minimize errors, to facilitate tracking and coordination, and to maintain the account balance, a system known as a chart or code of accounts is used. The following is an example:

1. All assets accounts may be identified as follows:

22.	Cash
22.1	Petty Cash
33.	Accounts Receivable
33.1	Allowance for Uncollectible Accounts

2. All liabilities and fund balances may be identified as follows:

40.	Accounts Payable
41.	Boards
42.	Long-Term Debt
50.	Fund Balance

3. All revenue and expense and expenditure accounts may be identified as follows:

60.	Personnel Services
60.1	Regular Employees
60.2	Replacement and Overtime
61.	Contractual Services
61.1	Utilities
61.1.1	Fuel
61.1.2	Water Sewer Fund
70.	Property Taxes
71.	Sales Taxes

The number of accounts is limited only by the degree of detail desired by the managers of the organization or enterprise.

Understanding Debits and Credits

According to the system of accounting logic, increases (+) in assets are accumulated on the left and decreases (-) on the right. By applying this system consistently, the balance in an account can be determined at any given point in time, as follows:

Assets	
Debit	Credit
+	-

The system is based on the accounting equation: assets = liabilities + capital, or

Assets		=	Liabilities		+	Capital	
Debit	Credit		Debit	Credit		Debit	Credit
+	-		-	+		-	+

In applying the accounting equation logic to liabilities and capital accounts, increases (+) are accumulated on the right side and decreases (-) on the left side, as follows:

Assets		=	Liabilities		+	Capital	
Debit	Credit		Debit	Credit		Debit	Credit
+	-		-	+		-	+

In accounting, the left side of an account is known as the debit side, and the right side is known as the credit side. There is no intrinsic value to debit and credit other than what the accounting convention has assigned to them.

So far we have dealt with items found in the balance sheet (assets, liabilities, and capital). Because the accounts in the balance sheet are not closed out at the end of the period, they are referred to as *real accounts*. The reverse is true for income statement accounts. They are known as *nominal accounts* and are closed out to the capital account at the end of the fiscal period. Thus, the debit/credit analysis of revenues and expenses is related directly to capital. Revenue (credit) increases capital, whereas expenses (debit) decrease capital, as shown in the following:

Revenues	
Debit	Credit
-	+

Following the same logic for expenses, an increase (debit) in expense produces a decrease in capital, as shown in the following:

Expenses	
Debit	Credit
+	-

By memorizing a few basic rules, the system of debits and credits can be easily applied:

	To Increase Accounts	To Decrease Accounts
Assets	Debit	Credit
Liabilities	Credit	Debit
Revenues	Credit	Debit
Expenditures/Expenses	Debit	Credit
Capital/Fund Balance	Credit	Debit

To determine net income/loss or net deficit or surplus (in not-for-profit agencies) all revenues are totaled and all expenditures are totaled and subtracted from revenue for each fiscal period.

BREAK-EVEN ANALYSIS AND REVENUE ESTIMATING

Break-even analysis is a tool that has been widely used in the private sector. While there are some constraints in applying it to the not-for-profit sector, (for example, the assumption that there is a direct relationship between revenues and outputs, which is not typically true), there are opportunities where it may be employed, especially in those agencies that are client oriented.

The break-even point is defined as that level of activity where total revenues equal total expenses or expired costs. At this level of operation the organization will neither realize a profit nor incur an operating loss-the ideal operating point for not-for-profit organizations. While break-even analysis can be applied to past periods, it is most helpful when used to aid in future planning, especially if curtailment of operations is an objective.

Break-even analysis assumes that costs can be broken down into variable and fixed components. The main purpose of break-even analysis is determining the level of output where revenue includes both fixed and variable costs. The break-even point can be calculated by means of a formula or it can be determined from a graphic presentation of the relationship among cost, revenue, and the level or volume of productive capacity. Before the break-even sales volume (known as the equation approach) can be determined, the following data are required: (1) estimated fixed cost and expenses for a given period, such as a year; and (2) total estimated variable cost and expenses for the same period. The second approach is based on the unit contribution margin.

The equation approach is as follows: sales (no. of units x unit price) = variable cost + fixed cost. Take an example where the sales price is $2 per unit, variable costs are $1 per unit, and fixed costs are $3,000.

Let x = the units at break-even
2x = x + 3,000
x = 3,000 units

In the unit contribution approach, the unit contribution margin (unit price minus variable cost) is available to cover the fixed cost. This approach calculates the number of units necessary to cover fixed expenses.

$$Break\text{-}even \ units \ = \ \frac{fixed \ costs}{unit \ contribution \ margin \ (selling \ price \ minus \ variable \ costs)}$$

Using information in the above example:

$$x = \frac{3,000}{(2x - x)}$$
$$x = 3,000 \ units$$

With the information from this example above (the equation approach), a break-even chart can be used to determine the break-even point as shown in Figure 2.3. A break-even chart is developed in the following manner:

Figure 2.3
Break-Even Chart

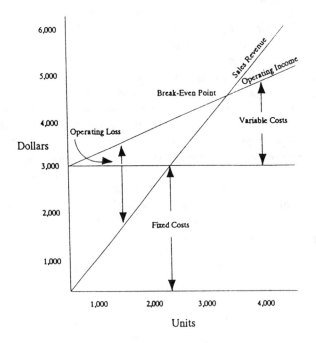

1. The number of units to be produced by an organization is plotted along the horizontal axis, and dollar amounts representing operating data are plotted along the vertical axis.
2. A diagonal line representing sales is drawn from the lower left corner to the upper right corner.
3. A point representing fixed costs is drawn horizontally, paralleling the horizontal axis.
4. The point where sales (revenue) and total costs intersect is the break-even point. The areas representing operating income and operating loss are thus identified.

Once the various cost components have been determined, break-even analysis can be innovatively applied to a number of not-for-profit organizations where unit cost information is maintained on the delivery of services. The following indicates an application: A state school for the blind produces knit floor rugs that are very popular. In order to encourage the development of multiple skills, however, the state sharply reduces its subsidy to rug making beyond the break-even point. It has been determined that the selling price for the rugs is $40, labor cost is $20, materials cost is $10, and fixed cost is $10,000. What is the break-even point?

$$\text{Contribution Margin(CM)} = \text{Selling Price - Variable Cost}$$
$$CM = \$40 = \$30 = \$10$$

$$Break\text{-}even\ unit = \frac{Fixed\ cost}{CM}$$
$$= \frac{10,000}{10}$$
$$= 1,000\ units$$

ALTERNATIVE BREAK-EVEN APPROACH

An alternate way may be employed to obtain the break-even point is as follows:

(FR - FC) = (VRPU - VCPU) x SV, where
    FR = Fixed Revenue
    FC = Fixed Costs
    VRPU = Variable Revenue per Unit

VCPU = Variable Costs per Unit
SV = Service Volume

This formula emphasizes the difference between fixed revenue and fixed costs. When fixed revenue exceeds fixed costs, a net fixed surplus is generated. Likewise, when fixed costs exceed fixed revenue, a deficit is produced. From the formula we can determine the contribution margin per unit of service. This is obtained by subtracting variable cost per unit of service from the variable revenue per unit of service.

Restatement provides the following break-even formula:

NFS/D = CMPU x SV where

NFS/D = Net Fixed Surplus/Deficit
CMPU = Contribution Margin per Unit
SV = Service Volume

The total contribution margin can be obtained from the following nonprofit case: In the program, Prevention of Teenage Drug and Alcohol Abuse, the contribution margin per unit of service is $4 ($14 - $10). The contribution margin percentage times the volume of service produces the total contribution margin. In the example, there are 8,000 client-sessions. Thus, the total contribution is $32,000 ($4 x 8,000).

Because of the restatement, a single measure can be used to determine the net benefits from volume changes. For example, in the not-for-profit program, Prevention of Teenage Drug and Alcohol Abuse, the purpose of the service is to counsel teenagers between the ages of 12 and 17. The fees are set to permit most high-risk teenagers to avail themselves of the services as they are based on family income. (This was stipulated by a foundation that provided a six-year grant of $40,000 yearly). The 1996 client sessions numbered 8,000. Each client revenue intake averages $14. The operating fixed cost is $60,000 per year, while the variable fixed cost is $10 per session. The revenue and costs figures will apply until 1997.

Operating Statement for Year Ending 1996
as Reflected in the Program Data

Fixed components:		
Fixed revenues	$40,000	
Fixed expenses	(60,000)	
Net fixed deficit		($20,000)
Variable components:		
Variable revenues	$ 14	
Variable expenses	(10)	

Contribution margin per unit	$ 4
Total contribution margin ($4 x 8,000)	$32,000
Surplus	$12,000

When fixed revenues and variable revenues are combined, they produce a revenue forecasting formula as follows:

$$TR = FR + (VCPS \times NCS), \text{ where}$$

TR = Total Revenue
FR = Fixed Revenue
VCPS = Variable Cost Per Session
NCS = Number of Client-Sessions

The application of the formula permits us to estimate the revenues at a given volume. Thus, if the Prevention of Teenage Drug and Alcohol Abuse projects 7,200 client sessions, the projected revenues would be $140,800, or $40,000 + ($14 x 7,200). This flexible budget for revenue generates the following formula:

$$\text{Total Revenue} = a + b(x)$$

where   a = the Fixed Revenue
         b = the Variable Revenue Per Service Unit
         x = Volume or Level of Service Produced

On the cost side, applying the same reasoning and analysis as was done for revenues, and assuming projected units of 7,000 per client-session, the following formula expresses the relationships between total cost due to changes in the volume of service:

$$TC = FC + (VCPS \times NCS)$$

where   TC = Total Cost
         FC = Fixed Costs
         VCPS = Variable Cost per Session
         NCS = Number of Client-Sessions

It generates the following formula:

$$\text{Total Costs} = a + b(x)$$

where   a = Total Fixed Cost
         b = The Variable Cost Per Service Unit
         x = Volume or Level of Service Produced

Again applying the flexible budget cost approach, the projected cost for projected volume of 7000 client sessions would be $123,000, or $60,000 + ($9 x 7,000).

Figure 2.4 provides a graphic alternate way for determining the Prevention of Teenage Drug and Alcohol Abuse program's break-even point. The figure clearly shows the fixed and variable costs and revenues. The break-even point shows the volume of service units at 6,000 on the *x* axis, while the *y* axis shows $124,000. If the existing relationships remain, the greater the number of sessions handled beyond the break-even point, the larger the surplus will be. The reverse is also true: as the number of client-sessions declines the deficit will increase. Whenever revenue decreases, whether fixed or variable, achieving the break-even point will become harder.

Figure 2.4
Prevention of Teenage Drug and Alcohol Abuse
Cost Volume Graph

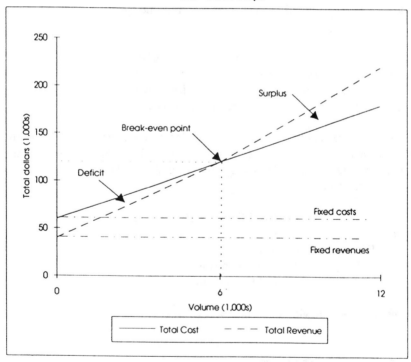

FINANCIAL RATIOS

The Private Sector

The dynamic and changing environment and the complexity of modern for-profit-oriented business requires the use of well-developed information systems for reporting and analysis. Accounting lies at the heart of such systems. Accounting techniques can provide a condensed, internally consistent picture of the firm. The *balance sheet* gives us a capsule summary of the financial status of a business at a particular point in time. During the period between two balance sheets, the *income statement* summarizes the firm's operations. Financial ratio analysis provides a useful means for interpreting these accounting statements, as it examines the relationships between the different accounting totals.

Ratios are calculated and interpreted in order to answer questions such as the following: How liquid is the entity? How well does it use its resources? Is the entity's debt financing reasonable? Are the profits reasonable for the sales level and the resources invested?

Financial Ratios as Predictors of Default

Typically, when funds are borrowed, debt contracts state the minimum compliance conditions in terms of balance sheet ratios. There are important reasons why ratios have been found to be useful predictors of financial distress and bankruptcy. The most useful ratio predictors have been: (1) cash flow to total debt, (2) net income to total sales, (3) total debt to total assets, (4) working capital to total assets, and (5) current ratio.

Ratios and Credit Quality

The key financial ratios that bond rating agencies, banks, insurance companies, and trade credit suppliers often use in assessing a firm's credit quality fall into four categories: (1) profitability, the ability of a firm to earn income by analyzing the ratios of net income to sales, earnings of operations to sales and return on equity; (2) activity, with creditors and owners assessing the ability of management to use the assets at its disposal by examining the ratios of a firm's sales per dollar of average investment for specific asset categories and the ratio of sales to the firm's average total assets (asset turnover such as receivable turnover, inventory turnover, and total asset turnover); (3) liquidity, estimating the ability of a firm to generate cash from assets to meet obligations, assessing the acid test ratio (cash, marketable securities, short-term notes, and receivables divided by current liabilities), current ratio (current assets divided by current liabilities), and the ratio of cash flow to total debt (earnings plus depreciation plus additions to the deferred charge divided by the total of short- and long-term debt and deferred income taxes); and (4) leverage, assessing the degree to which a firm's earnings must go to pay debt, obtaining ratios of total debt to equity, long-term debt to equity, total balance sheet and off balance sheet debt to equity, net income to net interest payments, and coverage on earnings before income taxes (EBIT) to interest payments.

The Public and Not-for-Profit Sectors

Unlike private firms, whose main purpose is profitability, the not-for-profit agency's goal is service delivery. The pursuit of surpluses, not the accumulation of resources, is the typical indicator of success. Resource accumulations should be made mainly to enhance future delivery of goods or service. From a historical perspective, the analysis of not-for-profit statements is likely to yield minimal benefits. As shown in Chapter 11, the amount of money expended on a given program or activity may tell us very little about the quality, quantity, adequacy or sustainability of results achieved or produced.

Not-for-profit ratios should be used only in the context of a given agency's mission, goals, and objectives (as they respond to the clientele, constituency, and political and legal environments) to provide useful clues about the efficiency and effectiveness of an agency's use of the resources entrusted to it. As in the for-profit sector, ratios may indicate potential financial dangers and be used to assess the credit worthiness of public and other not-for-profit agencies (see Chapter 19). Ratios provide only relationships between components in the agency. While there are no absolutes in ratios, careful and judicious interpretations and use can sometimes provide insights into internal agency operations and interagency comparisons in the application of resources. The maximum utility and meaning of ratios will result from the use of financial ratios only in cases where the analyst is thoroughly aware of an agency's total operations. In some cases, the analyst may have to modify or construct new ratios to fit particular agency situations.

Not-for-profit organizations should exercise caution when interpreting and using financial analysis. The first relate to the matching of the organizational goals with its available financial resources. There must be a continuing watch to ensure that programmatic commitments do not exceed organizational capability. To ignore this reality postpones a future day of reckoning, as was done during the 1970s following the boom years of the 1960s, when government and not-for-profit agencies overexpanded (cities such as New York and Cleveland, Ohio, became bankrupt and not-for-profit entities such as public libraries, and universities had to undertake major budget reductions). During the latter part of the 1970s and, especially part of the 1980s, massive retrenchment was required to bring programmatic expenditures into line with resource inflow.

The second caution focuses on the maintenance of intergenerational equity. The emphasis here is put on balancing spending for the generation today without robbing future generations of the benefits they should enjoy. Massive federal long-term borrowing increases the national debt and serves not only deny posterity future benefits, it also requires that tomorrow's citizen shoulder the burden of the benefits that Americans enjoy today. This practice has always been frowned upon, as it allows long-term debt creation to be used to satisfy short-term maintenance needs. This practice was followed in a number of public health schools during the 1960s and 1970s. Short-term grant money allowed faculty to be hired and be given tenure. As the grants were reduced and dried up, however, resources had to be reallocated from other priorities to meet tenure commitments.

Another concern is excessive dependence on one or only a few sources to maintain an agency. When problems with one source develop it puts the agency's viability at risk. When reduction in medicare health insurance reimbursements for the elderly occurred, it created major problems for a number of health care agencies because of their heavy dependence on federal inflows. Of course, it cannot be overemphasized that an agency that is overdiversified may have to contend with increased coordination and administrative costs.

In examining profitability in the not-for-profit sector, profit is viewed as an excess of revenues over expenses, or surplus. However, not-for-profit organizations (particularly those that are nongovernmental), viability requires the generation of a profit. Among the reasons included are: (a) the need to replace assets that are recorded at cost rather than market or replacement value; (b) the need to finance expansion; and (c) the need to build up reserves to ensure against uncertainties and the unpredictability of earnings.

When not-for-profit organizations fail to generate adequate surplus (profit) or return, they must use the current fund balance built up over prior years to maintain their existing purchasing power. Thus, it is useful to keep a close watch on important ratios/groups such as liquidation ratios, long-term solvency ratios, revenue expense assets ratios, and asset management ratios.

The Revenue-Expense-Assets Ratio

Ratios falling in this category are also commonly referred to as profitability measures because they provide indicators of an organizations' ability to generate funds from operations. The *operating margin* is a popular ratio. The operating margins for Bright Hospital, (Table 2.4) are as follows:

$$Operating \ \ Margin \ = \ \frac{Net \ \ Operating \ \ Surplus}{Total \ \ Operating \ \ Revenues}$$

$$1996 \ = \ \frac{75,000}{6,780,000} \ = \ .011$$

$$1997 \ = \ \frac{123,000}{6,690,000} \ = \ .018$$

Industry Average = .018

The operating margins indicates stability with respect to the excess of revenues over expenses. In 1996 Bright Hospital generated an operating margin of .011 (below the industry average). Results improved in 1997, generating an operating margin of .018 (equalling the industry average).

Return on assets(ROI) is widely used in profit-oriented firms to assess how well management has used its available assets to generate profits. Though this indicator is important to private and some not-for-profit agencies such as hospitals (for example Bright Hospital), it has little relevance to public sector agencies. For Bright Hospital, the return on assets is:

$$ROI \ = \ \frac{Annual \ \ Surplus \ / \ Deficit}{Total \ \ Assets}$$

$$1996 \ = \ \frac{\$75,000}{\$7,571,400} \ = \ .010$$

$$1997 \ = \ \frac{123,000}{7,435,000} \ = \ .020$$

Industry Average = .027

While there was improvement from 1996 to 1997 on Bright Hospital ROI, both years are still below the industry average. These results may suggest that revenue has been declining. Either a change in the revenue expenses relationship has been taking place or assets are not being employed productively.

Return on fund balances provides another measure to assess the return that an agency is internally generating from its invested resource in terms of fund balances. The ratio for Bright Hospital is as follows:

$$Return \quad on \quad Fund \quad Balance \quad (ROFB \ ) = \frac{Annual \quad Surplus \ / \ Deficit}{Total \quad Fund \quad Balances}$$

$$1996 = \frac{75,000}{2,968,000} = .019$$

$$1997 = \frac{123,000}{3,043,000} = .040$$

Industry Average = .07

Again the ratio for 1997 shows considerable improvement, but both ratios are still below industry averages. The ROFB indicates the extent to which the unspent surplus of prior years has been preserved and enhanced. It may also give early clues to prospective problems in revenue generation (earnings). When the ratios are rising faster than industry averages or a target historical average for the agency, the pricing structure of the fees needs to be modified. The increasing ratio average provides management with greater options to enhance the agency's capital base, setting the stage for greater stability, growth, and profitability.

Asset Management Ratios

These ratios are called activity or turnover ratios. They provide insights relative to the effectiveness with which total assets are being used to generate revenues. Asset management ratios involve four calculations: current turnover, current asset turnover, inventory turnover, and long-term assets turnover. The Bright Hospital turnover ratios are as follows:

$$\textit{Current Asset Turnover} = \frac{\textit{Total Operating Revenues}}{\textit{Total Current Assets}}$$

$$1996 = \frac{6,780,000}{1,661,400} = 4.80$$

$$1997 = \frac{6,690,000}{1,263,600} = 5.29$$

Industry Average = 3.98

Both 1996 and 1997 show excellent ratios. The high 1997 ratio may suggest that management is doing an excellent job in collecting its receivable, investing cash, and managing inventory.

The total asset turnover ratio is calculated as follows:

$$\textit{Current Asset Turnover} = \frac{\textit{Total Operating Revenues}}{\textit{Total Assets}}$$

$$1996 = \frac{6,600,000}{7,552,000} = .87$$

$$1997 = \frac{6,590,000}{7,435,000} = .89$$

Industry Average = .95

For each dollar invested, management generated $.87 in 1996 of revenue and $.89 in 1997, respectively. Both indicators are slightly below the industry average, though 1997 shows improvement. The below-industry average turnover rate suggests that assets are idle or, alternatively, that there was a relative drop in revenue. Bright Hospital's turnover problem relates to an increase in prepaid expense and new investment in equipment that has not generated the expected productivity.

The *Long-term* or *fixed asset turnover ratio* comprises mainly net property, plant, and equipment. For Bright Hospital it is calculated as follows:

$$Long\text{-}Term\ Asset\ Turnover\ =\ \frac{Total\ Operating\ Revenues}{Net\ Long\text{-}Term\ Assets}$$

$$1996\ =\ \frac{\$6,780,000}{\$5,640,000}\ =\ 1.20$$

$$1997\ =\ \frac{\$6,590,000}{\$5,900,000}\ =\ 1.13$$

Industry Average = 1.42

Both the 1996 and 1997 ratios are below average, indicating the agency is not using its assets effectively in generating revenue. Though the 1997 ratio suggests an improved delinquency collection rate, assets used to generate revenues, perhaps due mainly to the new equipment, has not generated the efficiency that was expected.

The inventory turnover ratio provides management with information about the acceptable or desirable levels of inventory necessary to generate required revenues. A large ratio indicates a lesser need required to generate greater revenues. Conversely, a small ratio may suggest excess or higher levels of inventory than necessary.

Liquidity Ratios

Liquidity measures provide indicators that tell us the extent of ability that an agency possesses to meet current and maturing obligations. Liquidity measures the gap between the current need for cash and the agency's ability to convert noncash assets into cash to settle outstanding obligations as they become due. The Bright Hospital current ratio is calculated as follows:

$$Current\ Ratio\ =\ \frac{Current\ Assets}{Current\ Liabilities}$$

$$1996 = \frac{1,661,000}{856,000} = 1.94$$

$$1997 = \frac{1,285,000}{762,000} = 1.66$$

Industry Average = 1.78

The 1996 Bright Hospital current ratio shows that it has $1.94 of asset for every liability request that is currently being made. This strong liquidity position is above industry standards. In 1997 the ratio was below the industry average. When the ratio falls to a point where current obligations cannot be met as they come due, the agency is put into a precarious position (which should be avoided). When the amounts of noncash items such as receivables becomes too high, better management of the receivables may be required.

The *quick ratio* (also known as the *acid test ratio*) is a stringent test of an agency's short-term bill-paying ability. The quick ratio excludes inventories and prepaid expenses from the current asset base. When problems arise concerning an agency's ability to convert inventories into cash in a timely manner, the quick ratio is typically used.

$$Quick\ Ratio = \frac{Cash\ +\ Short\text{-}term\ Investment\ +\ Receivables}{Current\ Liabilities}$$

$$1996 = \frac{\$305\ +\ \$20\ +\ \$1,179}{\$856} = 1.76$$

$$1997 = \frac{\$225\ +\ \$825\ +\ \$75}{\$762} = 1.48$$

Industry Average = 1.47

The 1996 and 1997 quick ratios for Bright Hospital are above the industry average. Accounts payable and current loan declines are two factors that played a role in improving the ratios, especially in 1997.

The number of days' revenue in net receivables is another liquidity ratio that measures the ability of an agency to collect its outstanding accounts receivable. The Bright Hospital ratio is calculated as follows:

$$Number\ of\ Days'\ Revenue\ -\ Net\ Accounts\ Receivable\ =\ \frac{Net\ Accounts\ Receivable}{Net\ Patient\ Revenue/365}$$

$$1996\ =\ \frac{\$1,179,000}{\$4,800,000/365}\ =\ 89.70$$

$$1997\ =\ \frac{\$825,600}{\$4,625,000/365}\ =\ 65.16$$

$$Industry\ Average\ =\ 61.20$$

Bright Hospital appears to have a problem with slower collection than the industry average. The year 1997 does represent a significant improvement from the previous year though additional improvement is still desirable.

When the ratio is restated so that the dollar amount of net patient revenues is divided by net outstanding receivables, the receivable turnover ratio is produced. The 1996 ratio is 4.1 ($4,800,000/1,179,000) or on average, account receivables has a turnover rate of 4.1 per year.

Additional insight may be obtained by making comparison between years (what is typically referred to as horizontal analysis). These useful ratios may be obtained as follows:

$$Percent\ Decrease\ of\ Accounts\ Receivable\ =\ \frac{\$1,179\ -\ \$8.25}{\$11,179}\ =\ 30.05\ --\ 30\%$$

$$Percent\ Decrease\ of\ Estimated\ Uncollectible\ Accounts\ =\ \frac{\$20,400\ -\ \$15,000}{\$20,000}\ =\ .27$$
$$--\ 27\%$$

$$Percent\ Decrease\ of\ Net\ Patient\ Revenues\ =\ \frac{\$4,800\ -\ \$4,625}{\$4,800}\ =\ .036\ --\ 3.6\%$$

Bright Hospital's 30 percent decrease in accounts receivable suggests a significant speed up in collection of outstanding accounts receivable. Uncollectibles have improved 25 percent, indicating that the quality of the patient receivables is improving. While revenue inflow is being reduced by 3.6 percent, it does not seem to present a problem at this time.

Long-Term Solvency Ratios

Long-term solvency goes beyond the short-term ability of an organization to meet obligations as they come due. Stress is put on the organization's ability to meet future payments on principal and interest on long-term debt, whatever the source of the outstanding commitment or obligation. The focus is on the entity's ability to generate sufficient cash flow to meet scheduled payment (coverage). The ratios are often used as indicators to assess long-term solvency as in ratios of total debt to fund balances, long-term financing to fund balances, and total asset to fund balances.

The *total debt to fund balance ratio* is a useful indicator of how externally borrowed funds are used to supplement internally generated funds. The ratio for Bright Hospital is calculated as follows:

$$Total\ Debt : Fund\ Balance = \frac{Current\ Liabilities\ +\ Long-Term\ Liabilities}{Fund\ Balance}$$

$$1996 = \frac{\$856\ +\ \$3,747}{\$2,968} = 1.55$$

$$1997 = \frac{\$762\ +\ \$3,630}{\$3,043} = 1.44$$

$$Industry\ Average = 1.10$$

The fund to financing ratio puts an emphasis on the percentage of assets that have been obtained from funds that were internally generated. The Bright Hospital fund to financing ratio is calculated as follows:

$$Fund : Financing\ Ratio = \frac{Fund\ Balance}{Total\ Assets}$$

$$1996 = \frac{\$2,968}{\$7,571} = .39 \; -- \; 50\%$$

$$1997 = \frac{\$3,043}{\$7,435} = .41 \; -- \; 41\%$$

Industry Average = 42%

A conservative capital structure generates a high percentage, indicating that most debt financing comes from internal sources. Conversely, a low ratio would suggest that most of the asset financing is obtained from debt, which must be paid in the future. Lending agencies are more disposed to those organizations that have a healthy fund balance. The amount and percentage of fund balance serve as leverage in attracting external funds.

CONCLUDING OBSERVATIONS

The importance of the accounting system cannot be overemphasized in public and other not-for-profit organizations. In many governmental units, it may be the only mechanism capable of bringing a semblance of coordination to the financial management system.

By means of the accounting system, a number of important accountability and control objectives may be achieved. Once the budget is passed, the breakdown of the component parts is recorded by means of a chart or code of accounts directly linking and identifying the division of authority and the responsibility centers in the organization. This operation facilitates responsibility accounting whereby individual units can be held answerable for the appropriated funds made available to them.

Accounting has multiple applications, depending on the objectives being sought for the organization, including accounting for funds, control, and compliance financial accounting. When the emphasis is put on improvement in efficiency and internal decision making, managerial accounting may be effectively applied. When the organization requires the costing out of programs, activities, and special projects, a cost accounting capacity may be developed to generate the data.

Based on the accounting data, balance sheets and income statements can be projected for future operations. Recently, public and other not-for-profit organizations have started to employ break-even analysis to aid in making projections.

NOTES

1. See, for example, Roger Hermanson, James D. Edwards and Cecily Raiborn, *Financial Accounting* (Plano, Tex.: Business Publications, 1984); Charles T. Hornigen, *Introduction to Management Accounting*, 3rd ed. (Englewood Cliffs, N.J.: Prentice-Hall, 1984); and Edward S. Lynn and Robert J. Freeman, *Fund Accounting: Theory and Practice*, 2nd ed. (Englewood Cliffs, N.J.: Prentice-Hall, 1982).

2. Leo Herbert, Larry N. Killough and Alan Walter Steiss, *Governmental Accounting and Control* (Monterey, Calif.: Brooks Cole Publishing Co., 1984), p. 5.

3. See Robert Simons, "Strategic Orientation and Top Management Attention to Central Systems," *Strategic Management Journal*, 12 (1991): 49-62.

4. Herbert, Killough and Steiss, *Governmental Accounting and Control*, p. 5.

5. Briget M. Anderson, "Using Activity-Based Costing for Efficiency and Quality," *Government Finance Review*, 9 no. 3 (June 1993): 7-10; Robin H. Cooper and Robert S. Kaplan, "Profit Priorities from Activity-Based Costing," *Harvard Business Review*, 69 (May/June 1991): 130-35.

6. Lynn and Freeman, *Fund Accounting*, pp. 627-28.

7. Robert N. Anthony and David W. Young, *Management Control in Non-Profit Organizations* (Homewood, Ill.: Richard D. Irwin and Co., 1984), pp. 17, 141.

8. U.S. General Accounting Office, *Accounting Manual for Guidance of Federal Agencies* revised, Title 2, (Washington, D.C.: U.S. General Accounting Office, 1978).

3

Internal Control Management

Despite the critical role that internal control plays in every phase of management, only minimal attention is typically given to it. The lack of attention is due, among other things, to the general view that internal control is purely or mainly a financial function to be controlled and managed by those charged with controlling finance. This is an inaccurate perspective of the true function of internal controls. Small governments and nonprofit agencies believe that they cannot afford a system of internal controls. However, evidence shows that internal controls are indispensable to agencies of all size.[1]

In small establishments, especially socially oriented not-for-profit agencies, managers are loath to implement internal controls because of the feelings of trust and camaraderie that exist among fellow workers. This view misses the special importance of internal controls. The system is established to keep honest people honest. Although it may be proper to assume that all employees are honest, it is unfair to permit weaknesses in the internal system to tempt individuals toward dishonesty. This guiding perspective aids in the generation of data and information is likely to prevent or minimize human error. Effective internal controls protect employees against unwarranted allegations as they fix responsibility and remove the cause of employees' temptation. A strong internal control system is most helpful to the independent auditor. The degree of confidence that is put in the internal control system has a direct bearing on the extent of the detailed checking that is required to assess the reliability of an agency's records. A sound internal control system requires the independent auditor to carry out fewer tests and checking of an agency's records, thereby reducing the time and cost of auditing. Sound internal control systems avoid laxness of procedures, minimize avoidable errors, and provide a built-in deterrence to easy temptation.

We should not forget that most people are defrauded by someone in whom the organization has reposed its trust. It is never good practice to put reliance and trust in only one individual. Too often, small social agencies and businesses tend to put their trust in long-time loyal employees. Most often such employees are viewed as being above reproach. However, it is important to note that employee circumstances do change in ways that may take precedence over employee-employer relationships. Individual circumstances may change due, among other things, to family illness and gambling debts, which create conditions that may tempt otherwise loyal and incorruptible individuals. Thus, it is seldom wise to put complete trust in one employee with no checks or constraints. Since no system is foolproof, it is always the greatest part of wisdom to obtain an insurance policy on all employees who are entrusted with cash or valuable assets. By taking out fidelity bonds, the agency hedges on the possibility of an occasional failure of the internal control system.

It cannot be overstressed that careful hiring practices and extensive and continuous on-the-job training are critical factors to reducing inadvertent errors. Particular attention should be given to the internal control system when personnel changes are taking place because this is a time when the system is most vulnerable to errors and irregularities.

Once a system of internal controls has been implemented, it requires monitoring to ensure that the objectives that were sought are being effectively achieved. The literature is replete with the failures of organizations that view internal control systems as self-executing. For example, the Phar-Mor Corporation's internal control system was in place, yet most of its assets were stolen. The president and a staff member (the controller) were charged with absconding with more than 50 percent of the entity's assets because systems were not carefully monitored and controlled.

This chapter is an examination of the principles and practices of internal control management in public and not-for-profit agencies. Six sections have been included: (1) principles and structure of internal controls are reviewed showing how it strategically facilitates the achievement of an agency's programmatic accountability; (2) the different types of internal controls are examined; (3) the importance of documentation and the audit trail are examined, showing how they provide the indispensable linkage fixing accountability for action taken; (4) the internal control system of authorizations is discussed, (5) the cost-benefit justification of internal controls is reviewed; and (6) designing and evaluating the internal control system are discussed.

UNDERSTANDING THE INTERNAL CONTROL STRUCTURE AND ITS RELATION TO ACCOUNTABILITY

Internal control encompasses every aspect (financial and nonfinancial) of an organization. An effective internal control system is the "nerve center" of an organization and is critical to the achievement of both the short-run and long-run organizational mission, goals, and objectives. The survival of each organization is tied to the effective implementation, maintenance, and monitoring of the internal control system. This includes the control system management; employee attitudes; the general control environment; the accounting system: the management philosophy and operating style; the organizational structure, the general oversight system, such as the legislature, the board, or the audit committee of the governing board; the control methods for monitoring and following up on internal auditing recommendation; and the quality of the personnel determining the effectiveness of the internal controls maintained in an agency.

Magnitude and Extent of Controls

The internal control system varies depending on the size of the not-for-profit organization. In organizations where the number of employees is few and the manager of the organization provides direct supervision and oversight, few controls are needed. The situation changes as the complexity and size of the organization increases, however, this requires that management delegate greater authority, making it necessary to put more reliance on the accounting system.

Accounting and Internal Control

Once an agency has decided on its goals and objectives, it must directly link each type of accountability that it wishes to realize with its internal control system. This requires the identification of all important decision points in each responsibility center in the organization. For each control decision point, the quantitative and qualitative measurement indicators must be clearly defined. Next, the process necessary to realize each measurement indicator must be clearly indicated.

Once goals, objectives, decision points, and the measurement indicators have been clearly defined, the type of accountability that the internal control system is seeking can easily be indicated and linked. It cannot be overstressed that the internal control system must be an organic and functional instrument if it is to be most useful in achieving the organization's financial and nonfinancial goals.

Defining Internal Controls

An internal control system is an organizational structure and the sum of the methods and measures that are used to accomplish the internal control objectives. The internal control system is a set of guidelines and parameters that are used to maintain control over the operations of the programs and functions that are undertaken by an agency. Table 3.1 provides a general overview of internal control evaluation improvement and reporting process consisting of six major steps or activities: the organizing process, segmenting the agency, that is, identifying the administrative functions or responsibility centers. For example, the Department of Health and Human Services (HHS) might be divided or segmented into the Social Security Administration, the Health Care and Finance Administration, and smaller units. Similarly, the Social Security Administration can be segmented into the Supplemental Security Income Program, the Old-Age Survivors Insurance Program, or smaller administrative functions such as eligibility determination systems, benefit payment systems, and quality controls. Internal controls facilitate the carrying out of a vulnerability assessment to determine an agency's greatest potential exposure to waste, loss, unauthorized use, and misappropriation of funds or other assets by identifying risk-creating factors in the environment.

PREPARING INTERNAL CONTROL REPORTS

Internal control comprises a clearcut organizational plan, method, and procedures that are designed to produce accurate data, providing assurance that the agency's objectives will be accomplished and that assets and resources will be safeguarded. The internal control plan should provide for: (1) definite placement of responsibility, with a clear division of duties between authorization and record keeping so that the activities of one employee act as a check on another; (2) use of forms, documents, and procedures that facilitate control and provide for proper approval; and (3) provision for facilitating compliance with policies and procedures. Alternatively, internal control involves compliance to a combination of policies, standards, and procedures that, when applied collectively, will minimize, prevent, or detect illegal or unauthorized acts and will preserve the assets and reputation of the agency. It is a top management responsibility that should not be carelessly delegated, yet most internal control activities must be assigned to specific members who will carry out the day-to-day operations. It must be kept in mind that the pursuit of the internal control objective must be balanced with the benefits to be achieved and with the costs incurred and the risks involved. A major internal control aim is to assure that assets are used as efficiently and effectively as possible, as directed by an authorizing body such as the legislature or a governing board.

The design of the internal control plan delineates the duties under which employees are expected to operate. Under the system of internal control, duties

Table 3.1
Overview of Internal Control Evaluation, Improvement, and Reporting

Organize the Process

1. Assign responsibilities to ensure efficient evaluation, improvement, and reporting on internal controls.

2. Give key consideration to responsibility assignment for internal reporting, documentation, personnel supervision, and scheduling the evaluation process, including vulnerability assessments and internal control reviews.

Segment the Agency

1. Divide the agency into components, programs, and administrative functions to facilitate the evaluation of internal control and vulnerability assessment.

2. Consider the following factors in identifying assessable units: existing organizational structure, special programs, administrative functions, agency size, number of programs and subprograms, the organization's operating programs, uniqueness of the operating systems, extent of centralization or decentralization, budget allocations, and number of personnel.

Conduct Vulnerability Assessments

1. Develop criteria and guidelines to determine program/functions susceptible to waste, loss, and unauthorized use or misappropriation.

2. Assess the potential existence of the following: lack of compliance of obligations and cost with applicable laws, lack of adequate safeguard of funds, property, and assets and exposure to waste, loss, or unauthorized use; and lack of properly recorded and accounted for revenues and expenditures generating unreliable financial reports and unreliable accountability over assets.

3. Vulnerability assessments comprise important steps:

• Analysis of the control environment, including management's attitude as expressed in written commitment to the maintenance of a strong internal control system; organizational structures delineating necessary functions and the required reporting relationships; competent, motivated and loyal personnel; policies and procedures disseminated to all employees showing how functions/activities are to be performed; budget-reporting practices; and utilization of clearly defined organizational checks and balances, indicating the strengths and potential weaknesses inherent in the system.

- Evaluation of potential and inherent risks, with an assessment of the functions of each to potential waste, loss and unauthorized use or misappropriation.

- Preliminary assessment of agency safeguards, making preliminary judgments about the existence and adequacy of internal control over selected programs and administrative functions. (This is not an in-depth evaluation. It is a judgment of the evaluator's knowledge regarding the satisfactory functioning of safeguards to protect the agency from waste, loss, unauthorized use or mismanagement.)

Development Plans to Subsequent Actions

1. Summarize the vulnerability assessment results to determine actions that may be necessary. (The objective at this stage is to strengthen the internal control system to achieve a more cost-effective result.)

2. Classify identified program/function vulnerability exposure, providing them with direction attention to achieve a timely and best outcome and enhance the internal control system.

3. Pursue the following actions that may bring about enhancing remedial action: scheduling and implementing required internal control reviews; recommending that auditing be initiated; setting in motion improved monitoring procedures, carrying out staff training programs, issuing clearly defined instructions, and modifying existing procedures and documents.

Conduct Internal Control Reviews

1. *Defining the event cycle.* It is the focal point of reference for the review of internal control. The event cycle consists of a series of steps that are required to be taken to carry out a specific task, activity or function. For example, in an entitlement program, a cycle of events is as follows: information gathering and verification obtaining, eligibility determination information, information processing and record keeping, payment and monitoring. An administrative function event cycle might involve payroll, supplies, and materials procurement, and letter wiring/correspondence handling.

2. *Analyze the general control environment.* This involves the management attitude, organizational structure, personnel, extent and type of delegation of authority, policies and procedures, budgeting and reporting practices and the extent, type, and quality of organizational checks and balances.

3. *Documenting the event cycle.* This provides an understanding of how activities, events, or functions operate. It requires the review of individuals in the event cycle, documentation and observation of the events, and the preparation of a narrative explanation or a flow chart to provide sufficient detail to assess the adequacy of the internal control system.

4. *Evaluation internal controls.* Assess the internal control event cycle to determine how the internal control objectives are being met, thus minimizing the potential for waste, loss, unauthorized use, or misappropriation. Attempt to determine from written documentation whether the internal control system as defined provides reasonable and adequate assurance that obligations and costs are in compliance with law. Appropriate safeguards must be in place to protect the agency's funds, property, assets, and revenue. Expenditures are recorded to permit and facilitate the preparation of accounts and reliable financial statements.

5. *Testing internal controls.* Determine if control objectives are being carried out as intended. This can be done by various sampling techniques, including making observations and reviewing documentation. This review should clearly identify problems that exist of control techniques that are not functioning as planned.

Prepare Report on Internal Controls

Preparing two types of reports. The final report, suggesting corrective action, is prepared for program managers. The second report goes to the agency head or the chief executive. Reports should detail weaknesses in the system and reasonable ways to rectify them. Recommendations for economy and efficiency should be made. Particular attention should focus on the following:

1. To what extent is the overall control system efficient in providing the required facilitative atmosphere for effective functioning of internal controls?
2. In what areas are the required control techniques nonexistent?
3. In what areas are the internal controls are functioning as planned?
4. In what areas are control techniques excessive and creating inefficiencies?
5. Are there executive and/or legislative requirements that are excessive and creating inefficiencies?

Source: Adapted from U.S. Office of Management and Budget, *Internal Control Guidelines* (Washington, D.C.: OMB, 1982).

are assigned to make it possible to exercise effective control over assets, liabilities, and expenditures. Summary requirements of the major objectives of the internal control system include a determination of the following:

1. Obligations, commitments, and costs are in compliance with applicable laws.

2. Funds, property, and other assets are safeguarded against waste, loss, unauthorized use, or misappropriation.

3. Revenues and expenditures applicable to agency operations are properly recorded and accounted for to permit reliable preparation of accounts and financial and statistical reports and as a means of maintaining accountability over assets.

4. Timely and accurate reports are provided to the different constituencies and users of information.

5. High priority is given to the development of professional integrity and the maintenance of the most affordable level of competence to enable employees to efficiently and effectively accomplish their assigned duties and responsibilities in accordance with an internal control system that has been tailored to maximize the achievement of agency objectives.

6. Due cognizance is given to the encouragement, facilitation and maintenance of a supportive employee attitude toward internal controls.

7. Internal controls objectives are identified for each decision point in each responsibility center.

8. Key duties and responsibilities such as authorizing, processing, recording, and reviewing of transactions are separated.

9. Effective and continuous supervision is provided to ensure that internal control objectives are being promptly and efficiently achieved.

10. Access to *resources* and periodic reviews of resources and records are limited to specifically authorized individuals, and the accountability for oversight, custody, and use of resources is specifically assigned and maintained.

11. Managers promptly evaluate audit findings and take necessary action in response to findings and recommendations, instituting corrective actions as required. When prompt resolution cannot be achieved, the matter is brought to the attention of top management or the board.

12. Personal accountability is clearly defined.

13. Accurate and reliable records are available from which

financial statements can be prepared in accordance with generally accepted accounting principles (GAAP).

CLASSIFYING INTERNAL CONTROLS

Internal controls are commonly classified as administrative controls and accounting controls. Accounting controls refer to procedures, records, and reports that have been designed to safeguard assets and to promote the reliability of financial accounting records and reports. They enable the management of an agency to ascertain that expenditures are properly authorized and made in accordance with appropriate laws and regulations. The accounting controls provide guidelines and specific procedures to ensure the recording of transactions in accordance with generally accepted accounting principles, assuring the reliability of financial records. In other words, the accounting controls relate to management responsibility for maintaining the assets entrusted to it and for providing information on the financial condition and results of the organization's operation.

Internal administrative controls are comprised of procedures and records that assist management in achieving the organization's goals. For example, when poor-quality work occurs in a particular responsibility center, the use of internal controls permits management to better evaluate personnel performance and attempt to improve the quality of the output.

SOME GENERAL PRINCIPLES OF INTERNAL CONTROLS

The following are broad principles of internal controls that should be considered:
1. Competent personnel and rotation of duties
   a. Employees should be adequately trained and supervised.
   b. Clerical personnel should be rotated periodically from job to job. This broadens the understanding of the employees and is helpful in uncovering irregularities that may have taken place.
   c. Annual leaves and reassignments of jobs to others during the absence should be encouraged.
2. Assignment of responsibility
   a. Clearly defined responsibility is a prerequisite for the efficient execution of assigned duties.
   b. To facilitate sound internal controls, an agency should have a formal plan of organization that fixes responsibility for the functions to be performed with the necessary authority to carry them out.

    c.   Overlapping and undefined responsibility areas should be avoided. Responsibility and authority for a given function should not be shared as this practice often results in a duplication of efforts. It may also result in jobs going undone as each individual thinks the other person is performing the assignment. When one person has responsibility for the function, praise or blame can be clearly assigned for specific results. In those instances where two people must be assigned the same cash register, for example, each should be given a separate cash drawer and register keys.

3.   Segregation of responsibility for related duties

    a.   Plan the organizational controls so that one individual is prevented from having complete control over a sequence of related transactions.

    b.   Divide related duties or operating responsibilities among two or more individuals to minimize the possibility of error, fraud, collusion, and inefficiency. For example, a single individual should not be permitted to extend credit on account to customers, record the account, and collect the payment. Individuals who receive and approve time reports of employees should not prepare or sign payroll checks. Employees who prepare the general ledger's trial balance should not be allowed to approve general ledger activities or prepare monthly statements. Similarly, one who reconciles the bank account should not prepare withdrawals or deposits.

    c.   Provide for checks and balances by distributing the responsibility over a number of departments. This requires that work in one department and its accompanying documents be compared to and agree with what is prepared in other departments. Similarly, when purchase orders and receiving reports are processed by different individuals, a third individual can compare the order, the receiving reports, and the vendor's invoice before payment is approved. This practice reduces the likelihood of fictitious conversion of goods. (Improper separation of duties increases the probability of fraud, carelessness and unreliable record keeping.)

4.   Separation of operations and accounting

    a.   Authorizing transactions, accounting transactions, and custody over assets should be segregated.

    b.   There should be separation of responsibility for the maintenance of the accounting records from those engaging in business transactions and those with the custody of the agency's assets. For example, the employees who handle cash payments should not have access to the journal or ledger in order to reduce the possibility of error and embezzlement.

5. Proofs are security measures
   a. Various techniques include separate bank accounts, provisions for safekeeping of cash and other valuable documents, and encouragement of possible observance and acceptance of printed receipts from clerks.
   b. Fidelity insurance can be used to ensure against losses caused by fraud due to shortcomings in the internal control system.
   c. An independent review of the internal control system should be carried out periodically to determine if the internal procedures adopted are being followed.

6. Proper accounting for transactions
   a. The system should ensure that all transactions are accurately and appropriately classified and recorded in a timely manner.
   b. All subsidiary ledgers must be reconciled with the general ledger on a regular basis.

7. Adequate safeguarding of assets
   a. The internal control system should ensure that assets are physically protected from fire, natural disaster, theft, and other problems.
   b. Both direct and indirect access to assets should be restricted.
   c. There should be an inventory of assets to reconcile the actual counts to the accounting records.
   d. Differences between actual assets and accounting records should be promptly investigated.

DOCUMENTATION AND THE AUDIT TRAIL

The audit trail is an important means to trace source documents through the accounting system, identifying individuals who are charged with the execution of particular duties. For example, as an employee authorizes a transaction, the document is typically initiated or signed to indicate authorization, while the individual requesting the custody of the assets or performance of an activity normally submits a requisition form. As the maintainer of the institutional memory, an accounting department employee puts an identifying mark on the documents to indicate that it has been checked for mathematical accuracy, reconciled with invoices or receiving reports, or has involved some specific action to guard and protect against improper use or loss of assets. When computers are involved, an audit trail may be automatically created. In this context a particular software may be used to identify users passwords indicating how long each person accesses the system and showing whether particular files have been read or changed. By means of the audit trail, the controller of the system has the ability to assess the effectiveness of the internal control system.

SYSTEM OF AUTHORIZATION

Every activity and transaction of a governmental unit should be authorized by statutes, ordinances, rules, or procedures. Authorizations determine by whom the conditions, functions, or duties of the agency will be carried out. It is by means of these conditions that a facilitative environment is established. As conditions, needs, and situations change, authorizations should be examined to determine their workability and utility. The review of authorizations provide an opportunity to assess the adequacy of their required documentation and the efficiency with which they are being communicated.[2]

Ideally, every transaction should be authorized by an individual who (1) has no interest in the transaction, (2) possess sufficient knowledge of the transaction, its purpose, and its legal ramifications, and (3) is at the appropriate level of the organization to issue the authorization and understands the procedures required to discharge the responsibilities involved. As an operating norm, the persons who are permitted to authorize transactions should have limits and the authorization should be in writing.

Authorizations may be either general or specific. General authorizations are set forth by laws, regulations, and basic management policies. Individuals are expected to execute general authorizations as prescribed laws, regulations, or policies of the governing board. Examples of general authorizations include tax rates, user charges, wage rates, and acquisition policies. The primary vehicle for general authorizations in governmental units is the budget under which most transactions are processed.

Some transactions require specific authorizations. Typically, these authorizations involve a case-by-case basis. They are nonroutine transactions that are established by the responsible official of a governing unit or agency. Examples include the purchase of capital assets and the issuance of bonds. Most specific authorizations are set forth by law or the governing board.

DESIGNING AND EVALUATING THE INTERNAL CONTROL SYSTEM

Risk exposure is the focal point in designing and evaluating an internal control system. A number of critical questions such as the following should be answered: (1) What are the probable things that can go wrong? (2) What are the specific components in the internal control system that are designed to prevent problems? (3) What components in the internal control system are designed to detect problems if they occur? (4) What specific consequences of the problem might continue or remain following the implementation of the prevention, detection, and control system?

Preventive controls are the most cost-effective means for avoiding or minimizing risks in a responsibility center, as they are intended to stop problems before they occur. For example, credit profiles of students requesting government loans may be checked before the loans are advanced and only those fitting the acceptable profile will be given loans. Dual check signing is another example of preventive control in which two individuals are required to review the supporting documents prior to expenditure authorization.

Detective control is initiated only after errors and irregularities have occurred. A good example is the reconciliation of bank statements, whereby the book balance is matched with the reported bank statement balance. Detective control is also used in determining pilferage of inventory supplies.

The design of an internal control system should give due cognizance to the cost that must be compared to the benefits that the system will reasonably generate in reducing risks. Sensitivity to cost-benefit considerations requires that each internal control system be tailored to the particular agency, governmental unit, or entity. This involves recognizing the size of the entity, complexity of operations, extent of computer use, and built-in flexibility to permit management to take appropriate action as each situation dictates.

Preventive control is likely to provide greater protection against risks than detective control. To obtain the best outcome (and prevent any losses from occurring) will necessitate the application of controls on all transactions. In comparison, detective control can be applied effectively to samples of transactions. Of particular note is that the very nature of most transactions in organizations precludes the use of preventive internal control such as bank reconciliation or dual authorization. Thus, in most instances, detective control is the most cost-effective means of reducing risks.

DESIGNING CONTROL WITH EMPLOYEES IN MIND

The employee represents both ends of the same control continuum. At one end, the employee represents the most important ingredient for the achievement of effective internal control. At the other end, the employee poses potentially the greatest risk to the agency. To promote the employees' greatest contribution, the organization must design a control system that integrates incentives in such a way that participants find it easy and compelling to comply in enforcing their internal control duties. One way to aid in achieving the internal control objective requires that employee responsibilities and duties be tied directly to the agency's performance evaluation system. Thus, raises, bonuses, and promotions should incorporate standards of both operating performance and compliance with the internal control system. The extent of the rewards should be commensurate with the quality with which the internal control functions have been executed. The linkage of these two important activities (control and operating duties) shows the seriousness and the priority that management gives to the control function. Sound management principles including planning, budgeting, clearly defined responsibility, and timely follow-through action, give important signals and cues to employees that management is fully supportive and committed.

INTERNAL CONTROL AND FLOWCHARTS

Flowcharts are important means for tracing the flow of transactions. Flowcharts provide a graphic representation of information flows that shows transactions, activities, processes, and interrelated decisions. They show lines of communication from the initiating point to the end. A flowchart is a shorthand way of depicting and simplifying complex relationships and could easily be achieved by using organizational charts or procedure manuals.

The system flowchart, representing the data throughout the system under review, is the most widely used technique for identifying information gaps, bottlenecks, redundancies, inefficient use of personnel, and poorly operating routing systems. Because the flowchart identifies sources of information, decision points, storage points, and the information flow direction, it can pinpoint the individuals responsible for processing the data.

If flowcharts are to be most useful, the individual preparer must have direct knowledge of activities as they actually exist. This demands a keen understanding of the organization and sequencing of operations. Figure 3.1 provides the standard flowchart symbols. Figure 3.2 shows the flow of information for the purchasing function in a small nonprofit agency.

Concluding Observations

Internal control has achieved greater visibility because its strategic role is gradually being recognized. Revelations of major deficits in internal control has led to significant losses in both the public and private sectors. When sound internal controls are maintained and effectively monitored they are an important aid to enhancing productivity and effectiveness. Finally, they are also a vital means for keeping honest people honest.

Figure 3.1
Standard Flowchart Symbols

Process-Manual, mechanical, or automated changes in data. For example, document preparation generating a computer run, recording accounting entries, proofing totals on an adding machine.

Decision-Involving two alternate procedures, solutions, answers, etc.

YES

NO

Document-Example of a record that supports an operation. This may be a form, report, computer printout, correspondence, accounting record, etc.

Multiple Documents-To identify disposition of copies, number each separately. Provide an additional document symbol to indicate any remaining copies.

1
2
3 - 4

Storage or File-Any media such as correspondence files, computer tapes, etc., used to retain information while it is not being processed. Notations such as "T" for temporary or "A" for alphabetical order may be made within the symbol.

Punched Card-A card with holes punched that signify information; used in data processing.

Terminal-Beginning or end of flow.

Information Flow-Indicating direction of flow of information.

Magnetic Tape-A file stored on magnetic tape.

Connector-Indication of information existing in one part of the chart but reentering at another point. Maintain continuity by entering the same number or letter with both connectors.

Figure 3.2
Purchasing Process Flowchart: Small Nonprofit Agency

Figure 3.2 (cont'd.)

Figure 3.2 (cont'd.)

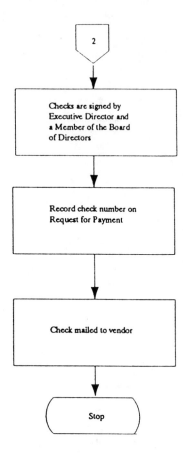

2

Checks are signed by
Executive Director and
a Member of the Board
of Directors

Record check number on
Request for Payment

Check mailed to vendor

Stop

Source: Adapted from Young Cho, Jesus M. Fernandez, and
Jeffrey J. Tolge, Class project in financial management, 1986.

APPENDIX: INTERNAL CONTROL QUESTIONNAIRE

General

1.	Is there a policy and procedures manual?	Yes	No
2.	Are there periodic physical inventories of supplies and equipment?	Yes	No

Control Over Checks

3.	Are all disbursements, except petty cash, made by check?	Yes	No
4.	Is the signing of checks in advance prohibited?	Yes	No
5.	Is the practice of drawing checks to "cash" or "bearer" prohibited?	Yes	No
6.	If not, are checks drawn limited to payrolls and/or petty cash reimbursements?	Yes	No
7.	Are the bank accounts independently reconciled by someone other than the employee who keeps the case records?	Yes	No
8.	Is the sequence of check numbers accounted for when reconciling the bank accounts?	Yes	No
9.	Are checks ever issued on the basis of verbal authority only?	Yes	No
10.	Is proper inventory control maintained over blank checks and voided checks?	Yes	No
11.	Are agency funds from major programs kept in a separate bank account?	Yes	No
12.	Are surprise counts made of the petty cash fund?	Yes	No
13.	Are vouchers or other supporting documents presented together with the checks submitted for signature?	Yes	No
14.	Are the supporting documents impressed with a "paid" stamp or other mark so as to prevent their use for duplicate payment?	Yes	No
15.	Are cash receipts recorded and deposited daily?	Yes	No
16.	Are checks issued in blank prohibited?	Yes	No
17.	Are checks issued to "cash" or "bearer" prohibited?	Yes	No
18.	Are alteration of checks or bank transfers prohibited?	Yes	No
19.	Are check protection machines used where appropriate and feasible?	Yes	No

| 20. | Is protective paper used? | Yes | No |

Control Concerning Cash Receipts

21.	Is surety bond required for employees handling cash?	Yes	No
22.	Are bank accounts authorized by the treasurer?	Yes	No
23.	Is the person performing the mail-opening function kept from making deposits?	Yes	No
24.	Is the person opening the mail required to give receipts in detail?	Yes	No
25.	Are cash receipts deposited daily?	Yes	No
26.	Is comparison made with the cashier's record and mail receipts by an independent person?	Yes	No
27.	Is there a system to independently control miscellaneous cash receipts?	Yes	No
28.	Are bank duplicate deposit tickets compared with cash receipts?	Yes	No
29.	Are postdated checks protected in a secure place?	Yes	No
30.	Are postdated checks required to be reported or logged in?	Yes	No
31.	Do people handling the cashier function engage in collection activities?	Yes	No
32.	Are vacations mandatory for people handling cash?	Yes	No

Control Concerning Cash Disbursements

33.	Is a system in place that accounts for all prenumbered checks?	Yes	No
34.	Are spoiled checks mutilated and secured to prevent reuse?	Yes	No
35.	Is the practice of making checks payable to "cash" or "bearer" prohibited?	Yes	No
36.	Is there a system that controls unused checks?	Yes	No
37.	Are people who sign checks prohibited from:		
	a) Handling cash?	Yes	No
	b) Approving disbursements?	Yes	No
	c) Recording cash receipts?	Yes	No
	d) Posting ledger accounts?	Yes	No
38.	Are signature facsimiles in use adequately controlled?	Yes	No

39.	Is there a system for counter signing checks?	Yes	No
40.	Are documents supporting payments destroyed or stamped "paid" when payment is made?	Yes	No
41.	Is the check preparation function and the approval of invoices separated?	Yes	No
42.	Are bank statements reconciled monthly?	Yes	No
43.	Is there a system to control and promptly record transfers from one bank to another?	Yes	No
44.	Are those charged with investing funds separated from:		
	a) Recording investments?	Yes	No
	b) Issuing confirmation of purchases?	Yes	No
	c) Matching securities purchases with broker, dealer, or institutional confirmation?	Yes	No
	d) Preparing bank reconciliation and periodic reports?	Yes	No
		Yes	

Control Over Payroll

45.	Are payroll checks issued prior to receiving time and attendance reports?	Yes	No
46.	Is proper authorization and documentation made in the hiring of additional staff and/or granting salary increases?	Yes	No
47.	Is official documentation presented to the payroll clerk to support the payroll?	Yes	No
48.	Is the payment of overtime properly approved?	Yes	No
49.	Are there procedural controls over the use of overtime?	Yes	No
50.	Are time and attendance reports countersigned by an individual in authority?	Yes	No
51.	Is a complete current record maintained on personnel and rates?	Yes	No

Control Over Purchases

52.	Is a separate bank account maintained for payroll funds? (If the answer is Yes, is a monthly reconciliation of the payroll bank account made by an employee who is independent of payroll preparation and accounting functions?)	Yes	No

53.	Are payment vouchers or invoices approved by a responsible official?	Yes	No
54.	Does he/she have a record of the individuals' signatures?	Yes	No
55.	Are there proper safeguards over undistributed or unclaimed checks?	Yes	No
56.	Are payroll checks distributed by someone other than the personnel?	Yes	No
57.	Are employees' names, salary rates, etc. checked against payroll by someone other than the payroll clerk on a test check basis?	Yes	No
58.	Are all invoices matched to the purchase order and/or approved by someone in authority indicating that the item was in fact received or the services were in fact performed prior to the preparation of the check in payment?	Yes	No
59.	Are all invoices examined to verify that the items, price, and quantity invoiced are proper and as ordered?	Yes	No
60.	Does the financial officer or department have a list of the individuals who are authorized to sign purchase requisitions, purchase orders, receiving reports, time and attendance cards, etc.?	Yes	No
61.	Are all requisitions for purchases approved by a properly designated individual?	Yes	No
62.	Are all purchase requisitions checked to the budget to verify that a budget line exists authorizing such purchases?	Yes	No
63.	Are purchase orders used to indicate receipt of all merchandise?	Yes	No
64.	Are receiving reports used to indicate receipt of all merchandise?	Yes	No
65.	Are purchase orders properly signed by someone in authority?	Yes	No

Overall Organization of the Agency Operations

66.	Is the overall management and departmental structure of the agency, including duties, lines of responsibility, and accountability or key employees, defined in organization charts and job descriptions?	Yes	No

67.	Are the organization charts and written descriptions reviewed periodically to determine if they are up to date?	Yes	No
68.	Are the duties, lines of responsibility, and accountability of the accounting staff adequately defined in organization charts or job descriptions?	Yes	No
69.	Are the organization charts and written job descriptions reviewed periodically to determine whether they are appropriate and up-to-date?	Yes	No
70.	Are there written policies regarding personnel that relate to delegation of duties when personnel are absent?	Yes	No
71.	Are annual vacations for all personnel enforced?	Yes	No
72.	Are the accounting policies reviewed periodically to determine whether they are appropriate?	Yes	No
73.	Is there an up-to-date manual of accounting procedures?	Yes	No
74.	Is there a list of account codes (charts of accounts)?	Yes	No
75.	Are there written policies relating to physical safeguarding of critical accounting forms, records, transaction processing areas, and procedural manuals?	Yes	No

Computer Department

76.	Are the duties, lines of responsibility, and accountability of the computer department staff adequately defined in organization charts and written job descriptions?	Yes	No
77.	Are the organization charts and written job descriptions reviewed periodically to determine whether they are appropriate and up-to-date?	Yes	No
78.	Are the organization charts and written job descriptions approved by appropriate levels of management?	Yes	No
79.	Are there written policies regarding computer staff that relate to delegation of duties when staff are absent?	Yes	No
80.	Are annual vacations for all computer staff enforced?	Yes	No

Fidelity Insurance

81. Are there written policies with respect to insurance
coverage and employee fidelity bonds?   Yes   No

82. Does the agency take appropriate steps to confirm
the adequacy of its insurance coverage (e.g. by
ensuring that the coverage is regularly reviewed by
a knowledgeable person who strives to make a
professional evaluation?)   Yes   No

83. Does the agency carry fidelity bond coverage of the
appropriate type and amount?   Yes   No

NOTES

1. See Jack D. Bakker and John Marts, "Internal Controls," *Small Business Forum*, (Fall 1990), pp.: 29-31.

2. Irwin T. David, *How To Evaluate and Improve Internal Controls in Governmental Units*, (Chicago: Municipal Finance Officers Association, 1981), p. 19.

4

Revenue Management

Governments have the responsibility for providing an array of public and quasi-public goods and services that are expressed through the expenditure process - the governmental budget, identifying who gets which portions, when, and how much of the available community resources. An important factor to keep in mind is that a budget reveals simply the other side of the same coin. Thus, every expenditure of dollars requires an equal amount of revenues to be withdrawn from the public. This results in a reduction of private consumption and a transfer of private savings to the public sector.

While there are numerous spending categories, typically, fewer categories are employed in collecting taxes. Especially at larger units of governments and in other not-for-profit organizations, revenues are seldom subject to earmarking (and this are not designated to be spent for specific program or activities such as education or old age pensions) except in those cases where funds are transferred in from other governmental units. Moreover, revenue inflows and sources tend to be relatively stable in contrast to expenditures. For these reasons, among others, revenue raising has seldom attracted a great amount of political attention. Additionally, politicians are loath to talk about revenues because they involve extracting resources from the public rather than giving them, as is the case with expenditure programs. The advent of California Proposition 13 in 1976 departed significantly from this norm and provided the impetus for a successful anti-tax movement throughout the country. This movement is still having negative impact on government's tax raising opportunities.

Unlike the expenditure process, revenue policies typically have a number of legal constraints. This is true for all levels of government and other not-for-profit organizations. The problem is particularly evident at the local levels of government. Constraints take such forms as uniform assessment, maximum rates, and specified accounting procedures. Other not-for-profit agencies, especially those participating as United Way members, are restricted in terms of whom they may solicit and when such solicitations may take place.

This chapter presents the different meanings and concepts of revenue, discusses the economics of revenue raising, and explains the determination and administration of the revenue plan. An analysis of selected methods for forecasting revenues is presented.

DEFINING REVENUE

Revenues are inflows or receipts (excluding cash in kind) from external sources less refunds, debt issuances, and the liquidation of investments. All levels of government and other not-for-profit organizations classify revenues by source. These entities also use the term *receipts* synonymously with *cash collections* while the term *revenue* is also typically equated with the accrual of funds (earned but not yet received). The types of revenues vary among the different levels of government and among other not-for-profit agencies. While the process for assessing, levying, and collecting taxes is similar in all forms of government, it differs significantly from that in other not-for-profit organizations.

Both by law and by tradition, there is greater reliance on certain kinds of taxes at different levels of government. For example, real and personal property are viewed almost exclusively as a local tax source, while at the federal and state levels, the income taxes, both corporate and individual, are important.

Meaning of Revenue: Federal Level

The General Accounting Office (GAO) has defined *revenue* as referring to the increase in assets or reduction in liabilities resulting from operations. GAO identified three important ways by which revenues could be generated:

- when the government performs services for which money is due;
- when tangible goods and other tangible property are delivered to purchasers from whom payment is expected; and
- when the government is owed amounts for which no current performance is required.[1]

At the federal government level, the Treasury Department (meaning predominantly the Internal Revenue Service and the Bureau of Customs) is charged with the main responsibility for the collection of receipts. Receipts typically include the following:

- individual income taxes;
- corporate income taxes;
- social insurance taxes and contributions;
- excise taxes;
- custom duties; and
- miscellaneous receipts.

Meaning of Revenue and Receipts: State and Local

The federal meaning of revenue and receipts differs somewhat at the different levels of government. Revenue may be defined as the inflow or receipt of money by a governmental unit that is not obtained by creating an offsetting liability. Stated another way, revenue consists of the total amount of money received by a governmental unit that does not represent a recovery or refund of an expenditure, the cancellation of a particular liability, or a decrease in assets or contributions from an enterprise or in intergovernmental service funds.

Receipts usually indicate cash received, unless stipulated otherwise. Note that this definition of revenue refers to those instances when revenue is recorded on the accrual, modified accrual, or cash bases. Some governmental units and other not-for-profit organizations use the term "revenue receipt" to mean cash. It should be kept in mind that revenue is synonymous with the operating income of a governmental unit.

Using the Accrual Basis

If a governmental unit billed property tax owner "A" for $2,000 in taxes in 1996 and received the $2,000 in 1996, this is revenue for 1996. If the governmental unit billed property owner "B" for $2,500 for 1996 but owner "B" did not pay until 1997, the $2,500 is revenue for 1996. Both the $2,000 and the $2,500 inflows relate to the 1996 operating activities and the services furnished for that year and to the expenses used for the provision of services. Thus, as of December 31, 1997, the $2,500 is an asset, and will be indicated on the balance sheet under accounts receivable or taxes receivable. Revenue is made up of revenue and receipts, it is generated from a number of sources grouped according to the recommendations of the National Council on Governmental Accounting, as follows:

- taxes;
- special assessments levied;
- licenses and permits;
- intergovernmental revenues;
- charges for services;
- fines and forfeits; and
- miscellaneous revenues.

Sales Revenues

Not-for-profit organizations, such as a hospital, typically operate on an accrual basis. Thus, sales of goods and services for a specific period are revenues for that period. Revenues are generated at the time a patient receives services and is charged, which may not coincide with the time when the patient or a third party was billed or when cash was actually received. (To simplify record keeping, some hospitals recognize revenue only as the patient is billed.) In those cases where there is a high probability that the patient is not likely to pay his or her bills, revenues are reduced by the amount established as an allowance for bad debt.

Membership Dues

When membership dues become payable they become revenue whether paid before, after, or during the period. Dues that are unpaid after the period become assets or receivables. At the end of the period, the amount of receivables is reduced for probable bad debt. Life membership is, however, treated differently in most cases. Instead of recognizing only the portion of life membership as it comes due, the total amount is typically identified as revenue at the time it is received.

Pledges

The principles stated under "Membership Dues" also apply to pledges. Future pledges are revenue in those periods to which the pledged contribution applies, even if the cash is not received for the same time period. Downward adjustments are made to recognize potential bad debts. Some analysts oppose the recognition of pledges as receivable because they are legally unenforceable. Additionally, uncollectible pledges are too unreliable to make reasonable estimates. The term *revenue* and *income* are used interchangeably in not-for-profit agencies. More recently, however, *income* has come to mean the amount left over after subtracting all expenses, though the United Way uses the term *revenue* to mean money donated or received from any given source.

Funders' allocation of resources to not-for-profit agencies typically coincide with one of the following practices in making payouts to recipient agencies:

1. A prearranged payment schedule (typically quarterly);
2. Prearranged payments based on actual expense flow (typically biweekly or monthly); or
3. Cost reimbursement based on actual expenses.[2]

There are, of course, contributions and special events that generate revenues that follow no specific patterns. Regardless, the funders or contributing organizations have found that they must live with the imposed payment plans.[3]

THE ECONOMICS OF REVENUE RAISING

Functions of government revenue include: (1) generation of resources to finance the delivery of goods and services, (2) income redistribution, and (3) a fiscal policy instrument for managing consumer demands. These activities may be referred to as the revenue, redistributive, and fiscal policy (manipulations of the taxing powers to affect consumer demand) functions of taxation.

The decision to pursue any one, or a combination, of the revenue functions involves value judgments, that is, determining who will pay and in what amounts. Many questions can thus be raised about the revenue function relating to concerns about the distribution, redistribution, and equity effects of the cost of government services on the taxpayers. The precise *distributional impact* on the incomes of individuals in a given community cannot easily be determined, though estimates of impacts may be derived by a careful study of the components of the tax base and tax rates. Importantly, it should also be kept in mind that the tax burden may not fall on the initial tax base object due to tax shifting (in the ultimate resting place of a tax impact). For example, the property tax on an owner-occupied residence cannot be shifted, but in those cases where the owner rents housing units, the tax can partially be shifted forward to the renters.

Taxes may affect the allocation of resources and economic efficiency by distorting economic decisions of individuals and businesses. When taxes are not related to the provision of goods and services, taxpayers will be unable to assess the costs and benefits of the goods and services.   Lacking such information, taxpayers cannot effectively formulate demands for public services, creating the likely possibility that their choice will be a suboptimal quality. This may result in faulty allocation of resources between the public and the private sectors. Tax differential rates among different jurisdictions may also have the effect of inducing persons, businesses, and even industries to relocate.

Our discussion suggests that taxes and revenue policy have important implications for the stability of the economy.   The concern for stability and growth are mainly national responsibilities, though local government units are keenly interested in stability, economic growth, and their taxing capacity. Singularly, an individual governmental unit has minimal effect on economic output, but where local governmental units provide tax incentives, they do induce some businesses to move from one jurisdiction to another.

Much attention has been devoted in public sector economics to the importance of distributing tax burdens equitably among taxpayers. A number of sophisticated theories and approaches have been developed to aid in explaining the distribution and equity consideration in taxation. In the discussion that follows, two benchmark criteria for evaluating taxes in public finance are discussed: (1) the application of the equity criterion and (2) the application of the efficiency criterion.

Tax Efficiency

The efficiency criterion accepts the view that different taxes impose varying degrees of distortion on the market economy, creating welfare losses by causing a departure from the pareto optimality (an inability to allocate resources to improve the well-being or utility of an individual without making at least one other person worse off). Ideally an objective of a society's tax system is to minimize the excess burden or welfare costs due to taxation when diverting a given amount of resources from the private to the public sector. The efficiency criteria evaluates a tax on the amount of excess burden it creates per revenue dollar collected. The taxes that impose less excess burden are said to be more efficient from an economic perspective. An effective tax is said to be neutral in that it affects consumption, savings, work, leisure, and other important choices only minimally. Ideally, a tax should transfer resources from the private to the public without affecting the overall performance of the economy.

Tax efficiency also relates to the way in which a tax is enforced. This is particularly important because tax equity must mean more than a theoretically rational tax system. Thus, there must be equitable enforcement of the tax on all those subject to it so that no one illegally transfers his or her tax burden to other taxpayers.   Also important for the efficient enforcement of a tax is the convenience, simplicity, and compliance cost to taxpayers of determining their tax liability. These factors ultimately affect the cost of collection and thus, the efficiency of the tax.

Horizontal Equity

A tax is viewed as being horizontally equal if it treats equals equally. For example, if two persons have equal economic circumstances before a tax is imposed they would be in the same economic circumstances after the imposition of the tax. Tax equity suggests that the application should not be arbitrary or discriminatory. Horizontal equity requires that taxpayers with the same income should pay identical amounts of tax.

Despite horizontal equity's popularity, it does have some drawbacks. To apply the criteria to a tax system, the point at which two persons have equal economic circumstances or welfare must be ascertained objectively, which is not an easy task. For example, should the size of the family be considered? How are income and wealth to be considered in determining ability to pay taxes? Will a distinction be made between capital gains and ordinary income?

Vertical Equity

According to the concept of vertical equity unequals should be treated unequally. The criterion suggests that persons of differential tax paying circumstances or abilities should pay different amounts of tax. In order to judge the degree to which the tax system is vertically equitable, value judgments about the desirable or appropriate way to treat people at different income levels must be made. To facilitate an understanding of vertical equity, the ability-to-pay and benefit principles are examined.

The *ability-to-pay principle* suggests that all taxpayers should bear "equal sacrifice" (based on their financial capacities) in the payment of taxes. Thus, taxpayers with more income would pay more taxes. How large or how small should the differentials be between taxpayers? The tax rates are typically based on three main alternatives: the regressive, proportional, and progressive concepts.

If the tax paid as a percentage of income declines as income increases, the tax is considered to be *regressive* as shown in Figure 4.1, part C. The reverse is true of the *progressive* tax (see Figure 4.1, part A). As income rises, the percentage of taxes rise. If the tax paid as a percentage of income remains unchanged as income increases, the tax is said to be proportional (see Figure 4.1, part B).

Of the three types of taxes, only the progressive type is normally viewed as being in accordance with the ability-to-pay principle. This is also

Figure 4.1
Tax Base Relationships in Distributional Equity Terms

A. Progressive Tax

Income (dollars)

B. Proportional Tax

Income (dollars)

C. Regressive Tax

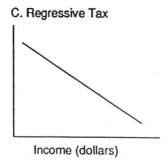

Income (dollars)

Tax paid as a percentage
of income regardless of tax base

partially true for a proportional tax, for as far as income goes, the absolute amount of taxes paid increases, despite the fact that the percentage does not change. Even a regressive tax system may have a degree of progressivity in its application if people with high income are required to pay a higher absolute amount of taxes, even though the percentage of tax paid to income falls. Only the progressive tax, however, accords with the ability-to-pay principle and distributional equity after taxes. It should be noted, however, that a particular tax should never be analyzed in isolation from other taxes because it is the total or combined effect of the taxes that ultimately determines the regressivity or progressivity of a tax system.

The *benefit principle* is viewed as the primary alternative to the ability-to-pay principle. Unlike the ability-to-pay principle, which more directly addresses the concepts of equity, the benefit principle addresses the goal of market efficiency. A major advantage of the benefit principle is that it directly relates the revenue and expenditure sides of the budget with each other. Basically, it provides a good approximation of market behavior in the allocation process of the public sector. The operation of the benefit principle permits individuals to voluntarily exchange purchasing power in the form of fees or the acquisition of government-produced goods, permitting the individuals to pay directly for the government-produced goods from which satisfaction or profit is derived.

It should be especially noted that equity is suggested, neither by the monetary nor the sacrifice benchmark, but by the dual facts that (1) the purchase of the government produced goods is voluntary, as in the private market sector, and (2) the payments are made according to the benefit received.

In practice, the benefit approach is restricted because of the inherent nature of collective consumption which typically characterizes the public sector. That is, individuals cannot be excluded from most of the benefits generated by government-produced goods, such as defense or police protection. Thus, unless compulsion is involved, requiring consumers to pay, they will benefit as "free riders" and avoid payment. For this reason, many public sector goods that are not susceptible to the market pricing mechanism cannot be provided under the benefit.

The tax paid as a percentage of income (regardless of tax base) approach, while useful in some cases, involves a benefit principle that is not comprehensive enough in its application to provide the desired benchmark of equity in the distribution of the tax burden. It has been found to be applicable in those cases where the government applies the user-charge approach, such as toll roads and garbage collection. Among the reasons why these services should be sold (involve user charges) are the following benefits:

1.   Generation of revenue intake approximating the value of the services produced;
2.   Motivation to determine whether the service is worth the cost;
3.   Creation of value-consciousness of managers about the service they receive;
4.   Generation of indicators to assess performance; and
5.   Creation of cost-consciousness with respect to the value of services exchanged between agencies, minimizing waste and overuse.[4]

The Property Tax

This is the major source of revenue for local governments. It accounted for 36 percent of all local revenue and 80 percent of all local taxes in 1982, though states had reduced their reliance on property taxes to approximately 2 percent in that same year. The property tax can be viewed as a tax on wealth levied against the value of property and based, at least partially, on the ability-to-pay and benefit concepts. There are a large number of defects associated with the property tax. They include its (1) regressivity with respect to income; (2) administrative inefficiency; and (3) creation of distortions in economic decision making.

The property tax involves both real property and personal property. Real property includes land and improvements to land. Improvement comprises the addition of such things as buildings and other structures that are permanently attached or fixed. Personal property consists of tangible and intangible property. Tangible property is comprised, typically, of movable objects such as machinery, inventory, furniture, and automobiles. Intangible property includes items that have no inherent, tangible value but rather they represent claims to value, such as stock certificates and bonds. For tax purposes, property can be categorized and differentiated by class of ownership (e.g., government, religious, and tax free) and by use (e.g., residential, commercial, industrial, and agricultural).

Because of the difficulty of administering personal property taxes, most states have exempted them, either partially or totally. Each state has its own property tax structure. Once the base has been defined, each governmental unit applies the tax rates to the base. Among the typical tax jurisdictions are the state, county, municipality, school district, and many other authorities.

There are three steps in the property tax process: (1) assessment, (2) determination of rate, and (3) collection. *Assessment* relates to the discovery and valuation of property (see Table 4.1). It is carried out usually by elected local officials, although some states may conduct this function for statewide

Table 4.1
Stages of the Property Tax Cycle

Appraisal determines the value of property for tax purposes, using legally specified standards of valuation.

1. Taxable and tax-exempt property are discovered.
2. Legal owners and taxable site of property are identified.
3. Property is appraised on the basis of use and estimated value as of the appraisal date.
4. Property owners are notified of changes in appraised value.
5. Appeals from property owners are heard by independent board of review.
6. Adjustments to appraisals are reviewed and approved by board and appraiser.
7. Final certified appraisal roll is prepared.

Assessment adjusts appraised value to determine the taxable value of property.

1. Appraised value is multiplied by assessment rate (or ratio) to determine assessed value.*
2. Assessments are equalized by state agency to the same percentage of full value across jurisdictions.*
3. Assessed value is adjusted for partial exemptions, such as homesteads.*
4. Truth-in-taxation notices are prepared and published.*

5. Public hearing is held on proposed tax rate and/or budget.
6. Tax rate(s) is(are) set by governing board.
7. Rate(s) is(are) certified as being within legal limits.*
8. Tax roll is prepared and certified.

Collection involves the preparation and distribution of tax notices to both current and delinquent taxpayers.

1. Tax bills are prepared and mailed to owners of record.
2. Lien is attached to property to secure payment of taxes, penalties, and interest.
3. Current tax payments are received, credited, and distributed.
4. Unpaid taxes become delinquent after due date.
5. Delinquent tax roll is prepared.
6. Delinquent tax notices are prepared and property owners are notified.
7. Court order is sought to foreclose on lien on outstanding delinquencies.
8. Property is sold at a public auction for payment of back taxes, penalties, and interest.

Note: Asterisks indicate activities that are not performed in all states.

Source: Robert L. Bland, *A Revenue Guide for Local Government* (Washington, D.C.: International City Management Association, 1989), p. 45, (with permission of the publisher).

property such as railroads.   The quality of the assessment activity is not uniform. The associated high administrative cost is a major reason for spacing the revaluation at lengthy intervals. Many local units underassess property but then take the opportunity to apply a higher tax rate to generate the locally needed revenue.

After the rate is determined, it is applied to assessed value to generate a given amount of revenue. The rate may be expressed in terms of dollars per hundred or thousand dollars of assessed value of property or in terms of mill(s) (1/10 of 1 percent) per dollar of assessed value. A tax rate of $5 per $1,000 of assessed value is also equivalent to 50 cents per $100 or five mills per dollar. The formula used to determine the property tax rate is as follows:

$$\frac{\text{Total Budgeted Revenue minus Anticipated Revenues from Other Sources}}{\text{The Assessed Valuation of Property within the Governmental Jurisdiction}}$$

$$= \text{Tax Rate of Assessed Valuation}$$

Collection involves the process of applying the tax rate to each property in the tax district (and involving the assessed value of all taxable properties). Tax bills are calculated and mailed yearly, semiannually, or quarterly. The tax is calculated as follows:

$100,000	(market value determination)
x .40	(assessment ratio)
40,000	(gross assessed value)
- 10,000	(exemption)
30,000	(net assessed value)
x .10	(tax rate, 100 mills)
$ 3,000	(tax liability)

.10 = tax rate
3,000. Thus the
effective tax rate =   100,000   = 0.03 or 3%

Economic Effects of the Property Tax

Three criteria are briefly discussed: (1) equity and distribution, (2) allocation and efficiency, and (3) stability. On the *equity and distribution* scale, the property tax scores poorly on both ability-to-pay and the benefit principles of taxation. It relates to the ability to pay in that property ownership can be equated with wealth and can be employed to generate income, which is an index of ability to pay. The benefit principle is involved because the owners of the property can avail themselves of a number of public services that are available directly to them, such as fire protection. As presently administered, the property tax is essentially a real estate tax and not a general property tax, and as such, it does not accord well with acceptable tax principles. For example, retired persons on small fixed incomes may become subject to higher taxes on the appreciating value of a home that was purchased many years earlier. Similarly, undeveloped land that earned no income is taxed as if it did. Another major distributional problem relates to disparities among governmental jurisdictions due to differences in the value of the tax base. Some jurisdictions have high per capita, rates while others have low rates. Jurisdictions with low tax bases are not able to provide the required services that citizens may need. This is a major reason why the California Supreme Court in 1971 held, in *Serano vs. Priest*, that reliance on the property tax for financing education discriminated against the poor. While this decision was later overturned, in 1973, by the U.S. Supreme Court, it acknowledged that the system in most states was inequitable and chaotic.

The property tax produces *allocation and efficiency* distortions for a number of reasons, including assessment practices and effects on locational decisions by business and industries that take advantage of specified tax breaks. *Stability* is not a strong factor in favor of the property tax because it is relatively income inelastic.

Economic Effects of the Income Tax

In varying degrees, all levels of government levy the income tax. The federal government is the most dominant of the three levels. The personal income tax is a prolific federal revenue source. It is essentially neutral in terms of allocational effects. Moreover, it acts as a positive economic stabilizer, is easy to administer, and can be adjusted to create equity. Because of the broad base nature of this tax revenue, yield (Tax rate times Base equals Revenue) is high. On balance, the personal income tax is viewed as the best among the major tax instruments.

Sales Tax Economic Effects

The sales taxes are employed by the federal, state, and local governments, with the major use taking place at the state level. There, two basic types of sales taxes are employed: the general sales tax and the excise tax. There are numerous variations to be found in each. The general sales tax (a percentage of retail sales) is usually based on a broad range of goods, and sometimes services. Excise taxes are imposed on specific goods levied as a percentage of sales, based on some specified unit (e.g., a gallon of gasoline).

The general sales tax, also known as the "broad-based," "gross receipts", and "ad valorem" tax, is based on a percentage of the sales value to the seller. Typically, the seller quotes the tax rate separately from the price of the goods, and it is paid by the customer. The sales tax is politically appealing and is a productive and steady revenue producer at both the state and local levels of government. The tax is easy to administer and, in some cases, local government uses it as a substitute for the unpopular property tax.

The general sales tax has an income substitution effect in that it does have the effect of raising prices to the purchaser or consumer, in essence lowering income. Since not all goods are taxed, it is not easy to generalize about the substitution income effect. Additionally, there are a number of means that have been used to reduce the regressivity of the sales tax, including exemptions on such items as food, medicines, and necessities.

MANAGING THE REVENUE PROGRAM

Besides the structuring of taxes to achieve an equitable and efficient tax system, the fiscal manager must develop and maintain a tax system that will generate sufficient revenues/resources to meet the community's demand for specified amounts of goods and services. A brief summary of general guidelines that should be considered in the development and management of a revenue system follows.

Determining Revenue Needs

The revenue requirement estimates are based on expected or proposed expenditure plans. Ideally, the revenue forecast should be carried out as soon as possible for the ensuing fiscal year to permit an evaluation of its adequacy to meet expected needs. When the analysis reveals a gap, the early time lead will permit the design and installation of new or enhanced tax sources. The following are factors that should be considered in developing the revenue plans:

- inflation rate factor;
- political philosophy of the policymaker and relevant interest groups;
- community growth and development;

- expanded and new programs;
- population characteristics and trends;
- nature and components of the tax base;
- stability of revenue over the business cycle; and
- tax efforts (low efforts, often typical of growth community, which has a large tax based from which to levy tax).

Typically, revenue needs in some units of government and not-for-profit agencies are not projected in advance. Instead, the amount of available revenue is surveyed and the agency programs are fitted to them.[5]

Fair and Equitable Distribution of the Tax Burdens

Tax rates are based, not only on the benefits received principle, but also on the ability-to-pay basis. As a tenet of good tax administration, the tax should be uniformly and equitably (nondiscriminatorily) applied. No one should be allowed to escape payment because of improper assessment, inefficient tax collection procedures, or an improper exemption allowance.[6]

Revenue Base and Growth

A tax should have elasticity in that it should be relatively responsive to growth in the economy. The expansion and/or growth in programs made necessary by economic growth should be financed directly from the expanded economic activity in the community. The normal assumption is that growth should always be attendant on expansion in revenues, provided that "the revenue base is tied to sources which are affected by the growth."[7] Lack of responsiveness of the tax base to economic growth or to inelasticity forces governmental units to increase existing taxes or to create new ones. While the revenue system base should be responsive to economic growth, the tax base should not be so structured that it is subject to widely fluctuating cyclical changes in the economy, which would create conditions of fiscal instability.

Making It Easy to Comply

This is one of the basic tenets of public administration. The objectives and structure of any law or regulation should be so administered that they motivate or enhance the possibility of voluntary compliance. Thus the tax procedure and administrative system should be developed to promote the ease and convenience of compliance. This approach minimizes cost and produces the greatest efficiency in collecting the revenue. It is said that whenever the cost of administration/collection is high in relation to better run tax systems, it may be desirable to revamp the administrative structure.

Revenue Collection and Cash Management

Finding ways to speed up the receipt of revenues is one of the principal objectives of effective cash management - a point that is elaborated in detail in Chapter 6. Each governmental unit and other not-for-profit agency should design revenue programs to generate an adequate amount of cash on a timely basis. The objective is to have sufficient cash to meet maturing obligations and other regular expenditures in order to minimize the need to borrow.

Ideally, a governmental agency or other not-for-profit agency should devise a revenue collection system that coincides with its expenditure or payment schedule requirements by developing revenue collection schedules to parallel spending schedules where state or local laws or funding agencies permit. As far as possible, revenue estimates should be provided on a monthly or quarterly basis. Receipts should be maintained on the same basis to facilitate the monitoring and tracking of the collection process.[8]

Maintaining Controls over Collections

Basic internal control norms should be observed. The receiving and accounting functions should be separated to minimize the potential for fraud and collusion. Prenumbered written receipts should be required for collection transactions. All receipts should be deposited intact in the governmental or agency's bank account. A procedure requiring prompt recording of billed revenues to taxpayers' accounts should be adhered to in order to minimize the possibility of errors and/or misplacement. It is essential to maintain up-to-date taxpayer records. A convenient time and location should be conveniently established to facilitate payment. Finally, tax statements should be designed to be readily understood, showing when and how much interest and penalty applies to delinquent taxes. When accounts become delinquent, taxpayers should be promptly informed. Especially in small governmental jurisdictions and other not-for-profit agencies where the separation of duties is difficult to obtain due to small staffs, intermittent audits may be necessary to maintain adequate controls.

A number of indices have been developed to assess collection performance. They include the following:

The *collection index*, which is used to indicate the progress made in reducing outstanding receivables is calculated as follows:

$$\text{Collection Index} = \frac{\text{Collection Made during the Period}}{\text{Receivables Outstanding at the Beginning of the Period}}$$

The *average collection index* indicates the average length of time for which receivables were outstanding. The estimate is obtained by employing the following formula:

$$\text{Avg. Collection Period} = \frac{\text{Net Collection Period}}{\text{Collection Index}}$$

The *past due index* shows the proportion of all accounts, either in amount or in number, that are past due. The index is obtained as follows:[9]

$$\text{Past Due Index} = \frac{\text{Total Past Due}}{\text{Total Outstanding}}$$

Enforcement of Collection

Enforcement comprises three main tasks: "controlling delinquency, discovering non-payers and auditing taxpayers."[10] Delinquency accounts require time notification and follow-up with legal action as the situation may dictate. Discovery involves collection investigations to locate and identify businesses or individuals who have failed to report their businesses or change of location. Compliance audits seek to ensure that taxpayers are properly reporting and accurately calculating taxes due.

There are a variety of enforcement actions that can be taken prior to and after delinquency to enhance revenue collection. They include the following:

- Charging penalties and interest sufficient (higher than short-term loans) to deter potential delinquent taxpayers and bad checks;
- Filing warrants to publicly record personal property on the court docket;
- Imposing tax liens on property to induce taxpayers to pay taxes that have been assessed;
- Seizing personal and real property (the most aggressive means to secure tax payment);

- Pursuing legal action;
- Withholding payments to vendors who owe the government taxes;
- Prompt reporting of delinquent accounts by government agencies to the collection division;
- Involving regulating agencies to withhold or suspend licenses and permits of those individuals and businesses that owe taxes to the government;
- Discontinuing utility service for nonpayment of taxes;
- Denying contracts, loans, and grants;
- Offsetting tax refunds;
- Arranging payment plans;
- Assessing corporate officers for the taxes owed by the business;
- Garnishing wages for taxes owed;
- Serving a levy requiring a bank to turn over a taxpayer's account to apply against a tax liability;
- Sending collection letters and making telephone calls;
- Promoting tax amnesties;
- Skip tracing (a system used to follow the taxpayer's whereabouts) to locate delinquent taxpayers; and
- Enforcing parking ticket violations by means such as the Denver boot, which makes cars undrivable.[11]

Managing Delinquent Accounts

Traditionally, there was a general reluctance (until recent years) to aggressively pursue delinquent accounts, especially in those cases involving unpopular taxes. This attitude has undergone an important change in recent years. The demand for more goods and services, the resistance to paying greater amounts of taxes, and the prolonged economic recession have forced governments to take greater initiative to motivate individuals to pay their taxes.

Increasingly, government officials have been employed new approaches to obtain quicker response from delinquent taxpayers (see the San Diego approach in Table 4.2). In some communities delinquent accounts have been farmed out to collection agencies that use procedures similar to those applied in the private sector. In other cases communities, publish the names of delinquent taxpayers in the local newspapers. Though this approach has been relatively successful, extreme care must be taken to avoid embarrassment to the taxpayers

Table 4.2

Streamlining Delinquent Collection Procedures: City of San Diego

Develop In-House Capability
- Hired experienced debt collection manager to develop in-house program.
- Treasurer's Office brought back all accounts from outside agencies. "Address correction requested" on envelopes allows the post office to put correct address on the letters of anyone who has moved, providing a critical tracing trail to taxpayer's whereabouts.
- Trained existing staff on appropriate collection procedures and how to collect on judgments in small claims court.
- Program initiated to enforce and collect treble damages and penalty on bounced checks not paid in 30 days. The enforcement of this provision provides significant revenue intake.
- Automated the manual tracking and billing procedures, enhancing the opportunity to produce an array of letters.

Streamlining Regulations and Centralizing Collection
- Payment arrangements are allowed to be set up *only* by staff of the collection division of the Treasury Department. This requirement centralizes the credit function, information relating to debtor's credit risk, and reporting to credit services.
- To protect the city's interest, bankruptcy notices were directed to Treasurer's collection division to arrange for proper court filing and appearances.
- All action on write-offs and bad checks are centralized. Writes-offs are made only after all reasonable efforts have been undertaken to collect debt. "Insufficient funds" notices from bad debts are pursued for treble damages up to $500 plus the face amount of the debt.

Relationship with City Attorney
- New regulations require that the city attorney provide quarterly updated reports on all outstanding delinquent accounts in its possession. Though the regulation limits the treasure's action to the small claims court, the collection personnel prepare the vast majority of the legal actions for the municipality with the necessary document for the city attorney's signature. This has been done due to the mutual trust and confidence that has been developed and the success that has been achieved.
- City attorney refers cases of award of court costs to the city from losing plaintiffs to the treasurer's office for collection.

Table 4.2 cont'd.

Credit Reporting
- Collection division subscribes to a credit-reporting service as one important means of prompting debtors to pay. It is the last resort before writing off their account.
- The credit-reporting system makes it difficult for debtors to obtain future credit, especially unsettled problems on real estate or on automobile loans.
- Debtors designated as "skips" are reported to the city when they seek credit.
- A debtor without assets but with a good credit rating may be counseled to borrow against his/her credit card or bank to settle his/her city account. When the debtor has exhausted his/her borrowing capacity, such an individual would be counseled to arrange a down payment plan.
- Credit histories reflecting extended amounts of unpaid debt or bankruptcy filings are likely to reveal hopeless opportunities for collection and thus should be written off.

Program Results
- Accounts less than $25,000 have seen 1,350 percent increase in collections since 1983, for a cost-benefit ratio of nearly 3 to 1.
- Improved documentation of records has resulted.
- Enforcement of appropriate penalties and fees has induced greater payments and generated greater revenue inflow.
- As a further inducement to spur voluntary and early tax payment, it is being recommended that a referral fee be imposed to aid in hiring more personnel for the collection division.

Important Considerations Prior to Program Implementation
- Assess the support from top organization officials. If the required support is not available, the program is not likely to succeed.
- Move slowly to avoid turf battles and friction. The San Diego program used the first two years to train, automate, and professionalize the collection division and to demonstrate its efficiency and effectiveness.
- Departments referring collection are given regularized updating reports and a final report indicating revenue collections that can be matched with cost of the given program.
- Responsibility for collecting delinquent accounts is centralized, whether located in-house or contracted to an outside agency. Whoever is assigned the collection must be knowledgeable about relevant laws and procedures to be able to assess the agency's capability for effectively carrying the collection function.

Source: Conny M. Jamison, "Collecting Revenues: No Stone Unturned in the City of San Diego," *Government Finance Review*, 7, no. 1 (February 1991): 25-28 whose names are erroneously included.

REVENUE FORECASTING

Forecasting has never been in wide use in the public or most not-for-profit agencies. The major exception involves the yearly budget, in which revenue is forecasted, planned expenditures are projected and cash flow projections are made (in some governmental and other not-for-profit agencies). In the private sector, it has become an accepted practice that has been integrated into the regular decision-making process. The use of forecasting, especially in a number of local governmental units, has been increasing, not because of the policymakers' desire for rationality, but because of the opportunity to use the forecast as a political instrument to get program directors and interest group advocates to lower their expectations for expenditure resources. For example, when the forecast is made, advocates for more resources are immediately informed about the constraints and are more likely to limit their requests based on forecasted revenue availability. Depending on the assumptions that forecasters use, the forecasted revenue may be affected either upward or downward. These projected figures can then become a guideline or parameter to get budget requests reduced.

Forecasts may be classified in terms of the length of time they cover: (1) the medium-range forecast may be used to tackle such problems as expected budget gaps or revenue shortfalls before they become crises. (Medium-range forecasting may extend across a budget period, involving problems such as the possible termination of a federal grant or revenue sharing.) (2) The short-range forecast relates predominantly to the development of the annual budget and related revenue forecasts and budget projections. (3) Long-range forecasting includes a wider range of internal and external macro-problems that must be examined. The past trends and present conditions of the governmental unit is carefully studied. Such factors as population, age, income structure, and employment (types and patterns) are correlated to determine the governmental unit's tax capacity or capability to undertake the projected expenditures.

Forecasting Methods

What are the appropriate methods that should be used in forecasting revenues? While the answer to this question cannot be completely determined, the degree of desired accuracy, the expertise available, and the available data base significantly influence the end product. A number of techniques have been suggested. These include the following: (1) the best-guess or expert approach, (2) time-series components, and (3) the least squares (simple regression) method of forecasting.

The *best-guess approach* is based on the use of experts who, because of their education, experience, and previous success, will be employed to determine the forecast. Although the experts may use a given formula, approach, or combination of existing methodologies, the methods used are not made explicit. The forecast is given credibility because of their expert reputation.[12] Therefore, it is very difficult to evaluate whether the approach is correct.

The *time-series components approach* relies entirely on the recent past as a means of projecting revenues. The approach assumes a continuing direction of the time series. The time-series component approach has been used to make relatively dependable projections of local government revenues. The results produced by time-series analysis "are affected by long-term trends in underlying economic and demographic variables."[13] Such variables are good predictors because they indicate whether the economy is moving, and its direction. For example, in a city where the economic activity is sharply declining, the potential revenue intake is likely to follow the same downward path, as in the case of parking meter revenue in Durham, North Carolina, in 1976. As the commercial and business activity began to move out of the downtown business district to other areas from 1960 to 1975, the parking meter tax fell from $60,000 in 1960 to just below $20,000 in 1976.[14] (See also Figure 4.2).

Cyclical factors or wavelike movements occurring irregularly over a number of years affect business activity, which impacts on revenue. The cycles impacting revenue include interest rate cycles, business cycles, and stock market cycles, with the cycle having the most effect on revenue stability being the business cycle.[15] In view of the potential impact that cycles may have on revenues in general, an understanding of the conditions of the economy and the phases of the business cycle is most desirable. Of particular note is that although the financial manager is not expected to make sophisticated economic forecasts, he or she must be cognizant of the state of the economy on a continuing basis.

Past cycles often provide guidelines. For example, cyclical fluctuations in interest rates tend to affect local government revenues in two ways: (1) they affect borrowing costs paid by government, and (2) they influence property taxes by affecting the level of new construction.

Seasonal components typically will not be discerned from annual or cyclical trends. Rather, seasonal variations can be effectively identified by examining monthly time series. An examination of sales tax collections can be used to highlight the impact of the seasonal factor. In examining the sales tax collection, it is possible to see that the collection for the month of December usually rises dramatically due to the Christmas shopping.

Figure 4.2 for Bright City reveals a constant upward trend in parking meter collection. This pattern is in sharp contrast with what Durham, North

Figure 4.2
Parking Meter Revenue Forecast, City of Bright

Annual Receipts in $

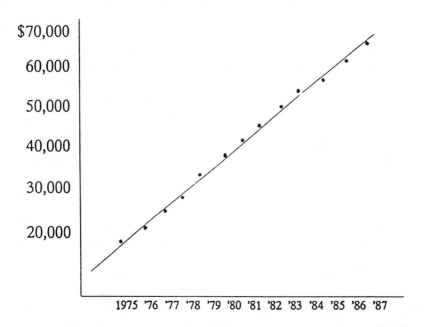

Carolina, experienced-a sharp decline due to out migration of business from central downtown commercial areas between 1960 and 1976. Because the variation from the trend line is small, it suggests that basic trends in determining collection are very significant and that cyclical or other components had only a minor impact on collections.[16]

Calculating the Trend Line Using the Least Squares Method or Simple Regression

Calculating the trend line in this manner (see Chapter 10) permits us to obtain an estimate of the slope and level of the trend and allows us to calculate (see Table 4.3) and plot future trend values (see Figure 4.3). A degree of caution is advised in using this method since it rarely produces an exact fit. Indeed, the actual trend may approximate a curved rather than a straight line.

To determine the variation of the actual data from the trend line and to adjust the data for trend, the percentage of trend can be calculated by dividing the actual data for each year by the calculated trend value for a given year (times 100), producing the "percentage trend" as was done in Table 4.4. If there are cyclical component effects, they will show up as a high or low percentage of trend value during the periods of contraction or expansion, respectively when major irregular components effects are present they will appear as one-time deviations.

In Table 4.4, the percentage of trend suggests that the year 1990 was affected by cyclical factors. Moreover, the greater the cluster of percentage of trend values around 100 percent, the greater the confidence in their accuracy. This would make permissible the assumption that variations occurring in the actual collection are caused by the underlying trend. When significant variations show up above or below 100 percent, many other factors may be affecting collection, suggesting that caution should be used in interpreting the results.

San Francisco's revenue-forecasting model uses a set of 23 econometric equations that are interrelated components consisting of the following: (1) 10 equations forecasting San Francisco's tax base, (2) 5 equations forecasting key local and regional economic variables, including San Francisco's assessed value, and (3) 8 equations forecasting revenues produced by the seven major local taxes (property, business, sales and use, utility, property transfer, parking, and transit and occupancy) and one state subvention (the motor-vehicle in-lieu of payment).[17]

In developing its revenue-forecasting model, San Francisco articulated three main objectives: (1) improving the accuracy of its forecasts, (2) providing a policy tool to enable the city to better analyze its tax and revenue policy, and (3) increasing the ease of revenue forecasting while achieving the undertaking with reasonable cost. Thus far, the model has had a degree of success. In the fiscal year 1989-1990 the seven main revenues were underpredicted by 0.1 percent, 0.7 percent and in 1991 they were overestimated by 1.9 percent. The most difficult of the taxes to predict has been the business transfer tax. In 1989 it underpredicted inflow by 15.1 percent. It overpredicted inflow by 6.5 percent in 1990 and by 4.5 percent in 1991. The view is that when the property transfer tax is removed, the model has a much greater predictability of the revenue flow.[18]

Forecasting in the Not-For-Profit Organization

In not-for-profit organizations, previous activities are typically used in preparing budgets. The manager responsible for making projections examines past trends and other factors considered likely to affect the revenue outlook. Subaggregate factors, such as the number of students, patients, and contact hours, may be used to make revenue projections.

Table 4.3
Least Squares Formula - Calculation of Future Trend Values

Let x = time deviation of years from middle year
    y = historical level of collection of taxes in dollars

Time Series Data:

Fiscal Year	Collections
1990	$150,000
1991	125,000
1992	180,000
1993	220,000
1994	250,000

Year (X)	Actual Collection (Y)	Time Deviation of Each Year (X)	Square of x deviation (X^2)	Trend Ordinates (Expected Values) XY	XY
1990	150,000	-2	4	-300,000	126,000
1991	125,000	-1	1	-120,000	155,500
1992	180,000	0	0	0	185,500
1993	220,000	+1	1	220,000	214,500
1994	250,000	+2	4	500,000	244,500
Total	925,000	0	10	+295,000	

Average = 185,000.

XY/X^2
Let xy = +295,000
    x^2 = 10
    = 295,000 = $\underline{295,000}$ annual increment = 29,500 annual increment   10

Figure 4.3
Graphic View of Least Squares Trend Line
(Revenue)

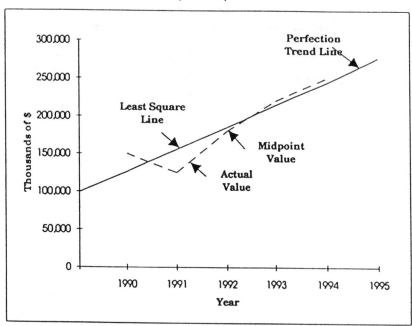

A number of external factors are likely to affect revenue projection. For example, a drop in the birthrate may effect elementary school enrollment, resulting in decreased demand for elementary school teachers.

Three types of revenue patterns may occur: regular, seasonal, and random. Regular revenue occurs as anticipated monthly, quarterly or annual payments. Examples are collections in a church, patient billing, and interest on bank deposits. At a private school, tuition may be received twice a year and fees from sporting events may come in during the summer. Random revenues from charitable institutions, grants, and other special requests may come in anytime during the year.[19]

SUMMARY OBSERVATIONS

Revenue is the fuel that runs financial management systems. Thus, an understanding of revenue is very important to the financial manager. It is not enough to have a knowledge of the technical aspects of revenue raising, involving the economics of taxation, forecasting, and administration. Political implications have become especially important as well, following the enactment of Proposition 13 in California in 1976.

The new consciousness among taxpayers about the desire to raise only necessary taxes and to reduce them when possible has created greater sensitivity on the part of financial managers and political officials to promote more efficient collection procedures. Additionally, it has motivated politicians to use revenue forecasting to obtain budget reductions and to seek alternatives to taxing sources, such as greater user charges, to finance government services.

Table 4.4
Calculating Percentage of Trend

Fiscal Year	Actual Collections		Calculated Trend Value			Percentage of Trend
1990	($150,000	-	$126,000)	x	100	199%
1991	(125,000	-	155,000)	x	100	80.6%
1992	(180,000	-	185,000)	x	100	97%
1993	(220,000	-	214,500)	x	100	102.5%
1994	(250,000	-	244,000)	x	100	102%

Revenue management in the not-for-profit agencies has many similarities, though there are significant differences in the funding sources. Of course, the not-for-profit agencies tend to be subject to greater uncertainties about the timing of their revenue inflows.

NOTES

1. See GAO, *Accounting Principles and Standards for Federal Agencies* (Washington, D.C.: GAO, 1978), pp. 1-25.

2. Robert D. Winter and Rhea K. Kish, *Budgeting in Not-for Profit Organizations* (New York: Free Press, 1984), p. 201; United Way, *Accounting and Financial Reporting* (Alexandria, Va.: United Way of America, 1974).

3. Winter and Kish, *Budgeting*, p. 204.

4. Robert Anthony and David Young, *Management Control in Non-Profit Organizations* (Homewood, Ill.: Richard D. Irwin, 1984), p. 182.

5. See Terry Nichols Clark, G. Edward DeSeve and J. Chester Johnson, *Financial Handbook for Mayors and City Managers* (New York: Van Nostrand Reinhold Co., 1985), pp. 36-37.

6. Arthur Mendonsa, *Simplified Financial Management in Local Government* (Athens, Ga.:   University of Georgia Institute of Local Government, 1969), pp. 88-89; see also Richard E. Wagner, *Public Finance* (Boston, Mass.: Little Brown and Co., 1982), pp. 43-52.

7. Mendonsa, *Simplified Financial Management*, p. 90.

8. Ibid., pp. 90-91.

9. David P. Dolter and Roger Mansfield, "The City as Debt Collector," in *Practical Financial Management*, ed. John Matzer (Washington, D.C.: International City Managers Association, 1984), p. 71.

10. Ian J. Allan, "Enforcement of Revenue Collections," *Government Finance Review*, 9, no. 3 (June 1993): 44.

11. Ibid., pp. 44-45.

12. See Hans Leverbach and James P. Cleary, *The Beginning Forecasters: The Forecasting Process Through Data Analysis* (Belmont, Calif.: Lifetime Learning Publications, 1981); and Steven C. Wheelwright and Spyros Makridakos, *Forecasting Methods for Management*, 2nd ed. (New York: John Wiley and Sons, 1978).

13. Charles D. Liner, "Projecting Local Government Revenues," *Popular Government*, 43 (Spring 1978): 33.

14. Ibid., p. 35.

15. Ibid.

16. Ibid.

17. Stephen J. Agostini, "Searching for a Better Forecast: San Francisco Revenue Forecasting Model," *Government Finance Review*, 7 no.6 (December 1991): 13-15.

18. Ibid, pp. 15-16.

19. James Gaestner, "Revenue Budgets," in *Financial Management for Nonprofit Organizations*, ed. Tracy D. Connors and Christopher T. Callaghan, (New York: AMACOM, 1982), pp. 27-28.

5

Purchasing and Inventory Management

The magnitude of expenditure for the purchase of goods and services is second only to the expenditure for personnel in most government and other not-for-profit agencies. In 1992 state and local governments' expenditures for the purchase of goods and services exceeded $190 billion. Because of the sizable allocation of resources to purchasing and procurement, considerable interest has been drawn to the area.

With the new federal drive to reduce or at least slow down the rate of increase in medical-related services, hospitals and other health care and service providers have come under closer scrutiny, and the intensity of the surveillance is likely to continue. Regulatory bodies and third party intermediaries (e.g., Blue Cross checks on the reasonableness and validity of cost for the federal government in supported health care programs such as Medicaid) have placed great emphasis on hospital cost containment and efficient purchasing power. The coming of the Bill Clinton administration and his health care plan, which is designed to meet the public demand to control costs and to provide coverage to more Americans, has increased the pressure on health care providers to reduce costs.

This chapter examines the purchasing function. Emphasis is put on the ways that are used to enhance the administrative structure and to improve its efficiency and effectiveness.

DEFINING PURCHASING

Purchasing may be viewed as a support service as shown in Figure 5.1A or as a management program as shown in Figure 5.1B. From a

Figure 5.1A

Purchasing as a Support Service

Figure 5.1 B

Purchasing as a Management Program

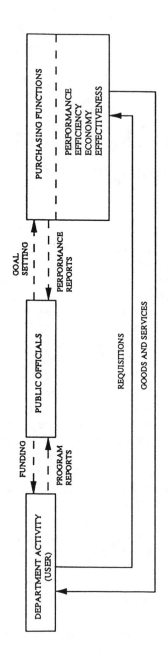

Source: GAO, Study of Selected Local Procurement Systems, Part I (Washington, D.C.: General Accounting Office, August, 1978),p.24

comprehensive perspective, purchasing is concerned in public and other not-for-profit organizations with the acquisition of all goods and services except those provided directly by employees of an organization.   This comprises the purchasing of materials, supplies, equipment, furniture, and all other services performed under contract. Included also is the construction of new public works in the provision of services when part of the regular operation of an agency.[1]

SCOPE AND OBJECTIVES OF THE PURCHASING FUNCTION

Purchasing seeks to procure required goods and services in order to achieve maximum value for the resources expended. Goods and services should be acquired in the appropriate quantity and quality at the place, manner, and time desired at the lowest cost possible. While the overriding purchasing criterion relates to the **lowest cost ultimately possible**, it is critical to understand that quality and price go hand in hand. A prompt delivery of goods and services of inferior quality is counterproductive.

A practice that has gained popularity among some governmental units and other not-for-profit agencies, especially when purchasing long-lived assets, is life-cycle costing. This is used to determine the total cost of goods and services. The approach evaluates, not only the initial acquisition cost, but also the maintenance, operating costs, energy, productivity potential, and any trade-in or recovery value that may be realized upon disposal.[2]

As a general rule, purchasing seeks to obtain goods and services at the appropriate time and at the best price from competent suppliers. As a universal expectation, purchasing in public and other not-for-profit organizations must be free from favoritism and arbitrariness or caprice. Among the duties, responsibilities, and objectives to which a purchasing system should give due cognizance are the following:

- Maintaining adequate supplies of materials at all times;
- Developing qualitative performance measures to aid in evaluating the performance function;
- Working individually and collectively (with vendors and using agencies) to achieve cost reductions;
- Conducting comparative cost-benefit studies to determine whether to undertake work in-house or contract out;
- Automating procedures and processes where this serves to promote efficiency and productivity;
- Developing and conducting training programs for buyers and supervisors;

- Employing team buying and other appropriate arrangements that will facilitate more effective performance;
- Arranging for alternative supply systems and sources to minimize or avoid interruption in the delivery of public goods and services;[3] and
- Maintaining open lines of communication with the news media.

Attributes of an Effective Purchasing Function

A well-run purchasing system should include the following features:

- A written and updated policies and procedures manual;
- A purchase requisition system to communicate purchase requirement;
- A purchase order system to communicate commitment to the vendor, the accounting department, the person who will receive the materials, and the requisitioner;
- An updated list of employees who are authorized to request purchases, with specific dollar limits;
- A preaudit system with which to compare requisitions before issuing the purchase order;
- A well-functioning system for evaluating "bill" type purchases;
- A system to expedite overdue orders; and
- Maintenance of a system to locate suppliers that meet specified requirements in terms of the most affordable price and delivery schedules.

The Purchasing Process

This process comprises the steps concerned with the acquisition of goods and services (See Figure 5.2). It is initiated at the time a need is identified and continues until the goods have been received and approved for use or the service has been delivered. While the steps required to carry out the purchasing function vary among governmental units and other not-for-profit agencies, typical activities include the following:

- Specifying quantities essential to meet necessary requirements;
- Preparing purchasing requisitions;
- Selecting sources or advertising;
- Soliciting bids;

Figure 5.2

Phases of a Purchase Transaction

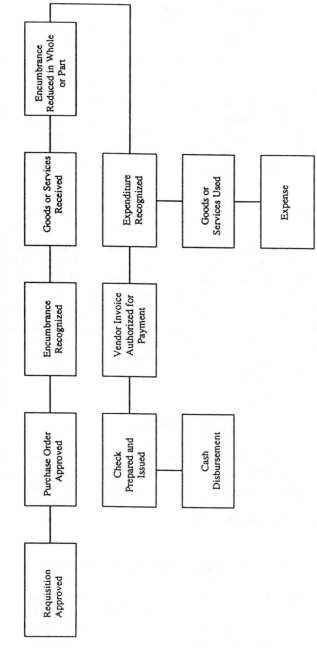

Source: Adapted From Ernst and Young, *Introduction to Accounting*, p.3-2.

- Conducting informal bidding;
- Analyzing bids;
- Issuing purchase orders;
- Following up or expediting purchase orders (when required);
- Receiving and inspecting goods or services; and
- Making payment for goods.

In addition to these purchasing activities, the process usually includes a provision for stores and inventory control and a clear delineation of responsibility for disposal of scrap or obsolete, or surplus inventory. An important point is that purchasing encompasses far more than the mere processing of orders. Because of the magnitude of resources devoted to purchasing, it plays a key role in helping to reduce agency costs.

CENTRALIZED PURCHASING

Centralization of the purchasing function is widely advocated in both the public and private sectors. The widely held view is that centralization is an optimal approach to realizing cost-effective procurement for a large number of activities. It does not permit individual entities to follow their own preferences in the selection of vendors or products and in the purchase of common items in small quantities. When appropriate authority and responsibility are combined with effective management techniques, a centralized purchasing system becomes an instrument that is accountable to the public and/or clientele for effecting sound procurement policy.[4]

Defining Centralized Purchasing

This may be defined as the concentration of the responsibility and authority for the government- or agency-wide purchasing function under the head of a single manager or purchasing agent. In governmental units, authority and responsibility to manage and coordinate purchasing activities are delegated by statute to the purchasing agent.

When Is a Centralized Purchasing Function Needed?

To determine this, a number of questions must be asked. What is the anticipated amount of savings to be gained? What are the amounts of poor-quality products being received? What are the needs for standardization and specification? Is there a need for an improved bidding procedure? Is there a need for better expenditure control? What are the costs of existing decentralized purchasing and storage systems versus documented benefits? How do the costs and benefits of the decentralized systems compare with the potential benefits from the centralized purchasing system?

How to Establish Centralized Purchasing

Several steps are necessary to effectively accomplish centralized purchasing:

First, obtain full administrative support. In government agencies, political support, including that of clientele and of interest groups, may be critically important. Secondly, "sell" the benefits to department heads and other relevant individuals and groups and enlist their cooperation. Finally, establish the purchasing department's credibility by carefully choosing the responsibility centers or departments for initial implementation; carefully map out or schedule other departments for joining the system. The process should begin with those departments with which good relations exist and that are the most disposed to accommodate change and innovation. However, before centralized purchasing is installed in any department, an assessment of the weakness and needed improvements should be conducted.[5]

Once it has been decided to consolidate purchasing activities with a centralized system, a number of activities are required. First, the basic objectives, responsibilities, and authority of the purchasing function must be determined. It is not enough to establish the scope of authority and responsibility. The regulation should define the degree of accountability desired and how it is to be enforced, and a clear delineation of limits should be put on the purchasing agent's delegated responsibilities and authority. With the establishment of the centralized purchasing unit and the appointment of the purchasing agent, the procedures necessary to effectively operate the purchasing function are then developed.[6]

Location of the Purchasing Function

The placement of the purchasing unit varies widely throughout governmental units in the United States. At the federal level, civilian procurement is carried out by the General Services Administration, which is directly responsible to the president. Procurement for the military is done by designated agencies which report to the service chiefs, who in turn have been appointed by the president.

It is interesting to note where the purchasing function is located in Canadian systems. In the Canadian system, "a case can be made for placing the purchasing function under the jurisdiction of the treasurer since purchasing has a greater affinity to finance than to any other central management function."[7] Another model has been emerging in the Canadian local government system, in which the purchasing head reports to a central administrative service group, especially when finance functions are attached to the group, as is the case in Thunder Bay, Ontario.

In a number of places in the United States, such as Chicago, the purchasing office is attached to the mayor's office. Purchasing accounts for a large portion of expenditure for public goods and services, and as such, it represents an important political investment that can be used to reward political friends and exercise direct financial influence over governmental resources. Thus, to ensure that the purchasing function operates creatively and professionally, due consideration must be given to its placement and authority, the training of its employees, and the mechanisms required for its control.

Advantages of the Centralized Purchasing System

The degree of centralization varies from organization to organization. Thus, the benefits to be gained will vary, depending on the extent of centralization. When a purchasing system is effectively centralized, it makes possible considerable savings and better maintains a system of internal controls over the procurement function. Among the common benefits that may be realized from a centralized purchasing system are the following:

- It permits lower prices of goods and services: (1) quantity discounts are made possible by consolidating like items to permit bulk buying; (2) due to an increased knowledge of the organization's needs, opportunity to participate in group purchasing is maximized.
- It permits the streamlining of management: (1) better scheduling and delivery of goods and services at the right place and time are facilitated; (2) surplus stocks and shortages are minimized; (3) a systematic disposal policy for dealing with surplus, obsolete, and scrap materials can be maintained; (4) the receiving, storage, and inventory controls are facilitated (for example, fewer orders are processed, reducing recurring cost, inspection time, and record keeping); (5) better purchasing practices and greater coordination of purchases are promoted; (6) the opportunity to develop in-house purchasing specialists is enhanced, and the chances for attracting high-

quality purchasing professionals are increased; (7) the number of employees required to perform purchasing activities is reduced; and (8) the receiving process is able to operate in tandem with inventory control. The receiving function is responsible for checking the status of incoming goods to ensure their acceptability in terms of condition, quantity, and proper placement. The receiving activity is charged with the following specific responsibilities: (a) assure that goods and services received correspond to a purchase order on file; (b) examine the goods to determine if they have been tampered with; (c) note any damage in the packing slip and the carrier's waybill in the presence of the carrier or on the form required for that purpose; (d) check the carrier's documentation to compare with the number delivered; (e) forward a copy of the receiving report to the accounting department and to appropriate location for use in central store; and (9) the purchasing manager is held accountable for the purchasing function.

- It improves administrative controls through better planning and control, standardization of materials, and implementation of improved funding techniques such as contracting and performance measurement.[8]

Competitive Bidding as an Effective Purchasing Tool

The competitive approach is the most widely acclaimed approach for the acquisition of goods and services, though it is not always used. In fact, at the federal level a significant amount of military procedurement is achieved through noncompetitive bidding. Typically, the competitive approach requires contracts above a specified monetary level to be submitted to competitive bidding or competitive negotiation. Public competitive contracting in state and local governments falls into three categories: (l) competitive sealed bidding (including multistep bidding); (2) competitive quotation bidding, also known as informal bidding; and (3) competitive negotiation.

Competitive sealed bidding is known by a number of names, including competitive bidding (the Model Purchasing Ordinance which was developed by the American Bar Association identifying and synthesizing the best elements of state and local procurement systems) and formal advertising (the terminology used by the federal Procurement and Acquisition Regulations). Competitive sealed bidding is the statutory approach employed most frequently at the state and local levels. Purchase by negotiation occurs only when competitive sealed bidding is not feasible or practical. Once it has been determined that a need to purchase exists, central purchasing initiates the sealed bidding procedure with the issuance of an initiation-for-bids (IFB). The IFB is intended to encourage competitors to offer the produce or service and to give all potential bidders an equal opportunity to bid. There are other important norms, duties, and responsibilities regarding bids that should be clearly set forth, involving (1) controlling the opening and tabulation; (2) public disclosure; (3) acceptance via telephone and telegraph; (4) modification or withdrawal; (5) acceptance of late bids; and (6) mistakes. With respect to mistakes, the National Association of State Purchasing Officials has observed, "The essential rule is that no change or correction should be permitted which would prejudice the interest of the public or would be unfair to other bidders."[9]

Multi-step sealed bidding is used in approximately 70 percent of state purchasing. Typically it is used for purchases requiring the provision of complex goods and services (such as a medical records system including personnel training and alternative approaches to performing the work). Multistep bidding employs the IFB with a two-step approach. Before commencing step one, potential suppliers may request information (a statement is usually attached indicating that no commitment is intended). Step one (the technical proposal) indicates the bidder's experience and resources for delivering the goods or services. Pricing most often comes in the second stage, and involves a sealed envelope. The proposals are opened and evaluated and negotiation about pricing follows.[10] If changes are made in the technical proposal, a revised pricing is allowed. Where a technical proposal is fully acceptable, negotiation is unnecessary and "award is made under sealed competitive bidding."[11]

Competitive quotation is a commonly used method to acquire goods and services where the dollar amounts do not require sealed bids. A kind of informal bidding takes place; potential suppliers provide a listing of their prices, which can be compared with those of competitors to facilitate the best price selection. About 90 percent of the states require a competitive quotation.

Competitive negotiation is not a recognized or authorized approach at the state or local levels and has thus been unavailable as a viable alternative procedure except as it may be permitted under emergency conditions.

Competitive Bidding versus Negotiation

While competitive bidding is the preferable procurement approach, it is not always possible to employ it because of the nature of the goods and services involved. A waiver is allowed in cases such as the following:

- sources are limited;
- prices are fixed;
- services are required to complete ongoing tasks;
- products are completed in correctional institutions;
- purchase is made from one unit of government to another;
- a needed item is available only for a short period;
- utility services are purchased; and
- a replacement part is available from only one source.

COOPERATIVE PURCHASING

Cooperative purchasing takes a variety of forms. Most often it involves arrangements among two or more governments to purchase goods and services under the same contract. The main objective in cooperative purchasing is to receive a cost reduction by making a volume purchase. The cooperative purchasing method provides a number of benefits:

1. It permits small units of government or agencies to obtain sizable discounts that would not otherwise be available, permitting significant savings.
2. It eliminates duplicate effort and improves technical support in defining requirements and soliciting, awarding, and administering contracts.
3. Officials can pool collective knowledge regarding when and where to buy and can share the benefits.
4. It can initiate a large enough dividend to encourage suppliers to produce and market new and modified products that are not commercially available.

Cooperative purchasing tends to encourage the sharing of information among purchasing units about where to get the best deals as they relate to the following:

1. new products entering the market;
2. alternative products located through value analysis;
3. development of cost-effective methods of supplying goods and services;
4. equipment repair experience;
5. breakthroughs in contracting methods; and
6. breakthroughs in prices being paid for specific goods and services.[12]

Sharing information may also provide valuable insights about the causes of significant price differences of similar items.[13]

It is important to keep in mind that cooperative purchasing will succeed only if it is supported by all participants, especially senior officials of the governmental units or agencies involved. Participation in cooperative arrangements should be based upon the evaluated benefits to be derived by the governmental unit. As a general rule, participants with cooperative arrangements should take turns making the purchase contract, giving all participants an opportunity to benefit from the learning process (except in those cases where the largest participatory unit's lead role permits superior benefits to be gained by all). A key element that must be observed in cooperative purchasing is that once commitments have been made for purchases, no withdrawals will be allowed. "All participating authorities must accept the group decision."[14]

Permission contracts involve those situations in which a third party (such as a local government that is allowed to enjoy the benefits of a state contract) that is not a participant in a contract is permitted to enjoy the benefits when and if it chooses. The contract price of the main contractor (in this case, a state) becomes a "ceiling price against which permissive users of the contract can bargain."[15] The successful bidder of the state purchasing contract permits the third party to use the bid prices as the target bargaining price. Though this practice is unenforceable, it is not typically challenged and is in wide use throughout the United States and Canada.

MEASURING PURCHASING PERFORMANCE

A successful purchasing system requires that the function be operated in an efficient and cost-effective manner. This accountability objective can best be facilitated when realistic and measurable goals and objectives are set and appropriate systems are developed to permit feedback to monitor and control it. This requires that performance be reported periodically and internal and external audits be performed from time to time. Performance measures can provide input information to aid management in assessing how the purchasing duties and responsibilities are being discharged and how performance can be improved. The purchasing system can:

1. aid management to better determine how well the purchasing responsibilities are being met;
2. be used to evaluate performance against set standards or historical indicators;

3.   be used to assess the cost-effectiveness of the purchasing function, pointing possibly to cost reduction; and

4.   be useful in showing time and money savings due to the purchasing agent's actions.

Measurement of the purchasing function is not an easy task because there are no generally agreed-upon standards or indicators for evaluating its performance. While indicators have been developed to assess the performance of the purchasing function, caution about their use has been expressed. The first concern is that management tends to give too much emphasis to quantitative indicators, such as savings, and too little to qualitative aspects, such as maintenance of effective levels of inventory and a purchasing manual that clearly defines authority and responsibilities.

The second caution expressed is about reliance on a single indicator to measure performance. Among the shortcomings inherent in the single-indicator approach are the following: it is only a partial performance measure; and it is subject to easy manipulation to show improved performance when this has not really occurred.[16] Despite the lack of consensus about the appropriateness of indicators as a means for evaluating the performance of the purchasing function, they are used in public and other not-for-profit organizations to assist in such evaluations. Among the indicators that may be used are the following:

1.   The ratio of goods and services purchased to the total expenditure of the governmental unit or agency;

2.   The cost-ratio of making purchases (buying) to total purchases made;

3.   Volume and percentages of purchases rejected due to defects;

4.   The average daily value of orders overdue;

5.   The ratio of price variance to budgeted purchases;

6.   Administrative savings resulting from blanket use of a purchase order;

7.   The ratio of purchasing employees to total governmental unit or agency employees;

8.   Reduction in the frequency of rush orders;

9.   Cost reduction attributable to standardization; and

10.   Cost reduction attributable to value analysis.

UNDERSTANDING ECONOMIC ORDER QUANTITY

Because inventory represents a large asset in government and other not-for-profit organizations, it is important that it be managed effectively so that it can make its appropriate contribution to the organization's purpose. This requires that management strive to achieve an optimum inventory balance and recognize the relationships of one inventory item to another.[17] In addition, management must be continually aware of three very important types of costs that are associated with inventory: (1) the inventory-carrying cost (e.g., storage, depreciation, and insurance) subsequent to its acquisition; (2) the purchase-ordering costs; and (3) the stockout or cost of running out of inventory.

A stockout results in service interruption and dissatisfaction to clientele and/or constituents. In the case of snow and ice removal, a shortage of salt may increase the time necessary to clean the streets. As a first step in minimizing stockout activity patterns, such as the flow and size of inventory orders, the dependability of suppliers and the length of time it takes to receive an order should be determined. Once estimates are made of the cost of stockout, the stockout loss probability factor can be determined. A stockout loss function is shown in Figure 5.3. As the size of the inventory grows, the stockout probability goes down, and vice versa. The objective of stockout analysis is to pinpoint the time when inventory should be reordered.

While avoidance of an inventory stockout is a desirable objective, inventory must be monitored closely because, as the inventory size rises, the carrying costs (e.g., insurance, storage, spoilage, depreciation or obsolescence, and opportunity costs) rise directly with it. Figure 5.4 gives an idea of the function.

Determination of the stockout or running out cost depends on the specific organization and the kinds of inventory items in question. In the case of a hospital, cost would have to be measured both in terms of tangible cash cost due to the liability of not providing patient care and in terms of intangible costs that are very difficult to measure, such as illness, increased pain, and death. Consequently, there are several basic decisions that management is required to make. Perhaps the more important are: (1) the size or amount of inventory to order at a given point in time; (2) the extra amount of inventory that will provide safety from stockout; and (3) precisely when to initiate or place an order.

Importance of the Size of the Inventory

If the inventory is larger than can be effectively used, it ties up unnecessary amounts of cash that could be employed for alternative organizational purposes or investment options. The longer the turnover period of the inventory, the greater the likelihood that it will succumb to obsolescence, deterioration, or damage, however, when the supply of inventory is too low, it creates impediments. Note that these management decisions suggest trade-offs between the different kinds of inventory costs. As the size of the inventory increases, the carrying costs increase, decreasing the chances of an inventory

Figure 5.3
Estimated Stockout as a Function of Inventory Size

Inventory Size

Figure 5.4
Inventory Carrying Cost as a Function of Inventory Size

Inventory Size

stockout. This, in turn, decreases the frequency of orders, effectively reducing ordering costs. Figure 5.5 suggests the trade-offs that are involved and the level of inventory that is required to minimize total inventory costs.

In Figure 5.4, part (b), note that the optimum safety stock is not at the point where the carrying cost and stockout cost intersect. The assumption is that optimum stock represents the point of an acceptable stockout loss, as opposed to the more ideal situation depicted in Figure 5.4, part (a). The same thinking applies in Figure 5.5, parts (a) and (b). The economic order quantity (EOQ) is not at the intersection of carrying costs and ordering costs. Thus, the size of the inventory is smaller than it would be under ideal conditions.

Management's Operation of the Organization

Rush purchase orders reduce efficiency and increase cost. These problems are compounded due to the perspective of the different department heads. The fiscal department views the lowest level of inventory possible as desirable because it permits greater cash flow. The operating or user departments typically insist on having the highest possible level of inventory to meet all departmental needs, irrespective of the cost. The purchasing officers take a balanced view of the situation in wishing to maintain low inventory, appropriate safety, avoidance of stockout loss, minimal orders, low costs, and rapid inventory turnover.

When considering the quantity of inventory to purchase, two opposing factors must be kept in mind: (1) as reduction in the quantities of inventories purchased occurs, carrying costs fall and ordering costs rise, but (2) as the amounts of inventories ordered rise, the situation is reversed. A critical concern in an organization is to find a way to satisfy material needs in the most economical manner.[18]   Thus, a way must be found to order and reorder inventory at the appropriate points in time.

Many approaches have been used to aid in determining economic order quantity in establishing optimum order volume for inventories, but the most widely used formula is as follows:

$$EOQ = \sqrt{\frac{2 \times annual \quad usage \quad \times purchase \quad order \quad cost}{unit \quad cost \quad \times inventory \quad carrying \quad cost}}$$

Example: Assume a nursing home uses 2,000 units per year at a cost of $40 per unit.

Order cost = $4
Inventory carrying cost = .28 (28%)
Annual usage = 2,000 units

Figure 5.5

Optimum Inventory as a Function of Stockout Costs and Ordering Costs

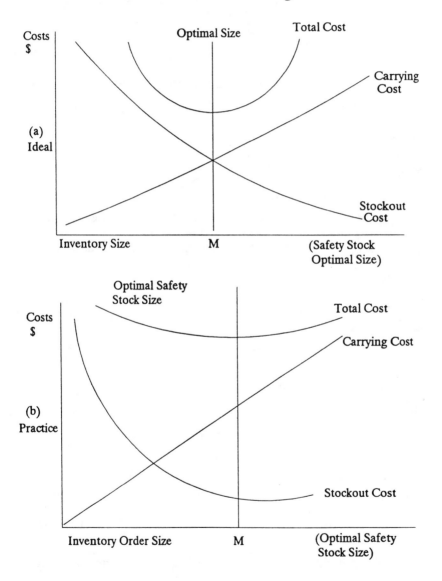

Figure 5.6
Optimum Ordering Quantity in Relation to
Carrying and Ordering Costs

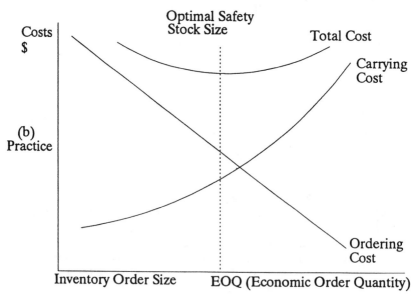

Cost per unit = $40

$$EOQ = \sqrt{\frac{2 \times 2,000 \ units \ \times 4}{\$40 \times .28}} = \sqrt{\frac{16,000}{11.2}} = \sqrt{1428.57}$$

EOQ = 37.74 units, or 38 units (rounded off).

In calculating the EOQ, an accurate identification of all costs involved is required:

1. *Annual usage* and *unit costs* can be determined by a careful examination of the inventory record. The unit cost may be taken directly from invoice copies, either from within the organization or from the supplier.
2. Purchase order cost is the total cost per line item. The following additional costs are involved: personnel, fringe benefits, office supplies, utility and maintenance, postage, and telephone.
3. *Inventory carrying costs* are those costs related to holding inventories. There are typically a number of costs that are incurred by government and other not-for-profit organizations; (a) obsolescence, deterioration, and pilferage; (b) storage costs and insurance; and (c) opportunity cost.

JUST-IN-TIME (JIT) PURCHASING

JIT provides significant contrast to the EOQ technique for managing the purchasing and inventory functions. JIT was developed in Japan as a means of reducing inventory storage, improving quality, and allowing purchase orders to be driven by customer-clientele expectations. The objective is to have only the right materials and products at the right place and the right time. This approach has been adopted in a number of private sector manufacturing firms. In the not-for-profit sector, hospitals have been most active in experimenting with JIT.[19]

Unlike the old-style purchasing system, Table 5.1, JIT involves far more than unloading materials onto a loading dock. The effective implementation of a JIT system requires maximum cooperation, communications, and synchronization of an organization's needs and production/service scheduling between it and its suppliers. The JIT system must ensure that products are not only delivered safely but also properly labeled,

Table 5.1
Comparison of Traditional and Just-In-Time (JIT) Purchasing

Traditional	JIT
Viewed as a tactical function	Viewed as a strategic function
Buying decision is driven by price	Buying decision is driven by quality
Quality defined by specification	Quality is defined mainly by customer/clientele expectations
Buyer dominates the purchasing function	Dealer dominates the purchasing function
Many suppliers are maintained	Single or few suppliers are monitored and maintained, with close partnership relations
Defects are tolerated as normal expectation	Zero defects are tolerated
Inspection is used as chief means to maintain quality	Prevention is used as chief means to achieve total quality
Quality is a static concept	Quality improves and changes throughout the process
Communication is based on the slow written-paper approach	Communication is electronically based
Delivery is determined more by supplier constraints than JIT	Delivery is synchronized to just-in-time requirements

Note: For additional ideas, see Kenneth A. Wantuck, *Just-In-Time for America* (Milwaukee, Wis.: Forum Ltd., 1989).

delivered in a timely manner, and available in the quantity and quality desired. This requires that both the supplier and the vendee firm have a clear understanding of the consumer/clientele expectations. To minimize confusion and maximize precision coordination, the number of suppliers must be kept to a minimum. This oftentimes means that long-term contracts must be signed and a partnering relationship must be developed and maintained. To become a dependable world-class supplier may require that suppliers tailor their system to make it compatible with the organizations they serve. To achieve this objective typically means that the supplier can focus on only a limited number of products and processes. To enhance the efficiency and maximize the synergy of the organizations, the supplier often installs its own software in the organization. In this new arrangement the role of the purchasing function changes "from placing orders to managing and monitoring a supplier's management, technical and process capability."[20] The view is strongly held that this is the best way to achieve the optimal product quality while simultaneously promoting continuous improvement. Because of the demanding criteria, including time constraints, proximity or nearby locations of suppliers is an important factor, that permits the supplier to more easily adjust to the organization's operations.

Among the benefits that accrue from the JIT system include the following:

- reduction in operating costs;
- improvement of cash flow;
- enhancement of quality;
- reduction in number of vendors;
- reduction in inventory obsolescence;
- improvement in space utilization; and
- enhancement of productivity.

CONCLUDING OBSERVATIONS

Because of the large amount of resources allocated to the purchase of goods and services in public and other not-for-profit organizations, the purchasing function attracts significant attention. Obtaining the biggest impact for the purchasing dollar requires expertise and professionalism. While this is possible in large governmental units and organizations, it is often too costly for small governmental units. A variety of means has been devised to aid these small units, such as cooperative and permissive purchasing arrangements.

In large and medium-size organizations, centralized purchasing has become synonymous with effective purchasing practice. That centralized purchasing is indispensable if the best deals and prices are to be achieved is the accepted view.

NOTES

1. Lennox L. Moak and Albert M. Hillhouse, *Local Government Finance* (Chicago: Municipal Finance Officers Association, 1975), p. 209.

2. League of California Cities, "Life Cycle Costing," in *Practical Financial Management*, ed. John Matzer, Jr. (Washington, DC: International City Managers Association, 1985), pp. 166-88.

3. Moak and Hillhouse, *Local Government Finance*, p. 210; Council of State Governments, *State and Local Government Purchasing* (Lexington, Ky.: Council of State Governments, 1983), pp. 18-19.

4. U.S. Government Accounting Office (GAO), *Study of Selected Local Procurement Systems Part I* (Washington, D.C.: GAO, 1978), p. 1.

5. S. Randolph Hayes, "Total Centralized Purchasing: Can It Ever be Achieved?" in *Hospital Purchasing*, ed. Charles E. Housley (Rockville, Md.: Aspen Systems Corporation, 1983), p. 29.

6. Ontario, Canada Ministry of Intergovernmental Affairs, *Managing Purchasing* (Toronto: Government Book Store, 1981), pp. 13-14.

7. Ibid., p. 15.

8. Ontario, Canada Ministry of Intergovernmental Affairs, *Managing Purchasing*, pp. 13-14.

9. Council of State Governments, *State and Local Government Purchasing*, p. 68.

10. Ibid., p. 68.

11. Ibid., p. 69.

12. GAO, *Study of Selected Local Procurement Systems Part I*, p. 17.

13. Ibid.

14. Ontario, Canada Ministry of Intergovernmental Affairs, *Managing Purchasing*, p. 55.

15. Council of State Governments, *State and Local Government Purchasing*, p. 104.

16. GAO, *Study of Selected Local Procurement Systems Part I*, p. 21.

17. Bruce G. Haywood, "Understanding Economic Order Quantity," in Housley, *Hospital Purchasing*, p. 161.

18. Ibid., p. 165.

19. See Jerry W. Wilson, "Stockless Inventory Systems for Health Care Providers: Three Successful Applications," *Journal of Health Care Marketing*, 12, no. 2 (June 1992): 39-45.

20. Greg Hutchins, *Purchasing Strategies for Total Quality* (Homewood, Ill.: Business One Irwin, 1992), p. 158.

6

Cash Management

In recent years attention has been focused on cash management at all levels of government and in other not-for-profit organizations. There are a number of reasons for this interest. The 1970s ushered in a period of high inflation, recession, and high interest rates. While in the 1990s high interest rates and inflation have subsided, citizens are currently demanding greater amounts of goods and services yet staunchly resisting paying the required taxes to fund them. Donors to not-for-profit agencies are finding it more difficult to maintain or increase their contributions. A better management of cash is seen as one means of stretching available dollars to meet the expenditure pressures. The process has been facilitated in large part by new computer technology that permits the use of more sophisticated methods of cash management, changes in federal laws affecting banks and financial institutions, and improved communication among cash managers.[1] As the rates of interest continued to fall during the 1990s, cash managers have had to be more creative and more careful as the options to generate greater returns narrowed. For example, the community of Seattle, Washington, developed a creative cash handling training manual to enhance its cash management system.[2]

This chapter reviews cash management practices, the development of the role of the cash manager, and techniques for effecting cash management improvements.

DEFINING CASH MANAGEMENT

The bank law changes enacted in recent years have increased the number of bank services and better defined their cost. In some ways, these changes have added to the complexity of the variables, constraints, and alternatives that must be understood in fashioning an effective cash management program.

Cash management may be defined as a process that is concerned with two important objectives: (1) providing and ensuring maximum cash availability, and (2) securing maximum yield on the short-term investment of idle cash. To achieve these objectives, a communication and monitoring system must be in place to identify the point at which revenue is earned and to track the point and time that an expenditure payment clears the bank. This action maximizes the cash investment yield because it minimizes the time lag between the recognition of revenue earnings and their conversion into cash and accurately times the dates of expenditures. Cash management is focused on "the conversion of accounts receivable to cash receipts, the conversion of accounts payable to cash disbursements, the rate at which cash disbursements clear a bank account and what is done with the cash balances in the meantime."[3] Cash must be managed to provide required liquidity to meet all maturing obligations, both expected and unexpected. The amount of cash that an entity holds to meet both routine and unforseen needs involves (1) its willingness to risk running out of cash to meet required demands, (2) the entity's ability to predict cash flows with a high degree of accuracy, and (3) the entity's available lines of credit or reserve-borrowing power.

EVALUATING AND ESTABLISHING LONG-TERM NEEDS

The cash manager must make certain that the cash management objectives and priorities are specifically defined and consistent with the entity's overall mission. Once this is done, these actions should be reflected in the subsequent policies to be adopted.[4]

Next, long-term expected cash flow patterns and targets of perhaps three to five years should be set forth. This step provides parameters and general guidelines about revenues and expenditure expectations that will be helpful in developing useful policies. Attention is directed toward those sources of revenues that are subject to wide and unpredictable fluctuations and long-term needs (including borrowing) that must be planned to effectively meet capital expenditure requirements and debt repayments.[5]

THE CASH MANAGEMENT SYSTEM

In the pursuit of maximum cash availability and maximum yield, as noted above, cash management objectives inevitably conflict, since cash that is maintained for use cannot be employed to produce a higher yield. This conflict can be avoided only if an ideal or optimum balance can be determined. While methods for estimating these balances do exist, determining the optimum balance is not an easy task, especially among smaller units of government and other not-for-profit organizations. Patitucci and Lichtenstein have suggested that the availability objective be pursued first, and then the yield goal.[6]

The effective operation of a cash management system (see Figure 6.1) requires the consideration and understanding of a number of elements, including the following:

- policies and constraints;
- bank-institution relations; and
- investment strategy.

POLICY OBJECTIVES AND CONSTRAINTS

Policies set the legal and procedural guidelines for facilitating the execution of the day-to-day activities of the cash management program, while guidelines typically identify its objectives and criteria for evaluating its progress and achievements. Within the context of the adopted policies, the cash manager should set specific annual objectives such as cash availability levels, desired yield, and amount of idle cash that will be invested throughout the year. These objectives can be used to periodically assess the performance of the cash management functions.[7]

Figure 6.1

The Cash Management System and the Operating Cycle

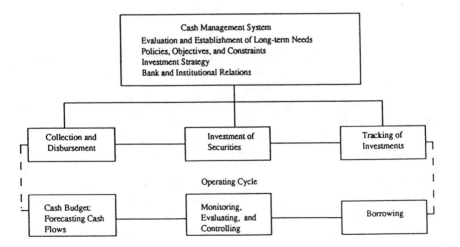

There are many constraining factors to the cash manager must give due cognizance, such as local, state, and federal laws that directly impact upon cash management practices, "determining when monies can be collected, when obligations must be paid, where deposits can be placed and what securities can and cannot be purchased."[8] Other not-for-profit organizations must conform to the funding agencies' stipulations. For example, the United Way requires agencies that have free cash or surplus to return amounts in excess of $5,000 at the end of a fiscal period. Though the policy is not rigidly enforced, it does create some degree of uncertainty.

Risk related to investment in securities is another constraint factor that public agencies must control. Unlike in private enterprise, government laws and regulations help to minimize this problem. For example, most governments are permitted to invest in relatively safe instruments such as Treasury notes and bills. Thus, most governmental units are not likely to lose large amounts of their investments. When government and other not-for-profit agencies move cash into investment that carries greater risks, extreme care must be exercised. Prudence requires that the drive for market yield be balanced with a high priority for risk aversion.

In the age of electronic transfer of funds and the numerous investment options that have been created, cash managers often find that brokers, dealers, and banks prefer to maintain control of the securities, given their need for flexibility to trade and negotiate with other institutions. This practice denies agencies or governments the opportunity to maintain physical control over their investments on the underlying security or collateral. As a measure against this external risk, governments have insisted "that collateral securities be physically delivered to the government as a condition for making the investment," a practice that may reduce yield, but provides an important form of protection.[9]

THE CASH BUDGET

Cash budgeting requires a keen understanding of the major and minor sources of cash receipts and disbursements in order to estimate cash availability. Unlike revenue and expenditure budgets that are based on obligations and commitments, cash budgeting requires the identification of specific receipts and disbursements as well as the relevant dates. Due to the length of time (from 1 to 60 days) between commitment and obligation indicative of the regular/traditional budget, this is not a useful predictor of cash levels.

To achieve a realistic cash budget, the historical experience of the past and the prospects of future developments must be studied carefully. The cash budget projection may be made weekly, monthly, quarterly, or semiannually. Whatever the projection period, the cash budget must be updated when information and conditions require. When estimates are made for quarterly or longer periods, the need for updating becomes more urgent. For larger governmental units and other not-for-profit agencies, prudence and accuracy may require weekly, or perhaps daily, cash budgets.

The cash budget is not used as an allocating instrument, nor is it concerned with programs or operating functions. Rather, it merely identifies projected expenditures and a revenue stream usually of six months to a year. These projections will enable the cash manager to determine how much cash will be available or idle at various times during the year and for how long. An analysis of information will permit the cash manager to develop an effective basis for making investment decisions.

CASH COLLECTION AND DISBURSEMENT

The collection and disbursement elements are critical to success in achieving the objective of maximum cash availability and meeting cash and investment needs. If cash collection can be speeded up, the twin aim of increasing cash inflow and enhancing the potential for greater earnings on investment will be achieved. There are a number of impeding or constraining factors. For example, (1) various tax due bills cannot be mailed out before a given date; (2) hospitals may not be able to influence third-party payers to speed up scheduled payments; and (3) cash inflows at universities are limited by registration dates.

There is always a lag between the time when checks are mailed and when the funds are credited to an organization's checking account. The period involved in mailing, recording, processing, and clearing is known as the float time, and its length directly affects the availability of cash. The objective, then, is to find a means to shorten or minimize the float time.

A number of methods have been used to minimize the float time, such as the *lockbox system*, which allows clients of public and other not-for-profit agencies to send their checks to a post-office box. The bank collects the checks daily from the lockbox and deposits them daily directly to the client's account, reducing the float time and making the money more quickly available (typically two to four days sooner).[10]

While the lockbox system is a useful innovation, it may not fit the needs of every organization. Before adopting this approach, cost versus benefits should be assessed. The positive side includes the returns that result from the added cash, speeded up inflow of funds, and/or reductions in costs associated with internal processing. The negative side consists of a fixed monthly charge assessed by the bank plus a per-item processing charge.

The following formula aids in assessing the costs and benefits of the lockbox system:[11]

$$BAL = (NUM) \times (AVG) \times (TIM) \qquad \text{[Equation 6.1]}$$

When BAL = usable balances generated due to the
lockbox system
NUM = number of checks per day
AVG = average value per check
TIM = reduced number of transit days

Based on the increase in the usable balances (BAL) and the annual interest rate (INT), the annual dollar returns related to the additional funds (ADR) generated from the lockbox system can be determined. They are represented by the following:

$$ADR = (BAL) \times (INT) \qquad \text{[Equation 6.2]}$$

To find the annual total cost (ATC) of the lockbox system, we need to identify the bank processing cost per check (UC) and the number of checks processed during the year (ANU), generating the following:

$$ATC = (UC) \times (ANU) \qquad \text{[Equation 6.3]}$$

Finally, the determination of the break-even point, where the benefit generated is equal to the system's costs incurred, is shown as follows:

$$ADR = ATC \qquad \text{[Equation 6.4]}$$

Whenever the benefits of the lock-box system exceed the cost, the system should be implemented (i.e., ADR > ATC). If the reverse is true, it should be rejected. An application of the lockbox approach may be analyzed from the following example.

The City of Bright is examining lockbox systems for possible implementation in the collection of its water bills. It has been estimated that a lockbox system will reduce float time by four days. The 10,000 participants in Bright have an average $200 monthly tax bill. Bright earns 10 percent on its short-term investments. The bank charges $.20 for each check it processes. Should Bright adopt the lockbox system?

Assuming that the number of working days each month is 20 and that checks flow at this rate, the number of checks processed per day (NUM) is:

$$NUM = \frac{10,000}{20} = 500 \quad checks \quad per \quad day$$

Using Equation 6.1 to calculate usable balances:

$$BAL = (NUM)x (AVG) x (TIM)$$
$$= 500 \text{ x } \$200 \text{ x } 4$$
$$= \$400,000$$

Note that the implementation of the lockbox system will provide an additional $400,000 for investing. This amount can be invested at 10 percent to produce an annual dollar return (ADR) as follows (using Equation 6.2):

$$ADR = (BAL) \text{ x } (INT)$$
$$= \$400,000 \text{ x } .10$$
$$= \$40,000$$

The $40,000 equals the annual benefit generated as a result of the implementation of the lockbox system.

The annual number of checks processed per year (ANU), assuming customers are billed on a monthly basis, is determined as follows:

$$ADU = 10,000 \text{ x } 12 = 120,000$$

The cost for implementing the lockbox system is calculated by using Equation 6.3:

$$ATC = UC \text{ x } ANU$$
$$= \$.20 \text{ x } 120,000$$
$$= \$24,000$$

Since the ADR is $40,000, and the ATC is $24,000, the benefits exceed the cost by $16,000.

Electronic transfer and *branch deposits* are other means for speeding up cash collection. By means of the Federal Reserve Wire System, banks may electronically move balances from one bank to another. Like the lockbox system, it is used to reduce transit time and speed up check collection. Since the cost of transferring funds ranges between $1 and $6 per transaction, it should ideally be used only for larger transfers. In those states and jurisdictions where branch banking is permitted, deposits can be made in outlying branches to be immediately credited to the individual agency account.

To determine when to use the electronic transfer method, a break-even analysis can be performed to determine the minimum amount that would be required to make this method cost-effective. The following information is needed to calculate the break-even point: unit cost of the transfer, float days gained/saved in transit time, and annual interest rate on idle balances, using Equation 6.5.

[Equation 6.5]

$$Breakeven \quad point \quad = \quad \frac{Cost}{Days \quad \times \quad \dfrac{Rate}{365}}$$

Assume the following for Bright City: cost for an EFT = $6, days of float gained = 2 and short-term rate = 8 percent.

$$Breakeven \quad point \quad = \frac{\$6}{2 \times \frac{.08}{365}} = \frac{\$6}{.0383} = \$13,689$$

This suggests that wire transfers are cost-effective in cases where receipts are in excess of $13,689.

An alternative way of calculating the break-even point can be achieved by using Equation 6.6:

$$Breakeven \quad point \quad = \frac{Cost \quad \times 365}{Rate \quad \times Days}$$

Using the data for Bright City, the alternative method generates approximately the same results.

$$Breakeven \quad point \quad = \frac{\$6 \times 365}{.08 \times 2} = \$13,688$$

Preauthorized checks are signatureless checks that can be used to accelerate the collection of fixed payments. Under this arrangement the client or customer signs an agreement with the public or not-for-profit agency to allow its bank to write a check, for a given amount, on his or her account. By means of a computer file, the agency sends the bank the necessary information to carry out the function, and by similar means, the bank informs the agency of the deposit and the availability of funds. The process has the advantage of reducing the float time while creating a greater certainty of cash inflows.[12]   Smaller agencies may wish to explore this technique.

COLLECTION PROCEDURES

The complexity of collection procedures increases with the size of the government or other not-for-profit organization. Small organizations typically have one bank account to which all the checks and monies are deposited, while larger organizations may have many bank accounts and many sources from which cash inflows originate. The objective is to get the cash into the organization's account as soon as possible and to keep it for as long as permitted in order to increase earnings on investments. Collection can often be facilitated by a number of simple common sense actions, such as billing outside agencies for services as soon as performance is completed, facilitating for citizens and clients the payment of taxes and fees; and establishing and maintaining good relations with funding agencies. Coordinating and making more likely the achievement of the cash management goals involve the following steps:

- Establishment of revenue collection policies and procedures for each major revenue source.
- Provision for special deposit procedures to deal with major revenue processing problems (such problems may result, for example, from the quarterly or annual collection of property taxes).
- Establishment of deposit procedures for each type of revenue base or location.[13]

To aid the collection procedure, a detailed checklist of each revenue source should be developed, identifying the specific activities to which close attention should be given. Rosenberg, Stallings, and Coe have suggested a good example, as shown in Table 6.1.

Letter of Credit

Streamlining the letter of credit payments system provide communities with the opportunity to better predict the time when federal funds will be available to make disbursements for federally funded projects. Improvement of the letter of credit process does not quicken the speed of the process but it does enable the entity or agency to accurately time the receipt of the federal funds with the project expenditures and disbursements. This avoids delaying application of funds (cash) to other projects, essentially avoiding a kind of internal loan.

The letter of credit is the federal government's method of choice for disbursing funds to local governments. Typically, the federal government grants authorization to the governmental entities to draw down federal bank accounts as the entity's cash needs dictates in order to meet grant disbursement obligations.

To be eligible to participate in the federal letter of credit system, the grantee must meet specific criteria. It must have had at least a one-year relationship with the federal government as well as a grant for $120,000 or more. The second condition requires that the grantee agrees to draw down the approved project funds only as needed. The grantee must also file periodic reports on cash and disbursements and balances to the agency that approved the project. Finally, the grantee agency must give the awarding federal agency the opportunity to review the awardee's financial practices and permission to take remedial action in cases where the terms of the grant are being followed. In those cases where state and local government laws and regulations prohibit local

Table 6.1
Checklist of Detailed Procedures for
the Collection of Revenues for Municipalities

Licenses and permits

- Deposit all monies intact.
- Maintain a list of all delinquent licenses or permits and strictly enforce collection of delinquencies uniformly.
- Require all licensees or permit holders to display their licenses and/or permits. Instruct government offices to look for such licenses and/or permits and notify the collection agency when violators are suspected.
- Utilize reports submitted to other government agencies, such as taxes paid to the state treasury, to verify gross receipts, if fees are based on gross receipts.

Parking lots, golf courses, swimming pools

- Indicate in plain sight at all locations a schedule showing the full range of fees.
- Design a standard format for use at all locations if tickets are used.
- Check all cash register receipts to ensure that cash and ticket counts reflect recorded frequency and monetary totals.
- Rotate attendants through different facilities and work schedules at frequent intervals.
- Practice close supervision and surveillance.
- Have all keys to lock boxes, cash registers, and similar equipment under control of authorized supervision and not available to attendants.
- Schedule frequent unannounced visits by internal auditors who will review inventory of tickets, count cash, require authorization for all exemptions, and so on.

Parking meter collections

- Establish, number, and describe meter routes.
- Select coin collection equipment that will be secure against theft.
- Consider maintaining weight records by route.
- Rotate the schedule of route collection periodically.
- Collect coins at hours that coincide with heavy traffic.
- Safeguard keys to coin meter receptacles; issue daily to coin collectors.
- Mutilate and destroy worn keys.
- Order new keys only on authorization of responsible persons.

- Require meter collectors to wear distinctive uniforms.
- Supervise the coin-counting process.
- Ensure the security of the coin-counting area.
- Have meter collectors report the location of all broken, stuck, or pilfered meters as they are discovered.
- Maintain dollar and/or weight records to provide for periodic comparisons of collections for each weight.
- Issue receipts daily to collectors.
- Establish procedures to make reconciliations of cash deposits. If coin-counting machines that register total values are used, such values can be reconciled to deposits.
- Schedule periodic unannounced reviews of all phases of operation. Spot-check collection and counting procedures, personnel rotation, revenue comparisons, and so on.

Property taxes, parking and vehicle code fines, sales taxes, gasoline taxes, cigarette taxes, liquor license fees, and motor vehicle fees

- Establish written contracts with other agencies as provided by law.
- Test receipts-to-treasury record periodically to verify that all receipts are deposited properly and in a timely fashion.
- Request confirmation from agencies doing the collection and distributing and compare information received from them with the municipal records.

Federal and state grants

- Prepare status reports for each grant. These reports show such data as:

  - grant description;
  - granting agency;
  - total amount of grant;
  - terms and restrictions concerning the use of the grant; and
  - anticipated payment terms of the grant.

- Bill granting agency as soon as permitted by grant guidelines.

Source: Adapted from Philip Rosenberg, C. Wayne Stallings, and Charles K. Coe, *A Treasury Management Handbook for Small Cities and Other Governmental Units* (Chicago: Municipal Finance Officers Association, 1978), pp. 54-55.

government and agencies from expending cash before it is physically in hand (in the treasury), the letter of credit system cannot operate smoothly.

DISBURSEMENT PROCEDURES

Ideally, cash should be disbursed only when absolutely required and at the last possible moment. While this practice should be carried out in a manner that avoids fines for late payment and minimizes poor vendor and community relations, efforts should nonetheless be made to hold or delay payments to clients.

Effective disbursement requires that accounts payable be well managed. Invoices should be analyzed and filed according to their dates for payment to permit discounts to be taken and to facilitate timely payment. Factors such as the following should be considered: "the discounts available, the standard policies for handling different types of invoices, the past history of the vendor for requiring rapid payment and the method by which the payment will be made (e.g., mail or pick-up)."[14]

A means that is sometimes used to improve the availability of cash is the use of the *warrant*. A warrant is like a non-interest-bearing note payable that the issuer promises to pay upon presentation at some specified future date. The warrant is typically presented to a clearing bank for payment. Subsequent to payment, the clearing bank presents the warrant to the governmental unit and receives payment. The warrant is unlike a check in that there need not be money in the bank when it is written. Rather, money does not have to be made available until the warrant is presented for payment. The ability to use the warrant allows the governmental unit to retain the cash for a longer period than might otherwise be the case. (Some opponents say that it denies vendors the opportunity to use their money). Normally, a higher fee is charged for the extra processing required.[15]

The *wire transfers* system can be used to delay disbursements in the same manner that it can be utilized to speed collections. Since wire transfers maximizes the time for which money can be used in an entity, it reduces the disbursement float time and minimizes the need to draw cash from other applications. The wire provides a definite time that permits funds to be invested instead of making rough estimates of how long it will take checks to clear the bank. This is very important in cases where large payments must be made at scheduled times. Moreover, when purchase of investment instruments are executed through brokers in another city, wire transfer may be the most suitable means. Since banks are required to pass on the cost, it is necessary to calculate the break-even point, as shown in Equation 6.4.

The *automated clearing-house* (ACH) method is employed mainly to process electronic payments, direct deposit of payroll, and, to a lesser degree, pension payments. The ACH method is costly and should be undertaken only if the net benefits or savings can be demonstrated. In the case where the ACH method is likely to positively affect employee relations, a good rationale can be established to implement it. Though float time is lost in the ACH method, there are some advantages associated with its use including reductions in check processing charges, account reconciliation costs, employee time lost for cashing checks, and storage costs for canceled checks.

CONSOLIDATING OR POOLING CASH

Governmental units and most other not-for-profit agencies use the fund-accounting system, which tends to have a negative impact on cost management. The fund-accounting practice requires that restricted funds be segregated and that receipts and the disposition of resources be accounted and reported separately. It is not uncommon to find government and other not-for-profit agencies maintaining separate bank accounts for each fund. The maintenance of separate bank accounts, which is useful perhaps for control, is an impediment to effective cash management because it requires that the cash manager keep track of the individual balances with their separate cash flow patterns. The proliferation of bank accounts leads to a number of unacceptable results: (1) administrative costs rise, (2) the cash manager's ability to make accurate projections of each separate cash flow decreases, and (3) uncoordinated and fragmented investments are produced. Review shows that consolidation and pooling of cash can minimize most of these problems.[16]

A number of methods have been developed to facilitate the pooling of cash while permitting separate fund bank accounts to operate. The single-concentration account has been gaining acceptance among municipalities because it permits the pooling of all cash receipts while allowing a separate, zero-balance account for cash disbursement.[17] The operation of a concentration account allows local banks to automatically transfer funds to it. Several advantages are gained by this method: (1) it permits separate checking accounts to be used for disbursements; (2) it permits cash consolidation; (3) it makes it easier and less expensive to invest idle cash in short-term market instruments; (4) it reduces the problem of maintaining a minimum balance in each account; and (5) it minimizes disbursement float time (the time between writing a check and having it charged against the bank account).[18]

BORROWING

Since debt management affects the flow of receipts and disbursements, it should be given due consideration. Long-term borrowing in public and other not-for-profit organizations is intended mainly to finance capital projects that are expected to have several years of useful life. Usually the money is received in large amounts and is held for specific time periods. During these periods, care must be given to the way in which the money is handled. In governmental units, for example, federal arbitrage regulations should be observed (borrowing at lower, tax-exempt rates and reinvesting at higher rates is also forbidden by most state governments).

Short-term borrowing should be used only during those periods when the paucity of cash inflow causes temporary gaps. Identifying the gaps before they occur and taking appropriate actions to deal with them is one of the principal objectives of effective cash management.

Among the most common types of short-term borrowing are the following: (l) tax anticipation notes (TANs), which are issued for a specific period of time, to be repaid upon the collection of a specific tax; (2) bond anticipation notes (BANs), which are short-term notes in anticipation of a bond issue and are retired from the proceeds of a particular issue; and (3) revenue anticipation notes (RANs), which are issued to obtain cash in anticipation of revenue that is not a tax source.

MONITORING, EVALUATING, AND CONTROLLING

The important inflow and outflow accounts such as receipts, disbursements, and balances in cash and investments should be monitored daily, and monthly, quarterly, and yearly reports should be regularly prepared. Periodically or as required, the performance of the cash budget managers is also compared with the predetermined performance indicators. From these assessments, performance reports are prepared and sent to administrators and elected officials. The reports are the used as valuable inputs to aid in forecasting and fine-tuning projections for the ensuing fiscal period.[19]

Because of the vulnerability of cash and securities to fraud and abuse, special care should be taken by the internal auditor to ensure that the internal control systems are operating properly at all times to safeguard these liquid assets. The internal control system to safeguard assets is also a focal concern of the independent auditor, whose recommendations are important in fashioning future cash management policies and objectives.

BANK RELATIONS

Banks occupy important roles in communities by providing access to primary and secondary markets and by providing essential services (see Table 6.2). In most communities the local governmental units are large depositors whom the bank usually attempts to attract. Many elements contribute significantly toward achieving the goal of effective cash management. They include:

Table 6.2
Available Banking and Financial Services

Collection Services	Disbursement Services
Wire transfers	Wire transfers
Automated Clearing House (ACH)	Payable-through-drafts
Collections	Balancing monitoring and reporting
Pre-Authorized Checks	In-bank services
Lock Box-Systems	Direct Deposit System
Depository Transfer checks	Account Reconcilement Service
Over-the-Counter Payment Systems	Pre-authorized check payments
Armored Car Services	Automated Clearing House (ACH)
Night Depository Services	Payments
Coin Counting Services	Concentration/Zero Balance Accounts
Special Deposit Messengers	Microfilm Checks
	Computer Services
Investment Services	**Credit Services**
Investment Advice	Line of Credit
Savings Accounts	Note purchases
Time Deposits	Bond underwriting
Investment Instruments	Bond Purchasing
- Certificates of Deposit	Bond Transfer and Registration
- Repurchase Agreement/Custodial	Services
Arrangements	Short-term Notes
- Short-term U.S. Treasury Securities	Municipal Commercial Paper
- Banks' Acceptances	
- Commercial Paper	
- Money Market Mutual Funds	

Source: Adapted from Phett D. Harrell, "Banking Relations Part I" in *Cash Management For Small Government* by Ian J. Allan, editor (Chicago, Ill.: Government Finance Officers Association, 1989), p. 65.

- keen knowledge of available bank services;
- information about the cost of each bank service provided;
- competition among banks for the deposits of the governmental unit;
- continual evaluation of the banking relations; and
- maintenance of day-to-day competition among banks in order to obtain the best values when making investment decisions.[20]

It is especially important that banks give attention to *community involvement*. Policies such as providing loans to individuals and businesses in the local community and participating in local government bond issues provide both tangible and intangible benefits to the community that cannot easily be expressed in quantitative dollar terms.[21] When a bank's community involvement policy is positively oriented toward the community, the bank may occasionally justify sacrificing a higher potential yield to encourage such relationships.

Banking Policies

Public and not-for-profit agencies' bank relations may not typically be able to escape political influence. Every effort should be made to minimize such influence, however, as it may negatively impede competition in procuring banking services at the best prices.[22] Banking policies that can economically permit the maintenance of bank accounts in all banking establishments in the community and require periodic rotation of banking services to each financial institution will likely minimize the political influence that may take place. This approach has its drawbacks.

The maintenance of the minimum deposit approach is not preferred for the following reasons: (1) it reduces the opportunity to pool cash and increase investment earnings; (2) it increases processing costs; (3) it reduces the flexibility to respond to emergencies; (4) it impacts on the accuracy in making a cash forecast due to the large number of accounts that may be involved; (5) it increases handling fees, especially in large communities; and (6) determining the size and length of time of deposits in a variety of banks can present problems.

Selecting Banks on a Competitive Basis

Law or precedent may dictate that the entity can conduct business only with the bank that provides it with the most competitive prices for timely and comparable service quality. Typically, the competitive approach will involve competitive bidding that specifies the services desired in a request for proposal.

Returned bids are reviewed and analyzed and a contract award is made (see Chapter 21 for details).

The *cost of bank services* is normally determined in two ways. The first is based on the cost accounting system of the bank. The information provides the bank with a basis for imposing a monthly service charge according to the number and kinds of services provided (for example, the number of checks processed or the number of coupon redemptions for a local jurisdiction's bonds, disbursements, and account reconciliations).

The use of compensating balances in non-interest-bearing accounts such as demand deposits is the second approach. These deposits represent "free money" to the bank, which invests them to generate earnings for itself. In those cases where banks pay interest on amounts in checking accounts, such interest is significantly lower than what the deposits actually earn. Banks sometimes use the float time (the period between depositing and paying funds) to earn money that helps to defray their costs.

The compensating balance may be calculated using the following formula:

$$\text{Required Compensating Balance} = \frac{\text{Annual charges for services}}{\text{Earnings factor (return bank expects to earn on deposits)}} \div (1 - \text{reserve requirement})$$

Example: for the city of Bright, assume annual charges of $4,500, earnings factor for bank of 5 %, and reserve requirements of 15 % of deposits.

$$\text{Required Compensating Balance} = \frac{\frac{4500}{.05}}{1 - .15} = \frac{\$90,000}{.85} = \$105,882.35$$

When the banks cannot or do not furnish an analysis of their compensating balance costs and minimum requirements, a third approach for paying banking services may be considered: many business firms and governmental entities avoid the problem of computing an amount as a compensating balance by the simple expedient of agreeing with the bank that the account will return a profit. To this end, the bank is asked to provide a monthly analysis of the account. The bank analyzes and records earnings from account balances, less the cost of all transactions, and subtracts costs from earnings, indicating either profit or loss.[23]

INVESTING IN SHORT-TERM SECURITIES

Engaging in short-term investment is necessary because of the uncertainty about how much cash will be needed to fully meet operating needs. The instruments used most for government investments are bank certificates, money market funds, U.S. Treasury obligations, time deposits, repurchase agreements, and U.S. agency securities. Collectively, these investments are known as *marketable securities*. They are relatively risk-free interest-bearing paper assets, having a high degree of liquidity in that they are easily sold. To make maximum contribution toward the achievement of cash management goals requires that the cash manager be knowledgeable about the characteristics of different investment securities, including their yield and their primary and secondary market statuses.

Treasury Bills

Treasury bills (commonly known as T-bills) and Treasury certificates are U.S. government short-term instruments. Treasury bills are initially issued in $10,000 denominations having 91 to 182 day maturities, while certificates are issued with 9 and 12 month maturities. Since T-bills bear no interest, they are sold at a discount. The interest return or yield is the difference between the purchasing and selling or maturity prices of the notes.

A testimony to the liquidity of the T-bill is the very active secondary market that exists. T-bills may be bought and sold at any time between the issuance and the maturity dates. This is a major reason why they are so attractive as an option for idle cash investment. For the same reason, however, T-bills carry the lowest yield of all money market instruments.

Government Agency Securities

A number of U.S. government agencies, such as the Farmers Home Administration, the Federal National Mortgage, Association and the Export-Import Bank, issue securities that are fully guaranteed, while organizations such as Banks of Cooperatives, Federal Home Loan Bank, Tennessee Valley Authority (TVA), Federal Land Bank, and Federal Intermediate Credit Bank issue securities that are not fully guaranteed. There is a large secondary market for these securities, but their liquidity is not as great as that of Treasury bills. This accounts in large part for the yield spread between Treasury bills and government agency securities.

Certificates of Deposit

These consist of negotiable and nonnegotiable receipts for monies normally deposited in large commercial banks for a specified period of time with a specified rate of interest. Certificates of deposit (or CDs, as they are commonly called) are, in essence, time deposits. CDs issued by larger banks usually have greater liquidity than those of smaller institutions. Like Treasury bills, they are traded on the secondary markets, though not as actively. Typically, CDs trade in secondary markets in $1 million amounts or multiples of $1 million, though odd lots can be obtained in multiples of $100,000 and $250,000.

Commercial Paper

These are business promissory notes specifying a future payment date. They are usually sold at a discount and are supported by the general credit of the agency or company. Maturity dates range from 30 days to 9 months, with a yield that is one-quarter to one-half greater than that of Treasury bills. Laws in many states prohibit local governments from participating in this type of investment.

Repurchase Agreements

A repurchase agreement is a type of short-term investment that permits governments to invest cash for short periods of time, typically between one and seven days. The governmental unit or agency enters into an agreement to purchase Treasury bills from banks which agree to repurchase the securities at some specified date for a specified higher amount. The investment is virtually risk free.

Money Market Funds

Money market funds are mutual funds that invest in marketable securities. This involves the pooling of cash from a number of investors to purchase different types of market securities such as CDs and Treasury bills. The return from the investment is shared proportionately. While no commission is normally charged, a small management fee is permitted. Money market funds have grown over the past 20 years due in large part to their returns, which have been significantly higher than the rates on passbook savings accounts.

For public and other not-for-profit organizations, money market funds offer a number of attractive features.

1. They permit small organizations to obtain expert management of their idle funds.
2. They provide yields that are much higher than those obtainable from savings banks.
3. They provide virtually risk-free investments since most instruments are Treasury securities, CDs, and commercial paper.
4. They provide flexibility for entering and/or withdrawing funds.
5. They require small numbers of participants.

TRACKING OF INVESTMENTS

An important function of cash management is the maintenance of accounts on-line, using an up-to-date tracking system of all outstanding investments. This system must be capable of providing information on the amount and source of money invested, the maturity schedule, and the yield each investment is generating. As an important risk management practice, collateralized investment values should be checked daily to compare them with market value. This minimizes the possibility that the collateralized investments will fall below required market value without this being recognized. Additionally, maturity dates must be constantly tracked to ensure that the appropriate interest and principal on investment are paid when due. Monthly and periodic reports as required are sent to the departments responsible for the funds.[24]

INVESTMENT STRATEGY

The investment strategy is an important element in the cash management program in that it provides guidelines for determining "what will be purchased, when, and for how long, and what the target investment mix should be on specific dates."[25] An investment strategy should ideally be written and aimed at assisting the cash manager to best invest available funds for the time period covered by the strategy. In preparing the investment strategy, consideration should be given to the following:

- Explicit assumptions about prospective market conditions, cash availability, and the desired mix of securities.
- Guidelines and timetables for purchasing specific types and amounts of securities.

- A clearly delineated system for selling or pruning securities if destabilizing conditions so demand.
- Clearly defined procedures for accelerating investment when excess cash is available to expand purchases.
- Development of specific performance indicators to assess the cash manager's achievement.[26]

DETERMINING OPTIMUM CASH BALANCE

In order to collect, process, and disburse cash in the most efficient manner, it is most useful to know the minimum cash balance that is necessary. Because of the uncertainties related to cash inflows and outflows, it is difficult to determine the optimum cash balance. A rule-of-thumb approach has been suggested. The rule is that the governmental unit or not-for-profit organization may hold cash sufficient to cover the expected average expenditure that is likely to be incurred for a specific period, such as a week. This amount is held as security against running out of cash. Amounts above this imposed level will be invested, while amounts below this target will trigger the selling of securities. When this rule is used jointly with an accurately projected cash budget, it provides a reasonable basis for meeting cash needs, especially those of smaller public and other not-for-profit organizations.

CONCLUDING OBSERVATIONS

Attention to cash management is a recent phenomenon that developed in response to the high interest rates and inflation of the late 1970s and early 1980s, the low interest rates of the 1990s, and taxpayers' resistance growing toward paying more taxes and decreasing donations to not-for-profit organizations. Improved cash management is seen as one way to increase available resources. Effective cash management requires the coordination of many factors, among them a well-thought-out investment strategy, an efficient and timely collection and disbursement system, an effective short-term securities investment program, and timely and strategic monitoring.

A successful cash management program requires that a way be found to speed up the collection of cash while slowing down its disbursement as much as possible. The objective must be perceived within the context of the organization's policies and implemented in a way that limits the impairment of client services and vendor relations. A number of improved procedures have been introduced to speed the availability of cash, such as the lockbox system, the electronic transfer of cash, the concentration account, and the zero-balance account. Finally, the pursuit of greater earnings on idle cash should be carried out with prudence to avoid unnecessary risk.

NOTES

1. Michael Dotsey, "An Investigation of Cash Management Practices and Their Effects on the Demand for Money," *Economic Review*, 70, no. 5 (September/October 1984): 3; see also Raymond L. McCabe, "Electronic Funds Transfer as a Cash Management Tool," *Governmental Finance*, 10, no. 4 (December 1981): 9-14.

2. See Lloyd Hora, "Bucks: Better Understanding of Cash Control Systems," *Government Finance Review*, 8 no. 2 (April 1992): 17-19.

3. Frank M. Patitucci and Michael H. Lichtenstein, *Improving Cash Management in Local Government: A Comprehensive Approach* (Chicago: Municipal Finance Officers Association, 1977), p. 4.

4. Paul L. Shinn, "An Overview of Cash Management," in *Cash Management for Small Governments*, ed. Ian J. Allan (Chicago, Ill.: Government Finance Officers Association, 1989), p. 13.

5. Ibid.

6. Ibid.

7. Ibid., p 15.

8. Ibid.

9. Ibid., p. 6.

10. Dotsey, "Investigation," p. 11.

11. Ronald Braswell, Karen Fortin and Jerome Osteryoung, *Financial Management for Not-for-Profit Organizations* (New York: Wiley and Sons, 1984), pp. 150-52.

12. Dotsey, "Investigation," p. 4.

13. Patitucci and Lichtenstein, *Improving Cash Management*, p. 27.

14. Ibid., p. 29.

15. Ibid.

16. See Walter P. Berg, "Selecting a Municipal Depository," *Municipal Finance*, November 1969, p. 94.

17. Dotsey, "Investigation," pp. 4-5.

18. Ibid., p. 4.

19. Shinn, "Overview of Cash Management," p. 18.

20. Patitucci and Lichenstein, *Improving Cash Management*, p. 32.

21. Ibid., p. 33.

22. Rhett D. Harrell, "Banking Relations Part I," in *Cash Management for Small Governments* ed. Ian J. Allan, (Chicago, Ill.: Government Finance Officers Association, 1989), pp. 62-63.

23. Berg, "Selecting a Municipal Depository," p. 94.

24. Shinn, "Overview of Cash Management," p. 18.

25. Pattitucci and Lichtenstein, *Improving Cash Management*, p. 40.

26. Ibid., pp. 40-41; See also Nathaniel B. Guild, Michael Clowes, William Deane, Peter F. Rousmaniere, and David A. Shepard, *The Public Money Manager's Handbook* (Chicago: Crain Books, 1981), chs. 3-4.

7

Risk Management

Until 1978 risk management aroused little interest in public sector and other not-for-profit organizations. This has radically changed during the recent past due in great part to the erosion of sovereign immunity of governmental units as a municipal defense following the case of *Monell vs. City of New York* (1978), in which the county extended the right of citizens to sue the government for negligent acts of their employees. Because of this ruling, governmental entities became vulnerable to a number of suits.

During the period of the mid-1970s through 1982, the insurance industry was able to obtain extraordinary earnings on its cash investments due to prevailing high interest rates. Simultaneously, the industry was experiencing low demand for its services, inhibiting it from aggressive pricing policies. However, as interest rates fell and market demand firmed in 1984, the insurance industry, which was mindful of its huge losses in 1983, instituted major increases in insurance premiums. Increases of 100 percent or more became widespread. It is significant that these sizable increases were taking place while deductibles were rising and the amount of liability coverage was falling.[1]

The repercussions of the New York City case made increases in insurance premiums inevitable. The number of the suits and the magnitude of awards could not be sustained on the old premium structure. Suits and awards such as the following have occurred since 1978:

- In Newport Beach, California, the court awarded a $6 million payment to a man who became paraplegic after diving into the water and hitting a sandbar.
- Merill, Michigan, with a population of 1,710 and a budget of $250,000, was ordered to pay its former police chief $250,000

for wrongful discharge.

- An award of $2.6 million was granted to a woman in Torrington, Connecticut, "because the police failed to protect her from her estranged husband."[2]

The city of Dallas, Texas, reports that when it solicited bids for insurance coverage in January 1985, it expected that its insurance would increase in cost by perhaps 100 to 200 percent and that a number of insurers would bid. The city received a sole bid asking for $1.5 million in premiums, compared to $154,000 only the year before.[3]

The risk management crisis is especially difficult for governmental units because unlike businesses, they are newcomers to the insurance field. Few public entities have developed expertise in risk management. A large number of governmental units operate fragmented risk management programs. The risk management crisis brought about rapid change, forcing government and other not-for-profit agencies to recognize the desirability of a systematic, centralized approach to protect themselves against loss.

DEFINING RISK MANAGEMENT

Until quite recently, risk management in the public sector has been oriented around insurance management. The manual on risk management by Charles K. Coe, (*Understanding Risk Management*, 1980), is indicative of the continuing approach. Although the author indicates that risk management is not insurance management, the manual reads that way.

In reality, risk management is a comprehensive and systematic approach aimed at identifying, measuring, and controlling an entity's exposure to accidental loss, theft, and liability involving human, financial, physical, and natural resources. Examples of these types of loss include: (1) damage or loss of property, (2) income loss due to destruction of records, (3) expense incurred in replacing damaged property or repairing a broken water main, (4) liability due to wrongful acts by an entity's employees or officials, and (5) personal liability due to job related injuries resulting in loss of productivity.[4] This chapter attempts to provide an understanding of risk management and the alternative options that are being used to achieve maximum safety at a reasonable cost.

RISK MANAGEMENT PROCESS

Though there are slight differences regarding the sequence or specific steps of the risk management process, there is general agreement that there are five basic elements: (1) discovery and identification of risk, (2) measurement and evaluation of risk, (3) risk control, (4) risk financing, and (5) risk administration.

Discovery and Identification of Risk

An important first step in risk determination requires the identification and inventory of the resources of an organization that are exposed to potential loss. This involves: (1) an examination and analysis of items such as liquid assets (cash, checks), capital assets, budgets, contracts, leases, organizational charts, policy and procedure manuals, annual reports, capital projects, and other financial records; (2) regular or periodic inspection of premises owned or leased by the governmental or not-for-profit agency; (3) use of well-conceived risk discovery questionnaires identifying major types of possible losses; and (4) use of reputable insurance brokers to aid in exposure analysis.[5] "Large-scale and long-term hazards have become increasingly prevalent in our economic system."[6] The consumer market has a number of products, such as saccharin and cigarettes that may produce harmful results and liability. External environmental disaster includes the Exxon Valdez oil spill, potential nuclear power plant accidents such as occurred at Three Mile Island, and toxic waste dumps that may present hazards to local communities' water supply.[7] Attention should be focused on those items or situations that have the greatest potential for financial loss.

Measurement and evaluation

Once the exposure has been identified, measurement and evaluation are the next logical steps. Measurement requires quantification, which relies heavily on the present records of insurance carriers. In measuring the risk, a thorough review of an agency's past loss experience, and the frequency and severity of each exposure must be carried out. This is not an easy task: "measurement of identified risk exposures is the most difficult and least precise step in the art of risk management."[8]

Data should be organized for each identified exposure and coverage as follows: (1) the frequency of a particular incident for a specified time period, perhaps four to six years; (2) amount of claims resulting from the incident for the same time period; and (3) the type of incident involved (e.g., injury to foot, to leg, or back) for the same time period.[9]

Risk control

This step is essentially an analysis of the relevant alternatives that might be selected to reduce or eliminate the identified exposure. This is perhaps the most critical step in risk management. A decision must be made to determine if the risk can be eliminated entirely, reduced significantly, assumed partially or totally by the governmental unit, or transferred to the insurers.[10]

Risk reduction in many local governmental organizations is complicated due to fragmentation among different departments that share the responsibility for risk management. This is a major problem operating against efficient management of risk control. The National Safety Council statistics for 1992 demonstrate this point in showing that the national average loss of time for hours worked due to personal injury was 14.4 per 100 full-time employees, costing $16 billion, or $27,000, per disabling injury. Industries such as auto manufacturing and chemical registered 23.4 and 6.4 respectively, while the government sector rate was 10.1. For police, refuse, and fire services, they were 12.16, 5.45, and 8.19, respectively, due to time loss because of accidents in 1992.[11] These figures represent a significant decline since 1983.

If improvements are to be realized, governmental units must reduce the frequency and possible severity of loss by eliminating hazards and unsafe conditions. This necessitates greater coordination than has been usual in local government to date. To achieve the risk reduction objective requires actions such as the following:

- Identify risk control areas, policies, and procedures relating thereto.
- Assist each department in interpreting and applying the rules.
- Monitor compliance of the policies and procedures on a periodic basis.[12]
- Establish safety and training programs (both in-house and external courses).
- Develop effective record-keeping systems.
- Centralize responsibility for risk management.
- Involve all levels of employees in helping to identify unsafe conditions.

Risk evaluation should ideally be viewed as a preventive measure in that the potential for exposure to loss is recognized and dealt with before it materializes. The main ways for eliminating risk are to change the way the things are being done or to terminate the performance of the risky activity or service.

Risk Assumption/Retention/Funding

This may occur in two ways - by unexpected or by planned assumption. Unexpected assumption occurs most often because of ignorance and neglect, or because the risk manager failed to thoroughly understand the implications of the actions taken, as follows:

- Ignorance that unless specifically stated, *actual value* (ACV) means current replacement less accumulated depreciation.
- Failure to carry the required insurance amount or percentage of coverage to meet the coinsurance clause stipulation.
- Failure to properly state or identify risks.
- Failure to take timely action to insure against risk exposure.[13]

Because of the public or other not-for-profit agency's difficulty in obtaining insurance coverage, risk retention has been pursued as a viable option. Before a final decision is made, a thorough evaluation of the governmental unit or agency's ability for risk retention should be undertaken.

Three basic ingredients have been viewed as essential for an effective loss financing program:

- The governmental unit or organization should have the financial capacity to meet its anticipated losses while accommodating its ordinary operating and capital needs.
- There should be exposure distribution across the entire organization sufficient to have an economy of scale that provides a relatively stable loss exposure.
- The entity should insure against losses. "Layers of insurance above the self-retained levels must be purchased so that the risk of loss greater than the entity is capable of absorbing is transferred to a commercial insurance carrier."[14]

The size of the governmental unit or organization is a particularly important consideration, as the larger the organization the greater will be its ability to absorb claims against it. Small and predictably recurring claims can be more economically handled by the entity, thus avoiding the extremely high cost of insurance carriers.

Once the conditions and basic criteria for evaluating the organization's capability for retarding risks are known, a decision can be made regarding the assumption of risks. To aid in this endeavor, a frequency severity matrix or protective pyramid may be used.

An examination of Figure 7.1 suggests that the left side of the matrix

Figure 7.1
The Frequency/Severity Matrix

High Frequency **Low Severity**	**High Frequency** **High Severity**
Low Frequency **Low Severity**	**Low Frequency** **High Severity**

containing the high frequency/low severity and low frequency/low severity loss can be assumed by the organization because one is predictable and the other has a low risk factor.

On the right side of the matrix, the low frequency/high severity condition provides a situation in which risks are such that the organization should obtain commercial catastrophic insurance. For the high frequency/high severity case, the situation is more problematic. Because of the high risk both in terms of occurrence and severity, the price and availability of such insurance may be too high to pay. Thus, an evaluation of the situation will heavily influence which risks might have to be retained or transferred.

The protective pyramid is analogous to the matrix approach in that the large number of exposure cases of high frequency/low severity are found at the base of the pyramid (capable of being handled by individual self-insurance). The smaller number of cases of low frequency/high severity is viewed as being at the top of the pyramid (requiring catastrophic insurance). In the middle of the pyramid, there are a myriad possibilities, such as pooling and harmless agreements.

Several types of risk insurance that are typically available to municipalities and other not-for-profit organizations including the following:

- damage to property, including automobiles, and machinery, by fires, water, earthquake, flood, or radiation;
- business interruption and data-processing equipment;
- loss of property due to dishonest acts or crimes by employees or private citizens;

- liability coverage for actions such as automobile-related accidents, workman's compensation, professional errors and omissions, and medical malpractice or public official liability; and
- loss of income-producing properties or increased cost due to fire to property, bridges, tunnels, boilers or machinery.

When the governmental unit employs the partial or total self-insurance option, there are two ways it may be used, involving large deductibles or coinsurance. Under the partial or total self-insurance approach, an insurance fund is set up and managed to provide payment for unexpected losses. If the fund is professionally managed, it has the potential of replenishing itself and perhaps in time may become a source of income.

Under the coinsurance approach, amounts are budgeted and appropriated each year. Coinsurance is essentially a pay-as-you-go concept. While the co-insurance approach is widely used, it has some possible negatives. If the amount of liability fluctuates widely, it can present a problem for governmental units and organizations that have inflexible budgets. This may also occasion steep rises in insurance premiums.

The drastic increase in insurance premiums for governmental and other not-for-profit agencies has generated pressure to find better alternatives ways to induce the insurance industry to cover risk at more reasonable costs. Self-insurance and pooling are becoming the only options for some governmental units if they wish to maintain risk coverage and avoid termination of private insurance policies. "There are 15,000 public entities being covered in these [municipally sponsored self-insurance pools] and other intergovernmental pools."[15]

In an effort to limit awards for damages, the state of Colorado has attempted to specifically define its Governmental Immunity Act by listing the areas for which it will be liable, including the following:

- Operation of state motor vehicles;
- Operation of public hospitals, parks, and correctional facilities;
- Dangerous conditions that interfere with the movement of pedestrian or vehicular traffic; and
- Operation and maintenance of any public facility, including water supply plant, electrical, gas and other power facilities, sanitation plants, and swimming facilities.[16]

Risk administration

In large units of government, risk management is likely to be a separate and distinct function headed by a risk manager. In small units of government, this function is performed by the financial officer. Clearly written policies and procedures should be an indispensable requirement. The main responsibilities are to oversee the implementation of the risk management process, which involves identifying exposure, evaluating risks, controlling and funding risks, and other duties and activities related to the risk management function. These would include evaluating and reviewing important leases and contracts, maintaining a risk management information system, and allocating costs, losses, and premiums. Finally, the risk manager acts as a communication channel for disseminating risk-related information and reports throughout the organization on a timely basis.[17]

RISK MANAGEMENT AND QUALITY ASSURANCE: THE CASE OF THE MEDICAL INDUSTRY

The skyrocketing liability insurance premiums experienced by doctors, hospitals, and other medically related functions have forced the industry to take a closer look at its risk management activities. Traditionally, hospitals have long practiced quality assurance as a normal way of attempting to maintain quality in the delivery of medical services. When the need arose to streamline the risk management function, it was found that many of the activities required under quality assurance paralleled those for risk management. The Joint Commission of Accreditation of Hospitals (JCAH) felt that: "the integration of risk management and quality assurance made good business sense as a means to improve patient care, reduce liability and maintain harmony in the labor force."[18]

In the 1974-1976 period, when the crisis in malpractice insurance became a major concern, commercial insurance carriers indicated that if hospitals developed acceptable in-house risk management programs, they would be given favored treatment. The "promise of reduced premium based on in-house risk identification, evaluation, reduction or elimination and consequential favorable claims history . . . provided the initial motivation of boards of trustees and administrators."[19]

Incident reporting

In 1978 a total of 3,293 incidents in one psychiatric center were reviewed. It was found that accidental injuries generated one-third of the incidents, while the major categories included: "leave without consent, patient fights and assaults."[20] This manual count led to the analysis of the incidents and the identification of possible trends and convinced the hospital officials that these reports had considerable potential, especially if more detailed information (for example, type of incidents, nature, frequency, witnesses, sex, age of patient, and particular days and hours of occurrence) was made available. It was felt that if this data could be obtained it would aid in achieving two important objectives: (1) improving patient care while minimizing risks to patients and staff; and (2) realizing an insurance savings due to claims reduction because the hospital would have its factual investigation report available to shield the institution from unfounded and unsubstantiated claims.

While judgmental factors still play a part in determining when a specific event should or should not be considered an incident, the following criteria will aid in identifying incidents:

- actions contrary to plans for the best-quality patient care;
- actions that place patients or staff at risk; and
- actions that put the program or facility in a tenuous legal or political position.[21]

Following the 1978 test year, a computerized incident-reporting system for hospitals, containing over 30 types of incidents (ranging from biting and assault to incorrect medication) was instituted in 1979, permitting answers to be obtained to a variety of questions. So far the system appears to be producing the intended results: reducing liability and producing a better utilization of resources in delivering cost-effective patient care. Expansion of the program to other areas of the hospital is underway.[22]

POOLING INSURANCE

Because of the insurance price rise, a number of units of governments have been moving to pooled risk. Pools are especially useful when a unit of government lacks clout with the marketplace commercial insurance to negotiate terms that fit its particular needs. When specialized coverage needs arise, traditional insurers may write a separate policy or issue an endorsement and add the cost increases involved.

The pooling approach has been instrumental in bringing about useful changes to risk insurance in governmental units. Pools have developed expertise and negotiating power to better provide customized coverage for needs that might have previously been uninsurable. These may involve exposure to such areas as:

- employment-related claims such as discrimination, sexual harassment, and retaliatory discharge;
- discrimination in the provision of services, creating potential

liability emanating from such laws as the Americans with Disabilities Act (ADA);
- environmental liability relating to pollution coverage resulting from court decision, lead paint, and leaking underground tanks creating first- and second-party cleanup claims; and
- special services, including recreational activities such as festivals and skate-boarding ramps.[23]

Before participating in a pool, an entity should thoroughly evaluate the pool versus the commercial insurance. The entity should evaluate the integrity and professionalism of the organization, the contractual agreement, the security that the pool provides, and the costs. The contractional agreement requires particular scrutiny. The joining entity must recognize the fact that it is taking ownership in the pool program. Typically, the enrollment document makes the entity liable for additional charges that may become necessary due to unforeseen excess cost incurred by the pool. Alternatively, members may receive dividends or rebates when pool costs are lower than was anticipated. This system of assessments and dividends tends to bind entities into longer-term relationships than they might have with most commercial insurance programs.[24]

When pools are not tailor made to the individual customer's needs, care must be taken to make sure that the entity knows the implications of its pooling arrangements. This caveat is reasonable when it is realized that joining pools often involves the acceptance of a packaged program that does not permit room to modify the coverage to meet the entity's specific needs. For example, there may be coverage that is not desired. It is likely that commercial insurance permits more flexibility. Often they permit self-insured extension and deductibles.[25] While tighter budgets are constraints on public entities, cost is likely to tilt the scale toward pooling arrangements. A careful assessment of the benefits, cost, and the needs should always be undertaken.

SUMMARY OBSERVATIONS

Emphasis on risk management is a recent development. The erosion of the governmental unit's sovereign immunity was occurring at the same time that insurance premiums were skyrocketing for liability coverage in the medical profession. In both areas, better risk management has been seen as one way to minimize the high cost of risk exposure.

The risk management problem has reached crisis proportions among governmental units. The insurance industry, which supported losses during the early to mid-1980s, saw two converging events taking place during the early 1990s: (1) demand for insurance improved, and (2) the number and amounts of awards continued to rise, though less dramatically. To recoup some of their losses as quickly as possible, the industry increased insurance premiums steeply in the late 1980s and less rapidly during the first past of the 1990s. This has forced governmental units to seek and develop alternatives such as pooling and self-insurance. Additionally, it has generated a keen awareness in the need to find better ways to manage risks.

NOTES

1. Dean G. Phelus, *Risk Management Today* (Washington, D.C.: International City Management Association, 1985), p. 1; Eric Wiesenthal, "Public Liability Woes Threaten Localities," *Public Administration Times* November 1, 1985, pp. 1, 12.

2. Wiesenthal, "Public Liability Woes", p. 12.

3. Ibid.

4. Phyllis Sherman, *Basic Risk Management Handbook for Local Government* (Darien, Conn.: Public Risk Management Association, 1983), pp. 5-10.

5. Charles K. Coe, *Understanding Risk Management* (Athens, Ga.: Institute of Local Government, 1980), pp. 13-14.

6. Al H. Ringleb and Steven L. Wiggins, "Institutional Control and Large Scale Long-Term Hazards," in *Government Risk Bearing*, ed. Market S. Sniderman (Boston, Mass.: Kluwer Academic Publishers, 1993), pp. 1-2.

7. Ibid., p. 2.

8. Institute for Local Self-Government, *Public Agency Liability: The Law and the Risks; Management, Avoidance and Transfer* (Berkeley, Calif.: Institute for Local Government, 1978), p. 58.

9. Jesus J. Pena, Alden N. Haffner, Bernard Rosen and Donald W. Light, "Combining Risk Management and Quality Assurance" in *Hospital Quality Assurance* ed. Jesus J. Pena et al., (Rockville, Md: Aspen Corporation, 1984), pp. 256-268.

10. Coe, *Understanding Risk Management*, p. 21.

11. Laurence C. Cragg and H. Felix Kloman, "Risk Management: A Developed Discipline," in *Risk Management Today*, ed. Natalie Wasserman and Dean G. Phelus (Washington, D.C.: International City Managers Association, 1985), p. 13 and National Safety Council (NSC) *Accident Facts* (Washington, D.C.: NSC, 1993), p. 49.

12. Ibid.

13. Coe, *Understanding Risk Management*.

14. Institute for Local Self-Government, *Public Agency Liability*, p. 96.

15. Wiesenthal, "Public Liability Woes," p. 12.

16. Ibid.

17. Cragg and Kloman, "Risk Management," p. 21.

18. Pena, Haffner, Rosen, and Light, "Combining Risk Management and Quality Assurance," p. 253.

19. Ibid, p. 254.

20. Ibid.

21. Ibid, p. 255.

22. Ibid, p. 269.

23. Betsy Kutska, "Pools Rush In . . ." *Government Finance Review*, 9, no. 1 (February 1993): 15.

24. Daniel S. Cullen, "Pooling and Insurance - One and the Same?" *Government Finance Review*, 9, no. 1 (February 1993): 14.

25. Ibid.

8

Borrowing and Debt Management

The responsibility for long-term borrowing and debt management is critical in public and other not-for-profit agencies. Particularly in smaller agencies, imprudent decisions can lead to serious financial problems. Because of this, it is very important for the officials that oversee borrowing and debt management to have a general understanding of, and a degree of familiarity with, the different types of debt, the structure of debt, debt instruments, and the process by which bonds are bid and sold.

This chapter examines the critical role of the management process for the sale of long-term debt, mainly as it takes place in governmental units. Attention is focused on the types of debt instruments and their proper use, the functions and responsibilities in the debt management process, and the many potential problems to avoid in the debt issuance process.

Debt financing takes place at all levels of government. Despite this reality, misunderstanding about the scope and nature of public debt is common, due perhaps to the minimal amount of information that is exchanged about public financial undertakings. Another contributing factor is the unwise attempt to equate public and private debt. Additionally, there has long been an antipathy against borrowing, suggested by the following comment: "It [borrowing] is a system which tends to make us less thrifty - to blind us to our real situation."[1]

Borrowing is a substitute for taxing citizens immediately, replacing present taxes with future taxes and thus necessitating the payment of interest on the debt. In essence, "public borrowing is a means by which people with relatively low preference for present consumption lend to those with relatively high preference for present consumption."[2] Until the late 1930s, government borrowing was considered a very abnormal event. It was referred to as "extraordinary finance," suggesting that "it was a method that was used only during extraordinary times such as war and depression."[3]

Government borrowing can be classified as either current or capital, depending on the purposes for which the money is being used. Goods and services to be consumed in a period of a year or less are viewed as current, while those that will be consumed over longer periods are capital expenditures, typically intended for long-lived physical assets such as schools, utility plants, and highways. Because of the long time span for capital projects, the benefits generated and outlays made cannot be easily synchronized.

While the federal government and a few states may run deficits as a permissible policy to fund current spending, this option typically is closed to local government and to most other not-for-profit agencies. Borrowing for current operations is not permitted for periods longer than a year. Such borrowing typically coincides with tax revenue inflows for the period or with grants from other governmental units. Short-term debts so created are known as *tax* or *revenue anticipation loans*.

Besides the restrictions on current borrowing, most states have constitutional provisions limiting their debt-creating capacity. More than half require a constitutional amendment beyond a specified debt limit. Most state constitutions require that a special tax be levied to cover debt service and stipulate that the state may not lend its credit to individuals or corporations.[4]

State restrictions on local government debt are quite specific and stringent. Usually there are stipulations regarding the following: (1) the purposes of the borrowing, (2) methods indicating how the debt should be incurred, (3) the amount of local debt, (4) the interest rate, (5) the term of the debt, (6) the retirement provisions, and (7) the form of the debt. The most common stipulation relates to the amount of allowable debt versus the assessed value of the local jurisdiction. In most cases, different assessment ratio debt limits are applied to the various types of debt. The greatest restrictions are placed on the smallest communities; less stringent provisions apply to school districts.

Debt limitation requirements have not been without their detractors. Property tax, which constitutes the major source of local revenue and on which the tax limitation is predominantly based, varies significantly among communities, permitting differing degrees of limitation. To compensate for this disparity, local governments have manipulated the assessed valuation of property in order to raise their debt limitation ratio. The assessed valuation of the property is raised, while the tax rate or millage is reduced. Particularly significant is the fact that the use of the property tax as the determining factor ignores the fact that an increasing source of local spending is grants from other governments.[5]

TYPES OF DEBT FINANCING

A number of avenues are open to public and other not-for-profit organizations to finance borrowing needs, typically for long-lived assets or capital projects. The financing option pursued will be influenced by a number of factors, among them the financial strength of the governmental unit or organization, the nature and scope of the project being financed, and the predictability of the cash financing flow. Among the general options that may be available are (1) pay cash, (2) set aside cash reserve for the prospective acquisition, and (3) borrow.

Before selecting from financing options, a thorough analysis of the costs and benefits of each should be made. Generally, a sound approach will involve a combination of three approaches.

The payment of cash or the pay-as-you-go approach (see Chapter 12) is essentially self-financing but allows interest payments to be avoided; it enhances the borrowing capacity of the organizational unit or other not-for-profit agency. Though very popular, it has distinct shortcomings. This approach assumes that a community or organization will have sufficient revenues to meet current operations plus an excess to meet capital facilities requirements. "Pay as you use" is a related concept, suggesting that the payment of the borrowed funds will be returned as people pay user charges for the services rendered.

Short-Term Debt

This comprises obligations that will mature within a year. Most often, short-term debt is assumed to provide temporary or interim funding. Short-term debt may be used for the following purposes:

- cash to initiate or begin a project;
- provision of cash as an interim financing means to await improved market conditions before issuing long-term debt;
- start-up cash for initial construction;
- provision of cash as a stopgap measure while resolving financial problems;
- provision of cash to accommodate underbudgeted expenditures; and
- minimizing cash flow fluctuations.[6]

There are a number of short-term *instruments* used to generate cash to meet expected spending needs. The following are three important instruments with which financial managers should familiarize themselves:

- Tax anticipation notes (TANs) are used to meet shortfalls occasioned by lags in tax collection; the anticipated revenue is used as security or pledged for the bank's advancing the loan (see the discussion in Chapter 6).
- Revenue anticipation notes (RANs) are used to provide cash to overcome lags involved in receipt of intergovernmental revenue. The anticipated revenues are pledged as security for the cash advance. Upon receipt of the revenues, the loan is repaid (see Chapter 6).
- Bond anticipation notes (BANs) are used to generate funds to initiate a capital project, especially in cases in which interest rates are volatile. In such situations, it may be necessary to wait until interest rates stabilize for long-term debt issues.

Long-Term Debt

This is typically used to provide permanent financing for major capital improvements, construction, and acquisition of capital facilities. As a general rule, long-term debt should not be used to fund current expenditures. It is important that the term of the bond issued be at least equal to the life of the asset being financed. There are several categories of long-term bonds.

- The general obligation (GO) bond indicates that the security standing behind the bond is the total credibility and unrestricted resource of the government unit or other not-for-profit agency. The bond is said to be issued with the full faith and credit of the issuer. In a governmental unit, the general tax revenue provides the ultimate source of funds. Though at one time, general obligation bonds were the only tax-exempt debt that was issued, this has changed significantly. Now, a large amount of tax exempt debt is represented by revenue bonds - approximately 56 percent in 1982.
- Revenue bonds are obligations issued to finance a revenue-generating project or enterprise. Both the principal and interest of revenue bonds are required to be paid exclusively from the generated earnings. The massive growth in revenue bonds has come about as a way of shifting the burden away from taxpayers to users, avoiding referendums and imposed debt ceilings. Typical uses of the revenue bond include financing of sewer and water systems, airports, toll roads, hospitals, or parking facilities, and industrial developments.
- Industrial bonds are issued by governments to construct

facilities for a private corporation that makes lease payments to the government to serve those bonds. Such bonds may be general obligation bonds, combination bonds, or revenue bonds. The state legislature enacts enabling legislation to permit local governments (typically municipalities) to finance the acquisition or construction of industrial facilities. The major purpose of these bonds is to encourage local economic development efforts. Originally, industrial bonds were used almost entirely to attract, expand, or retain industrial facilities in a community. However, the uses of industrial bonds have expanded in recent years to include financing of sports facilities/stadiums, hospitals, transportation, pollution control, and industrial parks.[7] The 1986 Federal Tax Reform Act severely restricted the use of industrial bonds.

Unique borrowing vehicles have been developed in recent years "to take advantage of the expanded public role in the delivery of goods and services [and] the desire of the private sector to capture the benefits of tax exempt financing."[8] Among the activities that have been undertaken are (1) resource recovery involving a privately owned waste disposal plant; (2) mortgage finance, permitting tax exempt bonds to be sold by a governmental unit or authority, which uses the proceeds to make low-interest mortgage loans; (3) joint action allowing governmental units to cooperatively own a power plant; and (4) municipal assistance corporations, permitting a city to issue tax exempt obligations supported by special revenue sources; this approval may be used especially in those situations where the city's credit does not make the debt issuance possible. The receipts obtained from the bond issue may be used for governmental purposes, as during the New York City fiscal crisis of 1975.

DEBT CARRYING CAPACITY

It is important to know the precise debt-carrying capacity of a governmental unit because it indicates how much that unit may reasonably borrow. In a governmental unit, debt capacity is dependent upon the quantity and quality of available resources that can be legally and practically drawn upon to meet the articulated needs.

Before debt capacity can be determined, the debt burden - the legitimate obligations that a governmental unit or agency is responsible for liquidating at some time in the future - must be calculated. The debt burden can, therefore, be compared to the amount of taxes or monetary resources that taxpayers are required to provide in order to finance outstanding debt service. When overlapping governmental units (e.g., school districts, public authorities, or special-purpose districts) extract taxes from the same taxpayers, those analyzing debt capacity must be cognizant not only of debt obligations in an individual unit but also of the composite debt responsibility in all the units concerned.

Among the main components that may be evaluated in determining relative tax capacity are the following:

- property value per capita;
- human resources in terms of age, employment, education, and type of occupation;
- per capita personal income;
- per capita disposable income;
- productivity of the tax system (indicators include per capita tax collections and per capita taxes as a percentage of per capita income);
- political, legal, and administrative constraints against expanding or broadening the tax base;
- property tax base;
- stability of the tax system; and
- the tax base growth rate.[9]

An underlying premise for evaluating fiscal capacity is that, given ordinary conditions, the debt of a governmental unit or agency parallels the size and growth of the governmental unit's tax base. It is important that schedules of debt repayment be prudently arranged to avoid excessive pressures on operating expenditures, minimizing the possibility of impairing the governmental unit or agency's credit rating. To aid in monitoring changes in debt structure which has implications for both short- and long-term solvency, the Financial Trend Monitoring System (FTMS) (discussed in Chapter 19) is most useful. The FTMS follows the change in debt, the scope, and the cost of capital items that will be purchased and overlapping debt.[10]

PLANNING A BOND ISSUE

An initial activity in planning a bond issue involves the determination of the purpose for incurring debt, the scope, and the cost of capital items that will be purchased or contracted. Ideally, bonds should be issues as part of a governmental unit's capital improvement program (CIP), involving physical involvements required to meet community service needs (see the discussion in Chapter 12). It is in the CIP that the definition of quantity and quality of services to be delivered is indicated.

Carefully determining the cost of the project to be financed is critical.

If the costs are overestimated, unnecessary interest and associated costs will be incurred. Underestimating the cost of the project is likely to be even more expensive because it may necessitate a supplemental bond issue. This requires that a bond be issued for an optimal amount.[11] To aid in selecting means to obtain necessary financial resources for funding the decided-upon project, the governmental unit or agency should seek expert assistance from consulting agencies, financial advisors, and bond counsel to minimize costs and legal problems and facilitate document preparation.

Once a decision has been made about the amount of resources needed, the available options other than incurring debt must be explored, including existing revenue sources, federal and state grants, and bond funds from prior issues. It should be determined how advantageous it would be to sell bonds through public bid versus private negotiations where this option is legal. The bond debt option should include a consideration of selling general obligation versus revenue bonds. A choice between the two options requires an assessment of the following:

- prospective beneficiaries (direct and indirect) over the expected life of the project;
- potential alternative revenues obtainable from user charges;
- legal authority to issue general obligation bonds;
- potential for the bond being approved by voters;
- political and legal authority to raise or increase taxes;
- implications and impact of the bond issue, especially demands on general obligation versus other financing priorities; and
- comparative costs of general obligation and revenue bonds.[12]

GENERAL OBLIGATION AND REVENUE BONDS: PARTICULAR CONSIDERATIONS

In cases in which revenue bonds do not require voter approval, fewer problems are encountered than with general obligation bonds, but revenue bonds typically carry higher rates because they are not secured by the full faith and credit of the issuer. The structure of the bond issue depends on whether it consists of general obligation (GO) or revenue bonds. A critical consideration by a prospective purchaser relates to the degree of coverage for the debt service from revenue pledged in support of the debt. As a general rule, the purchaser/investor will be more comfortable with a high coverage ratio than a low one. If possible, a comparative check of similar projects in other jurisdictions should be made. Another concern is the patrimony (undepreciated value of the facility or the net asset value), which may have been negotiated in earlier years but is not likely to provide enough security for interest payments in later years. This position accords with the view that the maturity of a debt should not be allowed to extend beyond the useful life of the facility financed.[13]

Unlike the revenue bond, which depends on revenue generated from a specific project, the GO bond relies on the revenue or total estimated annual revenue of the governmental unit. Since the same pool of revenue must be used to serve all GO bonds, it is important that current expenditure in any given year not exceed the project revenue.

Call Provision

When a bond has a call provision, the investor may be required to redeem the bonds at some time other than the specified maturity date. The call may apply to a portion or to all of the outstanding bond. If the optional payment of principal is not specified in the bond contract, the call option can be used only with the consent of the investor. The call provision is usually included to permit the issuer to achieve a number of objectives, including the following:

- voluntarily reduce outstanding debt;
- reduce debt in accordance with bond agreement (indenture);
- reduce interest cost by refunding; and
- reorganize debt voluntarily.[14]

The call provision provides flexibility in unstable markets. It also provides the issuer with the option to reduce the bond's interest rate when interest rates decline, allowing the issuer to reduce costs but reducing the earning potential for the investor. To compensate for this, the investor usually requires higher interest return on callable bonds than on noncallable bonds. Investors may also require a period of time by which the bond may not be called after issuance. This is known as the *deferment period*. When the bond is called, the different between the call price and its par value is referred to as the call premium.

Advance Refunding

In those cases where a deferment call provision exits but interest rates decline significantly before the deferment period, the issuer may issue bonds prior to the callable date when the outstanding bonds become due or callable. The proceeds from the advance funding are deposited in an escrow account and invested in securities, typically U.S. Treasury bonds or other authorized securities, to be used to redeem the underlying bonds at the maturity or call date

DEBT MANAGEMENT TERMINOLOGY

Consulting engineer. This is one who provides technical advice and conducts feasibility studies in areas such as designing and constructing roads, water and sewer facilities, and public buildings, making revenue and operation cost estimates.

Financial advisor. This is an individual who provides a wide spectrum of services to a debt issuer, including assessing the borrowing capacity; assembling an array of financial statistics and economic data such as tax rates and overlapping debt; making user charge estimates; projecting revenue flow estimates; advising on marketing methods; writing call provision features; assisting in preparing and distributing notice of sale and bid forms; determining the need for rating services; arranging analysis of creditworthiness; coordinating delivery of bonds; and ruling on acceptability of bids.

Bond counsel. The bond counsel's main objective is determining if there are conflicts with constitutional and other constraints such as monitoring/limitations, arranging required elections, reviewing bond-related statements for conformity with the law, ensuring that competitive sales are advertised and that an underwriter is secured for negotiated sale, rendering opinion on the status of tax exempt bonds, and answering questions posed by prospective purchasers and public officials.

Negotiated sale. This is a method that is used for selling securities in which the terms of the sale are arrived at through negotiation between issuer and purchasers without formal competitive bidding. This may include sales of securities directly to commercial banks or consortiums of commercial banks, investment banking firms or syndicates, and private placements by issuers.[15]

Callable bond. This is a type of bond which permits the issuer to call in and pay the obligation before the stated maturity date by notifying the purchaser of the redemption in the manner specified in a bond contract.

Maturity date. This is the date on which the principal amount of security becomes due and payable.

Debt service. This is the required amount of money necessary to pay interest and principal for a given year or years. When the term debt service payment is used it refers to the service of all bond payments that mature at some specific time.

Series bond. This is a bond whose principal is repaid in periodic installments over the life of the issue.

Debt Service Charge. It is an organization's ability to service its debt. Typically it is measured by a ratio called debt service ratio (see Chapter 2 and 18).

Municipal Bond Underwriters. It is the process in which bond dealers buy whole new bond issues from the state and local entities and then resell them in smaller blocks to investors. Typically new issues are underwritten by syndicates or a group of dealers who go together for each particular sale. By forming the syndicate, the dealer members share the risk of buying and owning an issue. This facilitates their cooperating to distribute the bonds to their customers in an effort to make a profit on their markup.

Municipal Securities Rulemaking Board (MSRB). Bond dealers and syndicates operate under MSRB rules with the approval of the Securities and Exchange Commission (SEC). The rules are self-enforced by the National Association of Security Dealers (NASD).

and to pay interest on the bonds refunded. It is important to note that refunding is normally desirable only when interest rates are high enough to generate a benefit.

Credit Rating Agencies and Investors

One of the most crucial factors influencing the success or failure of a debt offering are the governmental unit or agency's credit rating, regardless of whether the sale of a major bond issue rating is obligatory. Credit rating is used to designate the quality of governmental bonds and directly affects the interest rate that is required to be paid. Standard and Poor's Corporation, Moody's Investor Service, and Fitch Investors Services are the three main rating firms in the United States providing professional judgments or opinions concerning the quality and security or creditworthiness of debt issuers. Moody's and Standard and Poor's are by far the two dominant giants in the rating business. Moody's has been in operation since 1918 and rates approximately 15,000 municipal bonds and 4,500 new issues per year. Standard and Poor's began its municipal bond rating in 1940 and presently has 7,000 ratings outstanding. Each year it rates approximately 1,500 new issues.[16]

Each rating service charges a fee for its services based on rate schedules which vary according to the size and extent of the analysis desired. A host of factors is considered by investors and rating agencies, as shown in Table 8.1.

As can be seen from Table 8.2, Standard and Poor's rates bonds from AAA (highest quality and extremely strong capacity to pay principal and interest) to CC (highest degree of speculation) and D (indicating a bond in default). Moody's Investor Service ratings range from Aaa to C, with Baa having the lowest investment grade.

Bond Insurance

This is a relatively recent development, arising to insure government-related bonds against the possibility of default by the issuer. In such an event, the insuring company assumes the obligation to make all necessary payments for the coupons and maturity amounts required for investors. The initiating insurer in 1971 was the American Municipal Bond Assurance Corporation (AMBAC), whose objective was to reduce the interest cost to the issuer. For a one-time premium ranging between 0.3 percent and 3 percent of the total interest and principal amount of the bond, the issuer can receive insurance protection for the principal and interest.

In 1974 the Municipal Bond Insurance Association (MBIA) was created as a competitor to AMBAC. Unlike AMBAC, whose ultimate backing consists only of its net worth, MBIA is made up of five underwriters: Aetna Insurance Company, Aetna Casualty and Security Company, Fireman's Insurance Fund, Travelers Indemnity Company, and Continental Insurance Company. As with

Table 8.1

Factors Considered by Investors and Rating Agencies in Determining Rates

The Amount and Nature of the Debt and Debt Service Requirements:
- Total amount of debt and per capita debt levels
- Purposes for which debt has been created
- Rate at which debt has increased
- Debt repayment schedules and overlapping debt
- Degree of reliance on short-term debt

Economy of the Community and the Region of Which It Is a Part:
- Geographical area and past history of growth
- Educational and income characteristics of the population
- Location of area served and general character of future potential
- Sources of economic activity-employers, diversification, and dependence
- Maintenance of the economic plant
- Leadership
- Wealth of the community-taxable property, resources, transportation

Social Factors:
- Educational opportunities
- Cultural opportunities
- Recreational facilities
- Community record for handling social unrest
- Housing stock
- Characteristics of the population

Management of Local Government:
- Overall governmental structure--professionalism vs. balkanization
- Degree to which the government is well-administered
- Organization of financial administration
- Effectiveness of capital planning and programming
- Quality of revenue administration-passive collector of taxes vs. active
- Revenue base-new reliances
- Revenue calendar out of sync
- Reputation for prudent financial management
- Conditions of the physical plant
- Contingent liabilities
- Sinking fund management

Other Considerations:
- Debt limitations--higher regulatory controls
- Capacity of government to deal with local problems
- Security of deposits--guarantees of banks
- Bondholder's remedies--explicit or implied
- Subdivision controls--poorly planned expansions
- General regulatory codes

Table 8.2
The Major Rating Systems: Moody's and Standard and Poor's

Standard and Poor's Corporate and Municipal Rating	Moody's Municipal Rating	Description
AAA	Aaa	Highest quality, unquestionable ability to pay interest and principal.
AA	Aa	High quality and very strong capacity to pay interest and principal.
A	A	Upper medium quality, strong capacity to pay principal and interest.
BBB	Baa	Medium quality with adequate capacity to pay interest and principle, though subject to adverse economic conditions over extended periods.
BB	Ba	Predominantly speculative quality with low insurer's capacity to pay principle and interest.
BB, B, CCC, CC		BB is the lowest degree of speculation, CC the highest degree of speculation, and B medium speculation regarding issuer's capacity to pay principal and interest.
C		Income bond on which no interest is being paid.
D		Default on interest and principal.
	B, Caa, C, Ca	Speculation with low capacity to pay principal and interest.
	Con (...)	Conditional, requiring some act or fulfillment of some condition secured by a future project earning.

AMBAC, premiums are determined on the basis of the size of the total interest payment and principal and may be paid by either the issuer or the bond underwriter. While Standard and Poor's rates both AMBAC-insured and MBIA insured bonds as triple A, Moody's assigns no rating to insured bonds.[17]

Disclosure

Typically, about a month before a bond sale the issuer publishes a preliminary official statement or prospectus, describing the contents of the bond issue to enable potential investors to effectively price the bond. Subsequent to the sale of the bonds, the final official statement is developed, providing details relating to the issue and coupon rates. Governmental units are not required to comply with regulations of the Securities and Exchange Commission and other federal agencies.

The events of 1974-1975 relating to the financial crisis of New York City and the problems of a number of other cities, including Cleveland Ohio, raised the concern that the problems created were due in part to faulty reporting systems or manipulated reporting. Because of these developments, agencies, states, and a number of professional associations began calling for better disclosure guidelines. In some cases, legislation was introduced at the state and federal level stipulating minimum disclosure guidelines.

The Governmental Finance Officers Association (GFOA) published perhaps the most influential document, *Disclosure Guidelines for Offering of Securities by State and Local Governments* (1976). Two years later, (in 1978), GFOA issued *Guidelines for Use by State and Local Governments in the Preparation of Yearly Information Statements and Other Current Information*. GFOA also offers a Certificate of Conformance based on how well a governmental unit's financial statement conforms to generally accepted accounting principles (GAAP).

Negotiated versus Competitive Sale

The issuer has the option to sell competitively or by negotiated sale in revenue bond, while most states require general obligations to be competitively bid. The competitive sale permits underwriters to bid against each other to buy an issuer's bond. Acceptance of the competitive approach is widespread because there is a general feeling that it removes the possibility of favoritism, resulting in lower interest rates to the issuer.

In a negotiated sale there is no formal bidding; the underwriter is chosen beforehand. Typically, the issuer contacts a number of underwriters to solicit information regarding the expected interest rate or underwriter's spread (profit). The usual practice is that issuers exchange information on their proposed sale with underwriters with whom they have had satisfactory dealings in the past. The underwriter that is selected usually assists the issuer in a number of activities, including putting together the issue in terms of maturity date, maturity amount, and call provisions; preparation of the official statement; credit-rating assistance; pinpointing the market timing for the issue; the cultivation of potential investors; and compliance with legal requirements. Once the selection is made, the issuer and the underwriter work together to determine the structure, timing, and price of the bond for the underwriter. The negotiated bond approach is considered suitable when interest rates are high and volatile and the issue is   complex. Since 1973 the number of revenue negotiated bond sales has increased sharply - from 25 percent to more than 60 percent of the dollar value of municipal revenue bonds in 1993. For the same period, the total short-term negotiated expenditure bond sales have averaged 22 percent of municipal bond sales.

In both the negotiated and the competitive methods, the underwriter is a focal participant who buys the bond from the issuer and who in turn sells it to investors. For smaller issues, the underwriter buys the entire issue; larger issues are handled by a syndicate for later resale. Whether the sale method is competitive or negotiated, the underwriter assumes complete risk and responsibility for selling the bonds. Because of the negotiated underwriter's ability to time the sale of the bond and investigate the demand beforehand, the risk is limited.

When the underwriter decides to make a bid, he or she needs to determine the yield that will be necessary to attract investors, gain the winning bid to enable the bond to be offered to investors, and permit a profit. It is important that the underwriter make an accurate assessment of the market for the bond because miscalculations would result in its offering price being lowered, minimizing or eliminating the underwriter's profit. An important point is that the underwriter's costs for searching and preparing the bid are recovered only if he or she is successful in winning the bid. Thus, the potential risk for not recovering out-of-pocket costs restricts the underwriter's search and preparation efforts.

There are a number of options available to the negotiated sale underwriter that are not available to the competitive underwriter. If the negotiated sale underwriter recognizes that he or she can sell the offering at a lower interest rate or that investors want different amounts of bonds than had been planned, the underwriter can modify the terms of the issue to reflect the changed circumstances.

Precisely what types of bond sale are desirable for a given issue depends on a host of variables. Among the factors that might affect the choice are the following: the stability of the market, the experience of the issuer in the bond market, the size of the issue, the complexity of the issue, and administrative regulations in the state and/or local governmental unit.   In selecting a negotiated bond sales approach, the cost and benefits of six factors should be evaluated.[18]

●   The significance of the scope of the issue for the geographic tax-exempt market should be reviewed.

- Determining the lowest possible interest will make market-timing critical. When the number and/or volume of tax exempt issues is high or there is an unstable "roller coaster" market, the negotiated-financing approach can be an advantageous means to pinpoint a window of market entry.
- When the issue is complex or innovative, the negotiated route is likely to provide the greatest opportunity to explain and make the case for the issuer in the marketplace.
- When there is concern about the rating process and potential downgrading the expertise involved in a negotiated sale should be considered.
- In those cases where the issue requires a great deal of explanation because of significant economic or political developments or newsworthy or complicated building projects, the issuer may find the negotiated approach beneficial.
- A new issuer concerned about creating a positive image during its early tenure, monitoring a strong position in the secondary market (in the case of re-selling bonds of the issuer), and a contrasting style of management, ideology, or philosophy vis-a-vis the previous administration may wish to consider the negotiated sale option.

Notice of Sale

When an issue is to be sold, advertisements are placed, usually in national and local media, announcing the proposed sale. Thus, the traditional advertising document is known as the Official Notice of Sale. Active issuers will normally send copies of the Notice of Sale to prospective bidders and to legal publications. Because of its stature in bond underwriting, advertisement in the *Daily Bond Buyer* is typically required or recommended. The information in the Notice of Sale includes the following:

1. Amount of issue, including maturity and call features;
2. Authorization for the bond sale;
3. Type of bond (e.g., revenue, GO);
4. Names of the bond counsel (may be more than one);
5. Bid form and basis of award;
6. Amount of good-faith check, if required;
7. Denomination and registration privileges of investors;
8. Time, place, and date where bids can be accepted;
9. Maximum interest cost permitted; and
10. Statement of purpose of bond and security.

Basis of Award

When the issue is to be bid competitively, it is important that the issuer determine the basis on which the decision to sell debt will be made. The best known bases for award are the true interest cost (TIC) and the net interest cost (NIC).

The NIC is derived by determining the total interest payment for a debt issue and dividing it by the amount of the bonds outstanding times the number of years they are outstanding. When bonds are issued at a discount, the latter is added to the interest payments. Conversely, when the bond is issued at a premium, the latter amount is subtracted from the interest payments. The formula for calculating NIC is as follows:

$$NIC = \frac{Total \quad interest \quad payments \quad + discount \quad (- premium \;)}{Number \; of \; bond \; year \quad dollars}$$

For example, the interest payment equals $500. An amount of $50 is paid out for final maturity, due in one year and each year thereafter for the life of the bond.

Years to Maturity	Par Value	Coupon	Coupon Payment per Maturity	Bond Year (Dollars)
1	$1,000	5%	$ 50	$ 1,000
2	1,000	5%	100	2,000
3	1,000	5%	150	3,000
4	1,000	5%	200	4,000
Total	$4,000		$500	$10,000

There are no premiums or discounts. The bond year dollars equals $10,000. The NIC is 5 %.

$$NIC = \frac{Total \quad coupon \quad payments}{Bond \; year \quad dollars} = \frac{\$500}{\$10,000} = .05 = 5\%$$

A more involved example will help to clarify the NIC calculation. An issuer sells $20,000 of bonds with five separate maturities and no discount or premium. The serial maturities and coupons are as follows:

Years to Maturity	Par Value	Coupon	Coupon Payment per Maturity	Bond Year Dollars
1	$ 2,000	5.25%	$ 105	$ 2,000
2	2,000	5.30%	212	4,000
3	4,000	5.50%	440	8,000
4	6,000	5.70%	798	14,000
5	6,000	5.80%	1,160	20,000
Total	$20,000		$2,715	$48,000

$$NIC = \frac{Total \quad interest}{Bond \quad year \quad dollars} = \frac{\$2,715}{\$48,000} = 5.65\%$$

If the issue had been sold at a discount, the interest rate would be higher. For example, if the issue had been sold for an average price of $96, the issuer would have received $400 less. The NIC with the $400 discount added to the total interest payment is as follows:

$$NIC = \frac{\$2,715}{\$48,000} + 400 = \frac{\$3,115}{\$48,000} = 6.48\%$$

The TIC method is considered a superior alternative to the NIC. A major criticism of the NIC approach is that it ignores the prevent value or the timing of interest rate payments. Thus, it misleads the issuer to choose a higher bid than otherwise. The TIC accounts for the time value of money or present value.[19] It recognizes the interest rate that must be paid on the actual purchase price, which is the face amount minus the premium or plus the discount, in order to yield the bond coupon, giving a more accurate picture of the costs involved.

CONCLUDING OBSERVATIONS

Debt management, which was once relegated to relative obscurity, became a front-burner issue during the early 1970s due to financial crises in a number of cities such as New York and Cleveland. To be effective as a financial manager, (and, to some extent, as a chief executive), in a governmental unit or agency requires a degree of understanding that will improve the chances of recognizing potential problems and the ability to seek advice to avert them. Because debt represents a significant portion of spending in many governmental units, it requires close attention.

NOTES

1. David Ricardo, *Principles of Political Economy and Taxation* (1817; repr., Homewood, Ill.: Richard D. Irwin, 1963), p. 140.

2. Richard E. Wagner, *Public Finance* (Boston, Mass.: Little Brown and Co., 1982), p. 308.

3. Ibid., p. 303.

4. Alan Walter Steiss, *Local Government Finance* (Lexington, Mass.: Lexington Books, 1975).

5. Ibid., p. 75.

6. U.S. Conference of Mayors, *A Mayor's Financial Management Handbook* (Washington, D.C.: U.S. Conference of Mayors, February 1980), pp. 111-19; Lennox L. Moak and Albert M. Hillhouse, *Local Government Finance* (Chicago: Municipal Finance Officers Association, 1975), p. 250.

7. See U.S. Congressional Budget Office (CBO), *Small Issue Industrial Revenue Bonds* (Washington, D.C.: CBO, 1985).

8. Ibid.

9. Moak and Hillhouse, *Local Government Finance*, pp. 391-96.

10. See *Evaluating Financial Conditions Handbook 2* (Washington, D.C.: International City Management Association, 1980).

11. A useful approach has been identified by Philip M. Low, Jr., in *How to Calculate the Size of Your Bond Issue*, Special Bulletin 1976B (Chicago: Municipal Finance Officers Association, June 1, 1976).

12. George Kaufman, "Debt Management," in J. Richard Aronson and Eli Schwartz eds., *Management Policies in Local Government Finance* (Washington, D.C.: International City Management Association, 1981), p. 308.

13. Lennox L. Moak, *Municipal Bonds* (Chicago: Municipal Finance Officers Association, 1982), p. 232.

14. Ibid., p. 214.

15. See Center for Capital Research, *Planning, Designing and Selling General Obligation Bonds in Oregon: A Guide to Local Issues* (Eugene,: University of Oregon, 1978); see also Philip Rosenberg, C. Wayne Stallings, and Charles K. Coe, *A Debt Management Handbook for Small Cities* (Chicago: Municipal Finance Officers Association, 1979).

16. Public Securities Association, *Fundamentals of Municipal Bonds*, rev. ed. (New York: Public Securities Association, 1982), p. 40.

17. Ibid., p. 64.

18. Mark S. Farber, "A Negotiated Sale," in *The Price of Advice: Choosing and Using Financial Advisors*, ed. John Petersen and Pat Watt (Chicago, Ill.: Government Finance Officers Association, 1986), pp. 105-6.

19. See Chapter 12 for the method for computing present value.

9

The Budgeting Function

Public budgeting grew out of the political and social necessity to share power. It was through the budget that the English aristocracy, in Article 12 of the Magna Carta (1215), obtained both symbolic and substantive control over the king's absolute power of the purse. In this way, the barons obtained the power to say "no" to the king's revenue-raising objectives. Prior to engaging in domestic or foreign activities, the king was required to consult the barons and follow a recognized procedure before resources could be raised. The budget is thus "the product of the institutionalization of the rules and processes wrested from a sovereign, excessively jealous of his prerogatives."[1] Over time, the budget evolved as a formal instrument guaranteeing accountability and as an important means of control in the modern democratic state.

Whatever our political ideologies, the scope and significance of the budget cannot be ignored. Budgets are essential to every type of organization. Their impact on the fortunes of governments and agencies has long been recognized. The British statesman William Gladstone remarked, "Budgets are not merely affairs of arithmetic, but in a thousand ways go to the root of prosperity of individuals, the relations of classes and the strength of kingdoms."[2]

This chapter provides the reader with a brief overview of the components and issues that are essential to the understanding of modern budgeting techniques and philosophy. It also provides an introduction to Chapters 10 through 15, which examine the uses of budgets and the different types found in practice.

PERSPECTIVES ON BUDGETING

The budgeting function represents the third sequential step in the financial system, as shown in Figure 1.1. The budget makes the potential implementations of the planned programs specific and concrete.

Budget and Planning

All budget making involves some planning. The articulation of goals, objectives, strategies, and priorities is indispensable to the development of a sound budget. It is the planning function that sets the stage for all subsequent activities in budget preparation. Figure 9.1 presents a conceptual view of the linkage of planning and budgeting. Note that the budget amount of the prior period becomes a major input of the new planning cycle. Existing programs are evaluated; desired programs are identified; environmental or external factors are

Figure 9.1
Planning and Budgeting

assessed; changes in the government/agency are determined; strategic plans are formulated; and finally, the policy directive necessary to guide program development (program planning) and the detailed work plan (budgeting) are put together.[3]

WHAT IS A BUDGET?

A budget is an economic, planning, political, and social document. It is a comprehensive financial work plan covering a specific period of time. The plan outlines the services and activities or projects to be provided and indicates in quantitative terms, the necessary expenditures and available resources. The plan takes into account community preferences as competing claims and indicates how the resources will be allocated to satisfy these claims. All those whose preferences count are represented in the budget in dollar amounts, in other words, the particular group or individuals receiving the benefits - which may be subsidies in the form of welfare, tax relief, day care, and the like - will be indicated.

Table 9.1
The Budget as an Instrument

Planning Instrument--sets goals, priorities, and strategies and coordinates the community/agency resources into an expenditure plan identifying what programs or activities will take place and at what levels.
Political Instrument--involves competing interests attempting to influence a government/agency to form policy favorable to them.
Social Instrument--provides a vehicle to grant and deny privileges and disburse burdens and benefits to individuals and businesses.
Economic Instrument--offers powerful potential for affecting the growth and productive capacity of the community and its citizens.
Legal Instrument--grants authoritatively the rights, responsibilities, power, and guidelines that regulate the budget format, timing, and process.

Source: Adapted from Jerome B. McKinney and Lawrence C. Howard, *Public Administration: Balancing Power and Accountability* (Oak Park, Ill.: Moore Publishing Co., 1979).

The budget links the financial resources and human behavior necessary to accomplish policy objectives. Because the budget is an instrument (Table 9.1) for allocating scarce resources, it is an economic instrument. It is a political instrument because it settles conflicts in determining who will get how much of the available scarce resources and when. Finally, it is a social instrument because it is a device for distributing benefits and costs according to community preferences.[4] Every budget is a reflection of a particular kind of accountability as shown in Table 9.2. The type of budget that is used is directly dependent upon the user's desire to achieve a given type of accountability reflecting the goals and objectives, or value preferences, being sought.

Contrasting Public and Private Budgeting

The pricing and market systems act as the strategic resource allocation mechanism in the private sector, while the budget performs this function in the public sector. In the private sector, expected revenues are directly tied to the quantity and quality of goods and services produced and sold. Revenues are a good indicator of whether planned levels of activity have been realized. Unlike the private sector, public and nonprofit agencies must determine in advance the amounts that must be raised to achieve projected levels of activity, and the means to raise them. A failure to collect expected fees does not mean that the expenditure plans can be changed to match revenue intake. The public agency can resort to supplemental appropriations, but this is often viewed with hostility. Similarly, the nonprofit agency must rely on its reserve funds or on its funding sources. The latter most often do not like to provide additional funds, so agencies whose revenues are under budget learn to live with their mistakes.In both public and nonprofit agencies, yearly budgets are fixed and all funds provided are expected to be spent. Not spending the funds results in expenditure reductions according to the amount unspent. This approach is "counter productive and weakens the sensitivity of the budget as a measure of performance."[5]

The control aspect of the budget is far more critical to public and nonprofit organizations than it is to private ones. Several reasons may be advanced for this phenomenon. Particularly in private manufacturing companies, most costs are engineered costs. Thus, in these companies most costs can be identified with the products produced. In nonprofit agencies, however, most costs are discretionary because the amounts to be spent typically vary widely depending on management decisions.[6]

Unlike the fixed budgets of the nonprofit organizations, the budgets of profit-oriented companies tend to be tentative and management is expected to adjust to the changing conditions that affect sales. Managers are expected to revise plans so that the profit objective can be maximally achieved. However,

Table 9.2

The Budget Accountability Continuum

1 Line Item Budget ---------->	2 Performance Budget ---------->	3 Zero Base Budget ---------->	4 Program Budget ---------->	5 Budget for Social Purposes and Change (Emerging)
Objective:	Objective:	Objective:	Objective:	Objective:
inputs control accounting for object of expenditure	achieving desired standard outputs while minimizing inputs relating amount of input units to output units	achievement of articulated goals/ result objective at the lowest cost possible for identified clienteles and constituents, creating the opportunity to reallocate resources from lower to higher priorities	measured needs, demands, results, impact, effectiveness, outcome, relevance, sustainability and significance, determining congruence between stated goals and objectives to achieved results; and delivering the goods at the time, place and manner and in the quantity and quality desired to target clienteles and constituents	determining the extent to which programs make target groups or population better off over time than they were prior to the intervention
- Fiscal/Financial	- Emphasis on efficiency/ economy/productivity	- Emphasis on efficiency, productivity and economy for accomplishing targeted objectives	- Examples of program measurement indicators:	- Generating sustainability: percent of target group who failed to develop diseases after a vaccination, percent of school age children whose nutrition level improved as a result of school lunch programs
- Dollar accountability	- Using workload (no. of units of work to be done) as output	- Resource use constrained on the basis of benefit to be achieved	● need: quantifiable conditions or problem areas which require action if maximum welfare of the general public is to be served, requiring the identification of priority relationships among needs	
- Conformance to legal and procedural requirements	- Input dimension of efficiency, cost or some proxy measure such as man-hours worked	- Examples of program measurement indicators		
- Units of input: staff hours, materials used	- Examples of efficiency measurement indicators:	- Resource allocation based on priority ranking	● demand measures: identifying the need for a given public service measuring the dimension or scope of work to be performed in an entity such as miles of streets to be cleaned, number of businesses requiring protection	
	● Cost: input/output ratio such as solid waste collected per dollar spend or per employee hour	- Cost-effectiveness: specifics acceptable costs and benefits as a condition for acceptance or rejection		
	● Volume and quantity such as lunches served	- Incentives for inducing managers to exchange quality information up and down the hierarchy	● workload measures: indicating amount of work to be performed in a department or responsibility center linking with demand measures such as number of garbage pickup and number of patrol hours to be completed	
			● outcome: number of illnesses prevented due to vaccine	

Source: Jerome B. McKinney, "SEA Reporting: Linkage With Public Budgeting and Accountability", delivered at Government Standard Accounting Board, *Service Efforts and Accomplishments Reporting Concepts*, Vancouver, B.C., Canada, May 5, 1993 conditions in government and nonprofit agencies are viewed as essentially stable and predictable. For example, the number of miles of road to be built, the number of hospital beds, or the number of students enrolled at a university are not likely to change significantly from one period to the next during a single year.[7]

PURPOSES OF BUDGETING

One unarticulated objective of a budget is to minimize uncertainty and to make the future more predictable by identifying what is wanted, how much of it is available, and when it is available.[8] The budget quantitatively articulates planned intentions and priorities. Ideally, every proposed dollar of expenditure is specifically identified with an organizational unit known as a responsibility center, the manager of which has control over the use of that dollar.

Of all components of the financial management system, budgeting is perhaps the most important. The continuing pursuit of the balanced budget enhances stability in financial management because it fosters a matching of revenue (intake/inflow of resources or money) with expenditure (outflow/outgo of resources or money). As a detailed work plan, the budget gives direction to the implementation of articulated policies and significantly facilitates the achievement of organizational objectives.

Policy Direction

As a plan, the budget indicates a specific policy direction to be followed for a specific period of time. It contains a set of coordinated choices aimed at achieving articulated or implied goals and objectives.

Mutual Contract

The budget may be considered a mutual contract between the provider of resources and the deliverer of goods and/or services. This makes it especially important to involve those who will implement the budget. In spite of this desired norm, a number of nonprofit agencies exclude service deliverers from the budget process when crucial decisions are made. There have been cases when the budget submitted to the resource providers have been sharply reduced but the service provisions have been left intact.[9]

In the public sector the legislature and chief executives agree to provide the executing agencies with funds, with the understanding that they will expend them according to the previously agreed-upon objectives. In like manner, the governmental budget can be viewed as a contract between the legislature and the citizens of the governmental unit. The citizen implicitly agrees to pay taxes on the condition that the government provide certain general and specific services.

Communication

A budget should communicate the objectives and standards of performance expected of all decision makers. Externally, the budget can detail the costs and expenditures of operations by identifying the inputs, such as materials and equipment, and the outputs of specific goods and services, such as miles of road built or repaired, number of patients treated, or number of manuscripts submitted for publication. When management is concerned, not only with inputs and outputs, but also with results or effectiveness, such as the percentage of patients successfully treated (health care and/or welfare organizations), the number of degrees and diplomas awarded (universities), or a reduction in the crime rate (police departments), the budget can be a useful instrument in providing such information.

Motivational control

The budget can be used to motivate employees by dispensing or withholding rewards. The use of the budget as a means of control over departmental and functional expenditures has dominated much of the history of budgeting. The traditional line-item and incremental budgets (discussed in Chapter 13) were designed to control administrative discretion in the spending of agency funds. In fact, the orientation of line-item budgets is so directed at limiting specific expenditures (e.g., personnel and materials) that is has been referred to as the dollar accountability budget. Furthermore, each spending organizational unit is treated as a cost center to which responsibility can be specifically assigned and from which accountability can be obtained.

Monitoring of service

The budget can be used to monitor and assess the performance of various constituent units and programs by providing continuing feedback on their progress. Variance analysis of performance at timely intervals permits corrective action to be taken. For example, analysis of wages may show variance because of an increase in pay rate subsequent to the preparation of the budget, poor deployment of staff (for example, the use of more highly paid workers than planned), or both (see Figure 9.2).

Figure 9.2
Graphic View of Labor Cost Variance

The information equation needed to analyze a budget is as follows:

	Budgeted	Actual
Hours	5	3
Wages	$6	$8
Labor	30	24
Variance		6

- Budgeted Hours (5) - Actual Hours (3) x Budgeted Rate ($6) = Labor Use Variance ($12).
- Budgeted Wage Rate ($6) - Actual Wage Rate ($8) x Actual Hours (3) = Wage Rate Variance ($6).
- Budgeted Labor Cost ($30) - Actual Wage Cost ($24) = Net Wage Variance ($6).

Like labor, materials may be analyzed for variance because of price increases, excessive use of materials, or both (see Figure 9.2). The same conceptual approach employed for labor can be used to calculate materials variance.

- Budgeted Quantity - Actual Quantity x Budgeted Rate per Unit of Output = Materials Variance).
- Budgeted Rate per Unit Quantity - Actual Rate per Unit Quantity x Actual Quantity Used = Variance because of Price of Materials Input.
- Budgeted Cost of Materials - Actual Cost of Materials = Net Materials Price Variance.

In government and most nonprofit agencies, budgeted cost is a surrogate or substitute for standard cost, which represents the amount that a procedure or service should cost. Though the development and use of the standard cost are infrequent in the public sector, it is widely used in private industries and some nonprofit organizations such as hospitals. Standard costs have some very important potential and are a valuable aid in budget preparation. (1) They are objectively predetermined. (2) They can assist management in measuring performance by comparing actual cost with planned standard cost. They therefore provide information that permits management to isolate and explain variations from plans. (3) They provide a useful means of valuing or costing inventory that is transferred out or carried from one period to the next. (4) They provide a dependable basis for pricing goods and services.

Whether the objective standard (determined by rigorous engineering requirements) or the budgeted standard (amount appropriated by the authorizing body) is used, the responsibility center may regularly conduct variance analyses. A threshold point is established to permit top management to focus its attention only on those variances that exceed the threshold limits (see Table 9.3). This approach is similar to the management practice known as *management by exception* except that only a deviation above a given threshold level (for example, amounts that exceed 20 percent for supplies in Table 9.3), is reported to management.

Resource allocations

The allocation of resources to the most worthy alternative is a major goal of budgeting. The allocation criteria determine how limited resources are to be divided among alternative uses. If these criteria are defective, it is likely that a maldistribution of government resources will result. Resources will go to some centers that should not receive them, while units that do need them may not get enough. This outcome denies the organization or government the best potential use of its scarce resources.

Table 9.3
Variance Report: Police Department

Activity	Item	Budgeted Costs	Actual Costs	Variance	Allowable Variance	Remarks
Field Inspections	Personnel	$100,000	$130,000	$30,000(UF)	10%	Due to Overtime
Community Service	Materials	45,000	35,000	10,000 (F)	15%	Due to Reduced Price
Downtown Patrol	Supplies	5,000	7,000	2,000(UF)		Due to Increased Price
	Totals	$150,000	$172,000	$42,000		

Note: F = favorable.
        UF = unfavorable.

Accountability Instrument

The budget sets forth, in dollars, an agreement or compromise between the legislative and executive branches, on the one hand, and the administrative officials and relevant members of the community, on the other. In the nonprofit sector a budget sets forth an agreement between the governing board and the officials of the agency. The programs provided for in the budget are targeted implicitly or explicitly to clientele and constituents over a specified time period. By means of the performance indicators included in the budget, assessment can be made to determine whether the promised services and goods have been delivered at the time and place specified and in the manner, quality, and quantity desired.

By means of performance indicators (see Chapter 11 on performance measures), the budget permits managers to know whether they are perhaps using the same amount of resources to achieve more and better benefits for their clients and constituents or whether perhaps they are using a reduced level of funding to realize the same or better results.

In the final analysis, accountability can be most effectively accomplished only when the controlling instruments of performance measurement (i.e., the accounting, auditing, efficiency and economy, reporting and evaluation systems) are directly linked to responsibility centers, which are then linked to key personnel responsible for delivering specific goods and services to the target population. Take, for example, the manager of the dietary service in a hospital. He or she oversees the performances of subordinates responsible for patient food service, the kitchen, the cafeteria, and so on. The manager of the dietary service is, in turn, accountable for his or her performance to the head of administrative services.

It may be useful at this point to briefly summarize the attributes of a good budget. A budget is a device to:

1. Indicate policy direction for a specified period of time;
2. Explain the effects of budget requests on tax rates or charges;
3. Explain the effects of intergovernmental relationships;
4. Explain proposed expenditures of estimated revenues;
5. Identify the level of services to be produced based on the projected revenue;
6. Show the short- and long-range consequences of reducing or eliminating goods and/or services;
7. Facilitate control over expenditures;
8. Communicate the objectives and expected standards of performance that will be compared with results;
9. Motivate employees to achieve articulated objectives in their individuals units;

10.   Aid in maintaining a monitoring system to assess performance of the various units and provide timely feedback on their progress; and

11.   Assess the impact of goods and services on the target population.

DEVELOPING THE BUDGET

Budgeting is an ongoing and dynamic process that is typically marked by regular phases: (1) planning, needs assessment, and priority setting; (2) preparation, including expenditure forecasting and the development of performance measures; (3) legislative reviews of agency reports and appropriations; (4) the execution of proposed programs; and (5) audits and evaluations of agency expenditures. The budgeting phase takes place in a context that is characterized by "deadlines, reports, hearings, policy reviews, and work experience and is deeply immersed in politics."[10] Figure 9.3 provides a schematic view of the dynamic context of budget making. Five phases in budgeting resource allocation are indicated, each of which will be discussed in this section.

1.   The community (the general public, clients, constituents, and other relevant groups) expresses what it wishes the government or agency to do and not do.

2.   The gatekeepers (These are the people who typically decide what requests will or will not be seen by the policy makers. They can screen in or reject demands made on the system to obtain scarce resources.) receive the reports and compare them with available resources. Basing their conclusions on perceptions and on consultations with policymakers (executive and/or legislative officials), the gatekeepers accept, modify, or reject the requests.

3.   The policymakers review the existing resources and evaluate the power and influence of the participating interest groups. Through a process of bargaining and mutual compromise, policymakers determine the distribution of available resources as a balance between the vote that they are likely to obtain at the next election and what they feel is in the best interest of the public. Nonprofit agencies attempt to obtain the largest amount of resources that the funding agencies can provide and the largest amount of fees that can reasonably be collected from users. The objective is to expand or, at least, survive.

4.   The compromises become the basis for the allocation of resources, resulting in a policy that specifies services,

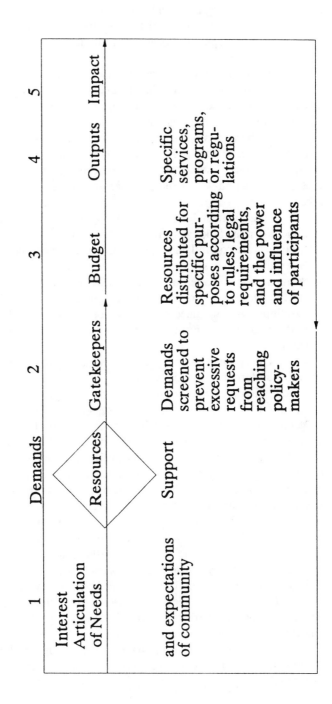

Figure 9.3
Budgeting Resource Allocation

programs, and regulations.

5.   The impact (i.e., the benefits and costs) on the target
       population is assessed and fed back into the system.

Despite the dynamics taking place in the allocation of resources, the emphasis is on maintaining the status quo. Few significant changes or innovations ever occur in budget making.[11] At the national level, neither the chief executive nor Congress has significant discretionary control over yearly expenditures because most of the budget is determined by previous commitments made at the federal level. These include programs such as social security and veterans' benefits. Additionally, there are required payments on outstanding contracts for public works and defense, and interest payments on the national debt.

Since in the budgets of nonprofit agencies there tends to be no ironclad agreement that the funding agencies will continue to support recipient agencies, these budgets are controllable. Once relationships have been established and the incremental budget system has been adopted, however, nonprofit agencies tend to be funded as a matter of policy. Like public sector agencies, recipient nonprofit agencies, especially those funded by United Way, cultivate relationships with volunteers, review committees, clientele, and corporate opinion makers in an effort to gain support toward their claim for a piece of the budget pie.

The approach to budget preparation has not been marked by a high degree of uniformity. Typically, budget projections tend to represent historical priorities. Resource allocation is based less on planning than on control, as noted earlier. If nonprofit and public sector agencies hope to improve their budget decisions, they must find answers to questions like these: What amount of service is needed? What level of service can be produced? What is the desired level of service? How can the available resources be used efficiently to achieve the stated objectives? Can the service be better provided by in-house staff or by contractors? To enhance the results of the answers to these questions, the planning process should precede the budgeting phase.[12]

In initiating budget development, a consideration of factors such as the following should be included in the information base: (1) the analysis of elements that affect public demand; (2) the constraints and limits on fiscal resources; (3) the extent to which federal, state, and other resources are available; (4) the adequacy of the current level of service; (5) the implications of population changes; (6) the political sensitivity of contemplated programs; and (7) the minimum standards of goods and services to be delivered to clientele and constituency.[13]

To aid rational decision-making in the budget-making process, needs assessment, cost projection of services, and priority setting should be considered.

NEEDS ASSESSMENT

Needs assessment is the examination of the aggregation of observed and articulated desires, needs, and expectations of individuals, groups, and the community. Needs may be reflected in each community. Data may be obtained by observing conditions such as poverty and the deterioration of bridges and crime and by evaluating inquiries obtained by direct feedback from clientele and constituents.[14]

To obtain reliable information on current needs, these procedures should be followed. (1) The quality of available data at all levels - federal, state, and local government - should be examined and the criteria for identifying the need should be established. (2) The policy statements of legislative and executive officials, position papers, the census, demographic information available from various planning agencies, departmental files, special studies on the target population, records of public hearings, and surveys conducted by other agencies (public or private) that may provide information regarding like or similar services should be analyzed.[15] This data should then be converted into specific demands for goods and services, suggesting the level and quality of services to be provided.

PRIORITY SETTING

Priority setting is a process by which an agency or entity articulates the functions or programs that are considered most important to the attainment of service objectives to be pursued during a coming fiscal period.[16] Priority setting is critical because of the scarcity of resources and the desire to optimize benefits. The director/manager of each responsibility center is responsible for identifying those programs that have the highest priority. This identification process may result in the shifting of resources among programs to improve an agency's objectives. For example, a district police station that experiences a sharp drop in crime or a hospital trauma center that has a significant decline in patients cannot continue to justify the same level of staffing; personnel should be shifted to other areas where they can be better utilized.

Priority setting is deeply immersed in values, especially in the public and nonprofit sectors, where resource allocation is not based on the profit criterion. Priority setting may be an exceedingly difficult process. The outcome of such a process is greatly influenced by the ability to mobilize power and exercise influence. The allocators determine what individuals, groups or organizations will benefit, when they will benefit, and to what extent. Priority setting is easier when there are generally agreed-upon norms and perceptions of the clients' and constituents' needs.

If economic rationality is a desired objective, the priority setting process can be facilitated when participants in organizations or communities agree in advance to abide by allocations made on the basis of cost-effectiveness and/or a ranking process similar to the one employed in zero base budgeting (ZBB) or a predetermined, objective rating scale. Such a scale could rate the functions of the agency in order of importance (with the numbers one to six representing descending order). Next, each function may be rated numerically in order of importance, as shown in Table 9.4. If equity is the main objective to be maximized in Table 9.4, it is given the highest rating - 1. Similarly, the importance of community development permits it to be rated 1. Maximizing the equity objective while pursuing community development gives a matrix score of 1 (#1 equity rating x #1 community development rating), the highest priority rating possible. On the other hand, the rating of the neighborhood improvement objective as 6 and the rating of the transportation function as 5 provide a total matrix score of 30. When priorities are articulated in public and nonprofit agencies they can be most useful in executive budget making.

BALLOT BOX BUDGETING

The regularized and predictable budget making process described thus far is not the only means for allocating scarce resources in the American federal system. California has shown that direct democracy may play a significant role when easy access to the initiative process is permitted. This process, if used prudently, can aid in promoting public accountability. Alternatively, it can be a very constraining and a disruptive instrument in the allocation of public resources.

Despite a projected deficit of $6.4 billion for fiscal year 1991-1992, public opinion showed that Californians believed their taxes to be too high. It was not until the deficit reached $14.3 billion that public opinion swung in favor (70 percent) of an increase in the state's income taxes. This receptivity to taxes has been rare in California from 1976 to the present. The ability of California's policymakers to resolve the state deficit crisis has been greatly hampered by the emergence of ballot box budgeting. California's easy access to the initiative process has produced many referendums that dictate fiscal policies. Table 9.5 provides a brief review of budgeting initiatives.[17]

Between 1977 and 1989, tax relief measures reduced potential state revenues by $178 billion. Proposition 13 accounts for nearly $120 billion of this amount. Initiatives now obligate approximately 70 percent of the state budget to local governments. No taxes may be passed in the state unless it receives a two-third majority. Additionally, between 1976 and 1992, tax indexing led to $40.1 billion revenue lost to the state while the phase out of inheritance taxes and rent credit cost $6.4 and $2.6 billion, respectively.[18]

Table 9.4

Priority-Setting Matrix

Maximizing Outcomes or Objective	Rating	Government Functions					
		Community Development	Human Resources	Environmental Resources	Health and Safety	Transportation	Legislative and Citizen Participation
	Rating	1	2	3	4	5	6
Equity	1	1	2	3	4	5	6
Economy	2	2	4	6	8	10	12
Standard of Service	3	3	6	9	12	15	18
Service Improvement	4	4	8	12	16	20	24
Service Coordination	5	5	10	15	20	25	30
Neighborhood Improvement	6	6	12	18	24	30	36

Source: Adapted from Barry M. Mundt, Raymond T. Olsen, and Harold I. Steinberg, *Managing Public Resources* (Stamford, Conn.: Peat Marwick International, 1982), p. 33.

Table 9.5

California's Key Constitutional Initiatives

Initiative	Year	Action
Proposition 13	1976	It cuts property taxes by 50 percent. Property tax rates were capped at 1 percent and property values were frozen at 1975-76 levels. Only a 2 percent yearly increase was allowed until the property was sold. At that time a fair market value could be established.
Proposition 4 (known as the Gann limit)	1979	It limited the growth of state expenditure to the increase in California's population and changes in the national inflation rate. Any revenue collected in excess of the limit had to be rebated to the people.
Proposition 98	1988	Forty percent of all discretionary tax revenues were earmarked for public elementary schools and community colleges. Later, the law was amended to permit excess above the limit to go to grades K-14 and not be rebated to the taxpayer.
Proposition 99	1988	A 25 cent per pack tax was imposed on cigarettes to fund antismoking and medical programs. (These expenditures were excluded from the Gann limit.) This action foreclosed state opportunity to increase cigarette taxes in the future. Thus the act allows special interests to dictate state expenditure policies.
Proposition 111	1990	The state gas tax was doubled and truck weight fees were increased and dedicated to transportation. The action recalculated the Gann limit. Spending was "tied to population growth and per capita income, rather than population and inflation."

Source: Adapted from James D. Savage, "California's Structural Deficit Crisis," *Public Budgeting and Finance*, 12, no. 2 (Summer 1992): 89.

THE EXECUTIVE ROLE

The executive role in budget making in the public sector has been influenced by a cultural fear of executive power and a concern for accountability. These influences caused the establishment of a system of checks and balances which led to fragmentation in financial management until the reform movement of the late 1800s. The movement culminated in the introduction of state and local executive budgets (which make the chief executives of these governments directly responsible for preparing budgets, submitting them for approval, and administering the approved budgets). With the passage of the Budget and Accounting Act of 1921, Congress instituted the executive budget at the national level. The act created the Bureau of the Budget, which is now known as the Office of Management and Budget (OMB), to serve as an arm of the chief executive and to assist in preparing the budget. The act gives the chief executive significant coordinating powers.

Further expanding the powers of the chief executive, Congress passed the Employment Act of 1946, which created the Council of Economic Advisors as a direct counselor to the president. The main aim of the council is to assist the president in forecasting and controlling fiscal policies. Under the 1946 Employment Act, the Joint Economic Committee was also established to provide Congress with additional means for examining the premises on which the annual budget is prepared.

Over the past two decades (1970s and the 1980s) many efforts have been made to improve the quality of the information used by the chief executive to make rational decisions. The introduction of the planning, programming, and budgeting system (PPBS) was the first major attempt at all levels of government to introduce analysis as an aid to decision making in the executive branch. This was followed by the introduction of the concept of management by objectives and zero base budgeting (ZBB). Like PPBS, ZBB is aimed at assisting central management to better allocate scarce resources and control their use.

An examination of the attributes and functions of the executive budgets of chief executives at the federal, state, and local levels (as shown in Table 9.6), reveals few divergences. Thus, it would be logical to conclude that the structure and operations of the executive budget at all levels of government are marked more by similarities than by differences.

Though seldom discussed, the physical location of the budget office holds particular symbolic and substantive implications for the allocation and control of available resources. At the federal level, the OMB is located in the executive office building. In some states the executive budget office is located in departments of administration directly responsible to the governor. The state constitution of Missouri places the budget office in the Department of Revenue, but relatively early in this state's history, it was moved to the governor's office, where it remains to this day.

Table 9.6
Chief Executive Comparative Executive Budget Functions and Responsibilities

Attributes/Functions	Federal	State	Local	Nonprofit
Balanced budget requirements	no	yes	yes	yes
Staff is requires to provide information/intelligence for better budget decision making	yes	mostly yes	mostly no	mostly no
Budget is effective coordinating instrument/extension of executive personality	yes	yes	yes	mostly yes
Executive is most visible political official	yes	yes	yes	no
Executive has exclusive power to prepare budget	yes	yes	yes	mostly yes
Executive authority to exercise item veto over approved budget or appropriation including:	no	yes	yes	no
- Allotment powers	yes	mostly yes	no	no
- Executive has problem with career bureaucrats	some	some	minimal	minimal
- Power over program execution	yes	yes	yes	yes
- Budget staff exercises strong management efficiency role	no	yes	yes	no

Local governments have experimented with a number of budget office locations. In some cities it is directly under the authority of the chief executive officer or in a department under the authority of a controller, department of finance, or division of a department of management. In all cases, however, the responsibility for control and decision making resides with the chief executive or, as in metropolitan Toronto, Canada, with an executive committee.

In the nonprofit sector, the executive budget is the norm, although it is not easy to make broad statements about this practice because of the variety of models found. Most often, the executive director of the agency is given executive powers similar to those found in governmental units. He or she exercises those powers under the scrutiny, whether close or minimal, of a finance committee. The interest, expertise, and activism of the committee members and/or the board determine the degree of vigilance.

Where an executive budget is the norm, executive influence over the budget process is pervasive. The chief executive's authority to recommend expenditures and revenues provides a powerful means for establishing the agenda and focusing attention on his or her preferred use for budget resources. Because of the dominance of the chief executive and his or her budget staff over budget matters, the chief executive exercises a monopoly over the information that is released to relevant publics and various participants in the budget-making process. The budget provides the primary tool with which to effect coordination and integration of agency or governmental activities. By means of the central administrative budget, establishment, planning, and management studies, the accounting control and personnel system become closely integrated.

Functions performed by the administrative budget establishment include: (1) establishing policy direction guidelines and service levels, (2) overseeing the preparation of the budget; (3) reviewing, critiquing, adjusting, and approving expenditure reports; (4) developing revenue estimates; (5) conducting economic research studies and salary surveys; (6) presenting proposals before the legislative or review committees or boards (the latter in nonprofit agencies only); (7) overseeing the administration of the budget; and (8) designing and implementing financial performance reports.[19]

The first phase provides the chief executive with an opportunity, via the "call for estimates" and the transmittal letter, to put forth budget policy as specifically as possible. This will include at least the following: (1) a general budget outlook that reviews the economic, social, and other critical factors likely to impact on the agency or the governmental unit; (2) assumptions about revenue from general and other funds, indicating tax rates, and about projections, indicating budget targets; (3) projections of expenditures (especially those from the general fund), indicating "the likely increment and opportunities for program substitution and displacements[20]"; (4) suggested changes and/or modifications in budget procedures; (5) contemplated changes in debt service policy and requirements; and (6) projected capital programs and special programs.

The budget timetable and specific procedures of budget making may differ significantly among units of governmental and nonprofit agencies. All these agencies perform essentially the same functions in developing the budget document.[21]

Hospital-Generalized Budget Process Steps

The following are the steps involved in making a hospital budget:

1. The authorizing board of trustees sets the goals and objectives that will guide the institution during the coming period.
2. The hospital budget committee identifies budget guidelines, which are then approved by the hospital administration. Within this context, the preparation of a number of internal and external factors, such as the following, are considered relevant to planned activities: how economic factors like inflation may affect the budget; statistical assumptions regarding patient days; changes in building requirements; the introduction of new services; the number of procedures that must be followed by the laboratory and major departments, such as radiology; outpatient visits; and proposed government legislation and regulations.
3. Budget packages are distributed to department heads or responsibility centers. They are also given technical assistance in preparing their individual budgets.
4. Departmental hearings are conducted. The budgets of responsibility centers are coordinated and reviewed, summarizing the hearings and promises agreed upon to assist controllers in future monitoring.
5. The budgets are approved and distributed to all department heads and responsibility centers.

The Executive Budget Cycle

Timetables for the completion of particular activities are especially important in public budgeting because designated times are typically established by statute and thus are legally binding. In addition, actions to be completed can have significant implications for resource allocation. For example, economic forecasts and revenue estimates may determine the level of spending within a program or determine whether the program can be undertaken at all. At the federal level, the executive budget cycle timetable is as shown in Table 9.7.

Table 9.7
The Budget Cycle of the Federal Executive

Actions to be Completed	Dates
Develop economic assumptions (by Council of Economic Advisors); review forecasts of international and domestic situations; issue policy guidelines regarding the preparation of materials for review.	March-May
Determine initial planning figures and cost projections for the coming year; compare total proposed outlay estimates with revenue estimates, present fiscal policy; program issues and budget levels of the president.	
Establish general guidelines and agency targets for annual budget; issue internal annual budget estimates. President (through OMB) provides agencies with policy assumptions and budget planning target for each agency.	June
Assist agencies in developing detailed estimates.	July-Sept.
OMB holds hearings to review agency budget requests. Economic assumptions and fiscal policies are reexamined in cooperation with the Council of Economic Advisors and the Treasury Department. Assumptions are discussed with the president and recommendations to the president are made. Agencies are notified and recommendations are revised to reflect the president's decisions.	Sept.-Nov.
Again, review economic and fiscal outlook with the president in cooperation with the Council of Economic Advisors and the Treasury Department. Draft president's budget and transmit recommendations to Congress within 15 days after Congress reconvenes in January.	Dec.-Feb.
With the approved appropriations, the Treasury Department and the General Accounting Office sign appropriation warrants and forward them to agencies.	Aug.-Sept.

THE LEGISLATIVE ROLE

By identifying policy direction and preparing and formally presenting the budget to the legislature or authorizing body, the executive limits and determines the legislative fiscal policy agenda. The budget-making process is essentially the same at the legislative and executive levels of government and nonprofit organizations.

Typically, the presentation of the budget contains a budget overview, namely, including major economic and social assumptions and a summary of major issues. The budget document is presented in a clear and understandable manner. (1) Revenue estimates are broken down and identified by source. (2) Statements of proposed expenditures are detailed. Budget format is designed to set forth the purpose, cost, and expenditure source of each service. (3) Amounts requested by each department or responsibility center and recommended by the chief executive are identified. (4) Finally, narrative statements justifying supporting requests are included.

At the federal and state levels, and to some extent in local governments, department heads are usually present during budget discussions to respond to legislative questions. However, department heads, especially those of local government units, may as a matter of strategy be asked to stay out of sight unless requested to attend. The apparent operating premise is, out of sight, out of mind.

The participation of citizen and interest groups in public hearings is an operating norm at all levels of government. Indeed, most states require local units to hold open hearings on the budget. However, while some local governments encourage citizen participation in budget discussions, many make little effort to build a well-designed system that works, despite the opportunities to build and promote better policies that such a system would offer. If due care is taken in designing and implementing a system of citizen participation, disruptions and delays in proceedings can be minimized.

Until recently, the legislatures at all levels of government were unable to influence and to participate in budget making and fiscal matters to the same extent as the elected chief executives (especially in systems operating on the executive budget model). Because of minimal intelligence gathering and lack of expert staff, members of these bodies have been limited to routine review and oversight. Except in a few states like California, there is no single head to coordinate and lead the legislative staff. Also, in only a few states (and in most local governments), there is no systematic coordination of revenue and spending bills. Typically, revenue and spending measures are parceled out to a number of different subcommittees. The vacuum created by the legislature's fragmented management of fiscal policies has given the chief executive a dominant role in fiscal policy-making. In most units of government, as much as 75 to 85 percent of all budget proposals are initiated by the chief executive or by the executive branch, over which the chief executive exercises control.

At the national level, the Congressional Budget and Impoundment Control Act of 1974 attempted to address the unequal influence exercised by the president vis-à-vis Congress. Until the act's passage, uncertainty and virtual chaos characterized the congressional process. A major feature of the act was the creation of the Congressional Budget Office (CBO) which attempts to add greater rationality to the legislative policy-making process (see Table 9.8).

Prior to this act there was no coordinating committee in the House of Representatives or the Senate that was capable of considering the president's budget as a whole. When the executive budget reached Congress, it was broken up and sent to a number of committees. Budgeting decisions were made without regard to their impact on the general economy. "No systematic procedure existed for resolving conflicts among authorizing, appropriation and tax committees on the basis of conscious congressional decisions related to the national goals and priorities."[22] As can be seen in the congressional budget cycle, the act created budget committees in both the House and the Senate that are responsible for developing priorities.

The CBO is headed by a nonpartisan official who coordinates the congressional budget staff in its functions as a research arm and as an aid to Congress in evaluating the president's executive budget. Congress is thus provided with the means to examine the premises on which the president's budget is based and of making independent projections regarding deficits, employment, and the general state of the economy.

GRAMM-RUDMAN-HOLLINGS (GRH): THE FAILURE OF BUDGETARY POLITICS

Figure 9.3 shows that budgeting is highly immersed in politics. Since politics is the art of the possible, compromise is a normal expectation, especially at the policy-making level. GRH is a testimony to the policymakers' stalemate and their inability to compromise about ways and means to reduce the U.S. deficit. When the normal budgetary decision making process fails to reach agreements on debt reduction, GRH provides an automatic way to achieve the budget reduction objective (specific amounts from identified categories such as defense are cut or sequestered) while moving toward a balanced budget. Despite the legally mandated objective the U.S. national deficit has continued to rise sharply, averaging more than $180 billion yearly.

The political pressure that gave rise to the passage of the GRH was also instrumental in allowing policymakers to keep changing the targets. Some were fearful that large cuts would produce a recession while others have been fearful of the political impact on targeted areas.

Table 9.8
The Congressional Budget Calendar
(Based on the 1974 Budget Act)

Actions to be Completed	Dates
CBO submits first year projection of current spending.	Oct. 1 or soon thereafter
President submits current services budget, indicating projected spending for existing programs.	November 10
Joint Economic Committee provides budget committee with analysis of current services budget.	December 31
President submits his budget.	15th day after Congress meets in January
Budget Committees conduct hearings and commence work on first budget resolution.	Late Jan.-March
All legislative committees submit estimates/reports to the budget committees.	March 15
CBO submits report to budget committees.	April 1
Budget committees report first concurrent resolution.	April 15
Congress completes action on first resolution, providing new budget authority and new spending authority. (Until the resolution is adopted neither the House nor the Senate may consider new budget or spending authority bills, revenue changes, or changes of the debt limit.)	May 15
Congress completes action on first appropriation and concurrent resolution on the budget.	May 15
House Appropriations Committee completes action on all bills.	June 10
Congress completes action on all reconciliation matters.	June 15
Congress completes action on bills and resolutions providing for new budget authority and new spending authority.	7th day after Labor Day
Congress completes second concurrent resolution. Neither the House nor the Senate may thereafter consider any bill, amendment, or conference report that increases budgeting authority amounts or decreases revenues beyond amounts agreed to in the second resolution.	September 15

Congress completes action on reconciliation bill or resolution. Adjournment of Congress takes place only after it completes action on second resolution and reconciliation measure.	September 15
Fiscal year begins.	October 1

The rise in the deficit is a reflection of decreasing revenue resources. It represents a decline in discretionary resources, leaving a smaller piece of the pie to share. The GRH moving target allows the president and Congress to avoid making hard choices - to avoid expressing "their priorities in cutting outlays to meet deficit targets."[23] GRH avoids the "realities of political consensus building between conservative and liberal ideologies that have traditionally traded tax increases and spending cuts to reach agreement."[24] The inability of Congress to follow the 1974 budget process or to meet GRH targets and the continuing political impasse over budgeting decisions led to the passage of Title 13 of the Omnibus Budget Reconciliation Act of 1990.

The Budget Enforcement Act of 1990 (BEA) changed the emphasis in the congressional budget process from controlling the growth of the deficit to limiting spending and puts the federal budget on the road to no-fault budgeting.[25] (See Table 9.9) This will allow the deficit to increase as before, as it now provides for the presidential adjustment of deficit targets at the time of "the budget submission to reflect changed economic or other factors."[26] BEA specifically excluded items (the savings and loan crisis and Gulf War's Operation Desert Shield) from the deficit in 1990. In effect, the act made it unlikely that sequestering will take place as the control factors limiting the deficit (specific target levels) have been greatly reduced by altering its calculation. The act allows the deficit to peak at $327 billion in the 1995 fiscal year. In the revised GRH target without the social security surplus, the deficit was allowed to reach $64 billion and then to decline to $83 billion by the fiscal year 1995.[27]

BEA is notable for the items it excludes, such as the line-item veto, greater recision powers of the president, a biennial budget, and a joint resolution that can be signed by the president.[28]

BEA is a process of reconciliation. It provides a road map for federal deficit reduction for five years. BEA has been "designed to enforce the spending caps and achieve deficit reductions as defined by the act. Because it also amends earlier legislation, complexity is built upon complexity."[29]

Table 9.9

Deficit Reduction: Budget and Enforcement Act of 1990

TIMETABLE

DATE	ACTION
5 days before budget	CBO sequester preview report
1st Monday in February............... (February 4th in 1991)	President submits budget and revises GRH targets
February 15	CBO annual report to Budget Committees
Within 6 weeks of president's budget	Committees submit views and estimates to the
April 1	Budget Committees
April 15	Senate Budget Committee reports budget resolution
	Congress completes budget resolution. If not,
May 15	Chairman of House Budget Committee files
End of previous session to June 30..	302(a) allocations; Ways and Means if free to proceed with pay-as-you-go measures
June 30	Appropriations report last bill
July 15	If an appropriations bill violates caps, OMB
August 10	sequesters 15 days after
August 15	enactment
August 20	House completes action on annual appropriation bills
October 1	President submits mid-session review
10 days after end of session	President's notification on military personnel
15 days after end of session	exemption
	CBO sequester update report
30 days after end of session	OMB sequester update report (with adjustments to caps and GRH targets)
	Fiscal year begins
	CBO final sequester report
	OMB final sequester report (with adjustments to caps and GRH targets)
	GAO compliance report

Source: Richard Doyle and Jerry McCaffery, "The Budget and Enforcement Act of 1990: The Path to No Fault Budgeting," *Public Budgeting and Finance*, Vol. 11 #1 (Spring 1994): 33, (reprinted with permission).

CONCLUDING OBSERVATIONS

This chapter contains an overview of the functions, structures and purposes of modern budgeting. Budgets are multipurpose in that they can be used to achieve accountability/control, political, social, planning, and economic ends. The interplay among the executive, legislative, and relevant interest groups in the budget process is examined. Throughout the chapter the emphasis is on the interplay of theory and practice.

NOTES

1. Jerome McKinney and Lawrence Howard, *Public Administration: Balancing Power and Accountability* (Oak Park, Ill: Moore   Publishing Company, 1979), p. 319.

2. Mark Mills and George Starr, eds., *Readings in Public Finance and Taxation* (New York: MacMillan, 1932), p. 763.

3. Michael J. Boskin and Aaron Wildavsky, eds., *The Federal Budget: Economics and Politics* (New Brunswick, N.J.: Transaction Books, 1982), p. 22.

4. Jerome McKinney, *Understanding ZBB: Promise and Reality* (Chicago, Ill.: Public Policy Press, 1979), p. 2.

5. Charles L. Harper, Curtis McLaughlin, and John W. Bartley, *Financial Systems for Community Health Organizations* (Belmont, Calif.: Lifetime Learning Press, 1982), p. 122.

6. Robert Anthony and Regina Herzlinger, *Management Control in Non-Profit Agencies*, rev. ed. (Homewood, Ill.: Richard D. Urwin and Co., 1980), p. 328.

7. Ibid.

8. In many public and nonprofit agencies, goals are not articulated but rather are implied based on the allocation of the budgeting resources.

9. Harper, McLaughlin, and Bartley, *Financial Systems*, p. 130.

10. McKinney and Howard, *Public Administration*, p. 322.

11. Ibid.

12. Phillip Rosenberg and Wayne Stalling, *An Operating Budget for Small Cities and Other Governmental Units* (Chicago, Ill.: Municipal Finance Officers Association, 1978), p. 40.

13. Lennox L. Moak and Kathryn W. Killian, *A Manual of Techniques for the Preparation, Consideration, Adoption, and Administration of Operating Budgets* (Chicago, Ill.: Municipal Finance Officers Association, 1963), p. 131.

14. Keith A. Neuber, *Needs Assessment: A Model for Community Planning* (Beverly Hills, Calif.: Sage Publications, 1975), p. 10.

15. Barry Mundt, Raymond T. Olsen, and Harold I. Steinberg, *Managing Public Resources* (Stamford, Conn.: Peat Marwick International, 1982), pp. 24-25.

16. United Way, *APPBS Approach to Budgeting Human Service Programs for United Ways* (Alexandria, Va.: United Way of America, 1972), p. 18.

17. James D. Savage, "California's Structural Deficit Crisis," *Public Budgeting and Finance*, 12, no. 2 (Summer 1992): 88-89.

18. Ibid., pp. 87-89.

19. Moak and Killan, *Manual of Techniques*, p. 29.

20. Edward A. Lehan, *Simplified Governmental Budgeting* (Chicago, Ill.: Municipal Finance Officers Association, 1981), p. 62. See also State of Massachusetts, *Approaches to Budget Preparation and Presentation* (Boston, Mass.: Massachusetts Division of Community Services, 1980), p. 23.

21. Hospitals may often break down their budgets differently, developing revenue, expense, operating, and cash budgets, about which there is more in Chapter 11.

22. Committee on Economic Development (CED), *The New Congressional Budget Process and the Economy* (New York: CED, 1975), p. 2.

23. Raphael Thelwell, "Gramm-Rudman-Hollings Four Years Later: A Dangerous Illusion," *Public Administration Review*, March/April 1990, p. 196.

24. Ibid.

25. Richard Doyle and Jerry McCaffery, "The Budget Enforcement Act of 1990: The Path to No Faulty Budgeting" *Public Budgeting and Finance*, 11, no. 1 (Spring 1991): 26.

26. Ibid.

27. Ibid., p. 27.

28. Ibid., p. 37.

29. Naomi Caiden, "Do Politicians Listen to Experts? The Budget and Enforcement Act of 1990 and the Capacity to Budget," *Public Budgeting and Finance*, 11, no. 1 (Spring 1991): 48.

10

Expenditure Forecasting

Because of the many types of expenditures that must be projected in both the public and private sectors, there is no single, all-encompassing approach to their forecast. No exotic mathematical model can be used to project expenditures with a high degree of accuracy. There is considerable evidence to support the view that simple approaches are as effective as the more sophisticated methods.[1]

This chapter examines a number of approaches that are employed in forecasting expenditures. First, traditional approaches used in budget development are examined. Then, expenditure components, standard costs, the least squares method, multiple regression analysis, and controllable and uncontrollable costs are considered.

PROJECTING THE COST OF CURRENT SERVICES

Projecting the cost of existing activities is based on factors typically outside the agency's control, such as population changes, inflation rates, as they affect items such as salaries, wages, benefits, materials, supplies, and contractual services; government mandates; existing staffing levels; discretionary and nondiscretionary expenditures emanating from policy commitments, such as the funding of pension benefits and subsidies; equipment replacement and repair schedules; capital costs, meaning expenses associated with construction, operation, and maintenance; debt amortization; and last, volatile cost centers that are subject to unpredictable cost changes, such as municipal convention centers, which are typically affected by the cycle of the economy. The projections are guided by assumptions and constraints set down by top management (the president, mayor, or manager in the public sector; the board of governors or trustees in the non-profit sector).

The cost projection of current services serves several useful purposes. It provides continuity between present and future cost and promotes the development of a dependable data base from which projections in each responsibility center can easily be made. Finally, it provides a dependable basis on which to evaluate whether future services should be improved, expanded, or reduced.

APPROACHES TO BUDGET DEVELOPMENT: SOME GENERAL GUIDELINES

Moak and Killian have suggested several orientations that may be used as general guidelines in budget development.[2] The methods may be used singly or in combination.

Open-Ended Budget

Managers who are given no explicit guidelines regarding budget amounts are allowed to submit whatever amounts they consider necessary to run the optimum program for the agency.

Fixed-Ceiling Budget

Unlike the open-ended budget, the fixed-ceiling budget (akin to the target base budget which is discussed further in Chapter 14) is constrained by a dollar amount that is specifically stated for each department prior to the preparation of the budget. Thus, the budget may fall below the fixed ceiling, but it may not exceed it.

Work Measurement and Unit Costing

This approach requires that a measuring criterion be established to determine the number of products or service units to be generated. Based on the number of products or service units desired, the cost per unit can be determined and the budget projected.

Increase versus Decrease Analysis

This method is closely related to the popular incremental approach to budgeting. Cost projections are made by identifying the costs to be increased or decreased in comparison with the previous year's costs. The items so determined are analyzed and projected.

Priority Listings

This approach, especially the ranking phase, is akin to the zero base budgeting (ZBB) approach (discussed in Chapter 15), and requests that projects be ranked in order of priority.

Shared Management Method

This approach encourages top and bottom managers in the middle and lower levels to share information and perceptions about the factors that are likely to affect expenditure projections.[3] The shared approach allows top management to contribute its overall perception of the organization, while middle- and lower-level managers in, for example, a health-care institution contribute insight acquired through their greater sensitivity toward physicians' needs, desires, and priorities relating to such activities as laboratory tests, changes in radiological procedures, and the physical condition of facilities. Additionally, middle- and lower-level managers will typically have knowledge about top management's short- and long-range plans and strategies, especially if the management style in the organization encourages some degree of management involvement in the shared decision-making system. Shared decision making requires that both top and operating managers study and exchange their knowledge of the following key resources:

1. Historical data and trends relating to inpatient and outpatient days;
2. Departmental goals and strategies;
3. Governmental and third-party decisions; for example, changes in federal law that alter the age requirement for medicare eligibility, impacting on the number of allowable inpatient days and causing changes in the reimbursement method;
4. Outside competition; for example, the establishment of neighboring health care facilities (hospitals, health maintenance organizations, and clinics); and
5. Other known facts or rumors.[4]

Item-by-Item Control

Like the priority-setting method, this approach contains come of the attributes of ZBB, particularly as it relates to the emphasis on questioning and justifying the necessity and desirability of each item. However, the item-by-item control method is more in line with the line-item/object budget focus.

Alternative Proposals

Attributes of the ZBB system are very evident in this approach. Emphasis is put on the basis budget (indicative of the ZBB minimum-level practice, as discussed in Chapter 15) and on the analysis of the consequences of pursuing each alternative (the ZBB consequences of not undertaking a level of service).

Historical Analysis

Requests for nonpersonal service items are evaluated in terms of past experience and current trends.

Factorial Estimating

Making budget projections by this method involves virtually no discretion or judgment. Program units are clearly defined and tables of organization and equipment are made up, providing a basis from which future requirements can be estimated.

Marginal Productivity Analysis

This approach emphasizes the optimal use of scarce resources. The application of this method shows that successive resource increments yield increasing benefits only up to a point. Beyond this point, each increment produces successively smaller (marginal) benefits or satisfactions, demonstrating that unlimited income is an inadequate reason for allowing unlimited expenditure on a large number of programs. The greatest total utility or satisfaction is realized when the application of resources is limited to a smaller number of uses (programs). Allocation of resources to alternative uses should be continued until the last additional increment of expenditure yields the same amount of additional satisfaction. The principle of marginal rule yields the following conclusions:

(1) Given available resources, the magnitude or scale of an activity should be expanded as long as its net marginal yield is positive, and up to the point where its net marginal yield is zero. (2) When resource constraint does not permit an activity to be expanded to the zero-yield point, the activity should be expanded to the point where its marginal yield is equal to the marginal yield of the alternative.

An application of the marginal rule principle may be demonstrated in the case of police assignments. Assume that a study of the records of two police department districts reveals the data shown in Tables 10.1 and 10.2. Assume additionally that a citation represents a reasonable output benefit (surrogate). A total of nine officers is to be assigned to Districts X and Y. Applying the marginal rule principle, District X would receive four officers and District Y five officers. Note that the five officers of District Y would yield a marginal benefit of 8, while District X would yield a marginal benefit of 6. Therefore, we assign five officers to District Y and four to District X, basing our decision on the marginal rule principle.

Applying Cost-Benefit Criteria

This approach, though not widely used, has potential because in the typical social service agency, it is very difficult to identify any single factor that may be used as the criterion for making program selection. Since selection decisions must be made, a basis for making them while maintaining a degree of uniformity among decision makers is therefore required.

The establishment of decision rules or selection criteria can be most helpful. Before the selection basis can be determined, the costs and benefits relevant to the programs must be estimated. An identification of the costs and benefits permits the display of data relating to each program, as shown in Table 10.3, which depicts, program alternatives, estimated costs, estimated benefits, the benefit-cost ratio, the decision rationale, and selection constraints for each decision. Given the constraints, alternative A is eliminated because it does not meet the minimum benefit constraint, and alternative C is accepted because it meets all the constraint factors.

The development and application of a particular criterion must depend on each individual situation, but once a decision rule system has been established, as shown in Table 10.3, it provides a useful method that permits a degree of decentralized budget making and decisions while maintaining a measure of central control.

Table 10.1
Marginal Cost Analysis - Police District "X"

Number of Officers Assigned	Total Citations	Average Citations	Marginal Citations
0	0	--	--
1	15	15	15
2	40	20	25
3	54	18	14
4	60	15	6
5	60	12	0
6	54	12	-6
7	49	9	-5

Table 10.2
Marginal Cost Analysis - Police District "Y"

Number of Officers Assigned	Total Citations	Average Citations	Marginal Citations
0	0	--	--
1	12	12	12
2	26	13	14
3	39	13	13
4	48	12	9
5	56	11.2	8
6	60	10	2

Source: Adapted from James Snyder, *Fiscal Management and Planning in Local Government* (Lexington, Mass.: Lexington Books, 1977), p. 245.

Table 10.3

Program: Benefit-Cost Estimates

Alternative	Estimated Cost	Estimated Benefits	Benefit-Cost Ratio	Decision Rationale
A	$100,000	$150,000	1.50	Eliminated due to minimum benefit constraints
B	$250,000	$225,000	.90	Does not meet minimum efficiency constraints
C	$295,000	$475,000	1.61	Meets benefit and efficiency constraints
D	$295,000	$310,000	1.05	Does not meet efficiency constraints
E	$125,000	$190,000	1.52	Meets minimum cost constraint and benefit constraints
F	$340,000	$510,000	1.50	Exceeds maximum cost
G	$125,000	$175,000	1.40	Does not meet benefit or efficiency
H	$299,000	$511,000	1.70	Provides maximum benefit and meets efficiency constraints
I	$280,000	$490,000	1.75	Provides maximum efficiency and meets other constraints

Source: Adapted from James Snyder, *Fiscal Management and Planning in Local Government* (Lexington, Mass.: Lexington Books, 1977), p. 245.

Constraints: Maximum budget = $300,000;
  Minimum benefit must be at least as great as program (E);
  Minimum efficiency must be greater than program (A).

EXPENDITURE: ANALYSIS OF MAJOR COMPONENTS

Personnel Services

These are the most important costs in public and not-for-profit organizations, amounting to more than 90 percent in some agencies. Close consideration must therefore be given to this input. Estimates of personnel services typically are based on one or more of the following: (1) experience in prior years; (2) workload trends; (3) staffing patterns, as shown on the current organizational chart; and (4) guesstimates.[5]

Additional factors to be considered in estimating the cost of personnel services include: (1) departmental staffing tables (an assessment of the tasks, functions, and duties of the personnel in each unit or responsibility center); (2) workload trends; (3) classification plans (defining position duties with the aim of reclassifying and/or allocating the duties to existing or new positions in the classification plan, in cooperation with the central personnel unit and with the appropriate operating line official); (4) estimates of salary savings; (5) use of overtime and premium time; (6) management studies (conducted to coincide with the budget hearings to provide information that will assist in evaluating personnel requests); (7) sick leave and annual leave; (8) quality of the work force; and (9) impact of new capital facilities.[6]

While staffing tables are confined to larger organizations, workload data are quite useful in smaller organizations because of the close relationship between the workload and the personnel needed for a particular job. Other factors that impact upon workload trends are: (1) new policies or changes in existing ones; (2) commitments to program changes; (3) workload consolidation; and (4) changes in systems or procedures.

Salary Savings

For several reasons the budgeted and the actual salary figures seldom coincide. Examples of reasons are vacations, vacant positions, and time lags in hiring for approved positions. This lack of coincidence has led to the common practice of adjusting the salary amounts downward at periodic intervals. The experience of prior years is the major determining factor in calculating the current percentage of gross and unused personnel services, adjusted for any known changes.

Overtime and Premium Time

A hallmark of effective management is the efficient use of human resource components. "Few operations move in such measured cadence that management can avoid some non-productive time or can avoid the necessity for overtime to help meet peaks in workload."[7] Many view overtime as an evil to be avoided. However, overtime has long been associated with well-managed operations. The problem is determining how to keep it in proper proportion and under control.

Contractual Services

The purchase of personnel services has become increasingly important in public and not-for-profit agencies. Some of the reasons why services are purchased are summarized by the following objectives: (1) to minimize costs; (2) to obtain task specialization; (3) to control the growth of permanent staff; and (4) to lessen the pressures brought on by seasonal and unplanned increases in workload.

Materials, Supplies, and Equipment

Efficient management of an agency's materials, supplies, and equipment requires that acquisition, maintenance, and control systems be instituted that facilitate achievement of the organization's purpose. Several key factors should be considered in assessing an agency's materials and supply needs: (1) existing inventory and agency policies in relation to current conditions; (2) price levels; and (3) changing patterns in the use of materials and material requirements in the light of changing rules and methods aimed at producing the best results. Budgeting for equipment from operating funds is done primarily for equipment replacement; however, some portion of the annual equipment budget for many departments represents a net increase in equipment inventory. These two aspects should be considered separately at all stages of the budget process. Of course, the line of demarcation becomes obscure when the replacement item is a substantial improvement over the item being replaced.[8]

The following should be established when the type, quantity, and quality of equipment necessary to achieve an agency's objectives need to be determined: (1) equipment replacement schedules, along with a dependable inventory system that includes the following information: (a) description and quantity of equipment on hand, (b) purchase data, (c) location of equipment, (d) condition in terns of number of operating hours and maintenance costs, (e) life expectancy, and (f) classification and code number.

Finally, the most efficient equipment replacement practices can be best achieved by clear policy development. Such policies should consider: (1) definition of the work to be performed, (i.e., planned maintenance schedules); (2) permanent inventory and service records; and (3) inspection procedures to ensure and validate that an item definitely needs to be replaced.

EXPENDITURE FORECASTING USING STANDARD COSTS

It is generally agreed that the critical category in expenditure forecasting is personnel service costs because this category is the largest and most frequently affected by changes in such items as salary, fringe benefits, and authorized versus actual levels of staffing.[9] Since each personnel position is assigned an identification number, all cost data can be used to control personnel service costs, determine seniority pay, and permit the development of a longevity profile. The latter can be used to "tailor seniority pay as an incentive to minimize turnover to reduce salary costs by granting increases to groups that are projected to turn over frequently."[10]

Position can be used as the centerpiece for accountability information on all related personnel costs, providing a high degree of versatility, and the data can be organized to serve a number of objectives. Unlike the traditional line-item categories (travel, material, and personnel costs), which conceal information about specific kinds of costs that are important to management decision making, the position technique permits identification of any costs that are of interest. Examples of such costs are: costs that vary directly in proportion to the volume of products or services produced, such as tons of concrete needed to build a street; semivariable costs; costs that vary, but not directly, in proportion to the volume or level of activity, such as the cost of maintaining equipment that requires varying amounts of periodic upkeep in quantities disproportionate to the volume or number of service units produced by the equipment; and fixed costs - which stay the same regardless of the volume or activity level, such as depreciation expenditures. Once cost has been identified and separated out, a standard cost system (one that determines the most desirable cost of completing an activity, given normal conditions) can be developed and from this system, a budget projection can be made.

Standard costs projections may be developed as shown in Table 10.4. Assume that a police department wishes to create three or more new beats. One police vehicle is required for every three officers or any portion thereof, at a cost of $10,500 plus $2,000 a year for maintenance. Additionally, the instruction fee per officer is $19,610. Up to 40 new officers can be trained for the fixed cost of $36,000. A beat consists of 24 hours a day for seven days a week, and six officers are required for each beat. The component costs projection is shown in Table 10.4.

Table 10.4
Calculating Variable Costs

Personal Service:		
Salary	$12,000	
Cost of Living	2,200	
Hospitalization	1,800	
Pension Contribution	2,300	18,300
Other Expenses:		
Supplies	400	
Uniforms	350	
Physical Examination	250	
Administration	300	1,300
Total		$19,610

Type of Cost	Units		Standard Cost Per Unit		
Variable	6 Officers	x	19,610	=	$117,660
Semivariable	2 Cruisers	x	12,500	=	25,000
Fixed	Classroom Instruction		36,000	=	36,000
			Total		$178,660
Three Beats Required:					
	12 Officers	x	19,610	=	$235,320
Variable	4 Cruisers	x	12,500	=	50,000
Semivariable	Classroom Instruction		36,000	=	36,000
Fixed					
			Total		$321,320

The standard costs approach offers much potential and can be used to effect service reduction or expansion. If care is taken in projecting individual items, it provides reliable projections with greater ease than other methods. "Additionally, if elements of budget preparation are decentralized," this approach allows the central budget staff to quickly check the expense estimates developed by the operating units.[11] Perhaps the greatest asset of this standard approach is that it enables management to change plans quickly in response to altered situations which often occur, especially in local government.[12]

Calculating the Standard Costs Requirement for a Laundry

The objective of creating any standard is to make it useful to those for whom it is intended. Consequently, it is important that the standard be accepted by the users. The participation of the potential users in the design and development of a standard is, therefore, a crucial factor that should not be ignored. By participating in the design and development process, the future users are unconsciously selling themselves on the acceptability of the standard.

In determining staffing requirements, managers must contend with both full-time and part-time employees. Additionally, employees never work at 100 percent capacity. Part-time and full-time employees can be converted into full-time equivalent (FTE) employees (one FTE equals 2,080 work hours per year). However, since employees cannot be divided, the employee staffing patterns must be determined in a step-variable or a production range, as shown in Figure 10.1.

The calculation of the normal annual hours of the step-variable range, in an example assuming a laundry worker who averages 90,000 pounds of laundry a year, is as follows:[13]

a.	Paid hours per week	40
b.	Weeks per year	52
c.	Annual paid hours (a x b)	2,080
d.	Less benefit hours:	
	10 holidays x 8 hours	80
	20 vacation days x 8 hours	160
	7 sick days x 8 hours	56
	Total benefit hours	296
e.	Normal annual work hours	1,784

The hourly production standard for the average employee can be determined in the following manner:

$$\frac{\text{Total annual units per employee}}{\text{Total normal work hours per employee}} = \text{standard per work hour} = \frac{90,000}{1,784} = 50.45 \text{ pounds per work hour}$$

The production standard calculation may be summarized as follows:

Figure 10.1

Weekly Staffing: Laundry Department

Pounds of Laundry
Processed

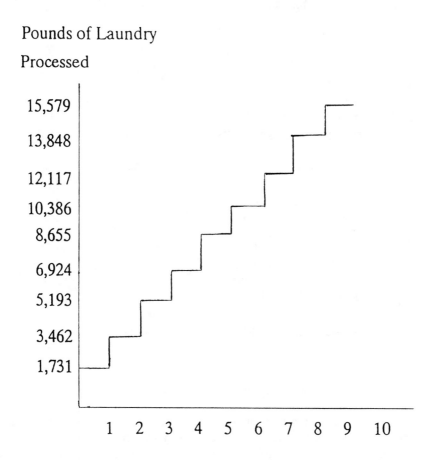

Description	Yearly Standards	Weekly Standards
Pounds of laundry	90,000	1,731
Total Weeks	52	1
Actual hours worked	1,784	34.31
Benefits allowed	296	5.69
Paid Hours	2,080	40.00

Applying the data indicated above, we can convert paid hours into FTEs, as shown in Table 10.5. Once standard rates are determined, calculation of the budget becomes a simple matter, as shown in Table 10.6.

Table 10.5
Weekly Laundry-Staffing Workload

Pounds of Laundry Processed	Actual Work Requirements	Paid Hours Requirements	FTE Requirement
1,731	34.31	40	1
3,462	68.62	80	2
5,193	102.93	120	3
6,924	137.24	160	4
8,655	171.55	200	5
10,386	205.86	240	6
12,117	240.17	280	7
13,848	274.48	320	8
15,579	308.79	360	9

Least Squares Method (Simple Regression)

This is the most commonly used mathematical method for forecasting expenditure level or volume. The method is based on the assumption that if a straight line is fitted to time series data or to a graph, it produces a trend line that can be used to project future years' volume.

Hamburg has indicated that the least squares method permits a line to be drawn through a series of plotted points in such a way that the sum of the squares of the deviations from the observed actual points above and below the

Table 10.6
Projecting Dietary Budget Using Patient Days and
Standard Rates, Bright Memorial Hospital

Cost Component	Standardized Rates	Computation	Budget*
Inpatient days	NA**	NA	$ 95,000
Patient meals served	3.25 patient meals served per patient day	Patient days x standard = meals served 95,000 x 3.25	$ 308,750
Person-hours paid	1.65 patient meals served per person-hour paid	Patient meals served/ standard = person-hours paid 308,750/$1.65	$ 187,121
Salary expense	$3.15 average hourly rate	Person-hours paid x standard = salary expense 187,121 x $3.15	$ 589,431
Food expense	$1.15 per patient meal served	Patient meals served x standard paid expense 308,750 x $1.15	$ 355,063
Other nonsalary expense	$.30 per patient meal served	Patient meals served x standard = other nonsalary expenses 308,750 x $.30	$ 92,625
Total expense	$3.35 per patient	Patient meals served x standard = total expenses 308,750 x $3.35	$1,034,313

*Numbers are rounded to the nearest dollar.
**NA equals not applicable.

trend line is at a minimum.[14] Thus, when the straight line is fitted to a set of data, the least squares method provides the "best fit" because the squared deviation is less than it would be for any other possible straight line (see Table 10.7).

Figure 10.2 uses a solid line to show the actual tons of garbage collected and an unbroken straight line to show the least squares trend. Examination of the graph reveals that the further the forecast extends beyond the middle year, the less accurate the trend becomes. Figure 10.2 and Table 10.7 illustrate the least squares fit to a progressive or advancing trend.

The least squares method is based on historical data, and it simply projects the trend line according to the available information. Attention is not given to other factors or variables, such as holidays, weather conditions, and vacations. Weaknesses such as these must be compensated for in each individual situation by the manager's experience and judgment. Finally, the annual forecasts must be broken down to reflect monthly variations and seasonal trends as needed by each organization.

Figure 10.2
Fitting a Trend Line to a Progressive Trend
Using the Least Squares Method

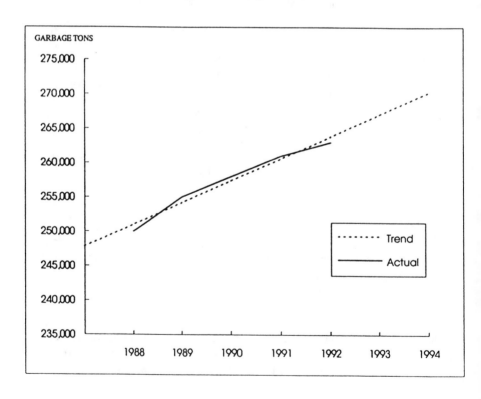

MULTIPLE REGRESSION ANALYSIS

Many of the problems associated with the least squares method (most of which are caused by the use of only one variable), may be overcome by the more sophisticated method of multiple regression analysis. Many variables that are likely to have an impact on future volume can be included in this method. A projection of tons of garbage, for example, might include time series data such as the number of garbage trucks, the condition and age of each truck, the number of garbage collectors, the weather conditions during collections, the population density served, and the economic and educational background of the population served.

The multiple regression analysis method holds much potential for sophisticated analysis, but a thorough examination of it is beyond the scope of this book. Moreover, it cannot be overstressed that the objective of forecasting is not sophistication but rather the ability to make accurate projections based on costs, benefits, political factors, and other constraints.

CONTROLLABLE AND NONCONTROLLABLE COSTS

For both program management and budget forecasting there must be a clear understanding of the specific costs that can be controlled and the specific times for controlling them. A controllable cost is one that can be restrained or changed by a responsibility center head. Ultimately, all costs are controllable in a relative sense at some level of the organization where the specific authority to do so resides. Since we cannot directly affect uncontrollable costs, the discussion will focus only on the controllable components.

Controllable and uncontrollable costs provide varying degrees of restraints and freedom of choice. Uncontrollable cost typically defines what the organization must do and cannot do.[15] These restraints and degrees of freedom emanate from statutes, regulations, federal, state, and local laws, funders' requirements, union contracts, and professional ethics.

Usually, controllable costs provide the greater leeway to exercise discretionary decision making. Among the factors that constrain controllable cost decisions are:

- agency goals and policies;
- program objectives;
- accountability and evaluation requirements;
- sound fiscal procedures;
- local situations: similar agencies and competition; and
- professional practices.[16]

Table 10.7
Projection: Garbage Expenditure
Progressive or Advancing Trend

Year	Tons of Garbage
1988	250,000
1989	255,000
1990	258,000
1991	261,000
1992	263,000

Year	Actual tons of Garbage	Time Deviation of Each Year From Middle Year	Square of X Deviation		Trend Ordinates (Expected Y Value)
X	Y	X	X^2	XY	Y
1988	250,000	-2	4	-500,000	251,000
1989	255,000	-1	1	-255,000	254,000
1990	258.000	0	0	-0-	257,400
1991	261,000	+1	1	261,000	260,000
1992	263,000	+2	4	526,000	263,000
Total	1,287,000	0	10	32,000	
Average	257,000				

Sum of XY divided by sum of X^2:

Let XY $= +32,000$

$\quad$ X $\quad = 10$

$$= \frac{32,000}{10} = 3,200 \ \textit{annual} \ \ \textit{increment}$$

The midpoint year, 1990, equals Q, with the average of 257,400 and annual increments of 3,200. Thus, to determine the trend ordinates, use the following method.

Year		
1988	257,400 + (3,200 x -2)	= 251,000
1989	257,400 + (3,200 x -1)	= 254,200
1990	257,400 + (-0-)	= 257,400
1991	257,400 + (3,200 x 1)	= 260,600
1992	257,400 + (3,200 x +2)	= 263,800
1993	257,400 + (3,200 x +3)	= 267,000
1994	257,400 + (3,200 x +4)	= 270,200

Controllable costs also offer opportunities to ameliorate restrictive factors. Discretionary decisions may be used to enhance program objectives and improve efficiency, working conditions, and staff and community relations.

Before cost projections are made, it may be helpful to identify all line-item costs in terms of three categories:

- fully controllable;
- partially controllable; and
- fully uncontrollable.

Once these identifications have been made, a strategy for influencing the cost may be devised.[17]

CONCLUDING OBSERVATIONS

There is no one best way to project the expenditures of public and other not-for-profit organizations. To date, the sophisticated quantitative methods that have been devised to project expenditures have not been notably more successful than the manual, incremental, and piecemeal approaches that are still in wide use. A major reason for this concerns political realities to which budget decision makers must give due cognizance.

If politics could be excluded from the expenditure equation, the calculation for each service unit would be a simple matter: service unit output measure times unit variable costs plus service fixed costs equals forecasted dollar amounts. Finally, in public and other not-for-profit agencies understanding of controllable costs is an important input in making cost projections.

NOTES

1. Charles Harper, Curtis P. McLaughlin, and John W. Bartley, *Financial Systems for Community Health Organizations* (Belmont, Calif.: Life Learning Publications, 1981), p. 131.

2. Lennox L. Moak and Kathryn W. Killian, *A Manual of Techniques for the Preparation, Consideration, Adoption and Administration of Operating Budgets* (Chicago, Ill.: Municipal Finance Officers Association, 1963), pp. 128-29.

3. Allen G. Herkimer, Jr., *Understanding Hospital Management* (Germantown, Md.: Aspen Systems Corp., 1978), p. 112.

4. Frank Maple, *Shared Decision Making* (Beverly Hills, Calif.: Sage Publications, 1982), ch. 4.

5. Lennox and Moak, *Manual of Techniques*, p. 134.

6. Ibid.

7. Ibid., p. 135.

8. Ibid., p. 142.

9. Robert M. Cramer, "Local Government Expenditure Forecasting," *Governmental Finance*, (November 1978): 4.

10. Ibid.

11. Ibid., p. 7.

12. Ibid.

13. Herkimer, *Understanding Hospital Management*, p. 100.

14. Morris Hamburg, *Statistical Analysis for Decision Making*, 2nd ed. (New York: Harcourt Brace Jovanovich, 1977), p. 368.

15. Robert D. Vinter and Rhea K. Kish, *Budgeting for Not-for-Profit Organizations* (New York: Free Press, 1984), p. 173.

16. Ibid., p. 175.

17. Ibid.

11

Budgeting as a Management Tool

The history of modern budgeting has been marked by a keen desire on the part of management to tightly control the expenditure of resources. In the private sector, the control orientation was once marked by emphasis on financial accounting (concerned primarily with preparing and reporting financial information to various groups, including investors/stockholders and creditors, outside the agency). This contrasts with the more recent emphasis on management accounting, which is aimed at providing information that is useful for internal management decision making.

In public and other not-for-profit agencies, the control orientation emphasizes compliance with legislative and administrative mandates and with the mandates and regulations of other oversight bodies. The widely used line-item budget was developed to meet the control need. The emphasis in this type of budget is on accountability in the narrow sense. Attention is focused on items like travel, supplies, and personnel expenditures. The major objective is to prevent allocated funds from being stolen or expended for unauthorized purposes. Though the control orientation is still important in public and other not-for-profit agencies, the demand for the better use of scarce resources has forced these agencies to seek more innovative approaches to the conservation of available resources. Al Gore's national report on performance review in government echoes the view that public agencies must go beyond present efforts because government can work better for less costs.[1] The Government Accounting Standards Board (GASB) has indicated its desire to press for greater use of performance measurements in reporting government results.[2]

This chapter emphasizes ways in which the management decision making role can be enhanced in allocating and managing scarce resources in the public and other not-for-profit agencies.

DEVELOPING PERFORMANCE MEASURES

The development of performance measures (see Figure 11.1) is essential before monitoring can be established as a basis for the effective evaluation of program execution. The development of performance measures is dependent on what the controllers (those in authority, whether individuals or groups) view as important or useful in assessing the implied or articulated objectives of the budget. For example, in most budgets, goals and objectives are seldom articulated, and even when they are articulated, they often remain unclear. When a budget identifies funds for a particular organizational or responsibility center and makes allotments for supplies, travel, repairs, and utilities, the implied objective is to control the amount of money to be spent on each. This control orientation is known as *dollar accountability*.

Once the goals and objectives have been established, the development of performance measures is the next logical step in determining how well the goals and objectives have been articulated. This facilitates the formulation and design of performance measures.

Performance measurement implies an evaluation of the possible consequences of directing resources to one use rather than another. It promotes effective resource allocation because it allows decision makers to predict what different uses of resources are likely to achieve. For example, the achievement of a welfare agency's goal to remove unemployed fathers from welfare dependency and the achievement of a health care agency's goal to reduce the incidence of lead poisoning among children can be measured using information showing the welfare agency's costs and its success rate in removing fathers from welfare dependency versus the health care agency's costs and success rate in reducing the number of children hospitalized and/or the mortality rate because of lead poisoning. Policymakers are thus provided with a rational basis on which to make decisions. Performance measurement can be used to promote the improvement of operations and output, to develop and control budgets, and to effect individual and organizational accountability. There are several general types of performance measures. The most common include need or demand measures, workload measures, efficiency/productivity measures, and effectiveness measures. The attributes of these performance measures are shown in Figure 11.2.

Needs are quantifiable conditions or recognizable problems that require attention and action if the public's welfare is to be maximally served.

Demand measures are articulated or implied recognition of the need for a given public good or service. This measure indicates the scope and magnitude of a problem. Examples of demand measures include: number of restaurant inspections required, number of citations and arrests to be made, number of patient days, number of people to be served, number of manuscripts to be

Figure 11.1
Linkage among Performance Measures

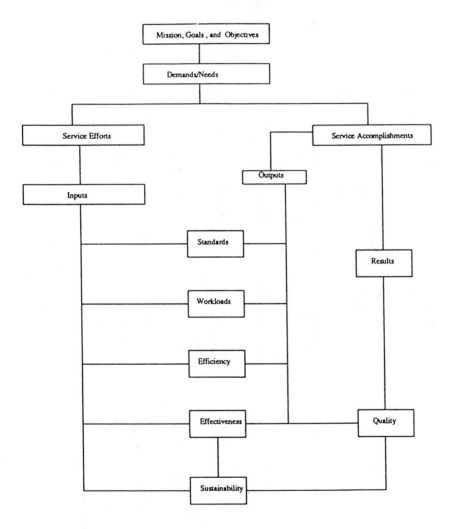

Figure 11.2
Attributes of Performance Measurements

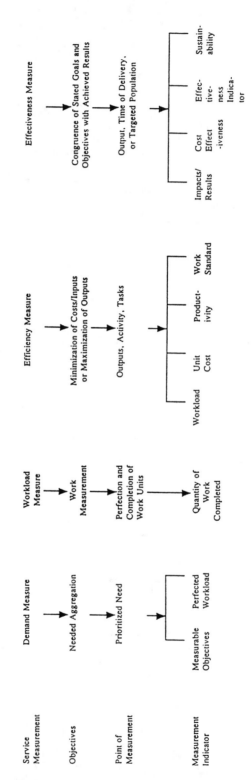

Source: Some ideas are drawn from Alan Walter Steiss, *Management Control in Government* (Lexington: Mass.: Lexington Books, 1982), p. 221.

submitted for publication, number of school children in need of inoculation against childhood communicable diseases, and number of burglaries in residential districts. Demand measures provide responsible officials with an important aid in understanding why particular services are needed.

Workload measures can easily be developed from demand measures. While demand measures identify what needs to be done, workload measures indicate the amount of work to be performed or actually executed on a given activity for a specific period of time. Based on the required workload, resources needed to realize the activity can be determined. Workload measures are the most widely used performance indicators in public and other not-for-profit agencies because they are easily quantifiable and readily understood by the public and by service recipients.

In normal operations planning, workload measures are used to project staffing requirements, develop plans, prepare budgets, and "establish work schedules and measure and evaluate operational output and efficiency."[3] Workload measures can assist management by showing trends in work performance from one time period to the next. For example, take the night patrol activity of a police department. Knowing the number of hours spent on patrol from period to period provides a basis for ascertaining and monitoring the amount to work being done by particular patrol teams. Moreover, the work performed can be compared with standard hours to determine what unit amount of time each officer or team needs to prepare standard budgets and work schedules.

Workload measures are operations indicators that typically provide little qualitative information.[4] They are often nonfinancial expressions of products or services produced. Examples include miles of street built in a given period, number of automobile licenses issued, number of welfare recipients visited, number of garbage pickups made, and number of examinations administered. An operation indicator may be expressed in financial terms, such as the amount of federal assistance to minority business programs, including grants, loans, and gratuities, from $X in 1996 to $X in 1997. Workload measures are not very useful in determining to what extent stated needs are being met. However, they are often used because they are simple and easy to understand.

Efficiency measures define the relationship between resources (money, personnel, materials, and capital) and outputs. The concept suggests the organization of resources for the purpose of carrying out a program, activity, or function at minimal cost.

When the maximum possible output is produced with the given supply of resources, technical efficiency is obtained and any reduction in input would reduce the volume of the output. A second kind of efficiency is referred to as allocative efficiency, meaning that "the cost of any given output is minimized by combining inputs in such a way that one input cannot be substituted for another without raising the costs."[5]

Once an agency has reached its limit, or output frontier in the use of its input resources, no additional outputs can be produced as efficiency is already at 100 percent level. Any attempts to add inputs would generate lesser amounts of output as the technical efficiency level would be breached. In view of this reality, management should keep two dimensions of efficiency in mind: (1) minimizing inputs to produce greater quantity of output (input efficiency) and (2) maximizing output with a given level of inputs. The output efficiency measure is a comparison of actual or achieved output with expected or standard output based on a given set of inputs. Similarly, input efficiency is a comparison of expected or standard inputs with actual inputs, given a specific output.[6]

Efficiency measures indicate the amount of service output in comparison with the input required to produce it. They provide managers with insight on how allocated resources are being used. For example, the number of inspection hours per health inspector, the number of nursing staff hours (inputs) per patient, and the number of patrol hours per patrol officer indicates how much time these personnel are spending on administrative assignments or duties other than their main tasks.

A major problem in the use of efficiency measures is that they are often considered interchangeable with workload measures. Thus, it is not uncommon to find that workload measures are used to justify budget requests. The additional brief descriptions of types of efficiency measures that follow may aid in understanding how they are applied.[7]   (1) The efficiency measure most widely used in public and other not-for-profit agencies is the *input-output ratio*, which permits the use of workload as a unit of output - for example, the number of tons of garbage collected per employee. (2) The *output-input ratio* (emphasizing effectiveness), though helpful, is seldom used. This indicator not only reports the cost of producing a product or delivering a service, it also tells whether the product or service is acceptable or satisfactory. For example, it is not enough to arrest suspected burglars; it is also important to know the percentage of burglars that are convicted. (3) The *equipment and personnel utilization ratio* shows the extent to which an important resource is in service. Typically, this ratio shows a resource's available hours versus the hours it is actually in use or the percentage of time it is utilized. (4) The *relative change measure* permits the tracking of the percentage of increase or decrease in productivity from one period to another or from a selected base period (usually given a value of 100), providing a measurement of relative rather than absolute change. For example, suppose 3,000 potholes were patched in the base year and 3,500 in the succeeding year. This gives a productivity index of 3,500 divided by 3,000, or 116.67 percent. Assuming that there was no change in resource inputs during the base period and the succeeding years, the change reflects a 16.67 percent increase in productivity. (5) Input efficiency (in which one input, such as cost of labor, is compared to total staff hours) is used widely, especially in public and other not-for-profit agencies that have a large personnel service cost. For example, the input efficiency ratio for a mental health/mental retardation program would be total costs divided by total staff hours compared to a standard.

Effectiveness measures show the degree to which program objectives have been achieved in terms of quality. Effectiveness indicates the congruence between legislative intent or policy objectives and the actual achievement of the program or function designed to achieve them. The measurement of effectiveness include the concepts of adequacy (how well the identified needs are met) and responsiveness (how the services are provided and whether they are convenient and timely). Effectiveness measures are the most critical factors in program evaluation and cost-benefit analysis. Their objective is to measure directly the benefits or service delivery to the target population. Examples are the percentage of reduction in air pollution following a new enforcement program; the degree to which the rate of arrest of individuals enrolled in a criminal justice rehabilitation program has decreased; the average amount of time and the minimum number of errors involved in operating a computer system; and the average police response time to emergency calls.

Effectiveness measures have a number of functional uses: (1) program planning (i.e., defining the intended results of a given use of resources); (2) defining management operation (i.e., showing to what degree services are achieving their objectives); (3) evaluating, analyzing, and developing program standards with which performance audits can be compared; and (4) establishing targets that enable the monitoring of employees, organizational units, responsibility centers, and contractors.[8]

Sustainability measures the duration for an extended time period over which the impact or efficacy of a program endures. Ideally, all five performance indicators should be used to evaluate each activity. Since this will not always be possible, especially in human service activities, it is highly desirable that performance measures be related directly to needs as much as possible. It is clear from the foregoing discussion that all performance measures are logically linked, as shown in Figure 11.3.

BUDGETING AND PRODUCTIVITY

Defining productivity

The most generally agreed upon definition of productivity views it as a ratio of outputs (goods and services produced) to inputs (money, materials,

Figure 11.3

Schematic Input/Output Linkage of Performance Measures

and labor). Productivity measures show how well resources are expended in accomplishing stated objectives. According to Mali: "Productivity is a measure of how well resources are brought together in organizations and utilized for accomplishing a set of results. Productivity is reaching for the highest level of performance with the least expenditure of resources."[9] Because productivity focuses on means or ways of delivering goods and services at the least possible cost, the process (the precise way in which resources are transformed into outputs) is a major concern in pursuing it. For example, a gas-guzzling Rolls Royce automobile could be used to deliver meals-on-wheels to elderly residents over a four-block area. While this use of a resource achieves the mission effectively, it results in the misallocation of resources because of the unnecessarily high unit cost of delivering the meals.

Productivity may be viewed as a combination of effectiveness and efficiency when there is equal concern for the quality and the quantity of services or goods to be produced. In this situation, productivity, efficiency, and effectiveness are inextricably linked. In determining how well resources are being utilized, a comparison can be made between the volume of the results produced (output effectiveness) and the volume of resources consumed (efficiency). The following is a formula for determining the productivity index.

$$\text{Productivity Index} = \frac{\text{Output Obtained}}{\text{Input Expended}} = \frac{\text{Achieved Performance}}{\text{Resources Consumed}} = \frac{\text{Effectiveness}}{\text{Efficiency}}$$

To enhance productivity improvement, it is necessary to develop measurable indicators for output (performance achievement) and input (resources consumed). Where measures cannot be developed for outputs and inputs, the organizational process should be reorganized to facilitate measurement.[10] Calculating the productivity ratio requires the identification of the output and input measures. When these two measures are lacking, productivity cannot be analyzed and the productivity index cannot be developed. To calculate the productivity index, assume the following:

Setting priorities and establishing a performance measurement system provides a solid basis with which to effect productivity improvement. Demand or need, workload, efficiency, and effectiveness are used to determine productivity. While Figure 11.3 is a general schematic representation of input/output linkage, Table 11.1 shows a more specific measurement linkage between social services, police control, and fire protection functions.

Examination of Table 11.1 reveals the following: (1) demand/need indicates quantitatively how much work clients and constituents require to meet their articulated needs and desires. (2) The workload indicates quantitatively the

Table 11.1

Examples of Performance Measure Linkages

Function	Demand/Need	Workload	Output
Social Services	No. of cases requiring services	No. of cases to be served	No. of cases served
Fire Protection	No. of places requiring inspection	No. of inspections to be made	No. of inspections made
Police Protection	Emergency call and no. of burglaries	No. of patrol hours beat-driven No. of arrests made (clearance)	No. of patrol hours; No. of arrests

Efficiency	Effectiveness	Sustainabiltiy	Goal
Cost per case served	Percentage of eligible cases satisfactorily served	Extended period over which cases were satisfactorily served	Ability to provide for individual needs
Cost per inspection made	Dollar amount lost due to fire	Duration over which dollar losses continued to decline	Fire prevention
Cost per patrol hour; Cost per citation issued	Dollars lost due to crime; cost per degree of security experienced by residents	Period over which loss due to crime continued to climb	Crime prevention
		Period over which residents continued to express increasing degree of insecurity	

amount of work necessary to carry out a given activity. (3) Output represents the amount of goods produced or services provided in the day-to-day activities of an agency without considering the quality of the work performed. (4) Efficiency is the ratio of inputs to outputs. It identifies the cost required to achieve identified objectives. In an examination of efficiency, attention is directed to such questions as the following: What is the cost per fire inspection? What is the cost per patient examined by the outpatient department? What is the cost per ton of garbage collected? Emphasis is directed to the process of converting inputs into outputs. (5) Effectiveness attempts to match the stated goals with the achieved or actual results. The greater the match (or congruence), the more effective is the result.

In Table 11.1 if all the social service clients are satisfactorily served, the match between stated and actual results is perfect and effectiveness is maximized. In the case of fire protection, no losses from fire means that maximum effectiveness has been reached.

To be most useful as a productivity instrument, the budget must be closely linked to the management decision-making process. The development of a performance measurement system, as shown in Tables 11.1 and 11.2, produces an important framework that can be used to enhance productivity. The management decision-making process involves the following: (1) an articulation of community needs and goals and the specification of policies to meet those needs; (2) specification of service objectives designed to meet the service level; (3) determination of the desired organizational and procedural changes; (4) provision for a performance monitoring system; and (5) evaluation of results and initiation of the action necessary to bring about the improvement (see Figure 11.4).

Figure 11.4
Activity Flow of the Management Process

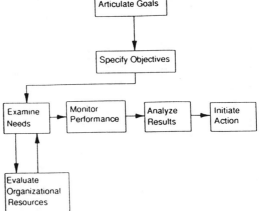

Once management decides that it will use the budget to actively promote productivity, the process must be institutionalized. The management information system must be designed to generate the kind of performance measures that will be emphasized in the controlling, monitoring, planning, and management decision-making processes. The performance measures thus developed can be used to aid budget justification and facilitate variance analysis.[11] To enhance decision making, management must develop performance indicators that will meet management needs at given levels of responsibility in the organization.

To be able to develop the most desirable performance indicators in public and not-for-profit agencies, managers must recognize the reality that there are no clear-cut and precise data to permit easy measurement. The linkage between resource allocation and performance result can seldom be directly and explicitly determined. This ofttimes, requires that public and other not-for-profit agencies' services be measured along a number of dimensions, which may be imperfect and incomplete, with multiple proxies or surrogate indicators. To develop the performance measure that meet a given agency or responsibility center needs will depend on the measure's utility (in terms of relevance and

Table 11.2
The Goal/Objective
Performance Measure Linkages

Department: Traffic Safety
Program: School Guards

Goals:

1. To provide for the safety and welfare of all school children walking or riding buses or bicycles to school.
2. To maintain order at school bus stops and to file written reports on motor vehicle violations that threaten the safety of school children.

Objectives:

1. To provide each school guard trainee with at least 20 class sessions.
2. To provide total safety and control of children entering and leaving school buses.
3. To provide 150 bicycle safety talks at local schools.
4. To reduce reported motor vehicle violations involving school children by 10 percent.

Table 11.2 (cont'd.)

Objectives

	Prior Year	Current Year	Projected Budget
Demand Measure			
Number of complaints from concerned parents about the lack of school guards at unattended school crossings	100	90	140
Number of accidents involving school children entering and leaving school buses	115	192	200
Number of dangerous street crossings at new school location	475	510	580
Number of safety prevention classes to be conducted for school children			
Workload Measures			
Number of school guard-training classes conducted	150	165	192
Number of school guards attending the training classes	NA	NA	NA
Number of hours spent watching children entering and leaving school buses	105	110	90
Number of hours in hearings	250	375	420

Efficiency/Productivity Measures

Number of school guard-training sessions conducted per officer	10	11	12
Average cost per training class	$205	$200	$195
Number of bicycle talks presented per officer	29	25	28
Average cost per bicycle talk	$48	$50	$43
Average number of accidents involving children entering and leaving buses	14	15	10
Average cost per report filed	$53	$75	$45

Impact/Effectiveness

Degree of satisfaction with school guard training classes	NA	NA	NA
Number of accidents involving school children entering and leaving school buses reported	5	6	1
Percentage of increase or decrease in bicycle accidents reported	15%	20%	5%

Percentage of decrease in motor vehicle violations involving school children reported	75%	85%	95%

Sustainability

Extended period over which satisfaction was expressed about school guard-training classes.	NA	NA	NA
Duration over which accidents involving school children decreased	15 Months	27 Months	39 Months
Period over which bicycle accidents decreased	25 Months	7 Months	9 Months
Extended period over which motor vehicle violations involving children decreased	26 Months	38 Months	50 Months

Prior Year	Current Year	Projected Budget	Over/Under Current Year Explanation
$189,000	$225,520	$251,520	$36,000, mainly for new officers' training and overtime report writing.

Note: NA = Not available
*All these amounts can be broken down by objects of expenditures.

significance) to each decision maker.

Instituting performance measures: Some practical concerns

Because adopting the use of performance measures in government and non-profit agencies typically means giving up old habits and modes of decision making, the time frame for the implementation of productivity measures should be based on each organization's situation. Some agencies may take several months to implement productivity measures, while others may require five years or more.

The introduction of a productivity system may take place as follows: (1) agency or unit that appears most receptive and capable is singled out; (2) line managers are involved in the development of appropriate productivity measures; (3) the central staff is allowed time to assist managers in formulating performance measures; and (4) performance measures are linked to specific services identified in the budget.

Besides the benefits that performance measures offer, they can also produce other, unintended, consequences. They tend to make managers concentrate their energies more on those programs that are easy to measure. Because the effectiveness of final results or other quantitative factors are harder to measure, much emphasis in both public and other not-for-profit agencies is put on intermediate output, such as the number of food inspections made by a health department inspector, the number of contacts made by an individual infected with a sexually transmitted disease, the number of inoculations given, or the number of grant proposals completed. Performance measures are often resisted by managers, who fear being evaluated on the basis of results over which they have little or no control. Often, managers fail to understand the linkages between the different kinds of measures. For example, a fire department that inspects buildings with the aim of minimizing or eliminating fire may fail to accept responsibility for buildings that are subsequently burned. If the linkage cannot be made in a case such as this, then no more resources should be provided for carrying out the inspection activity.[12]

SUMMARY OBSERVATIONS

This chapter presented the steps involved in the development and use of performance measures in the budgetary context. Throughout, attention was focused on how the budget performance measures are linked to each other and how these measures provide useful insights in assessing program results and accountability in public and other not-for-profit organizations.

NOTES

1. See Al Gore, *Creating a Government That Works Better and Costs Less* (Washington, D.C.: U.S. Government Printing Office, 1993).

2. See Government Accounting Service Board (GASB), "Service Efforts and Accomplishments Reporting" (Draft, September 15, 1993); Paul D. Epstein, "Get Ready: The Time for Performance Measurement Is Finally Coming," *Public Administration Review*, 52, no. 5 (September 1992): 5, 13.

3. Barry M. Mundt, Raymond T. Olsen and Harold I. Steinberg, *Managing Public Resources* (Stamford, Conn.: Peat Marwick, International, 1982), p. 14.

4. Robert G. May, Gerhard G. Mueller and Thomas H. Williams, *A Brief Introduction to Managerial and Social Uses of Accounting* (Englewood Cliffs, N.J.: Prentice Hall, 1975), p. 72.

5. Jack Diamond, "Measuring Efficiency in Government: Techniques and Experience," in ed. A. Premchand, *Financial Management*, (Washington, D.C.: International Monetary Fund, 1990): 142.

6. Ibid.

7. Mundt, Olsen, and Steinberg, *Managing Public Resources*, p. 16.

8. Ibid., p. 21.

9. Paul Mali, *Improving Total Productivity* (New York: John Wiley and Sons, 1978), p. 6.

10. Ibid., p. 7.

11. John R. Hall, *Factors Related to Local Government Use of Performance Measurement* (Washington, D.C.: Urban Institute, April 1978).

12. Allan R. Drebin, "Criteria for Performance Measurement in State and Local Government," *Governmental Finance*, 10, (December 1980): 4.

12

Capital Budgeting

The need for capital budgeting arises in public and other not-for-profit organizations because it is not always possible to find sufficient revenues to accommodate capital needs. Factors that have contributed to this condition include the increased demand for service, the upward pressures on costs due to inflation, the cutback/retrenchment movement in the public sector, revenue-raising limitations (e.g., Proposition 13 in California), the prevailing no-tax syndrome, and resistance on the part of donors to provide adequate resources to other not-for-profit agencies. The heavy expenditures that are usually needed for capital outlays cannot always be met by the popular "pay-as-you-go" method, which encourages a governmental unit or agency to spend no more than the revenues available for a specific fiscal period. This principle minimizes the unwise or premature commitments of resources and it avoids the interest payments and other related costs associated with debt financing, thus enhancing the entity's credit rating.[1]

Nonetheless, despite the public's acceptance of the "pay-as-you-go" approach, there are a number of problems that are associated with it. For example, current taxpayers pay for projects or investments from which they will only partially benefit. On the other hand, the argument can be made in the interest of equity that people should pay for capital facilities during their life span only as they benefit from them. When public agencies engage in long-term borrowing, current taxpayers are relieved from paying portions of their immediate tax burden, instead deferring it to future generations.

Unlike the business world or other levels of government, the federal government does not manage its capital facilities. There is a total lack of an effective national capital improvement plan. In fact, the federal government maintains no capital-budgeting system or procedure. As a result, most federally owned facilities "are deteriorating and the Government is faced with the prospect of either repairing or rehabilitating them, or risking a staggering replacement burden in the future."[2]

The chapter examines the capital-budgeting processes, financing approaches, and techniques for ranking and selecting capital projects. Throughout, stress is put on successful, as well as unsuccessful, practices.

DEFINING CAPITAL BUDGETING

A number of terms are used interchangeably to refer to capital budgeting, such as public works planning, capital improvements planning, capital facilities planning, and capital outlay planning. The use of so many terms creates an increased opportunity for misunderstanding the definition of *capital budget*. Most often, the term refers to the legislative plan for proposed capital outlays and the means of financing them for the coming fiscal period. The capital budget is often a part of the regular budget. When a capital facilities or program improvement is in operation, the capital budget will be the first-year component.

Capital Facilities/Program/Improvement

This is a plan made up of capital expenditures (the purchase of assets to provide service for many years) to be incurred over a specified number of years in order to accommodate capital improvements set forth in a long-term work program. Each project or planned expenditure is sequentially and specifically identified according to a schedule of priorities which sets forth the full estimated resources available to finance the projected expenditures. Typically, the projects are large, permanent, or fixed, with a life range of 15 to 20 years, and involve nonrecurring expenditures aimed at providing new or additional service. The construction of a public health clinic or a swimming pool is an example of a capital expenditure. (Salaries, supplies, or minor equipment replacements are operational expenditures and can be included in the yearly operating budget).

All recurring expenditures should be excluded from the capital improvement program (CIP). The following are suggestions to guide financial managers in developing the CIP: (1) capital items should have a life span of three years or more, (2) acquisition costs should be $5,000 or greater, and (3) all capital items "paid for from the proceeds of long-term debt [should be] included."[3]

Unlike the public sector, the business world tends to favor putting as many items in the capital area as possible to take advantage of the tax break.

CAPITAL BUDGET PROCESS

The capital-planning and -programming role of the chief executive varies according to statutory requirements and the size and type of government. Typically, the chief executive guides the capital-planning and -programming process and makes recommendations to the legislature. However, requests for projects are initiated in the operating departments. The guidelines for preparing and submitting the capital plan are determined by the legislatures, which establish the time frame on activity, extent of citizen participation, and planning and administrative responsibilities for the capital-planning process.[4] In recent years, outside experts have been used to advise agencies on financing options. Additionally, interdepartmental committees have been used to review and rank projects, while citizen advisory committees and citizen surveys, such as the type conducted in Dayton, Ohio, are used to facilitate community input into the capital planning process. Dayton polls its citizens on the priorities for capital improvements and their willingness to finance them, including taxing, the issuance of bonds, and public-private partnerships.

Implementation of the capital-planning process has been traditionally carried out by the planning departments or the central budget staff. These departments normally play the lead role due to their access to data and information (concerning, e.g., population, land use, transportation, and the economic base). This provides the basis on which to establish community plans. Infrequently, the public works department may be given the responsibility of the capital-planning coordination. The authority to analyze the financial implication and impact of the capital program on the operating budget and to make recommendations on financing approaches is assigned to the finance department.

Where a planning commission exists, its main responsibility is to review the capital project requests and make recommendations.

Benefits of CIP

A number of important results flow from an effectively planned and executed CIP. They include the following:

1. It forces communities to examine their goals and needs capabilities.
2. It promotes greater efficiency in the use of tax resources.
3. It provides an important guide to aid the growth and development of the community.
4. It encourages governments or organizations to improve their administrative systems.
5. It is an important means for promoting regional cooperation.

6.   It facilitates and promotes sound financial management.
7.   It offers an effective way for replacing or repairing capital facilities.
8.   It enhances the governmental unit or organization's opportunity for participation because of the many programs that federal and state governments maintain to aid in the planning and construction of the infrastructure.

There are many differences among governmental units, as the General Accounting Office (GAO) found in its assessment of capital budgeting in public and private organizations throughout the country. GAO stated that it could not find a comprehensive, precise discussion of the critical elements of a capital budgeting process anywhere in the literature. Thus, the process described here is a compression of a number of suggested processes. Among the basic steps that should be followed in the formulation of the capital budget are the following:

1.   Inventory and assess the existing condition of the infrastructure, establishing the short- and long-term physical needs.
2.   Develop alternative projects to meet short- and long-term needs.
3.   Select alternatives and establish priority classification for the short- and long-term needs.
4.   Estimate the required resources and short-term-funding allocation.
5.   Assess the impact on the governmental organization's financial policies.
6.   Establish a monitoring system, control work schedules,, and financing.
7.   Initiate a replacement and maintenance strategy.

Though the governmental procedures among jurisdictions differ, the chief executive traditionally oversees the capital-budgeting and planning process and make recommendations to the legislative body. The guidelines for preparing and submitting the capital plan are determined by the legislature.

The capital budget process begins with the development of the capital improvement program. This involves the identification of projects that will meet the entity's needs for a specified number of years. The vast majority of projects are identified by government agencies, though private organizations may make suggestions. Each project submitted is accompanied by a supporting rationale setting forth the cost data and a justifying narrative.

Planning departments or central budget offices typically direct the process of the capital budget planning. While these departments sometimes review the initial submissions, planning commissions usually perform these functions and make recommendations. In carrying out the review of the proposals, interrelationships are determined, costs are evaluated, and priorities are identified. As part of the review of the screening process, schedules for the proposed implementation of the projects are synchronized with each other to minimize the wasteful use of resources (e.g., surfacing streets before laying the sewage and drainage system). In addition, projects that can be reasonably postponed are identified.[5]

The Capital Improvements Plan (CIP)

This may be viewed as an instrument through which a community lays out its short- and long-term physical growth and development plan. Ideally, the CIP is linked to the community's master and fiscal long-term (10 - 20 yr.) plans, identifying public improvement needs.[6] The CIP is essentially "a schedule listing capital improvements, in order of priority together with cost estimates and the proposed method of financing them."[7] CIPs are subject to constant changes and should be reviewed each year and updated with regard to the changing needs and priorities of the community or organization. By means of the CIP, the following activities are undertaken:

1. Projects (e.g., library, community center) are scheduled over a five- to six-year period.
2. A budget is developed for high-priority projects.
3. A revenue policy is developed for projected improvements.
4. Departmental activities are coordinated to meet project schedules.
5. A system is developed to monitor, evaluate and inform the public about the proposed capital improvements.

There are three documents that emanate from or are closely related to the CIP. The first is the capital improvement budget, representing the first year of the CIP as approved by the appropriate legislative body or board which authorizes required funding to defray the cost of the improvements. The second is the annual operating budget, whose relationship to the CIP is significantly influenced by the way in which projects are implemented. The CIP is usually adopted prior to the completion of the annual operating budget to allow the capital improvement budget to be incorporated into it. This facilitates the linkage "between the CIP and the annual budget and appropriation process used by the community", as shown in Figure 12.1.[8] Note that the CIP programming approach is not a mandated process in most communities. Thus, though it is

Figure 12.1
CIP Linkage with Capital and Operating Budgets:
Conceptual View

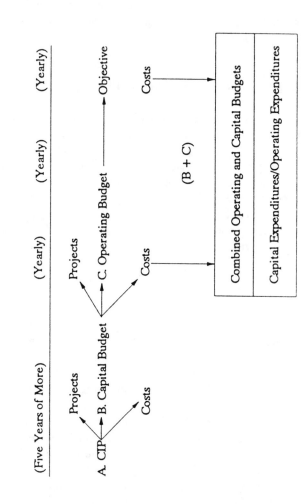

not desirable to ignore the CIP programming approach, most communities may institute a capital project's plan as long as they meet the legal requirements.

Priority Setting

Priority setting is a necessary activity because the scarcity of resources does not permit a community or an organization to undertake all the projects that it would like to implement. The agency charged with developing the capital budget can provide invaluable assistance to operating department heads in pinpointing cost projections.

The agency staff can stress the importance of long-range needs, interpret instructions, and complete the required forms necessary to promote a uniform application of policies and procedures. In addition, a number of officials (e.g., budget director, city engineer, and city attorney) may be needed to answer such questions as the following:

1. In what ways and to what extent will the proposed project impact on general city or government development?
2. Who will benefit or be hurt by this project?
3. Is this project a replacement of existing structure or a new, added responsibility to government?
4. Will the project expand the taxable property and economic base of the community? That is, what will be the impact on existing revenue (increase, decrease, or neutral)?
5. What effect will the project have on the efficiency and cost-effectiveness of service performance?
6. Can the city or governmental unit afford the proposed capital improvement?
7. Will the project be a revenue producer?
8. What is likely to be citizen and/or political opposition?[9]

In the priority-setting process, an initial review should be conducted to eliminate proposals that appear obviously impractical to implement during the ensuing period. Once this is done, a simple and precisely defined selection criteria should be established to enhance the community or organization's present and future financial viability. Perhaps a general criteria for a CIP priority system may be employed:

Table 12.1
Evaluation Criteria Matrix
for a University Complex

CRITERIA		PROPOSALS									
		1	2	3	4	5	6	7	8	9	10
1. Academic Mission of the University	Ratings 0-3 does not directly enhance mission 4-7 partially enhances mission 8-10 directly enhances mission										
a. Students training and research (closer proximity to labs and professors in own and related fields)											
b. Classroom teaching (improves access to teaching labs, equipment, Audio Visual, computers, etc.)											
c. Research (creates opportunities for new or expanded research endeavors, especially sponsored projects)											
d. Public Service (upgrades provision and quality, attractiveness, and visibility of public and community services)											
e. Quality enhancement responsive to/compatible with provost's priorities											
f. Recruitment and retention of faculty and students											
2. Integrative Planning and University -wide Considerations	Ratings 0-3 not consistent 4-7 somewhat consistent 8-10 consistent in all ways										
a. Consolidation of units located in multiple, nonadjacent, sites; meets long-term/permanent space needs											
b. Department/unit more consistent with existing understanding with the community											
c. Request consistent with building plans/limitations (accommodates parking, classroom, square footage, labs, etc.)											
d. Vacated space needed to solve other critical space problems											
3. Assessment of Existing Conditions	Ratings 0-3 suggests adequacy/acceptability 4-7 average to below average adequacy 8-10 extreme inadequacy/unacceptability										
a. Lack of adequate space to carry out required functions (implicit and explicit university commitments)											
b. Fragmentation and/or lack of proximity impeding use of department and university resources											
c. Need for general infrastructure improvements (sufficient staff, support facilities, etc.)											
4. Expenditures/Revenues	Ratings 0-3 does not meet expectations 4-7 meets some expectations 8-10 meets all expectations										
a. Reduces expenditures of (recurring) maintenance costs, deferred maintenance renovations or rental costs											
b. Provides for operating savings through consolidations											
c. Generates added revenues											
	TOTAL POINTS:										

Rank	Center	Applicable Criteria
1	Urgently needed (one year or less)	Immediate implementation to relive danger to public health, welfare, and/or safety.
2	Necessary or essential (two to three years)	Complete projects to bring about major improvements and to remove existing deficiencies and/or impediments.
3	Desirable improvements	Project identified to meet anticipated or projected future needs.
4	Deferable improvements	Foreseeable needs for projects cannot be effectively supported as part of the present CIP.

In recent years a numerical-rating system has gained popularity. For example, a specific number of points (e.g., 0 - 50) is given based on conformance to such factors as economic development, environmental quality, revenue generation, potential for revitalizing neighborhood, citizen neighborhood participation, and useful life expectancy. Jurisdictions where the rating system may be found include Dade County, Florida; Dayton, Ohio; Montgomery County, Maryland; and St. Paul, Minnesota.

In Table 12.1, a university uses the rating system to allocate proposed new construction space based on academic mission priority, integrating planning and university considerations, existing building conditions, and expenditure and revenue factors.

Table 12.2 shows how the Spearman's rank (Rho) correlation can be used to assess the degree to which project priority ranks and resource allocation priority ranks are aligned, meaning the extent to which the projects and resource allocations parallel the corresponding rank positions. A Spearman correlation coefficient (r_s) of 0.0 indicates no alignment between projects and resource allocation priority, while a correlation coefficient (r_s) of $+1.00$ indicates that the projects and resource priority are perfectly aligned. Negative correlation coefficients indicate disalignment, meaning a lack of match between project priorities and resource allocation intentions. A Spearman correlation coefficient (r_s) of -1.00 shows a perfect disalignment between projects and resource allocations. Ideally, projects with high ranks should receive the largest resource allocations. Table 12.2 reveals a moderate and positive alignment $(r_s = .55)$ between the Civic Center's projects and resource allocations, suggesting that projects and resource allocations need to be reconceptualized. The utility of Spearman's rank correlation is as an index of the strength of alignment between

Table 12.2
City of Bright, Civic Center
Project and Resource Allocation Analysis (Thousands):
Spearman's Rho Correlation for Ranked Data

Projects	Project Rank (R_1)	Resource Allocation (Y)	Resource Rank (R_2)	$R_1 - R_2$ D	D^2
A	1	250.0	5	-4	16
B	7	500.0	3	4	16
C	3	350.0	4	-1	1
D	9	100.0	6	3	9
E	2	700.0	1	1	1
F	8	150.0	8	0	0
G	5	125.0	10	-5	25
H	6	175.0	7	-1	1
I	10	135.0	9	1	1
J	4	650.0	2	2	4
N=10	$\Sigma(R_1)=55$	$\Sigma(Y)=3135.0$	$\Sigma(R_2)=55$	$\Sigma D=0$	$\Sigma D^2=74$

Spearman's Rank (Rho) Correlation

$$r_s = 1 - \frac{6\Sigma D^2}{N(N^2 - 1)}$$

$$r_x = 1 - \frac{6(74)}{10(100 - 1)}$$

$$r_s = .552$$

Since the Spearman rank correlation coefficient is .55, the projects and resources are moderately positive aligned.

Spearman's Rho Correlation Coefficients*

.90 - 1.0 = Projects and resource allocations are properly aligned.
.75 - .89 = Projects and resource allocations are highly aligned.
.60 - .74 = Projects and resource allocations are strongly aligned.
.45 - .59 = Projects and resource allocations are moderately aligned.
.30 - .44 = Projects and resource allocations are somewhat aligned.
.15 - .29 = Projects and resource allocations are slightly aligned.
.00 - .14 = Projects and resource allocations are not aligned.

---

*Spearman correlation coefficients range from negative 1.0 to positive 1.0.

projects and resource allocations, which ranges from 0 (no alignment) to $\pm$ 1.00 (perfect alignment or disagreement).

In summary, there are six specific activities that should be sequentially considered when officials attempt to establish project priority:

1. Development of clearly defined selection criteria.
2. Development of a point system to permit the assignment of points to each criterion.
3. Comparison of each project with the identified criteria.
4. Assignment of an appropriate score and ranking to each project.
5. Preparation of a priority listing of the projects.
6. Analysis of the projects.

Capital Budgeting: Elements Contributing to Success and Failure

In its extensive study of both public and private organizations' capital-budgeting practices, the GAO identified elements that either contribute to or jeopardize success. The elements found in a successful organization can be ranked on a continuum of critical to helpful attributes (see Table 12.3). Similarly, the elements found in an unsuccessful organization range from harmful to destructive attributes.

The successful organization is able to minimize the impact on its service delivery system when operating conditions change its environment. GAO stated: "A successful organization is one that can, even under adverse conditions, acquire and/or maintain physical capital without jeopardizing its mission or its clientele. By adverse conditions, we mean declining resources, political instability, or severe conflict among interest groups."[10]

FINANCIAL ANALYSIS

While the pay-as-you-go approach (discussed in Chapter 8) has been exceedingly popular in government and other not-for-profit agencies, most governments have not been able to adopt this option and still meet the needs of their citizens. Older communities (especially those with relatively stable recurrent expenditures) having most of their infrastructure in place are in a better position to adopt the pay-as-you-go approach, in contrast to newer communities and those experiencing rapid growth and development. The approach does have two particularly appealing features: (1) in the long run, it is more economical because financing costs are eliminated; (2) there is a generally held view among public finance experts that greater efficiency is

Table 12.3
Elements Contributing to Organizational Success and Failure

Elements Found in Successful Organizatons	Elements Found in Un-successful Organizations
Critical	Destructive
Extensively links planning to budgeting.	Does not link planning to budgeting when planning takes place.
Concerned about long-term effects.	Pays little attention to long-term effects.
Incorporates up-to-date information on physical capital into decision-making process.	Does not consistently feed information on the condition of physical capital into the decision-making process.
Important	Damaging
Recognizes the effect of deferred maintenance and minimizes it to the extent possible.	Has limited, if any, controls; misses many financial and work targets.
Protects capital investment funds from being used for operations.	Defers structural maaintenance; focuses on cosmetic repairs.
Considers related operations and maintenance costs when making capital budgeting decisions.	Cuts budgets with "closed eyes".
Considers alternative methods of meeting the objectives of capital.	
Monitors capital investments and the condition of physical capital.	
Does not have internal conflicts that disrupt capital budgeting activities.	
Sees individual projects as modernization, revitalization, and investment.	

Uses funding mechanisms to protect
priorities.

Uses incentives to meet work and
financial targets.

Helpful	Harmful
Figures out ways to allocate something for everyone (keeps things even, moves on all fronts).	Lets funding mechanisms drive priorities.
	Sees individual projects as pork barrel.
Uses categories for decision-making that are important to the organizations, (e.g., productivity items).	Lets special interest groups operate without control.
Routinely assesses physical capital and adherence to a maintenance schedule.	

Source: U.S. Government Accounting Office (GAO), *Federal Capital Budgeting: A Collection of Haphazard Practices* (Washington, D.C.: GAO, 1981), p. 40.

attained when taxpayers feel the burden/cost of the undertaking immediately.[11]

When the pay-as-you-go approach cannot be followed, a number of modified approximations may be pursued: (1) adopt a policy requiring that the length of all future debt instruments be successively shortened as they are issued, (2) make an initial down payment from current revenues and increase the portion until the capital outlay can be easily accommodated by current revenues, and (3) declare a moratorium until all outstanding debts are substantially reduced.[12]

When Pay-as-You-Go Is Appropriate

Despite the constant call for the pay-as-you-go approach, it may not always be the most desirable thing to do. (1) It should not be followed when capital projects expands the tax base; (2) it should be avoided when the capital expenditures will materially distort the entire tax structure of the governmental unit; and (3) when real interest costs are negative as during the period of the latter half of the later 1970s, it may be fiscally more prudent to borrow. During that period it was possible to borrow at rates lower than the inflation costs.[13]

A critical part of the CIP process is the development of the financing plan. The governmental unit or agency must determine how much can be spent, the sources from which the money will come, and the people and/or entities that will bear the burden. Satisfying the projected capital needs requires the identification and scheduling of funding sources (known as *financial programming*). Action must be taken regarding the following: (l) tax rates; (2) the desired balance between debt service and expenditures; (3) available aid from state and federal government; and (4) new revenue sources.

Analysis of Revenues and Expenditures

A review of the past five years of the revenue collection and expenditures record is an important first step as it provides a benchmark against which future revenue and expenditure can be measured. On the revenue side, special attention should be given to recurring items such as property taxes, user fees, and proposed changes affecting valuation tax rate, special limitations on property tax prospects for the local job market, inflation, trends in population, and other important changes that might be discernable.[14]

As illustrated in Chapters 4 (see Tables 4.1 and 4.3) and 10 (see Table 10.7 and Figure 10.2), the least squares regression models can be used to make revenue and expenditure projects. For revenue projections, the least squares model estimates the slope and level of the trend. More importantly, this method allows one to calculate and plot future revenues. To make the most accurate projections, the following underlying assumptions must be satisfied: (1) the time series must be linear (i.e., the data must increase progressively over time with an increase that can be plotted by a straight line), (2) past patterns must persist in the future, and (3) past patterns must be regular. More sophisticated regressions models that control for changes in population, industry growth, and other variables can also be used to obtain more precise trends and projections. Regardless of the regression model that is utilized, the precision of the projections depends on the extent to which the past revenue data are consistent with the assumptions. Assuming that the underlying assumptions have been satisfied, Table 12.4 shows that the Civic Center can expect an increase of $22.417 (b = 22.417) in summer concert revenues over time. Accordingly, the Civic Center can expect to obtain $613,335 in summer concert revenues for 1995. The utility of the least squares regression model is that it provides a statistical tool for assessing and quantitatively estimating revenue trends and projections.

When using data from the same period as the revenue review, the expenditures should be categorized as follows: recurring operating expenditures,

Table 12.4
City of Bright, Civic Center
Summer Concert Revenue Projections (in Thousands):
Least Squares Regression

Years (X) 1	Revenues (Y) 2	Coded Time Value (x) 3	Columns (2) by (3) (xY) 4	Column 3 Squared (x^2) 5	Trend Value For Revenues (Y_t) 6
1986	375.0	-4	-1500	16	y 411.582
1987	450.0	-3	-1350	9	435.949
1988	475.0	-2	- 950	4	456.416
1989	500.0	-1	- 500	1	478.833
1990	550.0	1	550	1	523.667
1991	485.0	2	970	4	546.084
1992	575.0	3	1725	9	568.501
1993	600.0	4	2400	16	590.918

$N = 8$ $\Sigma(Y) = 4{,}010$ $\Sigma(x) = 0$ $\Sigma(xY) = 1{,}345$ $\Sigma(x^2) = 60$ $\Sigma(Y_t) = 4{,}010$

$$Y_t = a + b(x)$$

$$a = \frac{\Sigma(Y)}{N} = \frac{4010}{8} = 501.25$$

$$b = \frac{\Sigma(xY)}{\Sigma(x^2)} = \frac{1345}{60} = 22.417$$

$$Y_t = 501.25 + 22.417(x)$$

Table 12.5
City of Bright, Civic Center
Expenditure Projections (Thousands): Least squares Regression

Years (X) 1	Revenues (Y) 2	Coded Time Value (x) 3	Columns (2) by (3) (xY) 4	Column 3 Squared (x^2) 5	Trend Value For Revenues (Y_t) 6
1986	350.0	-4	-1400	16	341.707
1987	375.0	-3	-1125	9	361.124
1988	345.0	-2	- 690	4	380.541
1989	400.0	-1	- 400	1	399.958
1990	475.0	1	475	1	438.794
1991	450.0	2	900	4	458.209
1992	435.0	3	1305	9	477.626
1993	525.0	4	2100	16	497.043

$N = 8$ $\Sigma(Y) = 3355$ $\Sigma(x) = 0$ $\Sigma(xY) = 1165$ $\Sigma(x^2) = 60$ $\Sigma(Y_t) = 3355$

$$Y_t = a + b(x)$$

$$a = \frac{\Sigma(Y)}{N} = \frac{3355}{8} = 419.375$$

$$b = \frac{\Sigma(xY)}{\Sigma(x^2)} = \frac{1165}{60} = 19.417$$

$$Y_t = 419.375 + 19.417(x)$$

capital expenditures, and debt service payment. Aspects such as changes in the work force (especially new employees), salary and benefit trends, and types and terms of existing bonded indebtedness should also be considered.

Least squares regression, along with more sophisticated regression procedures, can also be employed to make expenditure projections. Again, assuming that the underlying assumptions have been satisfied, Table 12.5 indicates that the Civic Center can expect an increase of $19,417 in expenditures over time. More important, the Civic Center can project expenditures to be $516,460 for 1994.

Future Revenue and Expenditure Projections

With the completion of the past revenue and expenditure review, revenue and expenditure for the duration of the proposed CIP may be forecast. This permits the linkage of the CIP with the community's resource capability. Whatever methods are used in making revenue and expenditure projections, various assumptions must be clearly defined. These assumptions involve changes in variables such as population, residential, commercial, and industrial growth. Once the new revenue and expenditure projections have been made, the capital facility plan for each year can be completed. The difference between projected expenditures and projected revenue represents the amount that the governmental unit or agency will need to generate to finance the proposed capital improvements.[15]

A number of options are available to a governmental unit or agency to obtain sufficient funds to carry out its CIP. Among the main options are the following:

- *General obligations (GO) bonds* are legal obligations of the unit issuing the bond. These are used to build public facilities such as jails, sewers, and bridges.

- *Limited* or *special obligation bonds* are unlike GOs in that they do not carry the same statutory and constitutional security as the general obligation bonds. They do not enjoy the "full faith and credit" of the issuing unit, though they have priority over all nonproject creditors. In many states, specific sources of taxes are designated to pay limited bond obligations. A few states do not permit bonds to be general obligation unless they are pledged by the property tax; others make a bond a general obligation if any revenue not generated from the project is pledged to pay for its repayment.[16]

- *Revenue bonds* are a type of limited obligation bond and

include those issues on which governmental units "promise to pay debt service . . ., exclusively from the revenue derived from user fees and charges from the project constructed. . ."[17] Examples are turnpikes and major public improvements, including special assessment bonds.

- *A lease-purchase agreement* involves a facility that is built by a private or not-for-profit organization.
- *Joint financing with other governmental units* may be arranged.
- *Private development funds* may be used, such as in cases where new infrastructure is required in new developments.
- *Sources of government revenues*, including taxes, special assessments, and user charges, may be employed.

The public sector pays for virtually all the country's infrastructure (roads, bridges, mass transit systems, sewers, water, etc.). The resources to fund most capital facilities were obtained mainly through federal sources and long-term debt issued by state and local governments. Historically, general obligation bonds have been the chief capital-financing source for state and local governments. (The general obligation bonds are secured by the units promising to pay the principal and interest from general revenue resources.)

Because of public resistance, the financing source for capital improvements has been declining in recent years. More popular are revenue bonds which permit the debt service (principal and interest payments) to be paid from the revenue produced by the specific project. While the revenue bond-financing approach is likely to enjoy popularity as a means of financing capital improvement, there is a distinct limit as to how many capital improvements can be self-financed. Limitations are caused by resistance to the amounts of user charges that people may want to pay. The demands on state and local governments to provide increased resources to finance improved capital facilities are likely to rise appreciably. Nonetheless, the major financing source (the federal government) has already begun to decrease the available funds in this area.[18]

CAPITAL BUDGET ANALYSIS

Since government and other not-for-profit organizations have limited resources or revenues, the costs of desirable programs and projects always exceed available revenues. If the best possible use is to be made of scarce revenues, only those projects providing the maximum social gain to the community should be undertaken. Capital budget analysis is comprised of techniques used for evaluating the social benefits of alternative uses for available scarce resources. Stated another way, the process consists of an orderly sequence of steps organized to produce relevant information for choosing investments.

The steps involved require the following:

1.   Identification of relevant investment alternatives.
2.   Estimation of the cash flow for each alternative.
3.   Selection of appropriate choice criteria to apply to the projected cash flow in order to facilitate a measure of comparison.
4.   Arrangement of data for each alternative (project), interpretation consistent with the specified criteria, and selection of the projects with maximum social gain.

Identifying Alternatives

This step demands that the various decision choices be clearly understood. The benefits to be gained from a project should be compared with the benefits that can be achieved from alternative applications of a resource.

Estimating the Cash Flow

Because the accounting system allocates costs on a responsibility or departmental basis, there may be confusion about which costs are relevant to decision making. Thus, a few useful rules have been suggested to aid in deciding which costs should be included in capital decisions, as follows:

- Include only those inflows and outflows that can be directly related to the project; exclude those that would occur irrespective of the project. A capital expenditure is a cash outlay over a number of years that is intended to produce a flow of future benefits. A capital expenditure may be viewed as consisting of three distinct elements: expected future benefits, time factor, and risk related to the realization of the expected benefits.
- Focus only on future cash flow, since all past cash flow discussions are *sunk costs* and cannot be changed.
- Pay close attention to cash flow and not to accounting reports, which may differ because of the accrual accounting system.

(The cash system and the cash flow approach will usually be nearly identical.) It is important to keep in mind that the data on costs and benefits are determined at this stage. That is, cost and benefits in dollars must be identified for the entire life of the project or program.

Applying Capital Budget Criteria: Techniques for Project Analysis

Decision makers in most not-for-profit agencies find it easier to identify cost (the input factor) than to estimate the benefits. The situation is even more difficult when the explicit intention of an expansion is to increase service capability or quality. It is critical to select the criteria that will generate information that is useful for ranking in order to enable the decision maker to accept or reject different investment objectives. Five criteria used from time to time in public and other not-for-profit organizations are:

- Simple rate of return/average rate of return,
- Payback period,
- Net present value,
- Excess present value, and
- Internal rate of return.

The simple rate of return (SRR) expresses the average net profits generated yearly by an investment as a percentage of the original investment or as the investment over its expected life. The following is one of a number of ways to calculate the simple rate of return:

$$SRR = \frac{Y}{I}$$

Where   Y = average annual profits (minus depreciation) projected for the new investment.
I = the initial investment.
SRR = the average annual or simple rate of return.

Each investment is ranked according to the relative size of its SRR. Its profitability is then judged by comparison with the investor's required rate of return (RRR). After due consideration of the risk, liquidity, and other relevant factors, the decision rules are the following: when SRR exceeds RRR, accept the investment; when SRR equals RRR, be neutral or indifferent; when SRR is less than RRR, reject the investment.

Table 12.6 shows the projected average annual rates of return for investments X, Y, and Z. Applying the simple rate of return criterion, investment X would be the first choice, followed by Y, and last Z. Since 8 percent is the required rate of return, the three projects are profitable.

Note that the simple rate of return does not consider the time element related to the different cash flows. When each flow pattern has large differences, the simple rate of return may lead to erroneous conclusions.

Table 12.6
Simple Rate of Return: Three Hypothetical Investments

Project	Net Costs plus Depreciation	Depression	Average Annual	Simple Rate of Return
X	31,000	20,000	2,000	10%
Y	30,000	30,000	1,800	9%
Z	29,000	30,000	1,600	8%

The Payback Period

This is a very simple quantitative technique and is widely used for evaluating investment opportunities. It provides an estimate of the time required to recover the cost of an investment. The payback period can be calculated as follows:

$$Payback \quad Period \quad = \frac{Original \quad Investment}{Annual \quad Cash \quad Flow}$$

In not-for-profit organizations, two approaches (see Table 12.7) are used: (1) the annual cash flow may be the actual inflow generated by the investment of a piece of equipment, or (2) the amount of savings produced as a result of the investment may be substituted for the annual cash flow. Either approach is acceptable.

As an illustration, assume that a hospital wants to purchase one of two comparable X-ray machines. Machine X costs $100,0000, with an annual cash inflow of $12,000.   Machine Y costs $120,000 and generates $16,000 in savings annually. The application of the payback criterion would require that

Machine Y be chosen.   The payback for the machines may be computed as follows:

Machine X:

$$\frac{108,000}{12,000} = 9 \text{ years}$$

Machine Y:

$$\frac{120,000}{16,000} = 7.5 \text{ years}$$

Because of the ease of the payback calculation, it may be conveniently used at lower levels of management to approve small expenditure projects. The chief advantage of the payback period approach is its ability to pinpoint the time it takes an investment to pay for itself. In addition, it is easy to calculate and understand.

Table 12.7
Three Investment Cash Flows

Year	Investment X	Investment Y	Investment Z
0 Present	-$20,000	-$20,000	-$20,000
1	2,000	6,000	10,000
2	4,000	6,000	8,000
3	6,000	6,000	6,000
4	9,000	6,000	4,000
5	10,000	6,000	1,000

Specific investments are ranked according to their relative payback periods and the projects with the shortest payback period are the most favored. The criterion for acceptance or rejection is based on the investors' required payback period (RPP). The decision rule is applied as follows: when the payback period is less than RPP, accept the investment; when the payback period equals RPP, be neutral or indifferent; when the payback period exceeds RPP, reject the investment.

A major disadvantage of the payback period approach is that it ignores all cash flows beyond the payback period. In the X-ray machine example, Machine X continues to generate cash inflows for three more years after the payback period, while the savings on Machine Y stopped at the payback period. When all this information is considered, Machine X will be selected rather than Machine Y. Because the payback period technique does not consider the time value of money, it is not accepted as a valid means of determining the economic feasibility of projects with long lives.

Time Value of Money

This approach is known as the discounted cash-flow method when applied to capital-budgeting decisions. Unlike the payback period and the simple rate of return approaches, the time value of money recognizes that the use of money has a cost. Interest is analogous to rent one pays on use of a piece of equipment or a building. The discounted cash-flow method recognizes the fact that $10 to be received or spent in the future does not have the same value as $10 received or spent today. To use a specific example, if you deposit $100 in a bank at 8 percent interest, at the end of the year you will have $108, assuming the interest is compounded annually. If the individual feels that $100 today or $108 one year from now are equivalent, then the 8 percent interest rate constitutes the *opportunity cost of time*, that is, the one-year wait for the money. The eight percent rate measures the willingness to exchange $100 today (*present value*) for $108 at the end of the year (*future value*). The present value is computed as follows:

$$Present \quad Value \quad = \quad \frac{Future \quad Value}{1 \quad + \quad Interest \quad Rate}$$

or, in this case,

$$100 \quad = \quad \frac{108}{1 + .08}$$

Note that the cash flow method is concerned only with *cash* inflows and outflows. This is in sharp contrast with the accounting method (e.g., the simple rate-of-return), which is affected by depreciation and other noncash transactions.

Net Present Value

Net present value (NPV) indicates the extent to which an investor will be better or worse off when accepting a given project as opposed to investing in other available options. The net present value (assuming a given rate of interest) is equal to the discounted inflow minus the discounted outflows. When the present value is greater than the outflows, the positive net present value is said to be the excess present value return that is earned on the project.

In evaluating NPV options, the sign and size of an investment's present value influences its ranking and acceptability. When all investments being considered are income generating, the one that has the largest NPV is given the highest ranking. The following decision rules apply: (1) when NPV exceeds zero, - accept the investment; (2) when NPV equals zero, - be neutral or indifferent; and (3) when NPV is less than zero, - reject the investment.

When the investment options are cost reducing, the projected cash outflows reflect outlays (i.e., expenditures). Cost-reducing comparisons require that the chosen criterion be based on the minimum net present value of each of the outlays.

To calculate the net present value, five types of data are required:

INV = the initial capital investment.
P_n = the annual net cash flows attributed to the investment that can be withdrawn periodically or yearly.
V_N = any salvage or other terminal investment value.
N = the time horizon (N) or the summation for n = Zero to N.
i = the interest rate or required rate of return.

The formula is set up for a nonuniform series of payments as follows:

$$NPV = -INV + \frac{P_1}{(1+i)} + \frac{P_2}{(1+i)^2} + \ldots \frac{P_N}{(1+i)^N} = \frac{V_N}{(1+i)^N}$$

If projected cash flows are a uniform series of payments (an annuity), USPV is designated as a simplified notation for the *uniform series present value* over N periods at interest rate (i). The formula is as follows:

$$NPV = -INV + A[USPV_{i,N}] + \frac{V_N}{(1+i)^N}$$

Assuming that an investor is evaluating investment X, Y and Z and requires a 10 percent rate of return, as shown in Table 12.2, the NPV of investment X can be determined:

$$NPV = -20,000 = \frac{4,000}{(1.10)} + \frac{4,000}{(1.10)^2} + \frac{6,000}{(1.10)^3} + \frac{8,000}{(1.10)^4} + \frac{10,000}{(1.10)^5}$$

The conversion factors $(1.10)^{-n}$ are found in Appendix 2, Table A.1, $i = .10$ and values of n range from 1 to 5. The NPV is:

NPV $= -20,000 + 2,000(.926) + 4,000(.856) + 6,000(.794) + 9,000(.735) + 10,000(.681)$

$= -20,000 + 1,852 + 3,424 + 4,764 + 6,615 + 6,810 = \$3,465$

An alternate way for computing net present value (NPV) requires determining the following:

1. Estimated annual cash flows (determined directly from each investment);
2. Estimated number of years or economic life for which the investment will generate cash flows;
3. Net amount of costs associated with the investment; and
4. The required rate of return.

The net present value may be calculated using the following formula:

Net Present Value = (Cash Flow x Present Value Factor) - Investment
$$NPV = (CF \times pvf) -1$$

Using the data in Table 12.2, investment Y, above and Appendix 2, Table A.2, the net present value is calculated as follows:

(1) Annual cash flow $= \$6,000$
(2) Economic life $= 5$ years
(3) Net investment amount $= \$20,000$
(4) Rate of return $= 10$ percent
     NPV $= (CF \times pvf) - 1$
            $= (\$6,000 \times 3.791) - \$20,000$
            $= \$22,746 - \$20,000$
            $= \$2,746$

This suggests that the investment is financially feasible.

Following the same procedure, the calculated net present value investment for Y is $2,746 and for Z is $4,443. While all three investment alternatives are acceptable, given the NPV decision rules investment Z is preferred over X and Y.

Internal Rate of Return

Though the term *internal rate of return* (IRR) is perhaps the most widely used, this is also known by a number of other names: discounted rate of return, the marginal efficiency of capital, or the yield of an investment. IRR refers to the rate of interest equal to the net present value of a projected series of cash flow payments at zero.

To find the IRR for an investment, apply the NPV formula with the appropriate projected cash flows (INV, P_n, P_N, V_n), set NPV equal to zero, and solve:

$$0 = -INV + \frac{P_1}{(1 + i)} + \frac{P_2}{(1 + i)^2} + \ldots \frac{P_N}{(1 + i)^N} = \frac{V_N}{(1 + i)^N}$$

The interest rate that satisfies the equation is the internal rate of return (IRR).

As an illustration, determine the IRR for an investment requiring an initial payment of $1,000, yielding $1,300 one year from today. The IRR is calculated as follows:

$$0 = -1,000 + \frac{1,300}{1 + i}$$

Transposing the equation, the yield is:

$$1 + i = \frac{1,300}{1,000} = 1.30;$$

$$i = .3$$

Thus, IRR = 30 percent.

Assume that the $1,300 payment was received after two years rather than at the end of year one. The IRR is then calculated as follows:

$$0 = -1,000 + \frac{1,300}{(1 + i)^2}$$

Transposing the equation, the yield is:

$$(1 + i)^{-2} = \frac{1,000}{1,300} = .7692;$$

thus, i = .14

Note that the conversion factor is determined by using Appendix 2, Table A.2, to find the value of i, given $n = 2$, and providing the conversion factor of .7692. In using the table, find the number of periods equated with n (in this case, 2). Then, move along to the right of the table until you find the conversion factor exactly or nearest to .7692. For this example, the conversion factor for $n = 2$ and i = .14 occurs exactly at .7692. Thus, the IRR is exactly 14 percent. When the factor for i falls in between two interest rates in the table, the best estimate of IRR may be determined through interpolation.

To find IRR for a series of payments, consider the IRR for $30,000 with a series of payments of $6,000 per year for five years. Appendix 2, Table A.2, is used to find the value of i where n = 5, given conversion factor of 2.941. When $n = 5$ the value for i = 21 is 2.991, while for i = .20 it is 2.926. Thus, the IRR for the investment falls between 20 and 21 percent. To obtain a more accurate approximation of the interest rate, interpolate as follows:

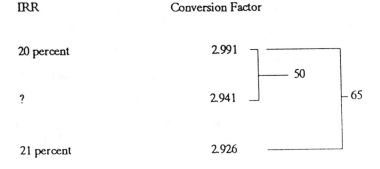

IRR   Conversion Factor

20 percent   2.991

                                                 50

?   2.941   65

21 percent   2.926

The estimate for the IRR is 50/65 or 20.77 percent. Like the capital budget evaluation techniques discussed previously, the IRR method can be used to accept or reject investment alternatives. The ranking system is based on the relative sizes of the IRR with the investments having the largest IRR being the most favored. Each investment acceptability is dependent on a comparison with the investor's required rate of return (RRR). The following decision rules apply: when IRR exceeds RRR, accept the investment; when IRR equals RRR, be indifferent or neutral; and when IRR exceeds RRR, reject the investment. It is important to remember that these decision rules are subject to a consideration of risk and liquidity.

It should be observed that the net present value is closely linked to IRR; each calculation uses the same discounting approach. However, while the NPV specifies a given interest rate, the IRR identifies the interest rate that yields a zero NPV.

Excess Present Value

This approach calculates the positive or negative percentage of streams of inflows over outflows of a project. By means of this approach, an index is calculated as follows:

$$Excess \quad Present \quad Value \quad Index \quad = \quad \frac{Present \quad Value}{Required \quad Investment}$$

This index can be used to compare and rank competing projects. Since it shows the present value of a project per dollar of investment, it provides a means of ranking projects of different sizes. This greatly simplifies finding the optimum solutions for competing projects when the budget for capital outlays have been arbitrarily determined. The criteria for selection and rejection are simple. Projects are ranked in order of profitability based on indices above 100 percent. Projects below 100 percent are undesirable because the cost of capital would exceed the adjusted rate of return. To illustrate, look at the example of a machine to process mail brought at a cost of $22,000.

Assume that money cost 16 percent and that the machine generates a cash flow of $5,000 per year for 10 years.

PV = $5,000 x 4.833 (using Appendix 2, Table A.2) = $24,165
Excess Present Value = $24,165 minus $22,000 = $2,615

$$Excess \quad Present \quad Value \quad Index \quad = \quad \frac{Present \quad Value}{Required \quad Investment}$$

or

$$\frac{214 \, , \, 165}{22 \, , \, 000} = 109 \, . \, 8 \ percent$$

Determining the Discount Rate

Though seldom discussed, the determination of the discount rate to be used in calculating the net present values and benefit cost ratios is critical. Two general ways have been used: (a) examining the cost of obtaining funds for the project and (b) examining the return on alternative investments. At the federal level, the Office of Management and Budget has endorsed 10 percent as a rate that may be used in government programs.

CONCLUDING OBSERVATIONS

Capital budgeting has great potential as a tool for public and other not-for-profit organizations. If effectively carried out, capital budgeting can aid a community's economic development and generate confidence in a governmental unit's ability to wisely manage its resources. Similarly, in other not-for-profit agencies, appropriate selection and good management of capital equipment can facilitate a better allocation of resources and minimize the possibility of fiscal strain.

Given the magnitude of resources required to fund capital projects, it is difficult for all but a few governmental units to use the popular pay-as-you-go funding approach for capital projects. Thus, capital budgeting requires that decision makers give serious thought to optimum methods for selecting a capital program mix to yield the greatest payoff for the amounts of dollars expended. The method of financing is especially critical since the selection of a particular option can result in either significant savings or additional costs.

Unlike in the past, a large number of public and not-for-profit organizations have begun applying varied techniques for analyzing and choosing among capital projects. Techniques such as internal rate of return (IRR), net present value, and excess present value approaches have been successfully applied.

NOTES

1. Alan Walter Steiss, *Local Government Finance* (Lexington, Mass.: Lexington Books, 1975), p. 4.

2. U.S. General Accounting Office (GAO), *Federal Capital Budgeting: A Collection of Haphazard Practices* (Washington, D.C.: GAO, 1981), p. i; see also Thomas M. Downs, "Reestoring Public Confidence in Infrastructure Investment", *Intergovernmental Perspective*, 29, no. 1 (Fall 1993-Winter 1994): 15-16.

3. International City Management Association (ICMA), "Planning for Capital Improvements," *Management Information Service Reports*, 16, no. 18 (August 1984): 5.

4. GAO, *Federal Capital Budgeting*, pp. 17-18.

5. ICMA, "Planning for Capital Improvements," pp. 2-3.

6. John L. Mikesell, *Fiscal Administration* (Homewood, Ill.: Dorsey Press, 1982), pp. 100-101.

7. Ibid., p. 3.

8. Ibid.

9. Steiss, *Local Government Finance*, p. 35; see also ICMA, "Planning for Capital Improvements," p. 13.

10. GAO, *Federal Capital Budgeting*, p. 39.

11. Steiss, *Local Government Finance*, pp. 104-5.

12. Ibid.

13. Bernard Smith, "The Pay-As-You-Go Concept in Municipal Financing," *Government Finance Review*, 6, no. 3 (June 1990): 21-22.

14. ICMA, "Planning for Capital Improvements," p. 8.

15. Ibid., pp. 8-9.

16. Dillion, Read, and Co., "Infrastructure Financing: An Overview" (November 1963), p. 4.

17. Ibid.; ICMA, "Planning for Capital Improvements," p. 10.

18. Dillon, Read, and Co., "Infrastructure Financing," pp. 1-2.

13

Line-Item and Performance Budgeting

While the last two chapters dealt with concepts and uses of budgets generally, this chapter examines two types of budgets that are found in practice - line-item and performance budgeting. Emphasis is focused on how each of these budgeting approaches allocates scarce resources among desirable courses of action. The development of the line-item and performance budgets is examined, as well as ways in which they are used for allocating, maintaining, and controlling financial resources.

LINE-ITEM BUDGETING

The line-item budget (also called the object-of-expenditure budget) is the earliest type of budget format to be used in public and nonprofit institutions. It came hand in hand with the development of modern budgeting. Its introduction was considered an innovative development by the reformers at the turn of the century. It replaced the lump sum budgeting approach.

The reformers sought to improve the economy and efficiency of organizations and to ensure the legality of expenditures in an effort to control graft and corruption in government. The line-item budget took prominence with the establishment of the executive budget, which reposed responsibility and accountability for government spending with the chief executive. This gave the chief executive a powerful instrument for controlling agency demands for money.

DEFINING LINE-ITEM BUDGET

Line-item budget is a technique in which line items (also known as objects of expenditure) are the main focus of analysis, authorization, and control. Typical line items include: supplies, personnel, travel, contractual services, and capital outlays. These are the items upon which major attention is focused and financial resources are controlled.

While there is no way of determining what the line-item budget will accomplish, it is easily understood. Table 13.1 clearly indicates the services or commodities to be purchased and the total amount of money that the City of Bright will spend for police services. The budget identifies items that administrators and elected officials can relate to in terms of their own experience. The fact that the line-item budget presents specific items that can be easily increased or reduced without debating the merits or demerit of a program enhances the opportunity for compromise.

A number of control objectives can be achieved with the line-item budget: (1) the avoidance of scandals by making sure that funds are spent for authorized purposes; (2) the accomplishment of the legislature's programmatic objectives; and (3) the maintenance of a balanced budget. Of the objectives, (3) and, most especially, (2) are the major concerns of the line-item/object budget.[1]

Line-item budgeting is the most widely used budgeting system today. It has wide appeal because of the type of accountability (narrow, with legal control) that it emphasizes. Attention is given to means for ensuring fidelity - preventing funds from being stolen and expended for unauthorized purposes. Emphasis is put on things or commodities to be bought rather than on the type and quality of services to be produced. For example, in a typical department, in Table 13.1, there are separate lines for wages and salaries; purchase of automobiles; equipment and supplies; and expenditures for other services, such as utilities; the list of items is limited only by the number of items or services requested.

A typical monthly budget report includes the budget category, the approved budget amount, amount expended this month, amount expended this year, and percent of budget expended and outstanding encumbrances (see Table 13.2).

The development of the line-item budget system involves the following steps:

1. The first step requires that categories of responsibility for expenditures be clearly defined. This action facilitates the development of an effective budget process, establishing clear lines for individual responsibility for each activity.
2. The amount of work and the kinds of skills required for each activity should be determined.

Table 13.1
City of Bright Police Department,
Simplified Line Item/Object Expenditure Budget, FY 1986
(Classified by Organizational Unit and Object of Expenditure)

Police Department:	Rate		
Salaries and Wages			
1 - Chief			
1 - Assistant Chief	40,000	40,000	
3 - Captains	30,000	30,000	
2 - Sergeants	25,000	75,000	
20 - Patrolmen	22,000	44,000	
4 - Radio Operators	18,000	324,000	
	14,000	56,000	569,000
Supplies/Materials			
Stationery and related supplies		1,500	
Janitorial and related supplies		800	
Gloves		400	
Gasoline and oil		5,000	
Uniforms		6,000	
Other		1,000	14,700
Other Service Charges			
Telephone			
Out-of-town travel		2,000	
Parking tickets		4,000	
Utilities		1,000	
Other		4,000	
		500	11,500
Capital Outlay			
2 - Motorcycles			
4 - Patrol cars		4,500	
Communication equipment		44,000	
		11,000	59,500
Total Police Department			$654,700

3. The budgetary unit desired to facilitate planning and controlling of expenditures should be defined.
4. A calendar is prepared specifically identifying individual or group responsibility and the target dates for completion.
5. Review of the object-of-expenditure classification chart should be undertaken to standardize and permit consolidation or summary of like items in departments.
6. Account codes should be examined and revised when necessary to make them consistent with the budgetary classification system.

The line-item process requires that agencies submit requests to the chief executive in terms of type of expenditures to be made according to established line items. The chief executive modifies these requests and submits them to the legislature or appropriate board. The latter then reviews, modifies, and appropriates funds on the line-item basis.

Once the budget is appropriated, the executive sets up the accounting system to record the line-item amounts as specified by the legislature or board. Additional controls are instituted for personnel hiring, transferring funds among intraagency and interagency accounts, and regulating amounts permitted to be spent from period to period. To facilitate the latter, an allotment system is set up to accommodate individual agency expenditure needs, based on past practice and the projection of likely expenditures during the fiscal period. Typically, each agency's appropriated funds are allocated on a monthly or quarterly basis (or whatever time period is considered acceptable). The allotment system provides a direct control device: amounts may not be increased without specific permission from the controlling budget official.

Whereas the allotment system tends to be used in larger agencies and governmental units, an expenditure plan (a less formal system) may be used by smaller agencies and governmental units. In this latter system the budget or staff official who has the responsibility for monitoring expenditures on a monthly or quarterly basis works with spending units to develop projections based, typically, on a five-year quarterly or monthly average corrected for any unusual events of the past and any expected abnormal occurrence in the coming fiscal period. When units or departments report that spending levels are higher than anticipated in the expenditure plan without an acceptable reason, prompt corrective action can be initiated. Among the actions that may be taken are transferring funds among activities, modifying work plans, reducing service levels, and cutting back expenditures on nonessential functions.

Table 13.2
City of Bright Police Department (Patrol)
Monthly Budget Report,
August 31, 1997

Budgetary Category	Approved Budget	Amount Expended This Month	Amount Expended This Year	Amount of Unexpended Budget	% Budget Unexpended	Outstanding Encumbrances*
Salaries and Wages	$128,000	$11,000	$88,000	$40,000	31.2	-0-
Fringe Benefits	32,000	2,500	20,000	12,000	37.5	-0-
Supplies/Materials	8,600	1,000	3,000	4,600	53.5	$2,500
Equipment	36,000	22,000	22,000	14,000	38.9	2,500
Total	$204,600	$36,500	$133,000	$70,600		$5,000

*Obligation or liability for amount of goods or services ordered but not yet delivered.

ADVANTAGES OF THE LINE-ITEM BUDGET

The line-item budget assigns expenditures on the basis of existing organization rather than on a responsibility center basis. There are a number of advantages associated with this type of budget. The line-item budget:

1. permits hierarchical authority to control inputs before the expenditure is made or obligated;
2. constrains the exercise of discretionary powers by managers;
3. helps to curtail the number of personnel positions, salary increases, and purchases - the largest cost in public and nonprofit agencies;
4. provides for uniform controls throughout an agency;
5. provides for the comprehensive control of all financial transactions and permits easy compilation of financial data, facilitating accounting and auditing systems and minimizing computational costs (records are collected in the everyday course of administrative activity with information is derived directly from vouchers, purchase order and other documents in use);
6. promotes clear-cut controls, minimizing the opportunity for circumvention of hierarchical controls (the controls can still be flexible for favored agencies and stringent for others that engage in unacceptable practices);
7. facilitates budget reductions. When agency spending exceeds revenues, cuts can be made without impairing the program objectives;
8. avoids the possibility of making large and costly mistakes;
9. provides continuity between the past, present, and future policy;
10. allows managers to operate with a greater degree of certainty; and
11. permits legislators to effect easier confirmations on dollar amounts rather than requiring agreement on program outcomes, thereby reducing or minimizing the potential for political conflict and deadlock in the political system.

INCREMENTALISM AND LINE-ITEM BUDGET

Incrementalism and line-item budgeting go hand in hand. Incremental budgets focus on limited alternatives that differ slightly from existing policy. Prior levels of expenditure become the major decision criterion for allocating resources. Typically, the budget makers accept amount X from the prior year budget and add a small increment, amount A, which is a percentage of X. The budget formula thus becomes $X + AX$.[2]

The incremental budget method has a built in upward bias. Small changes, when added together over successive years, can become significant. The incremental approach is accommodative to user advocates because it allows recurring programs to continue their growth with minimal scrutiny.

The Incremental Syndrome

The general orientation of budget makers directs them to add or subtract a percentage to last year's budget. When times are good, there is reasonable expectation that more money will be available. Additions are routinely made "to all line-items or selectively whenever it seems to make the most sense."[3] Likewise, in bad years small increments are added or subtracted, depending on the revenue outlook.

Decision rules (rules of thumb, generally agreed upon bench-marks, or criteria for facilitating decision making) typically characterize traditional incremental budget preparation. Once an amount is granted to a program or activity, it becomes the base or part of the basic budget from which "fair share" increases or decreases are added or subtracted.[4] Only amounts proposed above the "fair share" amount need to be justified, while expenditures for programs already in existence that do not exceed the fair share guideline go unquestioned and unchallenged.

Marginal or incremental changes constrain attempts to redirect social objectives. Policy-making tends to be short-range and tactical. Since no comprehensive analysis or weighing of cost and benefits of objectives is undertaken, no effort is made to make the best decision among available alternatives. The present budget is a mirror of the past and the future is a projection of the present.

DISADVANTAGES OF THE LINE-ITEM BUDGET

The main shortcomings of the line-item budget include the following:

1. There is a total preoccupation with material acquisition or inputs.
2. Accountability is focused on a narrow concept of what money can buy and not on output and impact (i.e., changes produced as a result of the program).

3.   Little attention is given to organization and/or program goals, making it difficult or virtually impossible to provide information for evaluating the efficiency and effectiveness of an agency's activities.

4.   Most budget items require no justification.

5.   Once a program has been funded, the program is likely to continue indefinitely barring major adverse publicity.

6.   It provides fragmented historical cost data that are not useful for program execution and evaluation.

7.   Reports based on the line-item budget produce very little financial data that can be used in planning, programming, and evaluating an agency's activities.

8.   Input-planning decisions are made at the lower levels if the organization.

9.   Goals and objectives of the organization are made on the basis of dollar amount allocated to the different activities. Operating procedures become policy. Thus, purposes are not consciously considered and achievement of objectives is due more to chance than to design (the City of Pittsburgh Department of Lands and Buildings budget provides a good illustration. The line-item budget has six responsibility areas. However, although there are no stated objectives for any activity; performance statistics are included in the budget, providing no basis for effective evaluation).

10.   Neither the executive branch nor the legislature is given information that permits them to allocate available resources wisely.

11.   Though it facilitates compromise, it promotes poor decision making.

12.   Emphasis is put on what is bought, and it fails to address policy or management issues.

POLITICS AND THE LINE-ITEM BUDGET

Despite the fact that line-item/incremental budgeting is viewed as stable, predictable, and conservative, the politics that surround its preparation, particularly in the public sector, may permit small increases to explode into unmanageable programs with huge costs overruns. For example, the Mark 48 Torpedo was sold to Congress as an almost invulnerable torpedo at a total cost of $680 million. A combination of participants, including U.S. Naval Ordinance Division, Westinghouse, and Penn State University, were selected to build the torpedo.[5] To minimize the possibility of cost overruns, Congress hired Peat,

Marwick, Mitchell and Company to monitor program costs. Between the time the project got started in 1963 and its completion in 1973, the cost grew from $680 million to $4.5 billion, a fourfold cost increase. Initially the torpedo system was estimated to appear low in cost but high in terms of effectiveness. The expenditure increments continued for several years before a more accurate cost for completing the project was estimated. If at the outset, the real cost had been estimated to be $4.5 billion, the project might never have been undertaken. This is a constant problem in public administration, especially in government contracting, where payment to the contractor is based on cost-plus-fee arrangement.

The political practice undergirding incremental budgeting has generated several rules that are used in preparing and submitting a budget. They include the following:

1. Avoid asking for sums smaller than the current appropriation.
2. When an implementing agency wishes to avoid close scrutiny and review, increases are put in the basic budget. Since new requests are subject to close scrutiny, it is good strategy to identify them with the basic budget or high-priority areas whenever possible.
3. Never give the appearance that you are making fundamental changes from existing policies. All necessary increases must be made to look small, appearing to grow out of existing operations.
4. Make it possible to permit budget reviewers to look good by leaving something for them to cut. This allows the budget reviewer to act while you nonetheless achieve your objective.[6]

Like the budget preparers, the reviewers or gatekeepers also employ decision rules, such as the following:

1. When new personnel are requested, decrease or eliminate the request.
2. Renovate and/or repair facilities rather than replace them.
3. As a general policy, avoid cutting safety or health-related requests, especially those programs that have substantial public support.
4. Decrease requests of departments with poor or bad reputations.
5. Reduce or eliminate by some fixed percentage all nonoperating requests.[7]

TARGET BASE BUDGETING (TBB): THE NEW ORTHODOXY

Many of the governmental units (e.g., the state of New Jersey, the city of San Antonio, Texas) which dismantled their zero based budgeting (ZBB) system have reverted to line-item budgeting or a variant of it called *target base budgeting*. This budgeting approach establishes a departmental or responsibility center spending ceiling. Within the prescribed limits, some shifting among expenditure functions or activities is permitted. The ceiling targets are set on the basis of projected revenue estimates. Thus, the amount or percentage approved as the target varies according to the expected changes in revenues.

In some jurisdictions such as Cincinnati, Ohio; Rochester, New York; Tampa, Florida; and Palatine, Illinois, where innovative target base budgeting has been implemented, creative features of ZBB and performance budgeting can be found. Target base budgets are prepared in two parts. The first part includes the funded service that is accommodated within the target while the second part contains the prioritized, unfunded list of service items. Because the targets are set at conservative levels, often a pool of resources is left "to allow for add-backs, new or expanded projects and political priorities".[8]

Advantages

Target base budgeting is attractive because it is very adaptable to the regular budgeting cycle flow and is based on a conservative and eclectic philosophy. The operating norm allows it to borrow from other innovations such as ZBB, PPBS, management by objectives (MBO), and performance budgeting as each situation dictates. As a "hold the line" budget it is a budget approach that champions fiscal responsibility. It virtually banishes, deficits while it tends to generate savings or surpluses. Budgets can easily be reduced or maintained during recessions and increased during times of prosperity. Target base budgeting provides politicians with the opportunity to affect priorities on short notice without creating undue problems. Agency managers are given strong incentives to improvise and take necessary action to enhance their chances to live within their prescribed resource constraint. This forces managers to develop decision rules to allow them to make hard choices and to prioritize when faced with a crisis. Thus, while targets are centrally determined (top down), any trade-offs, specific allocations, and changes between line items and programs are decentralized.[9] Finally, target base budgeting allows retargeting during the year. This forces managers to think about priorities early in the budget cycle.

Disadvantages

TBB is revenue driven, typically not by articulated goals and objectives, but by revenue projections, which are subject to changes as the revenue sources are affected by the economy, intergovernmental fund transfers, plant closings and a host of other factors. This reality tends to institutionalize a conservative orientation which leads to underestimation of revenues and, in turn, may lead to ill-advised staff reductions.

Since targets are often given in percentages, decisions tend to be ad hoc. The path of least resistance is to cut across the board. This may induce responsibility managers to play gamesmanship by cutting popular and high-priority programs, knowing that they are likely to receive supplemental resources from the pool of savings to fund them when reallocation is made.

TBB is essentially an emphasis on orthodoxy unless it is implemented and practiced as a hybrid budget, allowing the adoption of innovative features from systems such as ZBB and PPBS. While a number of governmental units have adopted this approach, a far greater number have reverted to the traditional ceiling line-item budget. As a budget that is revenue driven, there is no direct and systematic linkage between prioritized needs and the services/goods that are delivered. Traditional TBB is a tactical ad hoc, stop-and-go resource allocation system that does not look over the horizon but rather maximizes budget balancing and stability. This is a virtue that is definitely needed during recessionary periods and in declining communities but it is likely to be counterproductive in growing or stable environments. However, where the more innovative form of TBB is practiced, it has much to offer.

PERFORMANCE BUDGETING

At the national level, the Taft Commission of 1912 advocated a functional work-based classification approach to budget expenditures. This became known as *performance budgeting* (also identified as the cost data budget). It was first implemented in the Borough of Richmond, New York City, before World War I. Few units of government gave performance budgeting serious consideration until it was popularized by the Hoover Commission in 1949. The commission report stated: "We recommend that the whole budgeting concept of the federal government should be refashioned by the adoption of a budget based on functions, activities, and projects: This we designate the 'performance budget.'"[10] It was widely talked about and practiced throughout the 1950s.

Defining Performance Budget

The National Committee on Governmental Accounting defines performance budgeting as a budget that is "based primarily upon measurable performance of activities and work programs."[11]   Stated another way, performance budgeting comprises specific techniques directing attention to the service to be provided and the required work that should be performed. Services are broken down and described in terms of required inputs and projected outputs. The analysis of the efficiency of existing operations is a main objective.   Its main tools are cost accounting and work measurement.   The budget account is classified by organizational functions, activities, and object of expenditure, for example,

> Public Safety (Function);
> Department (Police);
> Activity (Patrol); and
> Object of Expenditure (Personnel Services, Materials, etc.).

Performance budgeting requires that standard unit costs be established. These permit budget projections to be determined by multiplying the unit costs by the number of work units in a given activity for the coming fiscal period. Each budget has a narrative description of proposed activities that are supported by cost estimates with expected accomplishments identified in quantitative terms. Input and output resource and total cost are clearly identified (see Table 13.3).

The major focus of performance budget is on economy and efficiency accountability.   Emphasis is put on the identification of activities (output) units for each activity, estimate of workload (output units) to be accomplished for each activity, determination of input (resources) required to accomplish the projected output for each activity, and projection of the unit costs and expenditure budget.

The performance budget is used as an important instrument to assess and improve service efficiency. It is most useful at the program-planning level that is staffed by middle management.   To facilitate work measurement comparison, with preestablished work standards and unit costing, expenditures are categorized by function and activity. Performance budgeting is most useful as a means for matching work to be done with the skills and training of the available work force. To minimize waste and create greater predictability in the pursuit of the goal of efficiency, the installation of a monitoring system is required.

The workload indicator is a critical component in the performance budget system. It allows management to plan work units, assess unit cost, and produce countable outputs. The development of the workload requires: (1) clear definition; (2) periodic updating of the entity's information system; (3)

Table 13.3
City of Bright, Sample Performance Budget

FUND:	General
DEPARTMENT:	Police
ACTIVITY:	Patrolling

PROGRAM AND PERFORMANCE

FUNCTION:

The Patrol Division of the Police Department provides prevention, suppression, and detection of criminal activity, traffic law enforcement, and general public safety to residents of the City of Bright.

PROGRAM COMMENTS:

The Patrol Division responds directly to calls for service received at its headquarters and through the county-wide emergency number 911. The program proposes twenty full-time patrolmen and two sergeants. This year's budget includes $20,000 in out-of-state funds to expand patrolling downtown. An increase of $24,000 is requested in this FY 1995-1996 budget.

PROGRAM MEASUREMENT:

	Actual 1995-96	Estimated 1995-96	Proposed 1996-97
1. Patrolling Residential Areas (hrs.)	9,825	10,927	11,308
2. Patrolling Business Areas (hrs.)	10,570	10,925	12,215
3. Issuing Citations #	6,514	7,528	8,721
4. Issuing Citations (hrs.)	1,500	1,800	2,312
5. Appearing in Traffic Court (hrs.)	1,395	2,189	1,556
6. Patrolling Special Events (hrs.)	2,007	2,500	2,715
7. Patrolling Events #	31	43	59
8. Arresting D.U.I. #	573	841	733
9. Patrolling for Crime Prevention (hrs.)	3,500	2,900	3,182
10. Patrolling School Crossing (hrs.)	2,967	3,100	3,300
11. Patrolling Supervision (hrs.)	2,537	3,528	4,176
12. Vacation Sick Leave (hrs.)	513	795	897

WORK DESCRIPTION:

1. Patrolling Residential Areas

Unit: Hours	9,825	10,927	11,308
Unit: Cost	$ 13.571	$ 13.651	$ 13.885
Total Cost	$133,335	$149,164	$157,012

2. Patrolling Business Areas

Unit: Hours	10,570	10,925	12,215
Unit: Cost	$ 13.726	$ 13.866	$ 13.707
Total Cost	$145,084	$151,486	$167,431

3. Issuing Citations

Unit: Hours	1,500	1,800	2,312
Unit: Cost	$ 13.902	$ 13.991	$ 13.893
Total Cost	$ 20,853	$ 25,184	$ 32,121

4. Overseeing Traffic Accidents

Unit: Hours	1,125	2,189	2,531
Unit: Cost	$ 14.229	$ 13.789	$ 13.774
Total Cost	$ 16,008	$ 30,184	$ 34,862

5. Appearing in Court			
Unit: Hours	1,395	1,556	2,217
Unit: Cost	$ 13.887	$ 13.728	$ 13.757
Total Cost	$ 19,372	$ 21,361	$ 30,499
6. Patrolling Special Events			
Unit: Hours	2,007	2,500	2,715
Unit: Cost	$ 14.037	$ 13.941	$ 14.120
Total Cost	$ 28,172	$ 34,853	$ 38,336
7. Patrolling School Crossing			
Unit: Hours	2,967	3,100	3,300
Unit: Cost	$ 14.037	$ 13.982	$ 13.941
Total Cost	$ 41,648	$ 43,344	$ 46,005
8. Arresting D.W.I.			
Unit: Hours	380	580	701
Unit: Cost	$ 13.900	$ 14.100	$ 14.21
Total Cost	$ 5,282	$ 8,178	$ 9,961
9. Patrolling for Crime Prevention			
Unit: Hours	3,500	29,000	3,182
Unit: Cost	$ 13.75	$ 13.82	$3.91
Total Cost	$ 48,125	$ 40,078	$44,262
10. Patrolling Supervisor			
Unit: Hours	2,537	3,528	4,196
Unit: Cost	$15.25	$16.10	$16.43
Total Cost	$ 38,689	$ 56,801	$ 68,940
11. Vacation, Sick Leave			
Unit: Hours	513	795	897
Unit: Cost	$13.52	$13.71	$13.87
Total Cost	$ 6,936	$ 10,899	$ 12,441
Grand Total	$503,504	$571,532	$641,870

determination of activities/programs susceptibility to workload measurement; and (4) locating the process for identifying workload measurement development within the responsibility center charged with carrying out the activity.

Once the organization has committed itself to the implementation of the performance budget system, it must decide, at an early stage, on the comparative benchmark or yardstick that will be employed to measure performance. The three most frequently used types of benchmarks involve one of the following: a historical standard (comparison of past performance), budgeted standard (the budget office benchmark), or engineered standard (based on rigorously and empirically determined standard). To illustrate the performance budget format for one function, the City of Bright budget for the Community Education subfunction (activity) of Crime Prevention is presented (see Table 13.4).

Crime Prevention - Community Education Budget

One full-time officer and one part-time assistant (equivalent to half a

Table 13.4
Projected Performance Budget for
Community Education
FY 1997

	Objective	Projected 1996	Revised 1996	Projected 1997
Workload Measures - Community Education				
1. Number of hours on crime watch education and related activities	1,2	720	700	710
2. Number of hours lecturing at schools and institutions	4,2	550	510	550
3. Number of hours in-house community relations	1,2	450	440	420
4. Number of hours distributing materials	3	420	460	410
5. Number of hours preparing materials	1,3	360	360	370
6. Number of hours responding to 911 calls	1,2	320	300	270
7. Number of hours of general seminars	1,2	300	320	310
Efficiency Measures - Community Education				
1. Cost per hour of crime watch	1,2	$13.54	$13.49	$13.15
2. Cost per lecture at schools and institutions	4,2	13.49	13.61	13.15
3. Cost per in-house community relations seminars	1,2	13.32	13.49	13.15
4. Cost per hour of distributing materials	3	13.49	13.49	13.15
5. Cost per hour preparing materials	1,3	13.50	13.50	13.15
6. Cost per hour responding to 911 calls	1,2	13.49	13.49	13.14
7. Cost per hour of general seminars	1,2	13.47	12.54	13.14

Projected 1997

Activity	Work Unit	Unit Cost	Number of Units	Expenditure
Community Education	Hours	$13.50	3,040	$41,040

full-time officer) have been assigned to this activity. Four objectives have been established: (1) the provision of 720 hours of community crime watch education, (2) reduction of reported "911" calls by 10 percent, (3) distribution of crime prevention brochures (420) to community residents, and (4) lecturing (550 hours) to schools and other invited places. The unit cost average is $10.50 (projected and actual). The number of hours projected and revised number of units in 1996 and 1997 were 3,120 units and 3,040 respectively (see Table 13.4).

A performance budget seeks answers to questions such as the following: What are the agency's objectives? What services are being provided to justify the agency's existence? What are the required activities to realize the agency's objectives? What is the volume of work required to achieve each activity? What are the level of expenditure and the unit costs for both inputs and outputs for the items requested? Note that attention is focused on major functions and work activities such as street cleaning, inspecting, and tree trimming. Each activity must be identified in terms of work or output unit, for example, a mile of street cleaned or an inspection completed. All major resource *input units* for items such as materials and supplies used and personnel hours worked are specifically identified. The cost per unit of input and cost of output per unit of things produced are determined by dividing the cost of resources used by the level or volume of items involved (e.g., 200 personal hours were worked at a cost of $1,000 or a per-unit input cost per hour of $5; thirty miles of streets were paved at a cost of $30,000 or at a cost per output mile completed of $1,000).

Successful performance budget development requires a lengthy period of strong leadership. In the initial implementation phase, attention should be given to the development of the budget structures, cost centers, performance measures, and account-coding system. Next, the recent past performance history of the agency should be organized. Given the new structure and the information on cost performance, the budget estimates can then be developed. The development of a performance budget involves seven steps:

1. Define individual work activities in terms that are measurable and can be related to resource requirements.
2. Inventory the work units and the kind of work that must be performed on each.
3. Develop quantity standards for each activity to permit estimation of the amount of work required during the year, expressed in terms of annual number of units of work (tons, cubic yards, gallons, acres mowed, etc.). Quantity standards are used to define the workload to be undertaken and the minimal acceptable quality of work necessary to carry out an activity.
4. Determine the number of work units per activity. This task is made

easy after the quantity standards and the inventory of the amount of work to be done on each activity has been established.

    5. Establish production standards. The efficiency with which work is performed is a function of how the workers are assigned and equipped and the methods used in performing work activities. Responsibility should then be assigned to investigate and evaluate alternative methods for accomplishing each activity.

    6. Compute resource requirements by applying production standards to the defined work program. For example, the production standard for premix patching, stipulates the following conditions:

Crew size:	3 persons or workers
Equipment:	1 dump truck
Accomplishment/crew day	3.75 tons premix
Production rate:	6.4 person-hour/ton

Activity	Quantity Standard	Work to be Done		Work Units
Mowing	3 Mowings x acres	2,500 mowable	=	7,500 acres
Pothole Patching With Gravel	2,500 cu. yds. x gravel/mile	400 miles	=	1,000,000 cu. yds.
Patching With Premix	7.5 tons x premix/mile	100 level miles	=	750 tons premix

Assuming the activity called for 750 tons of premix patching, the resource requirement would be:

crew days	=	750 tons - 3.75 tons/day = 200 days
person-hours	=	3 persons x 8 hours/day x 200 days
	=	4,800 person-hours

or

person-hours	=	6.4 person-hours/ton x 750
	=	4,800 person-hours
equipment	=	200 days x 8 hours
	=	1,600 hours for dump truck

materials   =   750 tons of bituminous premix
                              material

7. Collect cost data and convert the performance budget resource
requirements into financial terms. The procedures for each work activity would
be developed as shown as follows for premix patching:

Object of Expenditure	Resource Requirements	Average Unit Cost		Annual Cost
Labor	4,800 per hour	x $3.00/hour	=	$14,400
Equipment	1,600 dump truck hours	x $1.50/hour	=	2,400
Materials	750 tons of premix	x $6.00/ton	=	4,500
Total				$21,300

USES OF THE PERFORMANCE BUDGET

Performance budgeting is intended to help administrators assess and
improve the efficiency of an agency.   It is management oriented and is
especially useful at the middle-management level to aid in monitoring
performance and coordinating work activities and in providing useful
information for the review of operations.   Additionally, it promotes
accountability to top management and improves work planning and scheduling.
The advantages of performance budgeting are that it: (1) allows the
relaxation of control over inputs; (2) deemphasizes external control and puts
greater stress on internal control; (3) shifts the focus from budgeting control to
administrative control; (4) regularizes post-audit and post control; (5) promotes
better work planning and scheduling; (6) enhances the responsibility and
acceptability of management; and (7) facilitates the use of variance analysis and
performance reporting as an important management control device.

PERFORMANCE BUDGETS: SOME IMPORTANT DISADVANTAGES

Perhaps a major reason for the lack of success in the adoption of
performance budgeting in public and nonprofit agencies has been due to a
number of problems inherent in it.   The problems include (1) input and output

unit costing; (2) accounting and cost data requirements; (3) diffused organizational responsibility; and (4) its emphasis on volume of work done rather than on quality and effectiveness.

Input and Output Unit Costing

The unit-costing feature, which is an integral part of performance budgeting, has a number of potential problems. Factors such as inflation, strikes, and transportation delays may impact on unit cost, causing it to change. Thus, some opponents of performance budgeting advocate that unit costing be replaced by work measurement (the person-hours or the physical number of units used) in budget development. The use of person-hours makes especially good sense in public and nonprofit agencies since it represents about 80 percent of input cost factors.

Accounting and cost data requirements

Most human services organizations present particular problems with output unit cost measurements. In both government and, to a lesser extent, nonprofit organizations, accounts are maintained on the expenditure basis rather than full cost basis. This makes it exceedingly difficult to collect cost data that can be used to determine unit output costs. To overcome or minimize these problems requires extensive accounting and data-gathering facilities, which may be too expensive for small municipalities and nonprofit agencies.

Diffused responsibilities

Since the identification of work activities and unit (input and output) measurements are the critical components of performance budgeting, attention is focused on the contribution of each activity and little attention is paid as to how activities relate to specific organizational units. Table 13.5 shows five possible combinations of activities. While the matrix indicates four activities (#2, #3, #4, and #5) contributing to each other, activity #1 provides no input or assistance to the others. This is a typical problem associated with performance budgeting; it does not facilitate integration or coordination among activities. These problems must be overcome if public and nonprofit agencies are to be effective instruments in providing the public with goods and services.

Performance budgeting has enjoyed far less success than line-item budgeting because it demands a greater investment in time and skill. Performance budgeting demonstrates a method by which government and non-

Table 13.5
Activity Grid or Matrix Reporting

Unit	Activity #1	Activity #2	Activity #3	Activity #4	Activity #5	Total
A	$100,000	$ 25,000	$ 16,000	$ 14,000	$ 40,000	$195,000
B	--	80,000	5,000	12,000	35,000	132,000
C	--	10,000	70,000	30,000	5,000	115,000
D	--	6,000	8,000	4,000	25,000	43,000
E	--	13,000	21,000	90,000	20,000	144,000
Total	$100,000	$134,000	$120,000	$150,000	$125,000	$629,000

profit agencies could develop techniques to measure performance. Its emphasis on measurement and efficiency is its greatest strength. Performance budgeting's pursuit of efficiency is a narrow focus emphasizing the quantity and unit cost of things produced but not the impact or results they achieve. Minimal attention is given to the budget policy decision, limiting the effectiveness of performance budgeting in decision making.

Lack of Emphasis on Effectiveness

Performance budgeting focuses attention on process rather than on end purposes and results. Output units measure volume or the amount of work performed. Stress is put on countable quantities of things (e.g., miles of paved streets, tons of garbage removed, or number of library books loaned). The measures do not tell the quality factor of the goods and services produced (e.g., the quality of the road paved, the cleanliness rating obtained as a result of the garbage removal, or the number of books requested but not available at the library). However, in a number of cases, the quality attributes can be identified without too much difficulty. By incorporating the quality factor, performance budgeting proponents can blunt the criticism that the budget tends to concentrate on activities that are easily susceptible to output measurement while excluding or minimizing those that are not.

SUMMARY OBSERVATIONS

While line-item budgeting has many admirable points, there are also many weaknesses. Its simplicity, practicability, and understandability are major reasons why it has endured with great popularity. On the whole, however, the shortcomings of line-item budgeting outweigh its strengths. Its preoccupation with inputs, narrow control, and dollar accountability and its lack of issue and policy orientation are serious impediments. These problems must be overcome if public and nonprofit agencies wish to use their budget as an effective instrument for the delivery of public goods and services.

NOTES

1. Thomas J. Kane, Jr., "Budget Directors View Budget Control," *Public Budgeting and Finance*, 2, #2 (Summer 1982): 44.

2. Edward J. Luksus, "Strategic Budgeting: How to Turn Financial Records into Strategic Assets," *Management Review*, Vol. 70 (March 1981): 44.

3. Robert Leduc, "Financial Management and Budgeting," in *The Nonprofit Organization Handbook*, ed. Tracy Daniel Connors, (New York: McGraw-Hill, 1980), pp. 6, 51-52.

4. These amounts are the resources designated necessary to minimally carry out the functions of a program in order to prevent it from falling below an agreed-upon acceptable standard.

5. Daniel Guttman and Barry Willner, *The Shadow Government* (New York: Parthenon Books, 1976), pp. 42-44.

6. See Thomas Anton, *The Politics of State Expenditures in Illinois* (Champaign, Ill.: University of Illinois Press), pp. 6-51; and Aaron Wildavsky, *Budgeting* (Boston: Little, Brown, 1975), p. 24.

7. Wildavsky, *Budgeting*, p. 24.

8. Irene S. Rubin, "Budgeting for Our Times: Target Base Budgeting," *Public Budgeting and Finance*, 11, no. 3, (Fall 1991): 5.

9. Ibid.

10. Commission on Organization of the Executive Branch of the Government, *Budget and Accounting* (Washington, D.C.: USGPO, 1949), p. 8.

11. Municipal Finance Officers Association, *Governmental Accounting, Auditing and Financial Reporting* (GAAFR) (Chicago, Ill: Municipal Finance Officers Association, 1980), App. B-70.

14

The Planning, Programming, Budgeting System, (PPBS): A Rational Framework

The planning, programming, budgeting system (PPBS) was developed in response to dissatisfaction with traditional line-item budgeting and performance types of budgeting. It was felt that line-item budgeting was overly preoccupied with control and too little concerned with policy and results. Performance budgeting, which was expected to overcome many of the infirmities of the line-item budget, produced problems of its own. Performance budgeting is focused on things or work completed and unit costing. It draws attention away from alternative costing approaches which linked organizational goals and objectives. Emphasis is put mainly on things that are measurable or countable. Thus, while there is concern for output, little effort was made to link output with policy goals and objectives.

This chapter focuses attention on the theory and practice of PPBS. The reader is provided with the basic philosophy and techniques that underlie the PPBS approach to the allocation of scarce resources.

EARLY PROGRAM BUDGETING

The early development of program budgeting represented a bridge between performance budget and PPBS. Because of the different emphasis of program budgeting and PPBS, they are discussed separately. Like PPBS, the program budget emphasizes results.[1] The approach focuses on information more usable to the administrator than the accountant. The program budget includes a more comprehensive view of the budget process than either the line-item or performance budgets.

Program budgeting has the following attributes: (1) it encourages identification of program purpose, program development, and commitment to planning; (2) it brings considerable order to masses of detail in terms of understandable issues and specific plans; (3) like PPBS, it emphasizes multiyear planning and periodic reevaluation of program results; (4) unlike PPBS, it begins below top management, at the middle and operating levels, thus guarding against overcentralization; (5) it gives less attention than PPBS to the systematic consideration of alternatives; and (6) it stresses the input-output linkage, facilitating cost-benefit analysis.

Program budgeting is an extension of performance budgeting in that it defines program objectives and obtains measures (output) to assess these objectives. However, it differs from performance budget because its emphasis is more on program planning and assessment of output results. It is unlike PPBS in that it gives less attention to alternative analyses in making program selection. The definition of program is essentially the same in both systems, referring to a combination of resources, manpower, materials, and facilities (e.g., equipment, capital, and skills) that are put together to achieve a common set of objectives within a specified period of time.

PLANNING, PROGRAMMING, AND BUDGETING SYSTEM (PPBS)

Definition

PPBS is a planning, implementing, and control system. As a comprehensive decision-making instrument, it is designed to accommodate and integrate multiple functions (see Figure 14.1). It provides an important link between strategic planning (long- and medium-range) and operating plans. PPBS is a systematic effort concerned with the integration of planning, programming, and budgeting. It requires the articulation of explicit goals, purposes and objectives from which strategic output-oriented programs are identified. In turn, it generates output budget information from which effective resource allocations can be made. Viewed as such, PPBS is a subsystem of system analysis. Once the program outputs have been specified, expenditures can then be converted into the traditional line-item requests.

A major focus of PPBS is the purposes for which an agency is requesting funds. As a policy-oriented and decision-making system, PPBS seeks to improve resource allocation by assisting agencies in making the best selection among competing alternatives in the pursuit of organizational goals and objectives. PPBS is thus an important analytical tool designed to help decision makers achieve their assigned responsibilities with optimal results.

The underlying premises on which PPBS are based is perhaps best revealed in the answers to the following questions: (1) What are the basic goals and objectives being pursued? (2) What are the alternative means for achieving

Figure 14.1

PPBS as an Integrative Decision-Making Process: Conceptual View

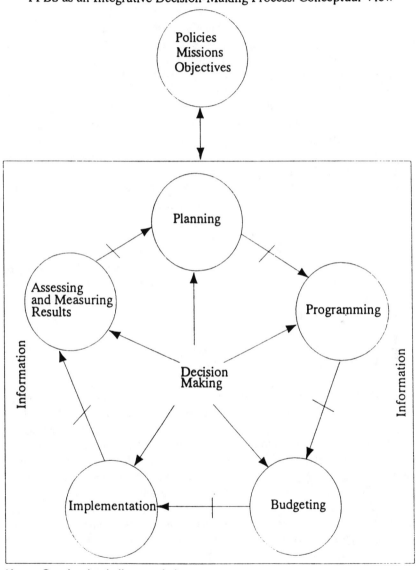

Note: Crosshatches indicate analysis.

articulated goals and objectives? (3) What are the costs (present, future, and full) of each alternative, in both financial and nonfinancial terms? (4) What are the benefits to be achieved from each alternative and how effective will each aid in achieving articulated goals and objectives? (See box, "Factors in Cost-Effectiveness Studies.)

Before PPBS can be initiated, an agency must develop an analytical capability to examine in depth its objectives and the programs identified to achieve them (see Figure 14.2). There will be a need to create an improved budgeting mechanism to facilitate broad program decision making and to translate it into budgeting outcomes to be presented to the chief executive and legislative or board officials for action. The schema in Figure 14.2 shows the steps that may be involved in developing a PPBS budget. Based on an assessment of needs and an evaluation of resource constraints, goals and objectives are articulated. Next, an agencywide program structure is developed. Programs are fitted into the structure and analyzed, after which a multiyear program budget and financial plan are constructed.

Figure 14.2 clearly indicates that a budget is an instrument for implementing long-range plans. Unlike traditional line-item budgeting, in which budget decision making is primarily done upward, PPBS decision making is mainly a downward aggregative process of information flow. In contrast to traditional budgeting systems which take a retrospective view in assessing what was done with resources, PPBS takes a prospective focus about the future impact of resource application. An unarticulated but implied premise of PPBS is that it is better to implement the right decision inefficiently than implement the wrong decision efficiently.

PPBS: ANALYZING THE CONCEPTS

PPBS comprises concepts, systems, processes, techniques, and formats. It is a management decision-making instrument that ties long-, medium-, and short-range plans into budgeting. The PPBS approach is designed to accommodate and integrate multiple management functions into an operating plan of action. Figure 14.1 schematically depicts the four main concepts (planning, programming, budgeting, and systems) in the PPBS decision-making system. The schema shows policies, missions, and objectives as the major input into the PPB system, which is held together by a decision-making network. This network links a dynamic and interactive process that must be maintained among the major components in the existing information system.

Figure 14.2
Schema of the PPBS Process ①

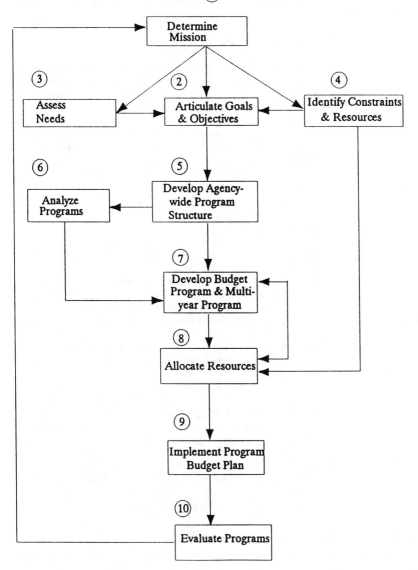

FACTORS IN COST-EFFECTIVENESS STUDIES

The cost-effectiveness study should result in a written document that contains all of the basic elements of good analysis:

1. A clear definition of the problem or problems.
2. Identification of the basic objectives involved.
3. Selection of "criteria" or "measures of effectiveness" that will permit an estimation of progress in relation to the basic objectives. These should not be limited to only those criteria that are believed to be quantifiable. So-called intangibles, if pertinent to program selection, should be included.
4. Identification and description of the key features and of the alternative ways of attempting to meet the problems. Alternatives may be in the form of different programs or different levels of a program, or both.
5. Estimates of the full cost implications of each alternative, including future as well as immediate implications.
6. Estimates of the full effects of each alternative (relative to each of the criteria identified as being important) to include future as well as immediate implications.
7. A clear presentation of the trade-offs among the alternatives considering the costs and effects as estimated in (5) and (6). Charts, graphs, and tables are useful presentation devices.
8. Identification of the major uncertainties and the quantification of the uncertainties, to the extent possible. Some uncertainty, and often, considerable uncertainty, can be expected to be present in any realistic analysis. The efforts of these uncertainties on the potential decisions should be estimated.
9. Identification of the major assumptions made in the study with an indication of the degree to which program choices may be sensitive to these assumptions.
10. Documentation of the study in such a manner to permit others to understand and evaluate what was done in the analysis and to obtain a feeling for how accurate the basic data and the findings can be expected to be. A cost-effectiveness analysis may use, if applicable, many of the techniques of mathematics, operations research, economics, and so forth. They may also draw upon various previously done technical and nontechnical studies that are pertinent to the study at hand. The cost-effectiveness analysis treats such problems as those identified in individual issue papers or perhaps will examine one category of the program structure or a group of interacting categories.

Source: Adapted from George Washington University, "State-Local Financial Projects ,"in Ralph G. Caso, ed., *Management Information Systems* (Nassau County, N.Y.: Fiscal Administration, 1971), pt. 3, p. 7.

Planning

Planning is the most fundamental activity in program budgeting because it is based on planned programs which give it a unique identity vis-à-vis other types of budgets. Since PPBS is a mission- and management-oriented system, planning (the first "P"), is the focal point and the ingredient that facilitates the effective clustering of activities around objectives. Thus, planning begins by defining objectives or outcomes to be achieved and concludes by suggesting the optimal way to realize the objectives. It is the formulation of a future course of action; it specifies and classifies long- and short-range goals. It is an important means for coping with a dynamic environment which generates uncertainty, a changing mission, evolving goals and priorities, and changing procedures.[2]

Planning does not take place in a vacuum. Rather, it is undertaken to achieve some goal or objective. Examples include welfare planning, comprehensive health care, and education planning. All organizations have goals and objectives, planning is the means that is used to achieve them. Typically, organizational goals and objectives are identified in a structure that may be broken down into subgoals (a goal-objective structure). Goals may be viewed in a hierarchical structure, as indicated in Figure 14.3, in which the goal is subdivided, becoming more specific and quantitative at each succeeding level of division.

Planning Constraints

Figure 14.2 indicated constraints as an important factor to be considered in the analysis and selection of program alternatives. What may appear to be a theoretically sound alternative might not be feasible in the real world due to operating constraints. Thus, constraints should be considered early in the planning stages so that they may be used as guidelines in the development of goals and the development of alternative methods of achieving them.

Program analysis is an important factor during the planning stages. It is especially critical during this stage, in which selection must be made among alternative courses of action in the pursuit of articulated organizational goals. Program analysis requires the establishment of selection criteria. The latter permits the elimination of clearly unfeasible alternatives without resorting to detailed analysis. Once these initial eliminations have been made, detailed analysis is undertaken to identify the alternative program that meets the established criteria. The analysis typically focuses on three aspects: (1) monetary

Figure 14.3
A Hierarchical Goal Structure in a Large Organization

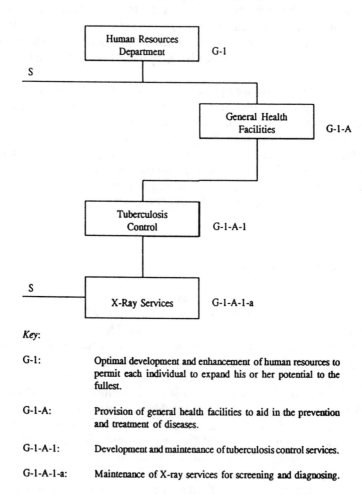

Key:

G-1:   Optimal development and enhancement of human resources to
            permit each individual to expand his or her potential to the
            fullest.

G-1-A: Provision of general health facilities to aid in the prevention
            and treatment of diseases.

G-1-A-1:   Development and maintenance of tuberculosis control services.

G-1-A-1-a: Maintenance of X-ray services for screening and diagnosing.

and other resources needed for the program; (2) kinds of benefits that will accrue from the program, and (3) comparisons of the total program costs with total benefits. A completion of these actions permits the program that is more suitable and implementable to be selected.

Implementing Points to Consider (Planning)

Three PPBS planning activities should be kept in mind: (1) the development of budgeting guidelines; (2) the identification and definition of goals; and (3) the development of needed information. Budgetary guidelines are indispensable if the budget request is to be more than an incremental resource allocation. The guidelines should contain three important components: assumptions, constraints, and priorities.

Assumptions identify the economic, political, social, and other external factors that are likely to impact the agency. It is important that both assumptions and constraints be dealt with as early as feasible in the planning process because it is vital to know the conditions that may impede or limit the scope and method of an agency. For example, it would be unwise to request an expansion of a program at a time when an influential group with direct access to policymakers feels that it should be cut back or abolished. Finally, the articulation of priorities shows the importance of the rank ordering that the agency or community attaches to the allocation of resources for the coming year.

An explicit, clear, and precise definition of goals is critical to program budgeting. The goal statement indicates to the public the kinds of problems that the government or other not-for-profit agency is mobilized to solve, the conditions to be ameliorated, and the extent to which articulated desires and expectations will be realized.

PROGRAMMING

Programming enters the picture after the mission, purpose, objectives and broad program outlines have been determined. It identifies program components, tasks, or activities and fits them into a time frame specified in the goal and objective structure. Programming aids in the generation of alternative approaches to the achievement of program goals and objectives. Perhaps the most essential step is the identification of activities surrounding program objectives and the development of operational plans (e.g., the assignment of resources such as personnel, materials and facilities) to achieve them. Programming occurs during the program analysis stage or after the program selection has been made. Importantly, programming acts as a bridge between planning and budgeting, assuring that all strategic decisions and projected expenditures are integrated into the program format for the fiscal and/or planning period. Answers should be sought to the following questions: Given the political, economic, and social reality, is the alternative feasible at this time? What are the legal constraints, if any, to this program? Given the available resource constraint, can this program achieve the most effective and efficient outcome for the resources applied? Considering the life span of the program, what will be the financial requirements to continue the program in future years? Is alternative funding available for this program?

A critical opportunity is present in the programming phase. This is the phase that permits the manager to consider whether changes in the agency programs are desired. The decision must be made to add new programs, and to eliminate existing ones or modify them. Obviously the action taken to add, eliminate, or modify programs must be based on a comparative analysis of benefits in which the advantages and disadvantages are clearly identified.

Implementing Points to Consider (Programming)

Through a process of self-study analysis, programming facilitates the best choice making among alternative programs. Through this process, programming is able to determine the extent to which existing or proposed programs complement or overlap other programs. The main activities undertaken to aid the programming process involve: examination of current programs, analysis of feasible alternatives, and identification of desired programs. This step requires: (1) a brief description of each program; (2) a review of the kinds of personnel employed in executing the programs; (3) a detailed description of the target groups or clients served and the time span over which the services have been operating; (4) materials and equipment required; and (5) the total and the different types of costs (direct and indirect).

BUDGETING

A program budget is much more than a listing of expenditures by program. Instead all dollars are systematically related to goals and objectives in the program structure. Based on the cost or expenditure allocations, a budget indicates where the emphasis and priorities of the agency are being put. The dollar amounts are incorporated into both the current-year program budget and the multiyear financial plan involving a projection of alternative programs for several years (usually five).

Implementing Points to Consider (Budgeting)

The budgeting phase has four steps that should be considered. These are the specification of financial support, budget request review, budget modifications, and allocation of available funds.

The completion of the programming phase, specification of the financial support or resources needed to implement the program selected, permits the budget implementation phase to begin. The quantity of the resources needed are estimated and required dollar amounts are entered in the agency books according to the standard chart of accounts. (Whatever system the agency uses, such as object of expenditure, functional, or program, the dollar amounts are expressed in terms that can be accommodated by the system. Depending on the system required, the budget amount may be broken out to show salaries, health and retirement benefits, and other items needed to implement the program.)

The design of the system to review the program budget requires that participants, other than the proposers, review the budget requests. Unlike other budgeting systems, however, the review is conducted in terms of program goals and objectives and program costs. This is done to ensure that the purpose of the program matches budgetary guidelines and that the identified accomplishments match accepted and articulated goals and objectives. Additionally, it must be determined if the proposed size of the program will adequately serve the target population and if the best alternative has been chosen. In those cases where program changes have been requested, it must be determined if they make sense within the budgetary guidelines. An examination is made to determine if the dollar amounts requested are adequate or exceed required limits; the amounts requested must be accurately calculated.

The completed budget requests are compared with projected revenues to determine if and where budget modifications may be necessary. In those situations where modification is required, the following options are available: (1) total or partial elimination of a program; (2) reduction of services in one or more programs; (3) identification of areas where resources could be shifted to effect efficiencies; (4) available sources from which to borrow funds or that provide access to external grants (in the case of government, tax increases; in nonprofit organizations, access to foundations, business donations, or campaign drives).

SYSTEM

The system concept implies that there are different parts in a network. These are organized to act interdependently in achieving a common purpose. In PPBS, planning, programming, and budgeting are interdependent activities that are synchronized to optimally achieve articulated goals and objectives. This

Table 14.1
City of Bright, Department of Housing
Suggested Program Budget*

Department Mission/Goal: To provide adequate, safe, and sanitary housing conditions for all residents in the City of Bright.*

Objectives:

1. To make it easier for private builders to construct new housing and rehabilitate old housing.
2. To present Bright neighborhoods as good places to live.
3. To protect the sound housing in the community through timely and effective repair and maintenance programs.
4. To develop and implement programs to prevent housing abandonment.
5. To rehabilitate or demolish already abandoned units.
6. To develop long-range plans for housing involving the public and private sectors and neighborhood residents.
7. To create a professionally and efficiently run Housing Department, responsive to the changing conditions and circumstances.

Program Area: **Housing Development**

Goal: To create a healthier development climate in the city, making it easier for private developers to obtain block grant funding, construct new housing, and rehabilitate old housing.

Objectives:

1. To encourage private developers to construct 25 percent more new homes.
2. To encourage private developers to rehabilitate 20 percent of the old and abandoned homes.
3. To obtain 25 percent block grant funding.

Demand:

1. The number of requests made to rehabilitate homes.
2. The number of substandard homes in need of rehabilitation.
3. The number of requests for block grants.

Workload Measures:
1. Number of housing units rehabilitated.
2. Number of rehabilitated units sold.
3. Number of new home buyers attracted to the city through its program.
4. Number of community block grants distributed.
5. Number of man-hours targeted for implementing each phase of the program.

Efficiency and Productivity:
1. Cost per unit of homes rehabilitated.
2. Numbers of homes rehabilitated per worker.
3. Number of community block grants processed per worker per period.
4. Number of home buyers attracted per marketing staff per period.

Impact/Effectiveness Measures:
1. Percentage of abandoned homes satisfactorily rehabilitated.
2. Percentage of substandard homes satisfactorily rehabilitated.
3. Number and percentage of people actually buying substandard homes.
4. Amount of Community Development Block Grants effectively allocated for rehabilitating homes.

Sustainability:
1. Extended time period over which rehabilitated homes are satisfactorily maintained and/or enhanced.

---

* Normally, a five-year budget is normally projected for each program.

requires that the mission, goals, and objectives be directly linked to programs and subprograms, objectives, activities, output, impact, and their costs, direct and indirect.

In summary, the system approach suggests that an organization is: (1) focused on a set of objectives aimed at satisfying a predetermined plan, (2) used to convert resources (inputs) into outputs; (3) viewed as having elements and components that are interactive and interdependent; and (4) devised to maintain a monitoring system to determine deviations from targeted objectives.

PROGRAM MEASURES

Table 14.1 shows different types of measures that may be developed for the City of Bright for the Department of Housing Development. From Table 14.1, we can see the linkage of a program mission, activities, and performance measures.

DEVELOPING THE PROGRAM BUDGET FORMAT

High priority should be given to the program budget format. There are two main elements, the program structure and the cost structure. Each program is broken down into subcategories with the presentation of cost estimates projected over the planning time horizon, which is typically five years (see Figure 14.4).

Program Structure

The program is the basic framework and building block in program budgeting. Thus, great attention must be given to program structure because it plays an important role in the success or failure of the program budget. The program structure translates an agency's fundamental mission, goals, and objectives into a program hierarchy, ranging from the largest program to the basic constituent or element. The program components are subdivided as desired by management to facilitate planning, budgeting, controlling, and reporting (Figure 14.5).

The program structure should ideally be a link between an agency's goals and objectives and the financial control system of the traditional object of expenditure budget, as shown in Figure 14.4. An agency output should be directly linked to articulated goals and objectives. The key aim in the PPB system is to develop appropriate classifications that will permit the measurement and evaluation of performance in relation to assigned responsibilities. The program is the highest level of work performed by an agency that carries out assigned responsibilities. All programs are directed at producing some product that is definable and measurable.

Some programs do not conform to existing organizational structures. For example, a state program (see Figure 14.6) dealing with alcohol-related problems may involve many other agencies such as Health and Welfare, Highway Department, Youth and Adult Corrections, Department of Employment, Department of Education, and the Attorney General's Office. The question is how these overlaps should be handled. Two approaches have been suggested. The first is simply to define programs across organizational boundaries. Thus, all related activities contributing to the program goal and

Figure 14.4
Program Budget Format

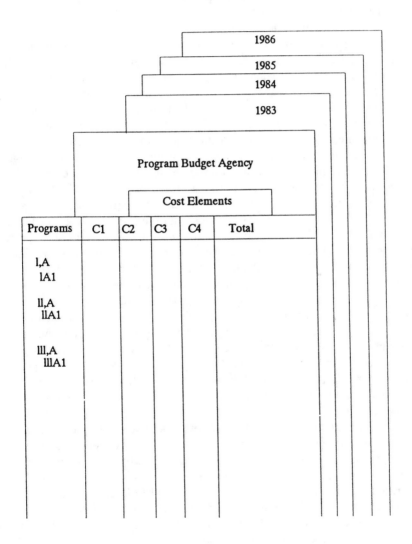

taking place in other departments are grouped together. The funding for the program is thus allocated to a number of departments. By means of a matrix or grid, resource allocation and responsibility can be displayed (see Figure 14.6).

Perhaps the most practical approach requires that programs be defined within major organizational units. This approach sometimes results in additional programs, but it enhances control and responsibility reporting. In addition, it provides sufficient information to permit program analysis to modify or eliminate duplicating activities.

An important and continuing question is how detailed should the program and subprogram should be made. Though there are no specific criteria, each situation should dictate the precise subdivision of a program budget hierarchy. A few observations may aid in understanding. Beginning with the mission of the organization, down to the smallest subdivision of the program, there must be logical linkage throughout the program structure. For example, once the mission/goal and objectives have been stated for an agency, each functional area must be consistent with them. Additionally, there must be as many functional areas as necessary to achieve the agency's mission/goal. Similarly, there must be as many programs as required to achieve the goal and objective of the function. At the program level, the number of sub programs identified is determined at the point at which the program goal and objective have been recognized. Note that for each objective stated, there should be at least one impact/effectiveness indicator to determine how well the objective was achieved. If there are, for example, five objectives but only two impact indicators that can be identified, it means that the other objectives are not important or that there is confusion about their logical relationships.

It is thus critical early in the program structuring stage to define precisely the legitimate services to be provided and their likely recipients. This gives a rough idea for relating the program goals and objectives with impact indicators and the particular intended clients. This provides answers to the question of "what" and "for whom" the program is intended. As far as possible, each program should be broken down to answer "what" and "to whom" until the point at which the question of "how" the activity is to be performed can be answered.

A basic function of PPBS is to relate the cost of the government and/or agency to the services provided. All program structures relate operating organizational units to functional areas, programs, subprograms, and activities. The functional areas identify the major purposes of an agency. The size of the functional area increases as we move from small to large organizations. For example, the state of Wisconsin divided the state's operation into five functional areas - commerce, education, environmental resources, human relations and resources, and general executive functions.

Figure 14.5
Program Classification System

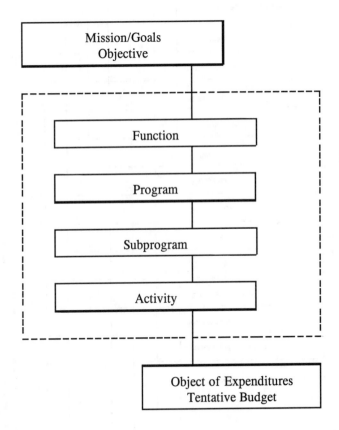

Figure 14.6
Expenditure for Alcohol Treatment Program

ORGANIZATION	PROGRAMS																		
	I. Prevention of Alcoholism	A. Education	B. Law of Economics	C. Research	II. Restoration (Early Stages)	A. Detection	B. Diagnosis	C. Treatment	D. Rehabilitation	E. Research	III. Care (The Chronic)	A. Detection	B. Diagnosis, Evaluation, Referral	C. Treatment	D. Rehabilitation	E. Domiciliary Care	F. Research	Etc.
Dept. of Welfare																		
Employment																		
Dept. of Education																		
Police																		
Youth and Adult Corrections																		
Atty. Gen. Office																		
Highway																		

Source : Adapted from C. W. Churchman and A. H. Schainblatt,
"PPB: How Can It Be Implemented?", *Public Administration Review* , 29, no. 2
(March/April 1969) 182.

A program is a division of a functional area providing services for an identifiable group or target population to achieve a specific purpose. The program combines a homogeneous group of services to meet similar needs, disabilities, or attributes. Stated another way, a program "is a clustering of activities and resources around one or more objectives focused on the production of similar outputs."[3] The Home Repairs Loan Program in the Department of Housing in the City of Bright provides a good example:

How	*What*	*For Whom*
Program	Home Repairs Loan	Home Owners
Sub-Program	Home Insulation	Home Owners Needing Insulation
Activity 1	Processing applications	
Activity 2	Applying cut off criteria	
Activity 3	Approving matching grant for insulation	
Sub-Program B	Emergency Home Repair Loan	Home owners having code violations
Activity 1	Processing applications	
Activity 2	Applying cut off criteria	
Activity 3	Granting loans to eligible homeowners	

As can be noted from this example, a subprogram is a breakdown of a program into more specific segments of the services being provided for a specific segment of the target population. Similarly, the activities are specific actions and techniques applied to implement the programs.

ISSUE ANALYSIS

Issue analysis (see box, "Outline of Issue Paper") attempts to identify, clarify, and analyze significant problems facing a government agency. Sometimes called *special study analysis*, issue analysis is an important supplement to PPBS. Issue analysis provides the analytic foundation for the PPB system. Issue analysis aids decision makers in making policy regarding program addition, rejection, or confirmation or it may simply provide vital input to the strategic-planning process. Two kinds of issue analysis have been used: one for resolving the budget or fiscal year issues and one having a time frame that extends beyond a budget year and aimed at aiding future development and resource allocation decisions. It is the issue analysis input that makes planning, programming, and budgeting substantive and dynamic.

CROSSWALK AND PPBS

A number of names such as *grid* and *matrix* have been associated with the term *crosswalk* in program budgeting. *Crosswalk* has come to mean the design of a program budget system that allows data to be converted from the problem system to traditional line-item budget, providing both a management and a control orientation. Typically the conversion is made only for one budget year at a time.

The need to make the budget conversion or classification occurs when the program budget differs from the existing budget structure. By use of the crosswalk, the program budget is transformed and regrouped from a policymaking format to one concerned with program implementation and control. With the use of computers, the conversion process has been made less difficult than it otherwise would be. An important requirement is the establishment of a coding method to facilitate ready reclassification of the budget items.

By means of the crosswalk system (Table 14.2), flexibility is increased to enable the provision and use of the traditional budget data to meet administrative, operations and performance requirements. Significantly, it provides the integration of planning, analysis, and budgeting.

PPBS: SUMMARY OBSERVATIONS

The PPBS system is an accountability instrument and a well-organized management information system that compels continuing self-study as a means of generating innovation and self-renewal. It is a means for examining the financial implications of programs over their expected life spans. This typically

Table 14.2

Expenditure Crosswalk Year 1

Account	Object Categories	Totals	Program I	Program II	Program III	Program IV
X 2	Salaries	75,000	30,000	10,000	15,000	20,000
X 3	Materials	85,000	40,000	5,000	20,000	30,000
X 4	Travel	20,000	8,000	2,000	5,000	5,000
X 5	Utilities	25,000	10,000	2,000	8,000	5,000
X 6	Rent	25,000	15,000	5,000	2,000	3,000
X 7	Consulting	110,000	50,000	1,000	4,000	10,000
X 8	Maintenance	35,000	15,000	2,000	10,000	8,000
	TOTALS	375,000	168,000	36,000	64,000	81,000

requires the examination of the consequences of expanding or contracting a program, as well as its spillover impact. PPBS provides a framework for planning and facilitating the organization of information so that planners can systematically analyze the fiscal and nonfiscal consequences of proposals and then select the best possible course of action.

PPBS: Advantages

(1) It can help decision makers focus on objectives and overall goals of an agency, indicating how it is linked with intra- and/or interagency programs and how it can be reached; (2) it links planning, programming, and budgeting into an integrated system; (3) it makes long-range and multiyear planning routine; (4) it promotes an efficient means for allocating resources; (5) it provides understanding that enhances interagency coordination and cooperation; and (6) it provides required information and data necessary to permit in-depth analysis of alternative courses of action.

PPBS: Disadvantages

PPBS requires massive amounts of data, expertise, and staff time, making it time consuming and costly to undertake. Its great emphasis on goal clarification and goal setting is highly conflicting because it forces more explicit value identification and operating philosophy, which may not be compatible with the philosophy of many participants in the budget process. The charge is made that PPBS minimizes politics, on which budgets heavily depend. Additionally, because of the PPBS emphasis on rationality, demand for performance, requirement for policy impact, and focus on explicit statement of objectives, the system is not likely to be consistent with participants' expectations in the budget-making process. Most participants prefer an inexplicit articulation of objectives because they believe it provides a better means for protecting their resource base.

OUTLINE OF ISSUE PAPER

The Issue Paper is a written document that attempts to identify and describe the major features of a major problem facing the government. It essentially attempts to define the problem.

The Issue Paper may either stand by itself as a description of the problem area in order to gain an improved perspective of the problem or, more important, can be used to set the framework, to act as the first phase, of an in-depth, cost-effectiveness analysis of the issue.

The Issue Paper should address such questions as:

1. What is the real problem?
2. What are its causes?
3. Who are the population groups affected? (That is, if other than the general public,
    identify characteristics such as: age group, race, income class, special handicaps, locations, etc.)
4. What is the magnitude of the problem? How widespread is it now and how large is it likely to be in future years?
5. Toward what objectives should programs for meeting the problem be directed?
6. How can estimates of progress against these objectives be made?
7. What activities are currently being undertaken by this government that are relevant to the problem?
8. What other sectors of the community, or other levels of government in addition to this government, are involved?
9. Are there major constraints, including political ones, that seem to affect the problem?
10. What are the types of alternatives that should be considered for meeting the problem?

Note that answering such questions does not answer the question of what should be done to meet the problem. Answering the question, "What should be done?" is *not* a function of the Issue Paper but rather of a cost-effectiveness-type analysis that ideally should follow the Issue Paper. The Issue Paper rather attempts to define the problem and direct attention to the specific information that will need to be obtained and examined before deciding what to do about the problem.

Some quantification might be attempted in the Issue Paper, such as providing estimates of the number of persons in the target groups that are affected by the problem (question no. 4 above) and providing estimates of the costs and pertinent outputs of current, relevant government activities (question no. 7). A government should not be surprised if the problem that is identified by the time the Issue Paper is completed is *not* the same as the problem that was conceived at the beginning.

Source: Adapted from George Washington University, "State-Local Finances Project", in R. G. Caso, ed., *Management Information Systems* (Nassau County, N.Y.: Fiscal Administration, 1971), pt. 3, p. 6.

NOTES

1. Harry P. Hatry and John F. Cotton, *Program Planning for Country and City* (Washington, D.C.: George Washington University, 1967), p. 16.

2. Jerome B. McKinney and Lawrence C. Howard, *Public Administration: Balancing Power and Accountability* (Oak Park, Ill.: Moore Publishing Co., 1979), p. 76.

3. Stephen Kenezevich, *Program Budgeting PPBS* (Berkeley, Calif.: McCutchan Publishing Co., 1973), p. 48.

15

Zero Base Budgeting and Total Quality Management (TQM)

Interest in zero base budgeting did not become widespread until the end of the 1960s and 1970s. The 1960s were marked by a period of full employment with inflation virtually unknown. When sufficient resources could not be found at the state level of government and at foundations for particular programs, the federal government became an eager partner. In the 1960s, federal revenue was growing so fast that federal policymakers were beginning to fear people would demand tax reductions. Chief Economic Advisor Walter Heller and others began talking about a fiscal dividend - a scheme (quite similar to the revenue sharing program that operated during the 1970s) whereby federal revenues are returned to local governments and distributed and spent according to federal formulae and criteria. The widespread practice of traditional incremental budgeting, with its built-in bias for continuity and growth, became ever more entrenched, and efforts at implementing PPBS and management by objectives (MBO) in the 1960s to achieve a more rational allocation of resources failed to make headway in the public-budgeting process. This chapter examines these practices and explores the forces that gave rise to the impetus for ZBB and Total Quality Management (TQM).

BACKGROUND AND DEVELOPMENT OF THE ZBB APPROACH

The economic, social, and political philosophies that shape priorities have been undergoing radical change. By the early 1970s, the long duration of the Vietnamese War, a continuing high level of unemployment, unmanageable inflation, a deep recession, and the apparent end of cheap and plentiful energy ushered in a period of conservation. People began asking for a greater degree of certainty, and it seemed irrational to continue to make choices by the traditional incremental, muddling-through approach. This was particularly true at a time when demands for government services were rising while available resources were falling, thus necessitating contraction and retrenchment rather than expansion.

As government attempted to cope with these problems, emphasis shifted to control by (1) direct citizen input; (2) reorganization; (3) legislative input (sunset laws); and (4) ZBB. The citizen input approach attempted to limit spending and revenue raising through referendums. For example in 1976 Proposition 13 cut property taxes nearly 60 percent in California.[1]   As McCaffery and Bowman have indicated, however, although direct citizen input may have good intentions, it does not necessarily produce the most desirable outcomes. Unintended results, such as reduced federal aid, shifting of taxes toward homeowners, and greater dependence on state government, often occur, and subsequently did take place in California.

Because of the ineffectual history of reorganizations (structural changes that deemphasize substantive social and political problems), the process of direct ditizen input gained few supporters. Sunset laws and ZBB received the greatest attention. The sunset approach (initially adopted by Colorado in 1976 for evaluating its 41 regulatory agencies) is a legislative instrument employed to control the cost and quality of government programs. Government programs, accordingly, are evaluated before a terminal date and are kept functioning only if the evaluation demonstrates satisfactory performance and a continuing need for the service.

The concept and practice of the sunset approach are commendable but, if inappropriately applied, it engenders opposition rather than support toward legislators for their policy-making. For example, in 1977, Alabama state representatives were expected to vote "yes" or "no" on 207 agencies in three hours. It is also said that if true sunsetting were practiced, high-quality individuals would be discouraged from entering government because promises could not be made about the tenure of an agency.[2]

Zero base budgeting is in some ways similar to sunset laws but permits a more comprehensive set of continuing controls and is executive oriented. In addition, it focuses yearly attention quantitatively on allocative, administrative, and economic efficiency and qualitatively on effectiveness. The emphasis shifts to control, not only of dollars expended, but of performance and the achievement of the greatest policy outcome for the fewest number of dollars. This requires that social changes be undertaken only as they are understood as trade-offs between benefits to be gained and costs to be incurred. This approach is important to governments, especially in those geographic areas that are experiencing general economic decline. It is in this context that the potential application of ZBB may be viewed.

DEFINING THE ZBB CONCEPT

Unlike traditional budgeting, "with ZBB nothing is assumed. Every function of every department is questioned. Existing programs are scrutinized as much as expanded or new programs. The entire budget is viewed as a series of supplemental requests with a theoretical base of zero and each supplement must be analyzed."[3] ZBB requires that managers defend every activity under their control before funds are allocated. To qualify for any allocation of funds, every programmatic activity or function to be performed must be identified, evaluated, and ranked in terms of costs and benefits.

ZBB is the only budget system that examines a budget request below its base. It aims to cut dollars, not service. Attention is drawn to the harm that cutbacks may entail, yet the greater emphasis is put on the decremental, in contrast to the incremental, orientation (which is standard practice in the traditional line-item budget).

ZBB is mainly a short-range tool employed in a managerial process to achieve objectives in the most cost-efficient manner. It is a bottom-up approach involving all management levels. The approach has built-in flexibility, for managers are given a range of choices to facilitate priority setting and the establishment of funding levels. Subordinates do not send their budgets up to higher management on a take-it-or-leave basis. Clear choices and options are an integral part of the ZBB approach in that every proposal presented to management for decision making must have at least three options. In writing about the system use in Garland, Texas, Leininger and Wong observed, "ZBB is a management tool which provides a systematic method for evaluating all operations and programs, current or new, allows for budget reductions and expansions in a natural manner and allows the reallocation of resources from low to high priority programs."[4]

A key consideration in ZBB is the search for alternative ways for achieving articulated objectives. The ZBB manager is expected to start from scratch by assuming that an activity (any activity that may be considered for implementation) does not exist. The manager can then reconstruct the operation from zero, asking the questions, should things be done the way they are now, or would the manager reorganize, consolidate, centralize, decentralize, subcontract, or implement the activity in an entirely different way? By employing this process, it is believed that more goods and services will be delivered at the same or lower cost. Innovative thinking is promoted, thereby enhancing productivity and improving economic performance.

Contrasting ZBB with the traditional line-item budget vividly highlights the differences between the two approaches, emphasizing ZBB's changes from the status quo (Table 15.1).

Table 15.1
Contrasting Traditional Line-Item Budgeting with ZBB

Incremental Budgeting		ZBB	
1.	Operating budget is estimated.	1.	Operating budget is developed by evaluating current activities and alternatives.
2.	Accepts existing base and estimates costs of new activities.	2.	Assumes a "clean slate" and estimates all costs associated with activities.
3.	Estimates costs and benefits for new activities.	3.	Identifies and evaluates costs and benefits for all activities including alternatives.
4.	Emphasis is put on dollars as the main initiating concern in preparing detailed budgets.	4.	Initiating emphasis is put on purposes and activities and on priorities.
5.	Little or no effort is made to examine alternative ways of accomplishing activities.	5.	New approaches are explicitly examined.
6.	Process results in take it or leave it budget.	6.	Process results in trade-off options/choices for different levels of service and costs.

WHERE SHOULD ZBB BE IMPLEMENTED?

ZBB should be implemented in any organization or unit where we can develop cost-benefit analysis and that does not presently have a standard cost system. Most governments and nonprofit organizations fall into this category. Typically, most service and overhead areas, such as personnel, counseling, accounting, legal, management service, and research also fall into this category. ZBB is most suitable for people and capital intensive activities where productivity standards are not easily obtainable to apply in making cost projections.

The ZBB process is used in organizations that have a desire and commitment to achieve speedy, favorable financial results and improve the effectiveness of managers. It is also used in communities and agencies where there is a concern to relocate resources to meet new and changing priorities, where there is the need to improve productivity and cost-effectiveness in program implementation, and where there is a need to reduce or minimize costs. In communities and agencies where the manager's attention is focused on specific objectives to be pursued and related to activities and resources required to realize the objectives, managers are encouraged to develop and reassess factors and constraints impeding performance; these managers are given the encouragement to carry out operational planning, better identify priorities, and improve organizational communication.[5]

The matrix in Figure 15.1 shows how we may conceptualize the extent of potential change and the degree of impact of ZBB implementation on an organization. The vertical arrow indicates minimal (very stable conditions) to extensive changes. This suggests that the success of ZBB in an organization depends on the prevailing conditions existing in the management environment. An examination of the latter will indicate how burdensome or how attractive the ZBB process is likely to be for the organization.

As can be readily seen from Figure 15.1, the greater the forecasted change (e.g., the likelihood of large budget cuts, high inflation, a large drop in the client casework, a sharp decline in revenue sources, a perceived lack of efficacy by clientele and constituency, and/or deteriorating public usage), managers will be more disposed to reassess and readjust their operations and programs. When this situation obtains (significant impact and extensive change), change can easily be imposed from the outside. When minimal change/high stability is the prevailing state, the environment for the implementation of ZBB is less attractive, creating the inclination to more easily revert to a traditional incremental budget. It is not enough to want to install ZBB because it is a good idea. There must be a defensible rationale for its implementation, which requires in-depth study of the organization's environment.

Figure 15.1
Evaluating the Impact of ZBB on an Organization

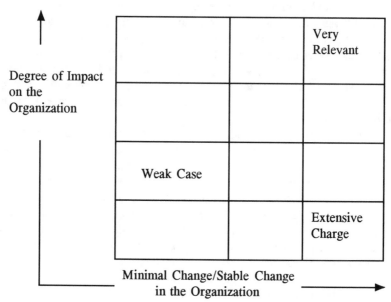

Source: Adapted from Henry C. Knight, *Zero-Based Budgeting Process: A Practical Guide to Evaluation, Implementation and Use* (Hamilton, Ont., Canada: Management Accounts of Canada, 1979), p. 11, (with permission of publisher).

EXAMINING THE ZBB PROCESS

Before the ZBB process can begin, an organization needs to clearly identify (1) its goals and objectives and (2) its structure. There must exist a framework for linking operations planning (identification of short-term objectives) and long-term planning (or what is called strategic planning). Answers to the following questions with short-term implications should be sought: What outcomes are desired from ZBB? What kinds of technology will be utilized? Who will be the main users of the information for which the ZBB process is being designed? What is the appropriate linkage between the present management information system and the ZBB process? What implementation strategies will be followed? The relevant questions about long-term implications include: Where is the government or agency now? Where should it be headed? Is it moving in the right direction?

Figure 15.2
The ZBB Process: An Overview

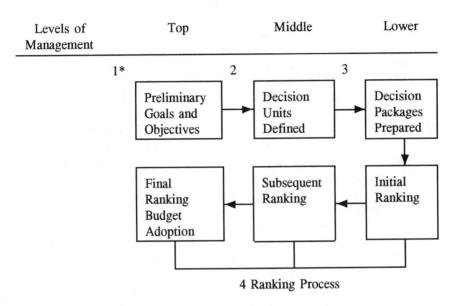

4 Ranking Process

* Numbers indicate steps or stages in the ZBB Process.

An organization should not attempt to apply ZBB without a clear understanding of its own structure and support, as suggested in Figure 15.1. For this reason it is essential to know at the outset if the existing organization is acceptable for the installation of ZBB. If the organization is not amenable to ZBB, what programmatic changes are presently being considered and what changes are planned for the future?

The ZBB process may be viewed as having four essential steps, as shown in Figure 15.2. The process begins with the development of planning assumptions and articulation of goals and objectives. The planning assumptions, goals, and objectives are the major inputs to the operating departments to aid in budget preparation. (As in the case of traditional budget making, managers also need to know projected inflation rates, salary increases, and service level requirements.) The next important step is the definition of decision units. (A decision unit is an organizational responsibility center for which a manager can be held accountable but budgets are required to be made.) The decision unit facilitates the grouping of activities and the analysis of inputs/costs and output/benefits. Typically, a decision unit is a program or organizational entity with common and measurable objectives for which budget requests are prepared and to which individual or specific accountability can be assigned.

With assumptions specified and planning goals and objectives defined, top management is in a position to identify agency activities/responsibility areas and the person responsible for performing each activity. The middle and lower-level managers can now sit down with the program managers and define decision units. The latter may be projects, training, maintenance, client service, budget units, specific activities, or a grouping of existing or proposed activities (a program) that management views as meaningful for planning and budgeting purposes. (A specific activity might be street paving, while a grouping of closely related activities, or program, would be street maintenance.)

Since each decision unit is viewed as a *responsibility center*, there must be a manager who can make important decisions about spending and the quality of work. A decision unit may be a line item, a project, an activity, a program, or an entire organization, depending on the level of management responsibility for the preparation of the decision package.

In most cases, decision units are formed within the existing organizational structure. This is especially true in those cases where PPBS has been operating, for it provides a logical structure that can easily accommodate ZBB. The fit or correspondence with the existing structure has the advantage of maintaining the linkage with the accounting system. Where a new decision unit must be designed, the accounting linkage must be incorporated and continued.[6]

Setting decision unit objectives is a function given to the unit managers in the initial implementation of ZBB. The pyramid of objectives is identified with the concurrence of superiors. As the ZBB system evolves and develops, unit goal setting is more closely integrated with the higher-level planning processes that set the overall organizational goals and objectives. Because of the conditioning role that the objectives play in the ZBB system, the organization that practices MBO will find its process readily accommodative with ZBB.

Developing decision packages is the third step in the ZBB process. It is through decision packages that goals and objectives are translated into concrete plans. A decision package is a request document (indicating in monetary terms the amount of resources a manager would like to have) identifying, describing, justifying, and providing information on a specific activity, program, function, or operation to permit managers to make informed judgments about the allocation of scarce resources. The information provided in a decision package should allow management to rank it with competing activities.

Decision packages contain the projected outputs that a manager believes are achievable and the required resources to realize them. A decision unit set should be complete, whole, and discrete. The activities of each decision unit

Figure 15.3
Schematic View for Developing ZBB Decision Packages

		Threshold
	Option 1:	
	Existing Approach	Level 2
		Level...n
		Threshold
	Option 2:	
Maintain Current Objective	Alternative Approach	Level 2
		Level...n
		Threshold
	Option m	Level 2
		Level...n

Eliminate Current Objective

		Threshold
	Option 1	Level 2
		Level...n
		Threshold
	Option 2	Level 2
Development Objectives		Level...n
		Threshold
	Option m	Level 2
		Level...n

should provide sufficient information to identify results, evaluate options, analyze costs, and assess benefits. It is important to note that a decision package is considered effectively prepared only when management is able to rank it with other packages. A schematic view for developing decision packages is presented in Figure 15.3. It should be recognized that the number of levels of efforts (n) typically equals three, while the number of options (m) is independent of the number of levels of efforts and may often exceed three.

Decision packages constitute the basic building block in the ZBB subsystem. Every unit has at least three or more decision packages except in those cases in which the cost of the program or activity is mandated for whatever reason. In such cases only one package is prepared. There are normally three decision packages: (1) *minimal level* or *base*, (2) *current level*, and (3) *advanced* or *enhanced level* (see Figures 15.4 and 15.5). Each decision unit package is prepared at the lowest operating level where the best cost-benefit information can be obtained.

Several related steps are involved in the formation of the decision package: (1) define the purpose or goal of the particular activity or function; (2) describe and document existing operations and resources, determining what will be done, when, and how; (3) evaluate the alternative ways or means of achieving objectives; (4) identify benefits to be achieved from specific funding levels (also known as levels of efforts) and the consequences that are likely to result from nonfunding (if funding for a described activity cannot be obtained, this information should be clearly outlined); and (5) define the performance measures upon which the activities will be evaluated (see Appendix 1).

Where capital outlays can be specifically identified with particular program improvement, this information should ideally be included in the decision package. For example, if the snow removal maintenance crew needs a new truck, this should be assigned a cost and be included in the budget as a separate package. In those cases where direct identification of capital outlays cannot be identified with a program, individual or consolidated packages are developed. Thus, before decision packages are funded, such items as debt service must be examined.

The Ranking Process

Once the decision package has been prepared the stage is set for the final step in the ZBB process - priority ranking. Properly done, this step allows management to achieve the most productive and cost-effective allocation of its scarce resources. Because of its multiple and hierarchical character, ranking allows managers with budget responsibilities to participate in determining the decision unit and overall agency priorities.

Ideally, the person responsible for subsequent rankings (all ranking

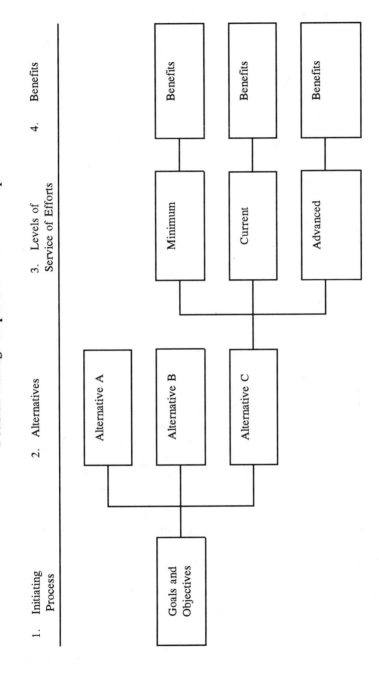

Figure 15.4
Decision Package Preparation Process - Perspective #1

1. Initiating Process	2. Alternatives	3. Levels of Service of Efforts	4. Benefits

Goals and Objectives

Alternative A

Alternative B

Alternative C

Minimum

Current

Advanced

Benefits

Benefits

Benefits

Figure 15.5

Graphic View of Levels of Service/Efforts and the Concept of Diminishing Returns Perspective #2

Outputs
(benefits)

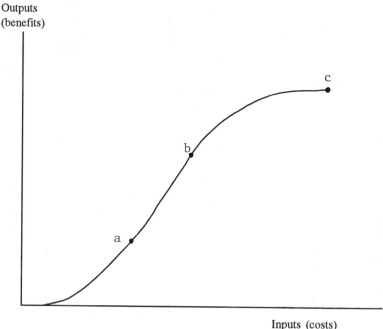

Inputs (costs)

Note: Point "a" represents the threshold minimum level of effort. From point "a" to point "b" there is a marked acceleration of the increasing benefits. This point ("b") may be considered the current level of effort or service. After point "b" benefits continue to increase but at a decelerating rate until point "c," the advanced level, is reached, producing the maximization of benefits. Most activities should operate at point "c" when possible because from that point onward there is rapid acceleration of benefits.

above the decision unit) should make a concerted effort to be familiar with the lower-level managers' submission. It may be necessary for ranking managers to meet individually with unit managers to obtain a clear idea. Additionally, all cost-benefit information, program measures, and evaluative materials that can sharpen the critical and analytical focus of the ranking manager should be provided. The ranking process permits the separate decision packages, representing the various levels of service for a given alternative, to be ordered to determine which proposed work item will be funded in the next budget year. The process then places a program function, or activity, in a descending order of priority based on the benefits to be gained from each undertaking at the various spending levels.

Decision unit managers rank the decision packages for which they are responsible. These rankings are then placed in competition with other decision units. Rankings within one division or between divisions or departments of an organization are shown in Figure 15.6. The consolidated decision packages are reviewed at different management levels until a final ranking is made. At some point in the process, top management will generally know (based on the best revenue projection) the budget cutoff point - that is, the total funds that will be included in the budget - and can determine which decision packages will be funded. For each level of service, the resulting benefits must be specified as they relate to profit margins in the private sector and to particular target populations in the public sector.

Ranking systems and criteria vary widely among governmental units and nonprofit organizations. The city of Mt. Lebanon, Pennsylvania, provides a good example (see Table 15.2). Decision managers are typically given a number of votes equal to the number of packages prepared and having a ranking value between one and six, with the highest priority decision packages given a value of six.

Using the same voting system, Mt. Lebanon uses a municipalitywide ranking committee "composed of all department heads, the finance officer, the personnel and purchasing officer and a student intern who ranks the decision packages, prepared and initially ranked by decision unit managers." Mt. Lebanon's manager participates but does not vote. He reserves the right to make changes in the decision packages' ranking before they are submitted to Mt. Lebanon's Township Commission. The department heads are given an opportunity to discuss their concerns with the commission, which determines the final funding priorities.

In ranking we cannot take a myopic view that seeks to maximize the short-run gain and ignore long-term applications. Lowering taxes by one or two mills, to win an election, (because of the insignificant material gain to most taxpayers, it is a symbolic gesture at best) but failing to plan to replace crumbling bridges is a dramatic example of shortsightedness.

Monitoring Performance

Once the ZBB budget has been approved, the development and implementation of a clearly defined and understood monitoring system is indispensable. Typically, the monitoring system will be established and integrated with the normal management review cycle.

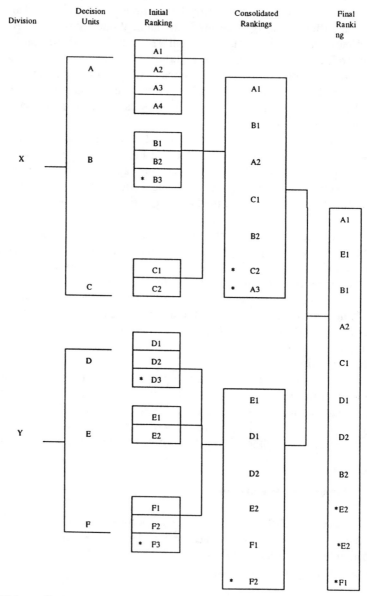

* Budget cutoff points represent nonrelevant packages not sent upward.

Table 15.2
Criteria for Vote Casting

1.	Importance of service levels in terms of perceived health, welfare, safety, and satisfaction of the township's residents;
2.	Statutory, charter, and contractual commitments met by the service level;
3.	Potential consequences (including political) if the service level is not provided;
4.	Federal and/or state funds received dependent on a particular expenditure or match of funds;
5.	Informal assessment of the quality of the service provided;
6.	Cost-effectiveness of the service level.

Source: Borough of Mt. Lebanon, Pennsylvania, *1979 Budgeting Manual*, (Mt. Lebanon, Pa. 1979), p. A-8.

ZBB AS A MEANS FOR DEALING WITH RECOGNIZED PROBLEMS

Once serious thought is given to the potential implementation of ZBB, there needs to be an evaluation of the extent of, and the need for, ZBB. Simultaneous with the examination of the ZBB system, the benefits and the costs of other methods that are capable of achieving the organization's identified needs should be explored. This is especially important when one realizes the changes in forms, relationships, procedures, and attitudes that may be necessary with the installation of the ZBB approach.

Among the factors that may indicate the need for the ZBB system is a desire to improve the effectiveness of managers. This may require a reallocation of resources involving a reduction in both costs and expenditures. Importantly, there may be a recognized need to improve operations due to unclear lines of authority, unclear policies and procedures, and poor channels of communication.

STATUS OF ZBB: FEDERAL, STATE AND LOCAL LEVELS

ZBB has undergone significant changes during the past 10 years. Government units such as the city of Garland, Texas, have incorporated a hybridized budget system (a different budget system is integrated into ZBB to make it more relevant and usable). Many entities have reverted to traditional budgeting or to various forms of performance budgeting and a type of ad hoc TQM. In most of the systems where ZBB has survived, the simplified approach has been adopted. The requirement that ZBB analysis be initiated from scratch has been discontinued. Unlike previously, once goals and objectives were decided upon, no specific number of decision packages is required. Greater flexibility is left to program or responsibility managers to determine the programs that are needed to be undertaken to implement the goals that have been agreed upon. In many instances, only the final decision packages are entered into the formal system.

Governments have modified their ZBB systems to enhance their efficiency and to adapt to the changing environment to reduce rigidity and to improve policy outcomes. Surviving ZBB systems have succeeded because participants are better trained, institutional influences are given greater recognition, and the legislative and executive branches of government have given increased support to the ZBB system.

With the coming of the Ronald Reagan administration, ZBB was allowed to be phased out at the federal government level and the traditional line-item budget became the norm once again. Despite the return to traditional budgeting, many of the agencies have maintained or instituted various performance measurements to complement their decision-making functions. In retrospect, it appears that ZBB has had a positive impact.[7]

THE RISE OF TQM

The late W. Edward Deming popularized the practice of TQM in Japan after World War II. Deming was sent to Japan as an advisor to help the Japanese to improve their shoddy image for products made in Japan. Despite the fact that the TQM method and concepts were developed in the United States, it did not receive visibility in America until Japan began to surge ahead in many commercial and industrial area during the 1970s and 1980s.

By the late 1980s, TQM had become the rage throughout America, in both the public and not-for-profit sectors. At conventions and meetings, TQM seminar rooms have been overflowing. Advocates promised government to save millions, cut budgets by 20 percent, reduce deficits and constituents complaints to all-time lows.[8] Governmental units such as New York City, Fort Collins, Colorado, the state of North Dakota, Palm Beach, Florida, Madison, Wisconsin, and Erie, Pennsylvania, have been implementing or examining TQM. The view is being expressed that if the right situation is matched with the right problem, TQM does seem to work. Unfortunately, TQM is not easy to execute well. "Despite the success stories, it is no magic formula for instant government rejuvenation."[9]

What is TQM?

TQM is a philosophy or a way of life comprising a set of principles, tools, and procedures for operating an organization to maximally achieve articulated goals and objectives. Everyone is expected to be mutually induced to participate in controlling and to continuously improve the quality of the work that must be done to satisfy customer/clientele expectations in every way possible. The TQM organization is characterized by constant change, teamwork, flexibility, sensitivity, and responsiveness to its environment. It is future oriented and mission and goal driven. To achieve continuous improvement and innovation, the organization must: (1) plan for change, (2) implement the change, (3) observe and evaluate the change, and (4) take action based on what is learned. These actions constitute what is sometimes referred to as the planning, doing, checking and acting cycle. This process (See Figure 15.7) is expected to lead inevitably to maximum improvement in quality output of product or service, decrease costs, increase productivity, lower price of outputs, and satisfaction of customers, clientele, or constituents.

The Deming View of TQM

Greatest success will come only from an organization that has a process-obsessed management culture that harnesses the know-how and natural initiative of its employees. This orientation is capable of fine tuning the organization to achieve the highest standards of excellence and innovation. In the United States it is exceedingly difficult for private firms to realize these goals because the heartbeat of the marketplace has been replaced with the singular pursuit of return on investment (ROI). Similarly, in government the reelection objective at any cost has replaced the drive to achieve the best quality outcome for constituents.

In Deming's view it is critical that decisions be made on the basis of data that is undergirded by required practical and theoretical knowledge and not on the basis of instinct. Eighty-five to 90 percent of all problems in organizations can be traced to systems or process. Only 10 to 15 percent are directly related to humans. When a blemished car rolls off the assembly, "gut reaction" may lead the worker to adjust the machinery. If the problem is em-

Figure 15.7
Continuing Process and Quality Improvement

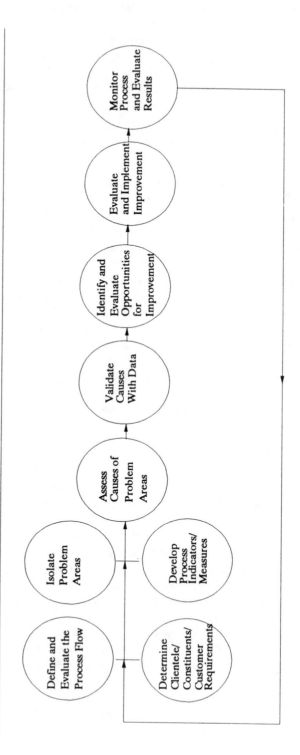

bedded in the machinery, the change may actually throw the machine out of adjustment. This might lead to more severe problems. Thus, it is critical that training be an accepted norm in every TQM organization as an indispensable ingredient to achieve maximum process improvement and innovation.[10]

Deming set forth 14 innovative TQM rules or commandments that must be followed if greatest end product results are to be realized:

1.   Articulate purpose and pursue it steadfastly.
2.   Improve systems constantly and forever.
3.   Avoid the use of MBO type goals and quotas.
4.   Eradicate fear in the organization.
5.   Create leadership that coaches rather than bosses.
6.   Allow quality, not just price, to guide all bids.
7.   Maximize the communication potential between departments by breaking down barriers.
8.   Provide for ongoing job training.
9.   Ban annual personnel evaluation ratings and the merit system.
10.   Create and institutionalize a program of education and self-improvement.
11.   Ban slogans and exhortations.
12.   Avoid dependency on traditional inspection.
13.   Inculcate the new TQM philosophy.
14.   Expect management to be the driving force of the new system if it is to succeed.

TQM AND ZBB

Not unlike the early days of the introduction of ZBB into the U.S. government, TQM is viewed with great expectations. TQM has an added advantage, in that it promises results without elaborate structure. Additionally, public officials see TQM as a cost-reducing instrument that simultaneously enhances the quality of services it delivers to clientele and constituents.[11]

The enhanced quality and cost savings that TQM promises do not provide budget linkage to enable us to effectively cost out programs. Project selection criteria is determined by a team committed process and outcome improvement. The critical linking role of the budget is missing. An examination of Figure 15.7 shows that TQM is silent on the budget requirement. Ideally, the budgeting phase should follow identification of improvement opportunities before initiating the next phase. The fact cannot be overlooked that most improvements have some cost constraint that is unexplained in TQM.

SUMMARY OBSERVATIONS: THEORY AND PRACTICE CONCERNS

Although ZBB is expected to be innovative and rational in practice, it tends to be status quo oriented and highly political. Although decisions are expected to be made based on a cost-benefit analysis, in practice, this is seldom the reality amd the generally perceived view that ZBB is an integrative planning tool is seldom obtained. The requirement that ZBB be initiated by goal clarification and goal setting by top management is not accomplished. Instead, most agencies permit goal articulation to be done at the department level.

The ranking process requires the greatest amount of trust and commitment to the ZBB objectives because it permits the exercise of a high degree of discretion; most critically, it is a focal point for determining the allocation of scarce resources. This discretionary element, the lack of quality information, and the significant influence exercised by the decision unit manager, has permitted the ranking system to be used as a means for political manipulation. The reasons for this outcome include the following: (1) the haphazard ways in which decision units tend to be defined within individual departments, making comparability difficult; (2) unspecific ranking criteria; (3) inadequate trust and lack of continuous feedback between upper and lower levels of management (decision unit managers fear that explicit identification of alternatives transfer control over their programs to potentially unsympathetic others); (4) lack of monitoring devices to check on ranking practices; (5) lack of an incentive system to encourage managers to minimize the manipulation of information and priorities, (6) lack of emphasis or productivity in the ZBB system; (7) lack of coordination between legislative sunset laws and executive oriented ZBB; and (8) loss of vitality to initiate change due to easy adaptation to traditional budget routines. (For a contrast between theory and practice problems in ZBB see Table 15.3.)

When implementing ZBB, it is useful to avoid viewing it as a set of specific techniques to be mastered and religiously implemented in every specific detail. Instead it should be viewed as a philosophy - a way of thinking that gives life and substance to the technique that may be usefully employed to effect resource allocation. Goals and objectives must be clearly understood and collectively agreed upon. The information system must be designed to meet user needs and be closely integrated into the accounting system. From the outset it should have the wholehearted support of top management.

The status of ZBB in governmental and other not-for-profit agencies has declined significantly since early to mid 1980s. It is no longer practiced at the federal government level. Many states and local governments have reverted to traditional budgets. In most instances where ZBB has survived (such as in the states of Tennessee and Missouri and the cities of Garland, Texas, and Welmington, Delaware), modified approaches have been adopted. The continuing uses of ZBB can be attributed to a number of reasons, including the

Table 15.3
ZBB: Theory and Practice

Category	Theory	Practice
Planning		
1. Budget base	None, minimum base	All programs have a base; true zero not considered; arbitrary service levels.
2. Overall	Explicit; expenditure-related	Not explicit; seldom considered
3. Decision-package objectives	Explicit; output and productivity measures	Not always explicit; seldom have links to productivity or output
4. Policy determination	Exhaustive consideration	Minimal; little consideration
5. Preparation of alternatives	Short-range and comprehensive; cost-benefit	Little or no cost-benefit analysis; no systematic criteria
6. Levels of effort (Service Levels)	Cost-benefit for each level; zero base identified	No explicit cost-benefit analysis; no systematic criteria
7. Programming	Not explicit	Nonexistent
8. Integrated	Not explicit	Nonexistent
9. Depth of analysis	In-depth	Minimal; superficial at best
10. Time span	Short-range; tactical	Short-range; tactical
Organization Theory and Management		
1. Organizational structure	Decision unit-oriented; responsibility unit	Decision units generally conform to existing organizational structure
2. Programmatic	Well developed	Well developed

3. Ideology	Innovative; dynamic; neutral	Conservative; status quo; highly political processes
4. Value agreement	Managerial efficiency	Minimal or totally lacking in practice
5. Management level involvement	Middle and lower	Minimum at top; maximum at bottom; inadequate feedback between levels

Decision Making

1. Focus of decision making	Participation at all levels	Focus on lower-level managers
2. Decision making flow between management levels	Bottom up	Bottom up, with high degree of reduction of information upward
3. Ranking Identified	Comprehensive, explicit, rational	Unsystematic, political rationality and expediency; minimal information
4. Administrative documents	Moderate	Many more than PPB

Productivity, Monitoring, and Evaluation

1. Emphasis for measuring objectives	Measures output	Heavy reliance on workload measures; unsystematic
2. Evaluating results	Required; pre-, continuing, and postanalysis	Haphazard, unsystematic
3. Evaluating on-going programs	Continuous	Seldom or not done at all; very unsystematic
4. Staff and time requirements	Minimal to moderate	High

following: attention was paid to demand; a simplified system and a unified philosophy were established; patience was exercised; factions involved in institutional politics were given an opportunity to participate meaningfully in resource allocation; and monitoring and evaluating systems were successfully implemented to permit the selection of high-visibility activities for closer scrutiny.

Among the reasons that have been given to explain the demise of ZBB in government units are the following: many viewed ZBB as an instrument for quick budget reduction; ZBB was used to demonstrate a unit's commitment and priority to innovation and the type of accountability (results) that were being sought were not clearly articulated or understood; and minimal support prevented ZBB from taking root strongly enough to replace traditional line-item and incremental budgeting.

The move to TQM reveals no clear theory, methodology, or practice. The TQM philosophy and practice do not provide a bridge or linkage between theory and practice as shown in Figure 15.4. Unlike ZBB, which is heavy on structure, TQM minimizes it. Nonetheless, both systems involve mission-driven, bottom-up management that is costly to introduce and maintain.

Many advocates like TQM because it does not require change or modification to the existing budget structure. This view should be accepted with caution and reflection before attempting to apply TQM. In the long run, TQM will not succeed unless the total human, political, and monetary commitment is given to it. The cultural change that TQM requires is not easy to achieve. Thus, the quick payoff that public officials typically expect is not likely to materialize.

Finally, it should be borne in mind that ZBB is not installed in a vacuum. Rather. it must compete with entrenched ways of doing things. Whenever a new system is instilled, participants want to know what it means to them individually. Placing emphasis solely on efficiency and productivity measures will produce anxiety and this may exacerbate latent fears. Perhaps, decision making in ZBB should be tempered by the view implied in Figure 15.8 that the most acceptable and best decision outcomes perhaps lay in a compromise between the political rationality and economic rationality producing the "mixed satisficing [*sic*] decision."

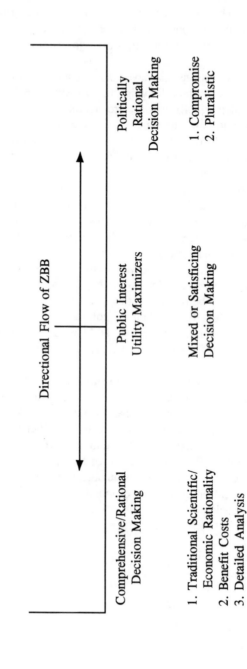

Figure 15.8
ZBB and Decision Making

Directional Flow of ZBB

Comprehensive/Rational
Decision Making

Public Interest
Utility Maximizers

Politically
Rational
Decision Making

1. Traditional Scientific/
   Economic Rationality
2. Benefit Costs
3. Detailed Analysis
4. Input/Output
   Efficiency

Mixed or Satisficing
Decision Making

1. Compromise
2. Pluralistic

NOTES

1. Jerry McCaffery and John H. Bowman, "Participatory Democracy and Budgeting: The Effects of Proposition 13," *Public Administration Review*, November/December 1978, pp. 533-36.

2. Jerome B. McKinney, *Understanding ZBB: Promise and Reality* (Chicago: Public Policy Press, 1979), p. 54.

3. City of Mt. Lebanon, Pennsylvania, "1979 Budgeting Manual" (Finance Office, May 1, 1978), p. 84.

4. David Leininger and Ronald C. Wong, *Zero-Base Budgeting in Garland Texas*, Information Report 8/4a (Washington, D.C.: International City Managers' Association, April 1976), p. 2.

5. Henry C. Knight, *Zero-Based Budgeting Process: A Practical Guide to Evaluation, Implementation and Use* (Hamilton, Ontario: Management Society of Management Accountants of Canada, 1979), pp. 25-33.

6. For more discussion, see United States. Executive Office of the President, Office of Management and Budget, *Zero-Base Budgeting 77-79* (Washington, D.C.: U.S. GPO, April 1979).

7. See U.S. GAO, *Performance Budget Experiences in the States* (Washington, DC.: GAO, 1992).

8. David K. Carr and Ian D. Littman, *Excellence in Government: Total Quality Management in the 1990s* (Arlington, Va.: Coopers and Lybrand, 1993), p. 2.

9. Jonathan Walters, "The Cult of Total Quality," *Governing*, May 1992, p. 38.

10. Andrea Gabor, *The Man Who Discovered Quality* (New York: Times Book/London House, 1991), pp. 4-5, 7.

11. See Al Gore, *Creating a Government that Works Better and Costs Less* (Washington, D.C.: U.S. Government Printing Office, 1993); and David Osborne and Ted Gaebler, *Reinventing Government: How the Entrepreneurial Spirit is Transforming America* (Reading, Mass.: Addison-Wesley Publishing Co., 1992).

16

Information Needs and Financial Management

There is a growing need for information management in government and not-for-profit agencies (see Figure 1.1). In the delivery of social services, the demand for greater efficiency and effectiveness of programs, the internal reporting requirements, and the availability of new information technology have made the management of information a critical, as well as a difficult, undertaking. These circumstances also point to the compelling need for the development of a coherent *management information system* (MIS). Despite this reality, a large number of government and other not-for-profit organizations have not given the problem the attention it deserves. This situation, however, has been changing, especially because of citizen and client demands for greater stewardship and accountability. This chapter focuses attention on the continuing changes taking place in the narrow, traditional financial management information system and examines the new, more integrated, user-oriented approach to financial management. The powerful capabilities of personal computers (PCs) has made the need for mainframe computers less compelling. The operations of networks and the server concept (software that can be easily "downloaded" to serve other machines) has created the opportunity for maximum flexibility, decentralization, and manager- or people-friendly systems. Data can be retrieved from far-flung places if the decision maker knows what is desired and understands the capability of the system. Thus, designing the information system to meet expectations and knowing how to utilize the system capabilities are important factors.

Government and not-for-profit organizations' responses to their information management problems have been hindered by the excessive attention to the "physical" aspects, such as computers, forms, and files, and by the minimal emphasis on qualitative factors and results. This has led to neglect of the ultimate goal for which all agencies have been created - the effective delivery of goods and services to clients and constituents. The design of effective information management systems, consequently, should be concerned primarily with the provision of information to enhance decision making.

During the last several years, state governments have been deploying multimedia computer kiosks to provide routine services and reduce administrative costs. The deployment of kiosks has been fostered by the desire of state governments to provide better services without increasing personnel. State governments can provide services such as car registration, job matching and information referrals via kiosks.[1]

In California, Info/California, a network of 15 IBM touch-screen kiosks, provides information and services such as job opportunities and ordering of birth certificates. After the Los Angeles riots, the California Health and Welfare Agency installed multilingual kiosks to provide data on disaster assistance. At present, the agency is evaluating the acquisition of 100 kiosks.

In April 1993, Maryland began providing Aid to Families with Dependent Children (AFDC) benefits via kiosks. The state of Maryland installed 1,800 automated teller machines at 3,000 grocery stores. The reduction of administrative costs was the main motivation for the implementation of the project. According to Betts, the traditional system cost the state $5.10 per client each month, while the electronic system costs the state $4.35 per client each month, a savings of 75 cents. It is anticipated that the electronic system will save the state $1.2 million yearly.[2]

States such as Arizona, Colorado, and Hawaii have also installed kiosks to provide basic services. In Colorado, kiosks have been used for obtaining citizen input in the budgetary process. In New Jersey, the Motor Vehicle Service has used kiosks for vehicle registration. Currently, the Pennsylvania Bureau of Motor Vehicles is considering deploying kiosks to improve its vehicle registration services. The use of kiosks can improve service delivery and reduce administrative costs. State agencies can provide routine services effectively and efficiently without increasing their staff. Further, state agencies can reduce waste, fraud, and abuse through the use of kiosks.[3]

While many management information systems have been developed around computers, others are not computer-based. Effectively operating MIS-dependency on sophisticated data-processing hardware varies according to the particular needs of each organization. In fact, there are some qualitative types of management inputs that are not readily susceptible to computerization. When excessive attention is given to the computer hardware and how data is processed, it may have a negative impact on the design of the MIS. Typical is this observation by Litechy and Wilson: "All too often, hardware vendors short-circuit the preferred approach by selling their own immediate solution to data processing problems."[4] The hardware aspects of the MIS should follow the initial determination of the user's information needs. Though certainly not unimportant, computer hardware needs should be relegated to a secondary position.

DEFINING THE MANAGEMENT INFORMATION SYSTEM (MIS)

While many tend to define MIS as an electronic data-processing or computer system in which the information flow is automated, this is not a complete definition. In fact, MIS is much more than a computer system. Essentially, it is a process for ordering information and communicating it on a timely basis to aid management in solving specific problems as they arise. What a management information system is may be better understood by considering each element in its name.

Management comprises activities that are concerned with resource use. These activities or functions involve planning, programming, organizing, budgeting, accounting, implementing, controlling, and evaluating the use of resources in accordance with stipulated guidelines and practices. A characteristic of effective managers is their ability to enhance the capacity and flexibility of an organization to respond to changing demands and conditions. The efficacy of the MIS can be evaluated in terms of its ability to facilitate management to effectively achieve its objectives - the communication of information for decision making.

Information and *data* are used interchangeably, but they are not the same thing. Data are facts and figures that have not been organized for specific use. Examples include accounting transactions, files, and reports. Data do not become information until they are organized to permit comparisons to be made and to identify relationships that can aid management to make decisions. Information, therefore, is data that are purposefully compiled and interpreted for management's use. The continual storage of information provides the MIS with valuable resources for potential use by management in the future.

A *system* consists of two or more elements that come together to collectively achieve a common purpose. Systems typically possess a set of subsystems arranged in a hierarchy from large to small. For example, the judicial system in the United States extends from the federal Supreme Court (the apex of the hierarchy) to the justice of the peace in a given locality. The effective operation of the judicial system requires that all courts consistently apply the procedures and rulings of the higher courts. This drive toward unison and the pursuit of the common goal of justice may be described as synergy, meaning that the elements of the system work better together than independently. Thus the MIS generates information that helps management to make improved decisions because of the synergistic context in which the information is derived and used.

THE FINANCIAL MANAGEMENT INFORMATION SYSTEM

Most financial management activities, especially in local governments, tend to be highly fragmented. A historical examination of the development of the financial information system reveals that it typically has had an independent beginning, arising almost entirely from within each independent financial function. Accounting personnel created systems to satisfy particular reporting requirements while budget personnel developed systems to meet their needs, such as expenditure estimating and budget control. Over time, such diverse systems, with their own terminologies and procedures, unconstrained by imposed or agreed-upon criteria and/or guidelines, were found to be duplicative, inconsistent, and counterproductive.[5]

In Chapter 1, the definition of the fiscal management system was given as consisting of three core financial processes: (1) financing - raising required financial resources; (2) budgeting - developing a work plan stated in both financial and nonfinancial terms; and (3) controlling - which is concerned with assuring adherence to the articulated budget plan. The operation of these financial components requires three basic, substantive management processes: (1) planning - defining the goals and objectives to be pursued; (2) programming - selecting the appropriate activities to achieve the goals and objectives that have been stated and planned; and (3) evaluating - assessing the quality and usefulness of the articulated goals, objectives, and activities that have been implemented.

The six different processes, ideally, should be incorporated and built into each organization as standard operating procedures. Transactions relating to such activities as payroll, purchasing, inventory, receiving, and disbursing should be guided by uniform procedures. To be effective, these processes must be serviced by an information and reporting system under the continuing surveillance of designated responsibility center officials.

Because this fiscal management system (FMS) follows essentially a rational approach, the question may be asked: Doesn't every organization use such a system? In varying degrees, the answer is definitely yes, despite the fact that management may not always be aware of the fact. The point is that each organization requires an FMS for its operations, regardless of whether the need for one is clearly understood.

The financial process has both financial and nonfinancial impacts. Thus, information generated from the financial system relating to both financial and nonfinancial activities must be stored and maintained. This is the job of the financial management information system (FMIS). The FMIS organizes and converts the financial data into information that enables management to monitor, control, and effectively direct the operation of the organization. This is what is traditionally referred to as the integrated financial management system. It is essentially a system that is coordinated to bring relevant financial information together to aid in developing policies and practices for raising, storing, applying, and evaluating the use of monetary resources.

More recently, the view and meaning of what constitutes an integrated financial management system has been changing. The new emphasis is no longer on planning, programming, and financing.[6] Instead, stress is put on three aspects of controlling - budgeting, accounting, and auditing - and on performance management. Performance management is a by-product of these components. Note that unless the budget process incorporates planning and programming, these aspects are likely to be minimized. This leaves accounting (a record keeping and expenditure control instrument) as the key information provider to managers and oversight legislative officials.

An integrated financial management information system should include information that will facilitate executive, legislative, and staff decision making about the allocation, administration, control, and evaluation of resource application (see Figure 16.1). The kinds of information useful to decision makers include:

1.   Budget:

   a.   comprehensive listing of all the funds expended by programs, functions, activities, and organizational units, including the objectives, functions, and activities;

   b   description of and qualitative data on service outputs of program functions and activities;

   c.   benefits increased or decreased at each service level;

   d.   cost-benefit analysis of existing and alternative methods for delivery of services;

   e.   established procedure for updating revenue estimates;

   f.   future expenditure of proposed programs;

   g.   a breakdown or listing of financial data for capital budget improvements and the projection of future program impacts on the operating budget; and

   h.   a multi-year financial plan.

2.   Budget/Accounting Implementation:

   a.   definition of periodic allotments (e.g., monthly, quarterly);

   b.   appropriated funds allocated to organizational units/responsibility centers;

   c.   budget modification criteria;

   d.   comparison reports of actual expenditures, encumbrances, and revenues versus approved budget;

   e.   maintenance of accrual accounting data for enterprise activities;

Figure 16.1

Financial Information and Resource Management (FIRM) System:
City of San Francisco

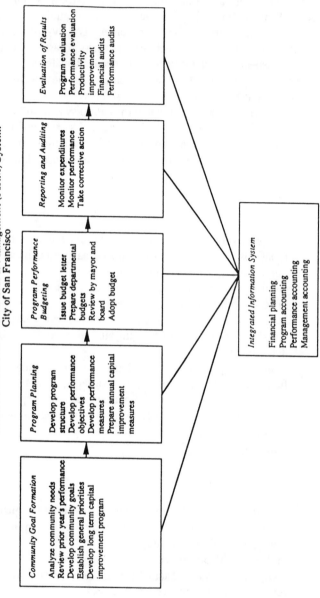

Source: Adapted from San Francisco, Office of the Mayor, *Program Measurement Handbook* (San Francisco, Calif.: Resources Management Program, City and County of San Francisco, Office of the Mayor, February 1980), Fig.5, p.33.

f.   a flexible accounting structure permitting the recognition of encumbrance for any given program or activity;

g.   a common data system to permit the recognition of expenditure and revenue programs, activities, and so on, to permit performance data to be collected; and

h.   ability to determine full costing of all undertakings.

3.   Performance Management:

a.   system for assessing performance of activities, programs, projects, and/or responsibility centers for measuring indicators, such as workloads, output, effectiveness, and quality of performance;

b.   periodic system for setting and reporting on planned performance targets with annual performance plan to the chief executive, clientele, or public;

c.   indicators showing performance measurement linkages to the budget;

d.   reporting of performance analysis with budget expenditure data and comparison of performance targets with recommended appropriations.

4.   Auditing:

a.   maintaining results data on important problems and recommendations emanating from independent audits and others deemed necessary;

b.   maintaining important findings and recommendations of performance audits;

c.   identifying systems for showing response and corrective actions taken due to audit recommendations;

d.   identifying systems, plans, and guidelines to be followed before each audit is undertaken; and

e.   process for selecting activities and/or programs to be audited.[7]

Advantages of the Integrated Financial Management Information System

Unlike fragmented financial management systems, the integrated financial management information system is able to respond effectively to citizens' demands. It generates performance data to enable decision makers to better evaluate agency and/or responsibility center accomplishments and facilitates the conduct of performance and effectiveness audits. The integrated system enhances policymakers' ability to organize data around significant issues instead of the expenditure or object classification, which is the norm under the existing, fragmented systems.

In summary, the following benefits are associated with the integrated system model:

1.   Information can be presented in a relevant framework.
2.   Data can be better analyzed and categorized before they are reported and/or disseminated.
3.   Information has greater opportunity for reaching decision makers on a timely basis.
4.   The opportunity to design the system to produce data to meet users' needs is facilitated.
5.   The opportunities for data analysis and for conducting cost-benefit analysis are enhanced.
6.   There is greater opportunity to standardize, centralize, and increase the consistency of information.
7.   Greater computerization can be justified.
8.   It forces the agency or governmental unit to train and upgrade staff. Typically, local governments and other not-for-profit agencies tend to hire consultants rather than develop in-house capability.
9.   The integrated system minimizes duplication and jurisdictional problems in exchanging information and facilitates efficient information sharing.

Disadvantages of the Integrated Financial Management Information System

Despite the many benefits to be gained from the integrated system, there are disadvantages as well. They include the following:

1.   It tends to be expensive and difficult to design and build.
2.   When a system is large, the problems associated with the system tend to be bigger and more involved.
3.   Since these systems are highly coordinated and operate to produce synergistic results, subsystem failures may disrupt the entire system.
4.   Maintaining accessibility, privacy, and security of information becomes more difficult.

DESIGNING AN INFORMATION MANAGEMENT NEEDS SYSTEM

In developing an information system (see the City of Pittsburgh example in the Appendix to this chapter), two critical points should be observed at the outset in determining information needs: (1) existing processing problems should be identified, and (2) the new types of information need should be developed to enhance management decision making.[8]   Also, it cannot be overemphasized that early in the design of the financial information system, key players (all major operating officials with financial responsibilities, e.g., the mayor, city manager, chief executive, legislative officials, and relevant financial officials) should be substantively involved.

A four-phase approach to designing the financial information system has been suggested. Phase one, organizational assessment, requires three activities: (1) needs determination, (2) assessment of the government or organization's capacity, and (3) system selection. Phase two, implementation, requires that management be alert and sensitive to personnel and other organizational problems attendant on potential changes. Documentation and testing are important in this phase. Phase three, operation, involves ongoing training, determining and delegating operating responsibilities, and planning for system enhancement. Phase four is the preparation of a control plan setting forth policies and procedures aimed at directing, controlling, and monitoring performance against plans. Since our focus here is on needs determination, our discussion will be limited to this aspect.

Organization Assessment Phase

The most important first step in system development is the definition of financial information needs, which typically fall into four basic management responsibility areas: planning, organizing, controlling and external reporting/record keeping requirements necessary to aid management decision making.[9]   A major objective of this phase is the definition of policies and objectives aimed at overseeing the acquisition and use of resources, ensuring they are effectively used in achieving objectives, and ensuring that the required activities are carried out with maximum efficiency and effectiveness.[10]   The needs determination may be carried out by any method deemed appropriate, though the small committee approach seems to be the most often preferred. When this approach is used, a consultant may be employed in an advisory capacity.[11]

A review of the existing information should be undertaken to determine what needs are being met as well as those that should be given more urgent attention and those that are not being adequately met. For example, if the payroll component is operating well while the expenditure control component is performing below minimal expectations, attention should be given to expenditure control problems before any attempt is made to upgrade the payroll system. It is particularly important that both current and future needs be projected when the needs assessment is being made. Planned improvements will help to prevent problems from arising in the future.

During the needs assessment determination, decision flow analysis may be used to reveal the interrelationships among decisions, identifying decisions that are required to be made and those that have no applicability to current problems. Decision flow analysis can be used to aid in showing "interdependent decisions that are being made independently," as well as responsibilities, organizational structures, and performance measures that should be modified.[12]

As will be pointed out in Chapter 18 ("Reporting"), there are differing information needs for different management levels and users. Needs of different kinds of users must be given due recognition if the best quality decisions are to be made. Thus, the design of the information system must provide flexibility to generate the appropriate information for each management level in the organizational hierarchy. In a given organization, let us assume four levels. At level one, the information is routine and standardized. The processing involves mainly collection, record keeping, and storage of data. Level two is characterized by low-level decision making. The decision criteria and rules are specific and clearly definable, for example, notifying delinquent taxpayers and determining eligibility for a tax exemption. At level three, information is needed to exercise greater discretion in decision making, such as revenue estimating and applying the tax laws and administrative rules. Finally, level four requires information to plan broad strategy and forecast needs, such as the analysis of the budget's impact on the poor and on unemployment.

There are fiscal users, both internal and external, for whom the information system must be designed to respond on a continuing basis. Drebin, Chan, and Ferguson have suggested five information categories that potential users may need to aid them in making informed decisions, especially as they relate to accounting statements:[13]

1. *Current financial conditions and flows of short-term financial resources*. This relates to information about liquidity and the ability to convert assets into cash in a reasonably short period of time. It is also concerned with solvency, or the ability to meet current and maturing obligations as they come due. Cash and equivalent items and other resources available for specific uses are identified.

2. *Economic condition and changes in economic condition*. Information about the health, the taxing base, and the economic stability of the entity or community is identified. The purpose is to indicate the entity's ability to deliver regular services, meet future maturing obligations, and maintain acceptable levels of capital improvements.

3. *Legal, fiduciary, and contractual assurance.* Information is included to permit "interested parties to monitor the execution of contractual and legal requirements."[14]   It permits public officials to discharge their accountability by reporting on the resources entrusted to them.

4. *Planning and budgeting.* The planning and budgeting system provides information to permit those responsible for it to make alternative analyses to effectively allocate resources to those options offering the best impact or results.

5. *Management and organizational performance.* This information relates to the efficiency and effectiveness with which management achieves articulated and implied organizational goals and objectives.

These information categories are directed toward two types of internal users and eight types of external users:

> Internal information users:
>> management;
>> employees.
> External information users:
>> voters;
>> taxpayers;
>> executives;
>> legislative bodies;
>> service recipients;
>> oversight bodies;
>> vendors; and
>> grantors.

CHANGING SYSTEMS: SYSTEM SELECTION PROCESS

The system design and the system selection involve essentially the same activities as explained earlier (see the definition of and discussion of the MIS). Important is the fact that management is seeking to modify or change from one automated system to another. A host of reasons may account for the decision to change, including the following: outmoded technology; inability of system to meet present, evolving and expanding information needs; excessive turnover in personnel; and failure to involve management and principal users to appropriately influence information need changes. Wold suggested a method that provides useful guides.[15]

THE INTEGRATED SYSTEM: THE DATA BASE MANAGEMENT SYSTEM VERSUS THE DATA MANAGEMENT SYSTEM

An important question to be asked sometime during the needs determination phase concerns the type of software to be installed to aid in retrieving information from the system. The debate centers around the choice between the data base management system (DBMS) and the data management system (DMS).

The data base management system contains data and procedures that permit a process to be added or subtracted. Such processes can be manipulated to modify or change/convert the raw data to produce desired information. The internal management operation of DBMS minimizes users' efforts to make the system responsive to their needs. The data base approach minimizes data redundancy by maintaining centrally stored data that can be collectively shared by a number of users and utilized for applications.

The data management system (DMS) has a broader and more comprehensive scope than DBMS. It consists of a combination of software programs that automatically generate and update fields. In addition, it selects, sorts, and retrieves data. From these data it has the capability to generate different kinds of reports. Perhaps the main differences between DBMS and DMS are the organization of the DMS files, users' access to the system, and the language utilized.[16] DBMS permits users greater freedom "to search, probe and query files' contents in order to extract answers to nonrecurring and unplanned questions that are not available in regular reports. . . [and] to 'browse' through the data until they have the needed information."[17] DMS permits less user interaction and is guided by structured programs to process information capable of satisfying user demands.

BUDGET AND ACCOUNTING INFORMATION

The budget and accounting systems are normally required to act in concert with each other. To do otherwise would raise the possibility of losing control over the raising and spending of resources. Thus, the code of accounts used to identify accounting transactions typically parallels the codes that keep track of budgeting expenditures. The budget amounts serve as the standards that the accounting system uses to track deviations from actual expenditures and allowed expenditures. When the accounting system recognizes deviations from a standard, it sends signals to appropriate officials to take corrective action. Viewed in this context, accounting is a powerful subsystem in not-for-profit organizations. In many local governments and other not-for-profit organizations, the accounting system is the only information system.

In the past, when recommendations were made to revamp and improve the effectiveness of the total information system in the public sector, the accounting system was usually ignored. Consequently, accounting, rather than being designed as an effective and integral subset of the total information system, has generally been designed only to meet operating, legal, and other budgeting control constraints. As was shown in Chapter 2, it focuses on aspects such as the liquidity of assets and their availability to meet maturing obligations.

Conceptually, in an information system accounting, must be viewed as a strategic part of the total system with an impact on all other areas. It must be recognized, however, that the conventional accounting system is not sufficient in itself to assess program performance. To assess more than narrow financial or dollar accountability, which conventional financial accounting permits, a variety of information is needed. It is important that the system be user oriented and designed to produce both financial and nonfinancial information. This requires that each entity organize its information system to capture information that will have multiple and comparative capabilities and applicability to the governmental entity.

Ideally, the accounting, budgeting, and management information system should be integrated as shown in Figure 16.2, which shows the interconnection of all the processes of management that are tied into the accounting system. The planning, programming, financing, and budgeting phases represent future orientation, while the controlling, evaluating, and accounting phases represent the past and present state of things.

BUDGETING AND INFORMATION REQUIREMENTS: A BRIEF LOOK AT CONNECTICUT

Budgeting (see Figures 1.1 and 16.2) is part of the continuous financial management system process and needs to respond to ad hoc program analysis requests and to new and changing fiscal situation. This necessity demands that governmental units and other not-for-profit organizations create "an organized consistent and reliable, timely set of data bases to support decision-making."[18] Because of this critical requirement, budget personnel should participate in the design and implementation of the financial management system to ensure that the budget function adequately meets the varied and changing needs of the organization.

The continuous budgeting function impacts on all phases of the financial management systems: (1) the policy-making stages; budget formulation and enactment of appropriations; (2) administration: budget expectation and expenditure monitoring; and (3) evaluation and reporting, including performance auditing and evaluation. If a program's efficiency and effectiveness are to be institutionalized, enhanced data are needed to be aggregated for multiple users, giving due recognition to both line and staff requirements.

Figure 16.2

Financial Information System

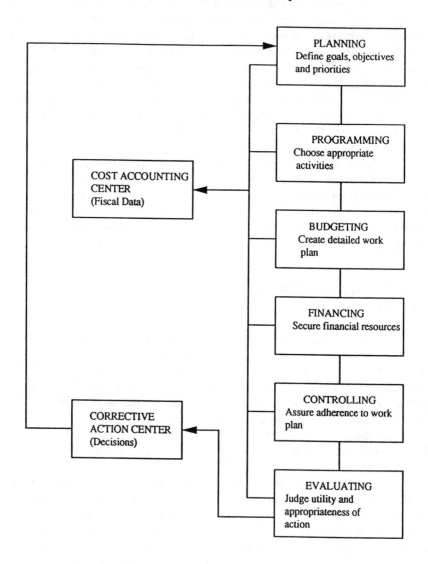

The state of Connecticut found that automating involved incremental or successive stages in moving toward a system that provides a programmatic format capable of generating timely and useful performance measurement data. Connecticut integrated payroll and 82 personnel and accounting systems "before expanding to more sophisticated approaches to budgeting."[19] In creating its Automated Budget System (ABS), a number of guiding objectives were established:

- creation of a common data base that was usable statewide;
- creation of an integrated, diverse, and flexible information base;
- provision of information to meet the needs of all levels of management;
- provision of oversight that minimizes micro and detail control;
- enabling agencies to decentralize decision making and accountability;
- planning for budget growth;
- establishing systems to enhance productivity and accountability; and
- improving information to better justify budget decisions.

The *cost center* "is the core feature of Connecticut's ABS." The cost center is the lowest level in the expenditure hierarchy directly identifying fund, organization, program or project.[20] Because of the specificity of the cost center, it can serve as a linkage for responsibility management allowing the organization to hold individual managers accountable for the execution and performance of their financial duties. Additionally, it provides high-level managers with needed information to carry out evaluation planning and policy-making.[21] To minimize implementation problems, the Connecticut ABS suggests the steps as shown in Figure 16.3.

CONCLUDING OBSERVATIONS

Fragmented and traditionally oriented information systems, while tolerable in small not-for-profit organizations, have limited usefulness in larger organizations. Due to the many demands to which these organizations must respond, essential information can no longer be collected, maintained, and compartmentalized in individual units. Public demands for efficiency and effectiveness in the delivery of public goods and services require that a whole range of substantive and financial information needs be coordinated and integrated into one system. Narrow object of expenditures or dollar accountability control data are still useful, but there is a greater need for data that are organized around issues that facilitate better decision making.

Too often, managers in not-for-profit organizations equate an information-processing system with computer hardware, leading many organizations to acquire expensive computer equipment that has produced unacceptable payoffs. This need not be so. The computer is only one important element in the development of an information system, and should be considered only after the information needs and the context of the organization, including the support staff, have been carefully considered. It should be kept in mind that "computer magic" does not happen by chance but through well-conceived and -designed plans developed to achieve specific objectives.

APPENDIX: DEVELOPMENT OF A MANAGEMENT INFORMATION SYSTEM FOR THE CITY OF PITTSBURGH'S DEPARTMENT OF FINANCE: A CASE STUDY[22]

In 1991, the City of Pittsburgh established a new Management Information Systems (MIS) division within the Department of Finance. This MIS division was established to compensate for weaknesses in the existing structure, increase the effectiveness and efficiency of the tax collection and -billing procedures, generate reports, and add integrity and reliability to the decision-making processes within the department. Several factors and challenges lead to the establishment of the new division, such as the lack of coordinated and accessible management and financial information and the real estate crash of 1991. With the establishment of the new MIS system, the Department of Finance and other departments sought to acquire a fully integrated information-sharing and report-generating system.

The objectives of the new MIS division include the following:

- Interface with other city departments, agency divisions, and sections to increase the effectiveness and efficiency of tax billing and collection.
- Improve productivity.
- Generate management and financial reports, analyses, and revenue and expenditure forecasts.
- Enhance the decision-making process and the retrieval and filtering of information.
- Examine and evaluate the activities of city departments and divisions.
- Organize and coordinate computer services and programming

needs between the Department of Finance and the City's Information Systems department (CIS), which has the responsibility of housing the centralized mainframe data base computer center.

- Utilize county data base systems for real estate property identification and tracking.
- Establish proactive mechanisms for future streamlining and networking for management and financial information needs as they arise.
- Eliminate excessive duplication of systems and programs.
- Hook up to the City and Planning Departments' PAGIS (Pittsburgh, Allegheny County, Geographical Information System) data base to allow the MIS division to access and make decisions on property values, density of population, and parking lots.

The Old System

Prior to 1991, the Department of Finance lacked a separate and distinct internal information system. The department had at most two individuals, who acted as liaisons between the city of Pittsburgh's City Information Systems and the department. Therefore, the internal decision-making process was decentralized, unorganized, and chaotic. There was no central focus, nor a single person responsible for supervising, coordinating, or prioritizing the functions and program needs of the department. The decision-making processes were ad hoc at best. Further, supervisors within the department did not know who was in charge nor what was involved in programming and assessing the needs of the division. Projects were prioritized by whomever had the most influence and depending on which projects were deemed the most important by the City Information Systems (CIS). CIS, in fact, had total control over systems operations. Department supervisors had no guarantees that CIS would address any specific requests. In addition, CIS reports were extensive and exceedingly long. This, in turn, contributed to decision-making processes and analyses that were cumbersome, faulty, and inaccurate, culminating in a lack of response to immediate needs. Additionally, the computer terminals, PCs, and printers within the department were not fully integrated with CIS. Thus, instead of being able to plan and take initiative by being proactive, the department was reactive.

The weaknesses of the department included the following:

- Information functions were decentralized.
- Lack of coordination with the City Information System.
- No clear job divisions, specializations, or responsibilities.
- Ad hoc decision-making processes.

- Unreliable management and information analyses, projections, and reports.
- No clear responsibility centers and controls.
- Workload inefficiency and ineffectiveness.

The Creation Of The 1991 MIS Division

The 1991 real estate system crash presented the newly established MIS division with its first challenge, and MIS was able to rebuild the entire real estate system within six months. MIS accomplished this by consulting analysts and completely revising and flowcharting the new system. MIS also educated personnel on how they wanted the system to work and hired the necessary temporary programmers to do COBOL programming. Without the newly created MIS division, it would have taken one to two years to rebuild the real estate system, indeed if this could have been accomplished at all.

After the revisions of the real estate functions were completed, the Department of Finance's existing files were linked to the CIS department through telecommunication systems. MIS now provided the department with the ability to analyze, prioritize, and assess the data bases and the networking and programming needs of its divisions. This also allowed management with the divisions to perform comparative analyses, projections, and forecasts to enhance revenue collections. For example, through the centralized MIS system, the investigative division is on-line with credit bureaus in order to conduct skip-tracing (i.e., locate individuals who have moved), which assists in the collection of delinquent taxes. The investigative and audit division is also on line with Dun and Bradstreet to produce reports on companies they are auditing. A tenant registration data base has also been established, which enables the investigative and audit division to locate nonfilers and those who fail to comply with tax laws. Finally, the establishment of the MIS division has made the system user-friendly throughout the department, allowing personnel to participate more readily by utilizing the system and encouraging them to make suggestions for possible enhancements, and thereby including the employees in the decision-making process.

The creation of the new MIS division has produced the following benefits:

- Real estate billing and collections are timely and accurate.
- Increased the Department of Finance's efficiency and effectiveness.
- Integration with the CIS department.
- Eliminated excessive duplication of programming.
- Improved the department's tax collection and billing processes.

- Improved the production of management and financial analyses, projections, and reports.
- Centralized core information functions with the department.
- Established a proactive mechanism for future modifications.

Implications of the Case Study

The creation of new MIS division has several implications for the City of Pittsburgh and its departments. They include the following:

- Centralized information functions facilitate the immediate utilization of information for decision making processes.
- Centralized information functions improve the data collection and processing procedures within departments and their divisions.
- Centralized information functions maximize the utilization of data with minimal expenditure of time and personnel.
- Responsibility centers and job specifications are clearly defined.
- Decision making processes and analyses are more systematic, eliminating ad hoc decision making.
- There is a greater level of certainty that accurate and reliable analyses, projections and reports are produced.
- Job effectiveness, efficiency and productivity are enhanced because information is specific and accurate to the needs of the user.
- The departments' and their divisions' priorities are clearly focused, preventing duplications of systems and reducing costs and wastefulness of duplicating systems.

By sharing, cooperating, and keeping the lines of communication open between the participants, decision making and program development is enhanced throughout the City.

Conclusion

The establishment of the Management Information System (MIS) in the Department of Finance of the City of Pittsburgh has added a positive and creative dimension to the scope and nature of the decisions made within and outside the division. This, in turn has added more depth and professionalism to their decision-making skills, the reports generated, and the projections, analyses and forecasts performed by the division. In the long run it should enable the city of Pittsburgh to function in a more cost-effective and efficient manner, thereby providing sufficiently high quality services and greater opportunities to the constituents it serves.[23]

NOTES

1. Mitch Betts, "States Redefining Public Service," *Computerworld*, 27, no. 16 (1993): 1, 20.

2. Ibid.

3. Ibid.

4. Charles R. Litechy and Earl R. Wilson, "Systems Development for Small Governments," *Government Finance* 10, no. 3 (September 1981): 11.

5. Frederick O'R. Hayes, David Grossman, Thomas Merchiling, and Rosenbloom, *Linkages: Improving Financial Management in Local Government* (Washington, D.C.: Urban Institute Press, 1982), p. 182.

6. David A. Grossman and Frederick O'R. Hayes, "Moving toward Integrated Fiscal Management," *Public Budgeting and Finance*, 1, no. 2 (Summer 1981): 41-42; see also Hayes, Grossman, Merchiling, Thomas, and Rosenbloom, *Linkages*, pp. 12-20, 131-37.

7. Hayes, Grossman, Merchiling, Thomas, and Rosenbloom, *Linkages*, pp. 12-20.

8. Litechy and Wilson, "Systems Development for Small Governments," p. 11.

9. Rhett D. Harrell, *Developing a Financial Management Information System for Local Government: The Key Issues* (Washington, D.C.: Government Finance Research, Municipal Fiance Officers Association (MFOA), 1980), p. 2.

10. See Geoffrey H. Wold, "Information Systems Planning" *Government Finance Review* 5, no. 3 (June 1989): 23.

11. William J. Kettinger, *Information Resource Management and the Use of Information in Local Government: A Policy Guide* (Columbia, S.C.: University of South Carolina Press, 1980), 31.

12. Alan Walter Steiss, *Management Control in Government* (Lexington, Mass.: Lexington Books, 1981), p. 123.

13. Allan R. Drebin, James L. Chan and Lorna C. Ferguson, *Objectives of Accounting and Financial Reporting for Governmental Units: A Research Study,* Vol. 1 (Chicago: National Council on Governmental Accounting, 1981), pp. 101-4.

14. Richard A. Bassler, "Data Bases, MIS and Data Base Management Systems," in *Computer Systems and Public Administration,* ed. Richard A. Bassler and Norman L. Enger, (Alexandria, Va.: College Readings, 1976), p. 203; Jeffrey D. Ullman, *Principles of Data Base Systems*, 9, no. 3 (Rockville, MD.: Computer Science Press, 1982), pp. 1-5.

15. See Geoffrey H. Wold, "The System Selection Process," *Government Finance Review* (June 1993), pp. 25-27.

16. Richard F. Schubert, "Basic Concepts in Data Base Management," *Datamation*, Vol. 18 (July 1972): 42-47; James Martin, *Computer Data-Base Organization*, 2nd ed. (Englewood Cliffs, N.J.: Prentice-Hall, 1975), pp. 4-7.

17. Norman L. Enger, "Data Management System," in Bassler and Enger, *Computer Systems and Public Administration*, p. 205.

18. John R. Fadoir, "State Financial Management System: The Connecticut Experience," *Public Budgeting and Finance*, 10, no. 3 (Fall 1990): 79.

19. Ibid., p. 82.

20. Ibid., p. 83.

21. Ibid.

22. Anthony Boule provided this review with the aid of the MIS personnel in the Finance Department, to whom thanks is given for their cooperation.

23. See Anthony Boule, "Management Information Systems in City Government: How Has the Institution of the MIS Division within the Department of Finance of the City of Pittsburgh Affected the Organization's Decision Making Processes?" (University of Pittsburgh, Graduate School of Public and International Affairs, Unpublished Graduate paper, Spring 1993).

17

Auditing

Auditing has been with us since antiquity. Records show that the Egyptians employed it as far back as 2000 B.C. to carefully control shipments in and out of the royal treasury (government storehouses). For example, containers of grain destined for the storehouse were accepted only if filled in the presence of overseers and a scribe, who duly recorded them. Effective delivery of the grain was made only after its receipt was recorded by a scribe stationed at the storehouse. Note that the activities performed by an individual were independently checked and confirmed (in a sense, audited) by another. Brown has observed: "Whenever the advance of civilization brought about the necessity of one man being entrusted to some extent with the property of another, the advisability of some kind of check upon the fidelity of the former would become apparent."[1]

The main purpose of government and not-for-profit auditing throughout history has been detecting fraud and, to a lesser degree, attesting to the fair presentation of an agency's financial condition, detecting technical errors, and detecting errors of principle.[2] Most individuals, due to lack of time or expertise, are unable to assess the credibility of financial statements or management's representation and assertions made therein. The auditor's report fills this gap by providing an expert's independent evaluation of financial reports.

Like the preceding chapter, this chapter is also about information. Auditing tests and validates the information generated by the financial management system. This chapter examines the processes, scope, and contrasting features and nature of the different types of audits found in public and other not-for-profit organizations.

Audits provide feedback information (see Figure 17.1) to those in authority (executive and legislative officials) for the purpose of reinforcing and strengthening control systems. Those reviewing audit reports will find three categories of information useful: (1) audits may be used to assess the reliability of subordinate officials' reports developed to meet stipulated accountability requirements aimed at providing verification of information. Such audits may focus on financial, program, or other performance indicators. (2) When officials need to be informed about existing conditions or results not included in submitted reports, the audits are concerned with information acquisition. (3) When the assurance need emphasizes adequate and appropriate controls for safeguarding and protecting resources and ensuring faithful, efficient, and effective performance, the audit may be referred to as independent assurance.[3]

Auditing suggests a basic responsibility and accountability relationship between top officials (recipients of audit reports), on the one hand, and subordinates (auditees), on the other. This principle directs subordinates to report all relevant information required to review and assess their performance.[4] This view was articulated by the former United States Comptroller General Elmer Staats when he indicated:

> A fundamental tenet of a democratic society holds that government and agencies entrusted with public resources and authority for applying them have the responsibility to render a full accounting of their activities. This accountability is inherent in the governmental process and is not always specifically identified by legislative provision.[5]

AUDITING: DEFINING ITS NATURE AND PURPOSES

There is no uniform meaning for the term *auditing*. Agreement on a single definition has been made more difficult by the changing nature, forms, and scope of auditing during the past forty years. An examination of Figure 17.1 shows that an audit is comprised of four parts: (1) the actors-auditors, the auditees (subordinates), and higher officials (audit recipients); (2) the accountability relationship between subordinate and higher officials (audit recipients); (3) the maintenance of independence between the auditors and the subordinates (auditees); and (4) the auditors' review and examination of subordinates' execution of the higher officials' delegated duties and responsibilities.

Participants in the audit process seek answers to several basic questions. Why is the audit being conducted? The typical objective is to achieve

Figure 17.1
Actors in the Audit Process

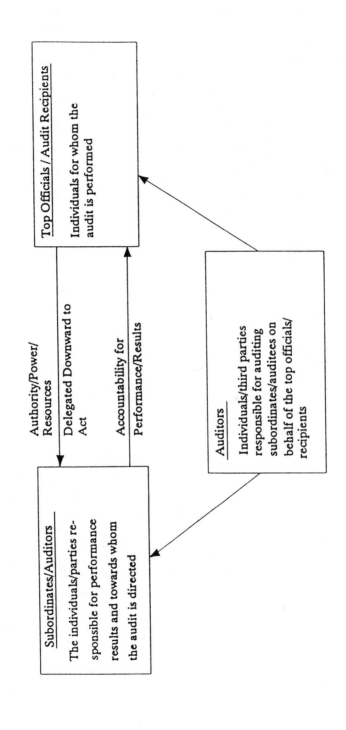

Top Officials / Audit Recipients

Individuals for whom the audit is performed

Authority/Power/ Resources

Delegated Downward to Act

Accountability for Performance/Results

Auditors

Individuals/third parties responsible for auditing subordinates/auditees on behalf of the top officials/ recipients

Subordinates/Auditors

The individuals/parties responsible for performance results and towards whom the audit is directed accountability and management control. What is the scope of the audit (it may be financial, compliance, performance, and so on)? Who are the parties (auditor, auditee, higher officials) involved? How is the process to be applied? The audit process consists of preparation, conduct (examination and evaluation), reporting (communicating), and settlement. Auditing, in general terms, may be defined as a process concerned with the collection and thorough analysis of the underlying information or evidence designed to render an independent, informed, and professional opinion about the representation and assertions made in management reports and supporting documents. Auditing is thus a means for independent verification and assurance about the completeness and creditability of financial and related records attesting to "the correctness of a calculation, the existence of an object, the accuracy of a statement, the reliability of a report, or the occurrence of an event."[6]

THE AUDITING AND ACCOUNTING LINKAGE

While there may be qualitative or effective audits without accounting records, there can be no financial or expenditure-related audits without supporting accounting data.[7] In fact, most audits conducted today in state and local governments and not-for-profit organizations are based on accountants' prepared records and financial statements of funds and account groups (records of nonfund accounts, such as land, buildings, and equipment) for the purpose of determining if the financial statements fairly present the financial position and results of an organization in conformity with generally accepted accounting principles (GAAP). Agencies are required to conform not only to GAAP but also to applicable local, state, federal, and other governing authorities' mandated accounting rules and regulations.

In the typical nongovernmental, not-for-profit agency, the accounting and budget systems are linked by conforming the budget account exactly to the code of accounts, and vice versa. For example, expenditure, appropriation, and revenue are used for both budgeting and accounting purposes. These accounting transactions usually provide the basis for audit reviews in determining whether obligations and expenditures have been accurately recorded. It is important to note that the auditor evaluates the internal control systems that agencies use for authorizing and recording financial commitments.

Finally, the test of an adaptable accounting system is that it leaves audit trails to permit transactions to be easily traced through accompanying supporting documentation. Adaptable accounting systems have clearly drawn procedures and guidelines indicating the lines of accountability to aid auditors in ascertaining how the accounting system is intended to operate. Accounting systems that lack these basic components provide an insufficient base upon which to perform informed and complete audit reviews.

TYPES OF AUDITS

Audits in Terms of Time

Preaudit is used to determine the propriety of proposed financial transactions and to control the accuracy of collecting and accounting for revenues and accounting for expenditures and disbursements. Postaudits occur at the end of the accounting period - after events have taken place and transactions have been recorded or approved for recording by appropriate officials. While preaudits are conducted by individuals internal to the organization and accountable to higher-level management, postaudits are conducted by individuals, usually certified public accountants (CPAs), external to the organization. The independent postaudit is what is usually meant when people talk about audits and will be the focus of attention in this chapter.

Pre-audits

The preaudit function is perhaps the most important type of audit carried out in an organization (see Chapter 20), yet typically, it has little visibility. Unlike the postaudit, which deals with activities that happened in the past, the preaudit permits action to be taken before the event/problem occurs. It thus may be viewed as a preventative instrument.

Whenever the use of resources is to be initiated, a series of affirmative questions such as the following should be asked: (1) Is the action consistent with articulated or implied policies? (2) If yes, is the action approved by the appropriate authority? (3) If yes, is the action approved to be undertaken now is reflected in the budget? (4) If yes, is the amount requested approved in the allotment agreement in the expenditure time table? (5) If yes, is the quality of the product or service consistent with the approved criteria? (6) If yes, is there sufficient cash available to expend the funds requested?

Internal and External Audits

Internal audits have all of the characteristics and attributes of preaudits but are much broader in scope and focus. They are independent appraisals (free of organizational constraints and pressures to avoid compromising objectivity) of the activities or operations performed within an organization to facilitate management and other controls. Indeed, the persons conducting the internal audits (internal auditors) have been referred to as the "eyes and ears" of management and as impartial providers of information to management. Additionally, internal audits may be conducted during or at the end of an accounting period. They may be used to assess employee compliance with managerial policies, to evaluate the effectiveness of various control systems, and to assist members of an organization to better discharge their responsibilities. Internal audits furnish management with analyses, appraisals, recommendations, counsel, and information relating to the activities reviewed. In summary, internal audits appraise the soundness, adequacy, and application of accounting, financial, and operating internal controls. In summary, the internal auditors perform the following functions:

- Act as an independent appraiser of important control functions;
- Performs advance, ongoing, and post functions of the organization;
- Aid members of the organization to effectively carry out their duties and responsibilities; and
- Provide managers with timely analysis, approvals, and recommendations on all matters reviewed.[8]

The external audit is synonymous with the postaudit. The individuals conducting these audits are independent and owe their allegiance to officials outside the agency. In government, they report to the legislative body, the public, or some authorized statutory official. In nongovernmental not-for-profit agencies, the auditors report to a governing board or an individual designated by the board. External postaudits may be divided according to scope - general and specific. General audits include a review of all financial operations pertaining to an agency at the close of an accounting period. Special audits are restricted in scope or time in that they include only a portion of an agency's financial transactions and records or cover all the transactions and records for a period shorter than a year. It is important to note that internal audits and independent external audits are not substitutes for each other; they are complementary.

Three kinds of groups perform independent external audits: (1) elected audit officials of the governmental unit being examined; (2) officials appointed or elected by a governmental agency other than the one being audited; and (3) independent public accountants providing service for a negotiated fee. Most states and a small number of municipalities elect an independent auditor or have one appointed by the legislative body. If appointed, the auditor reports directly to the legislative body. Elected auditors report directly to the people and are typically the chief accounting officers in their jurisdiction. The effectiveness of these officials has been mixed. This is especially true when auditors are elected as a result of political connections with elected executives or where only minimal qualifications are required for them to hold office.

In some states, elected or appointed state audit officials may audit selected state agencies, local governmental units, and not-for-profit agencies receiving government funds either at or without request. Though most local audits are executed by independent certified public accountants, state agencies have increasingly participated in prescribing standard minimal audit procedures, reviewing independent audit reports to assure compliance with statutes, and conducting spot checks or tests where audit systems and procedures appear weak.

Audits According to Purposes

As an overriding objective, each auditor's opinion assesses whether statements fairly and consistently present (in relation to prior years) the financial position and results of an agency's operations in conformity with generally accepted accounting principles. These objectives may be combined with others to achieve particular audit purposes. Figure 17.2 shows a schematic view of the four basic types of audits on which management relies: (1) the financial data found in the budget, financial statements, and reports comparing actual with planned targets; (2) a report on the efficiency measures, including nonfinancial output data; and (3) a report on the actual data on effectiveness or accomplishments of the agency. These are control reports that are intended to aid management decision making. Though economy and efficiency are shown separately, they are bridged by a connecting arrow. The economy component tracks the countable inputs, while the efficiency component oversees the system required to convert the inputs into outputs.

Financial and compliance audits or *fiscal audits* assess whether financial operations are properly conducted. They evaluate whether an entity's financial statements are presented fairly and in compliance with applicable laws, policies, procedures, and regulations. A determination is made about the adequacy of accounting records and procedures and the financial stewardship of the agency. Recommendations for improvement are usually made. This type of audit serves as an accountability and control device which aids in preventing misuses of public funds through inefficiency, inadequate security, and fraudulent practices.

Program results or *effectiveness audits* assess whether articulated or implied results and benefits as established by the legislature or other authorizing body are being attained and whether an agency is giving ample consideration to alternatives that might be employed to produce acceptable results at lower cost. This may require an analysis of the activities suggested in the statutes to determine if they have been properly developed or designed to achieve the legislative intent.

Program results audits are essentially a form of program evaluation. The implementation of program evaluation, like the audit, is designed to assure

Figure 17.2

Schema Showing Different Types of Audits

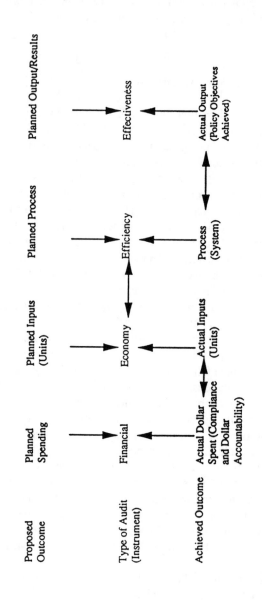

Source: Adapted from Henry A. Butt, "Values of Money Auditing Local Administration," *Public Budgeting and Finance* 5 (Summer 1985): 68

a high degree of independence for the auditors or evaluators vis-à-vis management. This type of evaluation, while very appealing conceptually, often has difficulty assessing congruence between expected and achieved results. A major reason for this problem is that "programs are conceived, justified and operated under assumptions that are never verified."[9]

Economy and efficiency audits determine whether an agency is managing or utilizing its resources, such as personnel, property, and space, in an economic manner toward achieving its legislative and/or administrative objectives. Explicit examination is made of the causes of any inefficiencies in agency practices, including inadequacies in management information systems; inefficiencies in administrative methods; defective work procedures; and ineffectiveness in the development, application, and use of automation and organization structure. Stress is put on economical acquisition and efficient use of materials and human resources. The economy aspect suggests minimizing expenditures, while the efficiency aspect implies maximizing benefits produced for the resources expended.

Responsibility and accountability on the part of public officials are at the heart of each type of audit. Few governments or other not-for-profit agencies use all types at any given point in time. Instead, audits are typically designed to achieve the specific articulated needs of an agency, its investors, the regulatory agencies that oversee it, or public interest groups. Usually, attention is focused on one type of audit, while the others, if considered at all, are considered to a much lesser degree. The greatest number of audits conducted are of the financial and compliance (fiscal) variety, although an increasing number of audits emphasize economy, efficiency, and program effectiveness. The financial and compliance audit opinions, moreover, are retrospective in orientation, while economy, efficiency, and program results audits render judgments, conclusions, and recommendations that are present- and future-oriented.

AUDIT AND INTERNAL CONTROLS

One of the important objectives of an audit is the examination of an agency's internal control system (1) to determine the reliability and accuracy of the accounting data and the information system in general; (2) to assess compliance with laws and regulations; (3) to promote efficient and effective operating procedures and policy implementation; (4) to evaluate methods designed to safeguard assets; and (5) to encourage adherence to managerial policies.

In determining the adequacy of internal control systems, several critical characteristics must be examined. These include (1) segregation of duties sufficient to safeguard an agency's resources, involving a prescribed system of authorization and record maintenance to obtain effective accounting control over assets, liabilities, revenue, and expenses; (2) a system to guide the execution of duties and functions in each unit or responsibility center of an agency; (3) staff capable of effectively implementing the responsibilities with which they have been charged; and (4) a defined system of internal review. These basic characteristics are so mutually interdependent that the absence or impairment of any one will impede the effectiveness of the internal control system. It should be noted, however, that detailed and minute specification of the internal controls can be prohibitive in terms of cost compared to available resources. Thus, each audit should emphasize only those controls that are relevant to the items being audited (see Chapter 3).

The reliability of the internal control system provides an important input in determining the extent and scope of an audit. Thus, an internal review auditor should give due attention to the process of the internal control system before commencing the audit. It is important to bear in mind that there is no one particular pattern of internal control that can be specified for all governmental units.[10] The state of Ohio has developed a risk-based methodology for financial audits.

RISK-BASED AUDIT METHODOLOGY

Traditional financial audits have been procedure driven. Certain standardized tests are used, sometime, without considering the context of the environment in which the audit is taking place. This might not be the most efficient way to carry out an audit. The Ohio risk model "requires the auditor to analyze the risks associated with auditing each particular government and to design a test procedure based upon those assessed risks.[11]

The risk-based auditing approach is initiated with an overall audit risk assessment. Emphasis is put on three risks:

- The first attempts to prevent errors from occurring prior to action by eliminating *inherent risk* occurring due to unintentional errors (mistakes) or an intentional act involving, for example, misstatement of financial information (government may want to hide revenue when adversarial union negotiations is about to take place by overstating expenditures).
- The second stresses *control risk* in determining extent to which controls are in place to timely prevent and detect the problems associated with inherent risks.

Figure 17.3
Risk-Based Audit Methodology

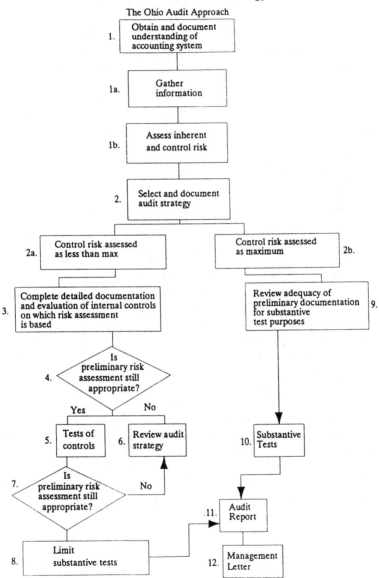

Source: Michael Howard, William Reidy, and William C. Serverns, "The Audit Approach: Ohio's Risk-Based Audit Methodology," *Government Finance Review*, 7, no. 2 (April, 1991): 17, (with permission of the Government Finance Officers Association, 180 North Michigan Avenue, Chicago).

- The third designs a system that combines the inherent and control risks assessments to test account balances minimizing the possibility of overlooking something significant. This is known as minimizing *detection risk*.

When the combination for inherent and control risks are low, the auditor can accept a high degree of detection risks as the chances of missing a maternal account balance are reduced. Conversely, when inherent and control risks are high the acceptable detection risk must be low. Risk assessment (the inherent, control, and detection risks, as shown in Figure 17.3) sets the parameter regarding the extent of the scrutiny that will be necessary to render the appropriate opinion of an entity's financial records.[12]

INSPECTORS GENERAL (IGs) AND THE AUDIT FUNCTIONS

Since the passage of the Inspector General Act of 1978, attention has been focused on the IG's Office to give leadership to auditing in federal agencies. While a few state and local governments have adopted some aspects of the federal IG model, attention here will be briefly focused on the federal IGs. Under the 1978 act, the IGs were given two main functions: (1) consolidation of the scattered audit and investigation units with a unified agency or department-wide responsibility and (2) pursuit of the reduction of fraud, waste, and abuse. Staffed by nonpolitical, knowledgeable professionals (in both auditing and investigation), they report to both Congress and the president. The IGs are expected to maximize the achievement of three types of accountability. The first is compliance, which promotes conformance to laws, rules, and regulations. The IG applies mainly negative sanctions (publicize violator's infractions) to individuals inside or outside the government agency such as contractors or other recipients of government resources aimed at achieving compliance with a visible display of punishment. The objective is to correct the existing problems and to deter future occurrences. Performance accountability stresses incentives and rewards to a accomplish desired outcomes. Capacity- or capability-building accountability attempts to create organizational competence by enhancing or investing in people skills and upgrading systems and structures.[13]

The view is expressed that the IG needs to put less stress on audit and investigation as these efforts do not get the greatest amount of results for the resources expended. Instead, the greatest emphasis should be put on performance accountability based on carefully defined indicators aimed at achieving the articulated or implied goals and objectives of the policymakers (see Figure 17.4 showing the IG performance measurement model and identifying

Figure 17.4
The IG Performance Measurement Model

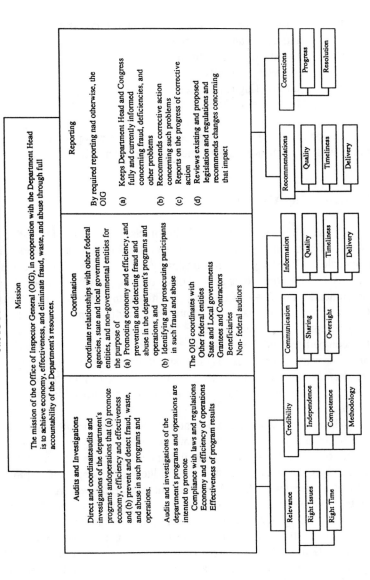

Mission

The mission of the Office of Inspector General (OIG), in cooperation with the Department Head is to achieve economy, effectiveness, and eliminate fraud, waste, and abuse through full accountability of the Department's resources.

Audits and Investigations

Direct and coordinate audits and investigations of the department's programs and operations that (a) promote economy, efficiency and effectiveness and (b) prevent and detect fraud, waste, and abuse in such programs and operations.

Audits and investigations of the department's programs and operations are intended to promote
Compliance with laws and regulations
Economy and efficiency of operations
Effectiveness of program results

- Relevance
  - Right Issues
  - Right Time
- Credibility
  - Independence
  - Competence
  - Methodology

Coordination

Coordinate relationships with other federal agencies, state and local government entities, and non-governmental entities for the purpose of
(a) Promoting economy and efficiency, and preventing and detecting fraud and abuse in the department's programs and operations, and
(b) Identifying and prosecuting participants in such fraud and abuse

The OIG coordinates with
Other federal entities
State and Local governments
Grantees and Contractors
Beneficiaries
Non- federal auditors

- Communication
  - Sharing
  - Oversight
- Information
  - Quality
  - Timeliness
  - Delivery

Reporting

By required reporting nad otherwise, the OIG

(a) Keeps Department Head and Congress fully and currently informed concerning fraud, deficiencies, and other problems
(b) Recommends corrective action concerning such problems
(c) Reports on the progress of corrective action
(d) Reviews existing and proposed legislation and regulations and recommends changes concerning that impact

- Recommendations
  - Quality
  - Timeliness
  - Delivery
- Corrections
  - Progress
  - Resolution

Source: Adapted from Dennis J. Duquette and Alexis M. Stowe. " A Performance Model for the Office of the Inspector General," *Government Accountants Journal* 42, (Summer 1993): 38

three focused areas and major goals and objectives). This will require a significant reallocation of resources away from audits and investigations.

The performance requirement model will necessitate a new orientation involving at least six steps:

- mission goals, objectives, and target identification;
- indicators and measurement identification;
- measuring achievement;
- analysis of results;
- interpreting results; and
- reporting performance results.

The belief is that the orientation performance will pay big dividends in the future as it will enhance performance by all concerned.

SELECTING THE AUDITOR

The requirement to audit and the precise procedures for auditing an agency are different among state governments, local governments, and not-for-profit agencies. Typically, the responsibility for selection of the independent auditor rests with the legislative body or the governing board of a nongovernmental, not-for-profit agency. While many governments attempt to select an auditor on the basis of competitive bidding, this approach is not generally accepted as a sound practice. Accountants have expressed the view that the competitive bidding method exerts unprofessional pressures on the auditor. This selection process may not permit the best auditor to emerge. The view is that qualitative factors required in an audit cannot be as easily as commodities, for which prices can be specified and allowable profits easily determined.

When the profit criterion becomes the major determining factor for the selection of an auditor, it is likely to impact on the professional independence of the auditor. Since judgment and situational factors (e.g., funding needs, internal controls, or other problems) may influence the scope and depth of the audit, this is a reason why the independent auditor should be given considerable latitude to explore important leads when necessary to determine if records are in order and if the agency's system is functioning effectively.

If competitive bidding is chosen over the negotiated approach, requests for proposals (RFPs) should be sent to potential independent auditors, clearly setting forth the scope of the audit and the kinds of services to be performed. Prior to the actual RFP some governments may issue preliminary requests asking independent auditors to submit statements showing their qualifications. Actual RFPs should go only to independent auditors who have been determined to be well qualified. A thorough review should be given to the submitted proposals and due recognition should be given both to price and quality as far as these can be determined.

Included among the information that should be obtained before selection is made are answers to the following questions:

1. What are the experience and qualifications of the independent auditor?
2. What is the time frame for conducting the audit? When the lead time is substantial, it gives both parties (management and auditor) an opportunity to review and resolve problems that may exist before the audit gets under way.
3. Will management or the auditor close the books? If the auditor closes the books, more time is necessary.
4. What kinds of clerical assistance will be provided to the auditor?
5. If an internal staff exists, will it be made available to the auditor?
6. What recent accounting changes have been made?
7. What is the scope of the audit?

In those cases where the audit price is determined by joint negotiation, both parties need the answers to these questions. In negotiated contracts, the independent auditor's cost estimate should be binding unless unforeseen problems arise, necessitating that the estimates be exceeded. Once all of the details of the audit have been determined, the agenda should be specifically identified in a contract.[14] Such aspects as the departments, programs, activities, and funds to be audited; the period to be covered; and the means of handling unexpected problems should be spelled out.

AUDITING STANDARDS

Private sector auditing performance standards are set forth by a wide variety of private organizations such as the American Institute of Certified Public Accountants (AICPA), and government agencies, such as the General Accounting Office (GAO). The "Standards and Guidelines" enunciated by the GAO basically incorporate and expand the AICPA standards to achieve the specific auditing objectives that are being pursued.

Audit Standards

In the private sector, the American Institute of Certified Pubic Accountants (AICPA) establishes audit standards. Firms falling under the preview of the Security and Exchange Commission (SEC), must follow generally accepted accounting principles (GAAP). Because of the relationship between the SEC, FASB, and AICPA, companies are encouraged to use GAAP. In an effort to obtain financing from investors and creditors and financial institutions, firms attempt to follow accounting practices that will result in their obtaining unqualified opinions. Moreover, auditors have an obligation to apply generally accepted auditing standards. To do otherwise would be in violation of professional standards of conduct and could lead to a loss of their CPA designations.

The AICPA has three groups of performance standards: general standards, standards of field work, and standards of reporting.

General Standards

Individuals conducting an audit are required to have appropriate and adequate technical training to effectively conduct an audit. The auditor is expected to have internalized values of independence so that they become an operating norm that influences the auditor's way of thinking and acting. The preparation and execution of the audit must be carried out with due professional care.

Standards of Field Work

There must be preplanning and effective supervision of all participants. A review and evaluation of an agency's internal control system is a precondition to all audits to determine the degree of reliance that can be put on the agency's system and the extent of auditing tests that will be necessary. The authority of the auditor's opinion is based on competent evidence obtained by means of inspection, observation, inquiries, and confirmation.

Standards of Reporting

The report is required to state whether the presentation of the financial statements is in accordance with generally accepted accounting principles. The report states whether GAAP have been consistently followed in the current report and the preceding one. Where disclosures are necessary to provide material information of the financial statements, the auditor must so indicate. Finally, the report is required to indicate an opinion regarding the financial statement as a whole or an assertion stating that an opinion should be clearly articulated. Whenever an auditor signs his or her name to an auditing report, the character of the auditor's examination must be clearly set forth along with the extent of responsibility that he or she is assuming.

GOVERNMENTAL AUDITING STANDARDS

Earlier we examined the various kinds of audits, but we did not discuss the auditing standards that are used in conducting public sector audits. Until 1972, when the U.S. Comptroller General issued *Standards for Audit of Governmental Organizations, Programs, Activities and Functions*, there was no comprehensive statement on governmental auditing standards.[15] The GAO audit guidelines were a response in the early 1970s to the explosion of interest in, and demand for, better assessment of both financial and nonfinancial activities at all levels of government. The guidelines are used by auditors in and outside of government and by both internal and external independent postauditors. The GAO standards were adopted by the federal agencies under OMB Circular A-73, which adopted the GAO audit criteria, and OMB Circular A-102, which was revised in 1979 to include the "single" audit (forces agencies auditing a program with multiple sources of funding to conduct one audit on behalf of all concerned). The GAO auditing standards were revised in 1988. In 1993 GAO provided a revised exposure draft of its 1999 standards for the audit of the government agencies which should be completed in 1994. Each kind of audit (e.g., financial, compliance, economy and efficiency, and program results) requires specific standards for use in conducting the audit. Many governmental units have incorporated the GAO audit guidelines as law for the conduct of audits in their jurisdiction.

Governmental entities first requirements is to operate within the constraints of state laws and local regulations. When these entities require practices that do not parallel GAAP, the Governmental Accounting Standard Board (GASB), or it predecessors, the auditors must conform to the government's stipulated practices. The potential for confusion does exists, but these problems are generally being eliminated, especially as states revise their practices to conform to GAAP. At the federal level, the GAO has incorporated the AICPA audit standards for federal audits unless they are formally excluded.

SINGLE AUDIT

The pressure to move to the single audit resulted from a number of developments during the 1960s and 1970s. Federal grants-in-aid grew from just over $2 billion in 1950 to nearly $95 billion in 1981. Though reduced to around $85 billion in 1985, they still represent a significant funding source for state and local governments. Hundreds and, in some cases, thousands of federal programs (1,100 in the Department of Health and Human Services, for example) were administered by different federal agencies. In many instances, each program established its own accounting requirements. A state or local agency that received aid for 40 different programs could have been required to have 40 or more accounting systems. Compounding the problem was the fact that each federal agency administering a program which awarded funds to a state or local agency had a right to have on-site audits. Thus, keeping track of the accounting, reporting, and auditing demands was a heavy burden to the state and local governments receiving federal assistance.

Efforts to bring about standardization in the 1960s met with minor success. It was not until 1979, with the issuance of Attachment P (*Audit Requirements to OMB Circular A-102, Uniform Administrative Requirements for Grants-in-Aid to State and Local Governments*) that the single audit got formal authoritative support. Attachment P requires that audits be done on an agencywide basis instead of grant by grant.

The review of the results obtained with the implementation of Attachment P led to passage of the Single Audit Act of 1984, which includes the following objectives:

1. The improvement of financial management systems of federally assisted programs;
2. The establishment of uniform audit requirements for federal assistance programs to state and local governments; and
3. Promotion of the efficient or effective use of audit resources, with the stipulation that all programs with revenues of $100,000 or more will be subject to the act as of January 1, 1985.

The law covers both direct and indirect federal assistance programs, including pass-through funds from another unit of government. Direct cash payments to individuals are the only item excluded. Only smaller units of government will not be audited annually. These programs may elect to have the single audit or be audited as required under the federal financial assistance requirement of the grantor agency or as prescribed by the federal comptroller general.

The audit conducted under the Single Audit Act of 1984 must be done in conformity with generally accepted government auditing and standards applicable to financial and compliance audits. The Single Audit Act does not require economy and efficiency and program results audits or program evaluation unless these approaches are required by plans, regulations, or contracts. Only independent auditors may perform the audits required under the act. All audits conducted pursuant to the act must be made available to appropriate federal officials 30 days after their completion and be made available for public inspection. When material internal control weakness or noncompliance with applicable laws and regulations are found, the audited agency must submit a plan to the appropriate federal officials for corrective action or indicate the reasons why corrective action is not necessary.

The Single Audit Act requires that OMB designate a "cognizant agency" (a specific federal agency) to oversee the implementation of the audit requirement in a given state. The cognizant agency has three main responsibilities: (1) to see that agencies conduct timely audits and conform to stipulations of the act; (2) to make certain that audit reports or corrective actions are transmitted to appropriate federal officials; and (3) where possible, to coordinate audits done by contract with those required under the act to aid in developing audit continuity and integration.

OPERATIONAL AUDIT

There is some confusion about precisely what an operational audit is because it is also a type of performance audit. An operational audit is different from a performance audit in that it is more inclusive. An operational audit comprises not only economy and efficiency audits and effectiveness audits but also financial audits. The performance audit, it is important to note, refers only to the economy and efficiency audits and the effectiveness audits as clearly set forth in the International City Management Association (ICMA) special reports on performance audit and *Governmental Accounting, Auditing and Financial Reporting* (GAAFR).[16]

Operational auditing facilitates decentralized management in that it is designed to keep agency management, top executives, and especially, legislative officials informed about whether an agency is using its resources both legally and effectively. Additionally, the operational audit is employed to review and appraise the soundness, adequacy, and application of all accounting, financial, and operating controls. This audit is not focused solely or mainly on accounting, but it considers how an agency's total resources are being applied. The operational audit attempts to determine the congruence between executive or legislatively articulated or implied objectives of administrative activities, functions, and programs that have been assigned for implementation with achieved results. The auditor is basically concerned with how well an agency is managed and the extent to which it realizes its objectives. Much that is presently done as performance auditing was formally carried out by management advisory services or consulting concerns.

Operational audits are more difficult to conduct because the standards and criteria to be applied are inexplicit. Many are derived from various sources, though legislative statements tend to be an important source, along with professional organizations which set standards of performance levels for specific fields. Typically, there are not explicit management indicators for accomplishments, economy, efficiency, and effectiveness. Additionally, legislative intent is not always clear. A number of general common sense standards or guides may be used in carrying out operational audits, covering such areas as: (l) the use of government property for personal benefit; (2) lack of coordination of agencies and/or units implementing related activities and programs; (3) lack of automation and up-to-date techniques; (4) excessive client complaints, unresolved disputes, and unsuitable policies, standards, and regulations; (5) nonadherence to policies, regulations, and procedures; and (6) unreliable reports.

The performance audit procedures parallel those of the financial audit. Financial and operating reports, administrative regulations, laws and contracts, agency policies, financial and operational information, and documentary evidence are examined. The auditor seeks answers to questions such as (l) What are the specific goals and objectives of the audited programs and activities? (2) What is the basis of authority (legal or administrative) under which the program is being operated? (3) How well are the audited objectives being achieved? (4) How well do the established procedures and practices aid in achieving the agency's goals and objectives? (5) What are the specific causes or reasons why existing procedures and practices are positively or negatively affecting the agency's goals and objectives?

Findings are categorized in terms of (l) those favorable to management and (2) those that are unfavorable. For unfavorable findings, the auditor is required to state how widespread or material they are and to indicate the direct and indirect impact on cost. It is not enough to simply identify the problems. Alternative ways for eliminating them must be identified.

Reporting for performance audits is divided into three sections. In section one the scope and objectives of the audit are stated. Section two contains an explanation of the findings of fact, indicating the causes and effects that management is having on the work environment in achieving the agency's objectives. Section three recommends ways to meet the identified problems, indicating the agency's enthusiasm and willingness in contributing to alternative solutions and stating previous recommendations that have not been implemented and current recommendations with which management disagrees.

AUDITS OF NON-PROFIT ENTITIES

Generally accepted accounting principles have particular applicability to colleges and universities, hospitals, and other nonprofit organizations. Each of these specialized areas has audit guides peculiar to itself. For example, colleges and universities have Audits of Colleges and Universities; hospitals have American Hospital Association guidelines and the AICPA's Hospital Audit Guide.[17] The voluntary health and welfare organizations (also known as human service organizations), which derive most of their resources from contributions, have the AICPA's *Audit of Voluntary Health and Welfare Organizations*.[18]

Other not-for-profit organizations need for solicitations, provides an incentive for them to follow GAAP. Bond-rating agencies have fostered the use of GAAP by these not-for-profit entities that enter the public bond market. There are still a number of not-for-profit agencies that use accounting practices because they are acceptable to the governing boards.

THE AUDIT REPORT

The various types of audits typically follow the same audit report format, though the operational audit tends to be more extensive. The general standards to be observed in writing the audit report have been summarized by the U.S. Comptroller General, as follows:

1. Be concise yet complete to facilitate ready user understanding.
2. Present accurately, completely, and fairly all material and factual information.
3. Present findings and conclusions clearly and as simply as the subject matter permits.
4. Include only factual information that can be adequately supported by evidence included in the working papers. Include supporting information only to the extent that it is necessary to make a convincing presentation.
5. Where possible include recommended actions for operations improvement, providing information on the problems and recommended courses of action to assist management in taking corrective action.
6. Put primary emphasis on improvement, minimize past criticisms, and point out unusual difficulties faced by operating officials.
7. Explain issues and questions requiring study and consideration.

8.   Direct attention to noteworthy accomplishments, particularly when the improvements may be applicable elsewhere.

9.   Give recognition to the views of responsible officials on the auditor's findings, conclusions, and recommendations.

10.   Explain the scope and objectives of the audit.

11.   Direct attention to significant and pertinent information that has been omitted because it is deemed privileged or confidential, giving the legal basis for such action.[19]

Audits containing financial reports are required to state the auditor's opinion as to whether the information contained in such a report is presented fairly. When the auditor is unable to express an opinion, the reasons should be indicated in the audit report (when the auditor cannot agree with the fair presentation of the report, he or she renders a qualified opinion). Additionally, the auditor states whether the audit is prepared in accordance with generally accepted accounting or prescribed principles applicable to the organization, programs, and functions or activities audited. Appropriate supplementary explanation about the financial reports is included as deemed necessary for full disclosure, including violations of legal or regulatory requirements and other instances of noncompliance.

CONCLUDING OBSERVATIONS

Auditing serves a strategic role in financial management in that it validates and attests to the accuracy of financial statements. In the public sector, it can cost a governmental unit thousands or perhaps millions of dollars if a negative opinion about its financial statement leads to a downgrading of the unit's credit rating.

Auditing can be used as an important management tool. The preaudit is employed to ensure that policies and activities take place in accordance with management policies and administrative procedures. The post-audit acts typically as a legislative or board oversight and accountability instrument when it evaluates the fairness and compliance of financial statements with statutory requirements and generally accepted accounting principles.

Of the different types of audits found in practice, the financial audit is the most widely used. In recent years, management decision-making requirements and public demand have made it necessary to go beyond the narrow dollar accountability approach that typifies the financial audit. Thus economy and efficiency, effectiveness/results, and operational audits are gaining support.

NOTES

1. Richard Brown, *A History of Accounting and Accountants* (Edinburgh, Scotland: T. C. and E. C. Jack, 1905), p. 74.

2. Robert H. Montgomery, *Auditing* (Chicago: American School of Correspondence, 1909), p. 12.

3. Lennis M. Knighton, "Four Keys to Effectiveness Auditing," *Government Finance Review*, 8, no. 2 (September 1979): 3-4.

4. Ibid.

5. Comptroller General of the United States, *Standards for Audit of Governmental Organizations, Programs, Activities and Functions* (Washington, D.C.: U.S. General Accounting Office, 1972), p. 1.

6. Ibid., p. 4.

7. Note that the term *expenditure* is used in the not-for-profit sector, while *expenses* is used in the private sector. *Expenditure* emphasizes things bought or acquired, while *expense* refers to actual consumption or expired costs.

8. See Seth Allcorn, *Internal Auditing for Hospitals* (Germantown, Md.: Aspen Systems, 1979), pp. 4-5.

9. Frederick R. O'Hayes, David A. Grossman, Jerry E. Mechiling, John S. Thomas, Steven S. Rosenbloom, *Linkages: Improving Financial Management in Local Government* (Washington, D.C.: Urban Institute Press, 1982), p. 154; for an extensive discussion of effectiveness auditing, see Richard E. Brown et al., *Auditing Performance in Government* (New York: John Wiley and Sons, 1982), pp. 73-101.

10. See Price Waterhouse, *Enhancing Governmental Accountability* (New York: Price Waterhouse, 1983), ch. 3.

11. Michael Howard, William Rerdy, and William C. Serverns, "The Audit Approach: Ohio's Risk-Based Audit Methodology" *Government Finance Review*, 7, no. 2 (April 1991): 15-20.

12. Ibid., pp. 15-16.

13. Paul C. Light, *Monitoring and the Search for Accountability* (Washington, D.C.: Brookings Institution, 1993), pp. 2-3.

14. Municipal Finance Officers Association, *Governmental Accounting, Auditing and Financial Reporting* (Chicago: Municipal Finance Officers Association, 1980), p. 90.

15. Comptroller General of the United States, *Standards for Audit*. This was revised in 1981.

16. International City Management Association, *Performance Audits in Local Governments: Benefits, Problems, and Challenges*, Management Information Report 8 (Special Report, April 1975), see Municipal Finance Officers Association, *Governmental Accounting*.

17. American Institute of Certified Public Accountants (AICPA), *Audits of Colleges and Universities*, 2nd ed. (New York: AICPA, 1975); American Institute of Certified Public Accountants (AICPA), *Hospital Audit Guides*, 4th ed. (New York: AICPA, 1982).

18. American Institute of Certified Public Accountants (AICPA), *Audit of Voluntary Health and Welfare Organizations* (New York: AICPA, 1981).

19. Comptroller General of the United States, *Standards for Audits*, pp. 7-9.

18

Reporting

Whenever resources are obtained from sources other than the individuals using and/or spending them, reporting to some external group or individual to render stewardship and accountability is a normal expectation. Such accountability may be based on law, contract, policy, or moral obligation. Stewardship refers to the execution of efficient administration. Importantly, "reporting on management's stewardship . . . is a principal purpose of financial statements."[1]

Basically, financial statements in not-for-profit organizations must provide information that can be used to assess management's ability to effectively utilize resources to achieve implied or articulated organizational goals. Certain questions immediately arise such as: To whom should fund users report? What kinds of information should be reported? What should be the format of the reports, and what are the authoritative guidelines and criteria to be followed? Though the answers to these questions appear obvious on the surface, in practice they tend to be difficult to find. Events such as the prolonged recession of the late 1980s and early 1990s, the national spiraling deficit, the total quality management movement (TQM), the interest in reinventing government, and the Gore report, *Creating a Government That Works Better and Costs Less*, have caused the chief rule-making body (the Governmental Accounting Standards Board, or GASB) for governmental entities to take a closer look at these questions, culminating in the *Service Efforts and Accomplishments* (SEA) draft proposal to aid in understanding government performance.[2]

This chapter contains an overview of the different types of reports and suggested general guidelines typically followed in preparing reports on the financial status and achievement of public and other not-for-profit organizations.

Historically, the financial reports of both public and other not-for-profit-organizations' present funds flow information. Data are organized to show the sources from which funds are derived and the applications to which they are put within the legal restrictions placed upon each fund with the aim of promoting budget and fiscal compliance. Financial reporting is a useful aid, helping public officials to show how they are faithfully discharging their fiscal responsibility to the electorate. The National Council on Governmental Accounting (NCGA) views the goal of financial reporting for governmental units as providing financial information that is useful for making economic, political, and social decisions; for assessing government accountability and stewardship; for assessing government's ability to meet maturing obligations; and for providing information that is useful for evaluating managerial and organizational performance.[3] The successor rule making body to the NCGA, the Governmental Accounting Standards Board (GASB), in its Concept Statement No. 1, "Objectives on Financial Reporting "subscribes" to the NCGA's position, culminating in the generation of a comprehensive annual financial report (CAFR) or the component unit fiscal report (CUFR) designed to achieve the objectives.[4]

Financial reports have been directed predominantly at meeting the needs of administrators, legislators, service recipients, resource providers, accountants, investors, public employees, and observers interested in public finance and administration. Although the general public's interest in financial statements has increased during recent years due to taxpayers' revolts and the cutback management movement of the 1970s, the average citizen shows little interest in the principal operating funds that generate deficits or surpluses.

An effectively presented financial statement of a governmental unit should describe the principal facilities and the capital improvement program for at least a period of five years, identifying the proposed yearly expenditure application by specific type of asset, planned use, and source of funding. Aggregated original and the replacement costs for fully depreciated assets over a five-year period and replacement policy regarding those assets should be presented. Comparative data showing planned versus actual operating and debt service expenditure, including the presentation of the past four years' actual results, should be described and any recognizable trends should be explained. The report should discuss the past year's accomplishments and the proposed objectives for the ensuing year. Citizens should be told where to obtain available reports, especially those analyzing the efficiency and effectiveness of operations. While this is an inexpensive and relatively effective way for promoting good relations, it is often handled poorly by most public and other not-for-profit organizations.

To be eligible for consideration for fair presentation and to be in conformity with generally accepted accounting principles (GAAP), three general types of financial statements have been suggested: (1) a combined balance sheet, (2) a combined statement of revenues, expenditures, and changes in fund balances, and (3) a combined statement of revenues and expenditures - budgeted and actual.   While the five types of governmental funds (general, special revenue, debt service, capital projects, and special assessment) are required to be shown separately, a memorandum column indicating totals is permitted.

INTERIM AND INTERNAL REPORTING LINKAGES IN THE FINANCIAL MANAGEMENT SYSTEM

Internal control and public accountability require that timely reports be issued throughout the fiscal year.   Depending on administrative needs, daily, monthly, weekly, and quarterly reports may be developed.   These interim reports assess ongoing programmatic activities and potential problems that may be developing.

Most governmental units do not publish interim reports; rather, they are produced to assist administrative officials and budget examiners at all levels of the organization or governmental unit.   Occasionally, the legislators may find them useful, especially when they provide data showing how budget plans are being followed.   Interim reports help management evaluate the extent to which administrative agencies are complying with budgetary, financial, legal, and administrative procedures.   Such important reports aid in disclosing deviations or variations from operating plans and permit corrective action to be taken.   In expressing the need for interim reports, NCGA noted that (1) they reflect monthly and quarterly current financial positions comparing financial results with estimates, indicating limitations for the month and/or the year to date; (2) they are mostly for internal use; (3) they exclude general fixed assets; and (4) they provide information on budgetary and cash flow projections aimed at facilitating management control.[5]

Annual Reporting

Every governmental unit, in the view of NCGA, is expected to publish a comprehensive annual financial report (CAFR) consisting of all funds.[6]   This activity represents the final step in the financial management-reporting system, indicating how well executive officials have discharged their responsibilities. The purpose of the report is to indicate the extent to which there was compliance with appropriations and contractual, legal, and other requirements.

All reporting systems are normally expected to have at least two types of reports: (1) internal reports required for agency use; and (2) external reports for administrative, legislative, and other interested parties.   Reports should be prepared to meet particular guidelines.   Accountability for the achievement of assigned responsibilities must be clearly identified.   A measuring system that is capable of comparing preplanned objectives or standards with actual achievements must be maintained. To be useful, the results must be reported with sufficient promptness to permit corrective activities to be taken. If maximum utility of the results is to be obtained, presentation must be consistent for all levels of management from one reporting period to another. Importantly, simplicity should be a guiding objective. Clear and concise presentation will enhance the use and understanding of the report.

Ideally, the reports intended for internal use should provide information to management that will be useful in effectively overseeing the agency operations. These reports should assist management in controlling operations (for example, the use of workload analysis) by monitoring how approved plans are being implemented. The reports will facilitate the management of funds, pinpointing the need for supplementary estimates or adjustments of allocations. The product of each report should typically provide the basis for the development of next year's budget and aid in the review of plans and priorities.

External reports satisfy a number of requirements, among them legal, contractual and fiduciary ones. Such reports provide information to assist interested parties in monitoring performance of the agency or governmental unit to determine if the resources have been utilized in accordance with requirements. External reports aid taxpayers, grantors, and service recipients to determine whether resources have been applied effectively.

Frequency of Reports

While comparative expenditure reports should be provided to management on at least a monthly basis and showing both actual and budgeted expenditures for a given period and for the year to date, particular programs or activities may require weekly or even daily reports.

The introductory section of the annual report should contain a letter of transmittal to the mayor and council or legislative body, and more recently, a second letter, from the mayor or chief executive to the council and/or the general public briefly describing changes in financial policies and the important areas of financial management, has become customary; other materials, such as a description of the reporting governmental entity, an organization chart, and a listing of elected officials may also be submitted. Recently, additional reports have been appended to annual reports. The opinion of the independent auditor or other required postaudit reports are appended. Where the unit of government has qualified for the Certificate of Conformance from the Government Finance Officers Association, it is included.

Each governmental unit is expected to prepare an official annual report also known as the comprehensive annual report (CAFR), containing all funds and account groups. Two major components of the CAFR are (1) the general purpose financial statement (GPFS) showing the fund type and account group (e.g., fixed assets); and (2) a combined statement by fund type and individual fund statements.

The Annual Report: A Pyramid Perspective

In Figure 18.1, the pyramid concept shows various levels of fund data groupings which offer different options for annual reporting. The apex (highest level) of the pyramid suggests a financial statement that is greatly aggregated and consolidated while the reverse is true at base or bottom of the pyramid. The lowest level is made up predominately of detailed transactions. Neither of these levels of reporting is recommended; a report falling between these two extremes is recommended.

The NCGA recommended the comprehensive annual financial report (CAFR) as the primary report (also known as the official governmental unit annual report). The General Purpose Financial Statement (GPFS), which is included in and accompanies the CAFR, is attached to bond offerings material and is distributed to general users who are uninterested in specific financial details.

It is important to keep in mind that the governmental unit or agency should go to that level of the pyramid where the details are sufficient to show the financial position and operating results of individual funds and account groups, to show compliance with legal and contractual requirements and to provide adequate disclosure of the individual fund entity level.

The Financial Section

This section contains the NCGA recommendations for the auditor's report and the general purpose financial statement which is made up of the combined statements, as shown in Figure 18.1. The following are the statements found in this section:

1. Combined balance sheet, including all fund types and account groups;
2. Combined statement of revenues and expenditure and changes in fund balance, including all governmental fund types;
3. Combined statement of revenues, expenditures, and changes in fund balances, including budgeted and actual, and general and special revenue fund types;
4. Combined statements of revenue and expenses and changes in retained earnings or fund equity, including all proprietor and

Figure 18.1
The Financial-Reporting Pyramid

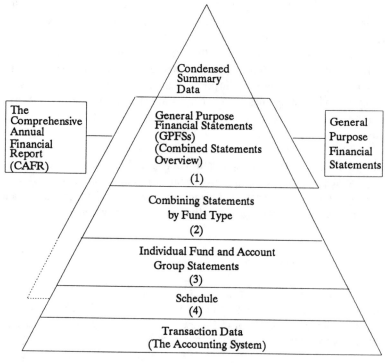

Key:
———— Required
·········· May Be Necessary

fund types;

5.   Combined statements of changes in financial position, including all proprietary fund types; and

6.   Notes to financial statements.

Statements of Other Not-For-Profit Organizations

The American Institute of Certified Public Accountants (AICPA) *Audit Guide* lists several types of financial statements that comprise the annual report of an organization.

The *Statement of Support, Revenue and Expenses and Changes in Fund Balance* is essentially a summary of the financial activities indicating all the sources of support and revenues and all expenditures. The AICPA recommends that the statement of changes in fund balances be made part of this statement, showing balances at the beginning and at the close of the year. Important interfund transactions are included and summarized.

The *Statement of Financial Expenses* contains a summary presenting an analysis of the entity's object of expenditure by program, function, and support. This statement, in essence, indicates how the resources (money) were spent in carrying out the agency's *program services* and *support services*.

The *Balance Sheet* presents the assets, such as cash investment, building, and equipment, and the liabilities, such as payables and encumbrances, toward which the assets will be applied. The difference between the assets and liabilities gives a balance - a deficit or surplus.

INTEGRATED ANNUAL REPORTING

The American federal system is made up of many layers of governments, often serving the same political community. Not infrequently, a number of governmental units, comprising the county, the city, special districts (e.g., schools), corporations, and authorities, can be benefitted if the service delivery performance can be rationally integrated through a single annual report document.

The presentation of a clear, comprehensive, and concise overview of local government finance is the principal objective in putting together the integrated annual report. Thus, all changes taking place during the fiscal year should be set forth in a section devoted to changes taking place in the operating and/or capital budgets during the fiscal year.

The Introductory Section

A number of general guidelines may be suggested for integrating such a report. Each of the participating, independent entities, structures, and frameworks may be briefly described, pointing out the formal and informal linkages with the dominant local government. Common features include accounting structure (such as titles and terminology), accounting basis or bases, and the fiscal year of the dominant local government and deviations therefrom). It is important to direct attention to "overlapping and underlying local governmental units and authorities."[7]

The Dominant Local Government: Budgeting Processes

The annual financial report of the major unit of local government describes the basic preparation and review process, as well as the adoption and administrative processes of the annual operating budget. A comparison of operating budget funds for several preceding years should be included. As far as possible, the linkages between the operating budget and the capital budget and capital program should be reviewed, indicating the support flowing from the operating funds. The authorization and application made on behalf of the capital budget over several years should be indicated.

Cooperative capital facilities planning is the most useful outcome that is likely to result from these undertakings, though integrated planning need not be the only vehicle to bring this about. Finally, the integrated budget system may be an important vehicle to provide statistical information on the following:

1.   Assessed and taxable property valuation;
2.   Exempt properties;
3.   Revenue sources;
4.   State aid;
5.   Federal aid;
6.   Operating expenditures; and
7.   Capital expenditure.[8]

GASB SERVICE EFFORTS AND ACCOMPLISHMENTS (SEA) REPORTING

A main premise of GASB is that public entities do not presently report on how well resources are being used to enhance the well-being of citizens. Because of the lack of the dissemination of SEA-type information, the public is denied the knowledge that is necessary for assessing accountability relating to the delivery of public goods and services. GASB views the existing provision of information, which emphasizes acquisition and use of resources, as inadequate. It should be complemented with performance information that shows linkage between resources used and the accomplishments they generate in terms of output, efficiency, and effectiveness/impact (see Chapters 11 and 16), in the form of a separate report. This should be a part of all general purpose external financial reporting (GPEFR) to aid in producing informed citizen decision making.[9]

Characteristics of SEA Information

To provide maximum utility to the public, SEA-type reporting should contain a number of characteristics:

- *Relevance* - including has data essential to understanding the extent to which the goals, objectives, and accountability have been achieved.
- *Understandability* - ability to make the entity's performance readily understood through means of graphs, charts, and tables.
- *Comparability* - provision of a frame of reference for assessing an entity and its subunits and program activities, and the opportunity to compare performance with similar entities.
- *Timeliness* - provision of information at the time needed for assessing accountability and to make decisions.
- *Consistency* - reporting on the same basis from period to period.
- *Reliability* - generation of information from controlled and verifiable data.[10]

POPULAR REPORTING

The most prominent organization presently promoting effective government reporting is the Government Finance Office Association (GFOA), through its certificate of conformance, and recently, by means of its popular reporting award. The University of Connecticut Institute of Public Service, in 1946, and the Michigan Municipal League, in 1944, initiated programs to promote better understanding of public financial reports. The objective of both organizations was to promote greater public recognition, acceptance, and comparison of reports with other jurisdictions.

Popular Report Reward

As the financial reporting for government has become more complex, information in the CAFR/CUFR reports has been increasing in difficulty for the general public to understand. As the reports have become more technical they have become usable mainly by investors, creditors, and other financial experts. "Popular reports are intended to communicate financial status and results of an entity to users who are nonaccountants types or are less technically oriented in governmental GAAP."[11] Because popular reports are not prescribed by any set format, individuals putting them together are constrained only by the limit of their imagination and creativity.

GFOA eligibility requires that the reporting entity satisfy a number of stipulations as follows:

- Be recipient of GFOA certificate of achievement of excellence in financial reporting and have CAFR/CUFR statements for the most recent fiscal year.
- The report must be prepared in conformity with generally accepted accounting principles; otherwise the report must give an explanation for nonconformity.
- All U.S. governmental entities must indicate fund types from which report data are derived.
- Financial information should be derived from CAFR/CUFR.
- Participants must include the American certificate of achievement excellence award and the Canadians include the financial reporting award.
- Canadians must in addition include aggregated or consolidated report and an auditor's report free of qualification. Moreover, financial information should be derived from a government general aggregated financial report.

The efforts of the University of Connecticut Institute of Public Service continue, but the Michigan Municipal League was terminated in 1966. The criteria that have been used in judging the quality of reports were the following:

1. *Attractiveness.* This indicator is measured by citizen willingness to examine the report due to the appeal of the external appearance and design of the report and the organization and presentation of the materials inside the document. Appeal features include "practical use of type for text and headings, legibility, and effective use of pictures."[12]

2. *Reader understanding.* This indicator attempts to assess the average citizen's ability to better understand local government undertakings. This is determined by an evaluation of the logic, organization of materials and clarity

of the written text. High marks also go to conciseness, brevity, and creative and informative use of appropriate charts and photographs.

3. *Content.* An attempt is made to determine how well the report summarizes the governmental undertakings and the perceived contributions toward the public's understanding of the kinds of services being delivered. This section presents data on the financial status of the community's budget, income and expenditure providing comparative analysis of costs, volume and other statistics on fiscal trends.

4. *Utility.* This attribute is assessed by determining if the size of the report permits easy filing, ready carrying and handling. Facilitative "directory-type" information items include: table of contents, lists of government officials and organizations, important phone numbers, and calendar of important dates.

Though not specifically identified, the audience must be kept in mind at all times. After all, it is the audience that the publication is attempting "to inform, influence or entertain."[13] Like commercial enterprises, not-for-profit organizations seek to predict, compare and evaluate benefits and sacrifices in terms of dollars, time and risks, despite the fact that the results sought are nonmonetary. Not-for-profit organizations cannot use the commercial-oriented profit yardstick. Rather, they seek to achieve goals whose performance involves indicators such as reduction in delinquency, improved health care, or reduction in crime. Ideally, financial statements must permit users to assess the attainments past organization goals, and the ongoing efforts to realize present goals and the probability of future goal attainment.

The AICPA identified seven qualitative characteristics that should provide useful guidelines in preparing financial reports.

1. *Relevance and Materiability.* To meet this test the following question should be asked: Is the information germane, and would its inclusion or exclusion influence or make a difference in the judgment of a reasonable person reading the financial statement? A positive answer indicates that the information in question should be included.

2. *Form and Substance.* Substantive economic and program characteristics should govern informative reporting, not the form of the report. Legal and/or technical criteria should establish the guidelines for accounting transactions and other events.

3. *Reliability.* Separate facts from interpretation. Disclose uncertainties and assumptions related to the information presented. The main point is that users of financial information should be informed about the data limitations.

4. *Freedom from bias.* This test does not imply absence of judgment, but rather that neutrality, objectivity, and fairness should be guiding aims. The financial statement should not be slanted to benefit any particular reader or

group.

　　5. *Demographic data.* Analysis of population characteristics provides the kind of information that is especially complementary to the financial data. The following are examples of useful demographic data: (1) changes in the population; (2) per capita income, per capita tax burden, and changes therein; (3) description and stability of industries; (4) comparative growth rate of main local revenue sources, expenditure, and per capita income; (5) taxable and nontaxable property value; (6) average change in long-term per capita debt; (7) discussion of population and age changes, education levels, school age children, ethnic characteristics, income levels, and unemployment rates; (8) number of government employees funded from own source; (9) percent of employees participating in collective bargaining; and (10) types of clientele.

　　6. *Comparability.* This guideline suggest that like things be reported alike and unlike things be reported differently. This task is made more difficult in not-for-profit agencies because of the variations that characterize the different kinds of services that are provided. However, if the guideline is followed, these problems will be minimized.

　　7. *Consistency.* The operating norm is that comparable events should be treated in a similar manner from period to period. For example, once an accrual system is adopted, to change to a cash system during the period would be considered a violation of this guideline and GAAP.

REPORTING: SOME INADEQUACIES

　　There are a number of continuing concerns about financial reporting in the public sector and a number of other not-for-profit organizations. The expenditure-reporting system used in the public sector emphasizes the acquisition of goods and services rather than the application (how much is consumed) approach employed in business. Expenditure accounting assumes an immediate expiration of resources. The incurrence of debt (e.g., a loan or, especially, the floating of a bond) is viewed as a source of resource, and the purchase of fixed assets is recorded as the application of resources, irrespective of the useful life of the asset. In order to maintain some degree of control over fixed assets, a separate General Fixed Asset Group of accounts (GFAG) must be developed. It is generally believed that use of the expenditure-reporting system is responsible for the poor record keeping concerning fixed assets in many not-for-profit organizations. Because of the expenditure practice, public sector funds require five governmental funds (general, special revenue, capital projects, debt service, and special assessment), two proprietary funds (enterprise and internal service), two fiduciary fund types (trust and agency), and two groups of accounts (fixed assets and long-term liabilities).

Many close observers of the public sector financial scene express the view that the present financial reporting system is plagued by too many shortcomings. They contend that (1) it is not possible to determine the cost of services; (2) government financial reports are distorted; (3) there is no system for measuring capital maintenance; (4) there is a commingling of sources and uses of funds with interfund transfers; and (5) the heavy emphasis on budgetary compliance does not facilitate meaningful information reporting.[14]

Disclosure Issues

There is no total consensus by accountants and agency managers on precisely what should be included in financial statements. This is a continuous problem - deciding whether government should develop combined balance sheets including all funds while excluding interfund balances. The same could be said about consolidated balance sheets that factor out interfund balances in presenting the balance sheet with one "superfund." The demand for a consolidated balance sheet is based on a number of concerns including the following: (1) there are too many interfund balances which tends to obscure or distort the financial position of a governmental unit, and (2) the present system does not present the true "net worth" of the governmental unit.

Rentals, leases, pensions, fringe benefits, and depreciation and other expenditure items are not always uniformly treated, though there is emerging convergence of views on this point. The biggest area of concern is related to accrued pension liabilities. The method that accounts for pension expenditures only as they are paid to reserve funds ignores significant benefits that have been earned but not paid. Nonetheless, such benefits are commitments and debt that must be paid out at some future date to present employees. Governmental units that fail to reserve funds at the time they become due can bring about major financial crises, as has been the case in several local governments during the last several years.

SUMMARY OBSERVATIONS

An examination of the not-for-profit financial statements clearly show the basic differences between the for-profit and the not-for-profit sectors. The not-for-profit organizations require a set of financial statements unlike those of their commercial counterparts.

To whom accountability and/or stewardship must be rendered is a basic principle underlying all reporting. To be acceptable, reports are expected to conform, not only to legal, professional, and regulatory standards but must be readily understandable to specific or general types of audiences. For the users to whom financial statements are directed, they are expected to assess the efficacy with which management is discharging its responsibilities.

Despite the socially oriented objectives of not-for-profit organizations, most reporting is still based on financial accounting. It is a legal "spend for" concept that emphasize dollar accountability. Though this approach is changing, it still has some way to go. Finally, the kind of financial statement needed is situational in that each organization must find the level of aggregation that fits its needs, as shown in Figure 18.1.

NOTES

1. American Institute of Certified Public Accountants (AICPA), *Objectives of Financial Statements* (New York: AICPA, 1973), p. 25.

2. See Al Gore, *Creating a Government That Works Better and Cost Less* (Washington, D.C.: Government Printing Office 1994), David Osborne and Ted Gaebler, *Reinventing Government: Entrepreneurial Spirit Is Transforming the Public Sector* (Reading, Mass.: Addison-Wesley Publishing Co., Inc., 1992).

3. National Council on Governmental Accounting, *Concept Statements, Objectives of Accounting and Financial Reporting on Governmental Units* (Chicago; 1982), p. 2.

4. See National Council on Governmental Accounting, Statement No. 1, *Government Accounting, Auditing, and Financial Reporting Principles* and *The Needs of Users of Governmental Fiscal Reports*, (Stamford, Conn.: GASB, 1985).

5. National Committee on Governmental Accounting, *Concept Statements: Objectives of Accounting and Financial Reporting for Governmental Units*, pp. 18-19.

6. Ibid., p. 19.

7. Lennox L. Moak and Albert Hillhouse, *Local Government Finance* (Chicago, Ill.: Municipal Finance Officers Association, 1985), pp. 428-430.

8. Ibid., p. 432.

9. See Governmental Accounting Standards Board, (GASB), "Service Efforts and Accomplishments Reporting" (Exposure Draft, December 15, 1993, p. 11).

10. Ibid., pp. 30-31.

11. Barbara R. Hennessy, "Communicating Financial Data to Nonaccountants: A Case for Popular Reporting," *Government Finance Review*, 7, no. 5 (October 1991): 7.

12. Hal Peger and Gerald Lonergner, "Popular Financial Reporting in the Public Sector, *Government Finance*, 5 (May 1976): 33.

13. Ibid., p. 36.

14. See Coopers and Lybrand and the University of Michigan, *Financial Disclosure Practices of American Cities: A Public Report* (New York: Coopers and Lybrand, 1976), pp. 9-11.

19

Evaluating Fiscal Health

Interest and concern for the fiscal health of governmental units and other not-for-profit organizations, especially colleges and universities, heightened in the early 1970s with the financial crises in New York City and Cleveland. Numerous cutbacks were necessary due to the reduction in revenues at all levels of government. The fiscal problems of the cities followed more than a decade of continuous growth in expenditures. Beginning in the early 1970s, an era of seemingly endless growth throughout the economy was replaced by increasing inflation, a stagnant national economy, rising costs, and declining productivity. Many larger cities that had expanded social and other types of services found them difficult to maintain as the stagnation and the malaise in the economy continued.

A number of cities, among them Pittsburgh, Pennsylvania, and Chicago, Illinois, slowed expenditures significantly, adapting to the changing economic environment. However, other cities such as New York and Cleveland, continued their incremental budgeting habits, making no adaptation to the decline in revenues; this led to fiscal strain and, ultimately, fiscal crisis.[1] The experience of a government-supported nonprofit agency such as the Smithsonian Institution shows how an entity can develop effective strategies to deal with retrenchment. Out of a budget of nearly $400 million, the Smithsonian Institution recognized early in 1990 that an impending recession would likely influence the generation of a shortfall of $10 million. The Smithsonian mobilized management to undertake a zero base review based on clearly defined and articulated priorities. The downsizing and restructuring were carried out within specified time frames. Simultaneous with the recession and downsizing, the Smithsonian adopted TQM. To build maximum momentum for the goals and objectives, visible TQM successes were highlighted.[2] This chapter explores the theories and practices relating to the fiscal health of governmental

units and agencies. Particular emphasis is placed on the analysis of fiscal strain
and the ways in which it can be identified, monitored, and prevented.

FISCAL STRAIN: REVIEW AND ANALYSIS

As an area of study, fiscal strain was formerly barren of theories and
the analysis of such concepts as fiscal stability, economic viability, decremental
budgeting, fiscal monitoring, and fiscal strain. Not until the mid-1970s was
serious attention focused on the problem of fiscal strain, following a number of
financial crises experienced by local governments. Though the theoretical
underpinnings of concepts are beginning to emerge, as evidenced by Clark and
Ferguson's **City Money** (1983), most of the literature still tends to be
descriptive. Despite this reality, many theoretical and practical insights can be
obtained from these sources.

A paradox during periods of fiscal strain and retrenchment management
is that the greatest opportunity to develop effective management systems (e.g.,
management planning, internal control systems, fiscal health-monitoring systems,
and information systems) occurs during periods when resources are plentiful.
However, these are precisely the times when such systems appear superfluous
or irrelevant.[3] Under conditions of abundance, habit, intuition, snap judgments,
and other forms of informal analysis and decision making often suffice because
the costs of making mistakes can be easily absorbed without threatening an
organization's survival.[4] However, during austerity periods, because resources
are restricted, the innovative management systems that were not previously
found necessary cannot be implemented, despite the critical need. Additional
problems abound when retrenchment comes; among them are the following:

- lack of resources to motivate managers, to seek consensus-
  building solutions, to provide incentive payments, and to
  minimize resistance to change;
- lack of resources to provide promotion incentives (necessary
  to motivate and keep successful managers);
- lack of resources necessary to expand (especially in the public
  sector) due to merit and tenure practice that leads to
  organizational entropy because new and creative talent cannot
  be attracted; and
- lack of resources leading to adoption of inclusionary practices
  to ensure that participants do not avoid paying their share of
  increased burden (the exclusionary practice is used during
  periods of growth to exclude people from enjoying benefits
  unless they share in the burden).[5]

Defining Fiscal Strain

Most writers fail to give a definition of fiscal strain. One prominent writer in the field, Charles H. Levine, observed that fiscal solvency means the provision of services at a level and with the amount of "benefits that are adequate, equitable and stable."[6] He went on to further define these terms:

- *adequacy*--suggesting sufficiency of goods and services to maintain individual well-being;
- *equity*--guaranteeing equal access and opportunity to benefits from goods and services; and
- *stability*--referring "to the maintenance of goods and services commensurate with the needs and expectation of the citizens."[7]

While intuitively appealing, this definition cannot easily be operationalized because it is too vague. Thus, attempts at measurement would be exceedingly difficult. A more useful and operational definition would permit measurement so that we can determine when the organization is moving toward an acceptable state and when it is experiencing increasing fiscal strain. Perhaps the most acceptable definition is one that permits the matching of private sector resources (e.g., employment or population) to government spending and debt. In this way, fiscal strain can be determined by the degree to which the expenditures of an organization or government are matched against private sector resources. Once an acceptable match is decided upon, expenditures may be adapted or manipulated to maintain the desired fiscal balance. This can be done by developing fiscal strain indicators or ratios using an equation, such as the following:[8]

$$\text{Urban Fiscal Strain} = \frac{\text{Government Spending and Debt}}{\text{Private Sector Resources}}$$

Note that unless approximate or proportionate changes occur in both the numerator and denominator at the same time, the system will become unbalanced. Thus, when a change occurred in Pittsburgh's denominator factor (a decline in the tax base) in the early 1970s, it reduced spending (the numerator), averting a fiscal strain crisis. Similarly, Cincinnati coped with its fiscal pressure by increasing user fees for a number of functions (e.g., water, parking, and the airport), by reducing demand on the general funds, by reducing the municipal work force, by regionalizing services (e.g., transferring the University of Cincinnati to the state and the municipal court to Hamilton

County), and by reducing planned capital expansion.[9] When the same events occurred in New York City, its government made no effort to reduce spending, which caused a financial strain crisis.[10] The point suggested here is that fiscal strain is determined by two major factors: the governmental fiscal policy output (government spending and debt) and private sector resources (employment, jobs, etc.) of the governmental entity. If the city leaders or organizational officials are able to adapt to changes that occur in the determinants, the governmental units need not reach fiscal strain.[11]

The Making of Fiscal Policy Outputs

Fiscal policy output is the response to the demand by important relevant groups and individuals for a particular program, project, or benefit. The resultant policy is affected by the philosophy of the participants, who advocate that government spending take a specific direction. Four examples have been suggested: (1) The mid-1960s saw the New Deal Democrats such as Lyndon Johnson in Washington and his imitators in many cities. They were fiscally liberal and saw government social programs as important instruments for disadvantaged blacks and the poor. (2) The ethnic politicians, such as the blacks, resemble the Democrats in that they strove to increase social services and to expand job opportunities for the unemployed members of their constituencies. (3) The New Deal Republicans viewed taxpayers as having more legitimacy than labor unions and organized interest groups. They believed in keeping taxes low and minimizing social programs. (4) The new fiscal populism was exemplified by President Bill Clinton, Jimmy Carter and former Mayor Peter Flaherty of Pittsburgh. Though they were fiscal conservatives, they attempted to respond to the needs of the disadvantaged while attempting to minimize the burden of the average taxpayer.[12]

The making of each policy output typically involves a complex of dynamic, interacting forces. Of the many factors (e.g., citizens' preferences, interest groups, leaders' preferences, and residential choice) impacting on the policy makers, it is important for us to know which has the greatest influence.[13] This knowledge can provide insights about the decisions that produce fiscal strain.

Fiscal Strain: New York City

New York experienced windfall increases in revenue from 1966 to 1970. During this period, revenues increased about 14 percent per year. This increase was generated by growing local revenues and supplemented with state and federal increases, the latter averaging a 39.7 percent yearly rise between

1966 and 1970. However, in the period 1971-1975, New York's operating revenues experienced a declining rate of increase.[14] The various periods of revenue decline were characterized by distinct administrative responses:[15]

1. During the initial decline, officials engaged in denial and delay, hoping that the increased revenue would mitigate the problem. The denial was complemented by budget manipulation, such as raising operating funds via the capital budget and postponing required maintenance.

2. The second decline was marked by the resistance of agencies and clients to cutbacks and vigorous efforts by agencies to stretch resources. Cutbacks were evenly distributed across departmental programs. Because of an attrition agreement with the labor union, few layoffs were necessary. At the same time, management instituted a number of improvements, such as the automation of the budget to enhance the city's credibility with the financial community.

3. Between 1975 and 1978, across the board cuts continued while few targeted cuts were made.

4. The 1978-1980 period saw the city making deeper, "more targeted cuts," along with significant organizational changes.[16]

It is also worthy of note that maintenance postponement and user fee increases took place during each of the periods.

Change in the level of resources was the most crucial factor (variable) in New York's fiscal strain. Each of the five identified levels of resource changes (moderate continuous growth, windfall revenue growth, no revenue growth, moderate decline, and severe decline) affected the political structure and administrative strategies in specific ways. For example, no revenue growth generated weak central control and fragmented interest groups in the political structure, thereby negatively influencing demand and delaying administrative strategies. The fiscal pressure was not great enough to force decisive reductive action.[17]

Each level of service produced different types of outcomes at the departmental, program, and client levels ultimately determining who received and who was denied the benefits of scarce public resources. The macro consequence manifested itself in areas such as the quality of the physical infrastructure (buildings, sewers, roads, etc.), the city's capacity to deliver services, and the quality of the city's living conditions.

Cause of Fiscal Strain

In the early analysis of fiscal strain (sometimes also referred to as fiscal distress), the causes were descriptively and loosely identified. The following are some of the principal symptoms or causes:

1. extended and severe economic decline, including unabated population and employment losses;
2. long periods of excessive reliance on federal aid and inelastic revenue growth of fixed costs;
3. decline in public productivity compared to the overall local work force, perhaps due to unionization;
4. deferment of current costs, including maintenance on fixed facilities and incurred pension liabilities; and
5. financial management practices, including manipulation of accounting and reporting systems.[18]

There is wide disagreement on the specific causes of fiscal strain. A grouping of the causes into three categories has been suggested:

1. The *migration and tax base erosion explanation* holds that population migration has been a dominant factor in creating fiscal strain. Migration into the cities was marked by the influx of poor blacks and Hispanics, which overloaded the capacity of cities, especially in the areas of education, welfare, job training, and health. The migration of upper- and middle-class residents out of the city to the suburbs left the cities with a disproportionate number of poor and unemployed, eroding the revenue base. The residents moving in required considerably more services than those moving out. Additionally, the residents moving out caused a significant shift in the base upon which taxes were being levied, creating a revenue gap. Finally, the out-migration movement saw the population moving to the Sunbelt, taking with them industries and technology and creating job loss and population and tax base erosion, not only in the city, but also in the region.

2. The *bureaucratic growth perspective* relates to the public choice model, which relies on nonmarket economics. Proponents of this model posit that the rapid growth of government has negative implications. The growth of government leads to increases in services. People are willing to pay for some services but not for those they believe are unnecessary. This model suggests that the services tend to grow larger than required because requests for services are not regulated or restrained by the cost factor. That is, all residents enjoy the benefits of the services produced, while only a few may be required to pay for them. The greater the number of residents enjoying these benefits without the tax burden, the greater the number of individuals supporting these services.

Likewise, bureaucrats find it in their interest to expand the bureaucracy, enhancing their own career opportunities. Thus they help to use their voting power to expand the bureaucracy when the opportunity arises.

3. The *political vulnerability approach* suggests that cities are more likely to reach fiscal strain as political officials (policymakers) are subjected to demands that compel a positive response. Three conditions occur that increase exposure to political vulnerabilities: (a) voter coalition breakdown, in which important political figures, such as the mayor, are unable to muster a working majority of groups, making it necessary to spend revenues in order to maintain and attract support and leading to fiscal strain; (b) weaknesses in the formal authority structure, in which a strong mayor and machine government are seen as incapable of resisting demands, while city managers' reforms, which permit the delivery of efficient services at lower cost, could minimize the potential for fiscal strain; and (c) shifting power among interest groups, in which the strongest groups impose their demands on a vulnerable political leadership, having a negative impact on fiscal policy.[19]

FISCAL STRATEGIES THAT FAILED

Intergovernmental revenue and legal reform play important roles in local fiscal policy. The impact of intergovernmental revenues may be significantly affected by the terms of the grant to the local government. Two models that guide grant distribution have been suggested. Under Model I, the local governments are passive actors executing the policies determined at a higher level of government (state or federal). In Model II, local units play a more active role, using intergovernmental revenues to implement local preferences. The Model II approach parallels the traditional decentralized role that most local governments desire. The national government typically favors Model I because it permits greater influence for the implementation of national policies and permits better accounting of the intergovernmental fiscal flows.[20]

Clark and Ferguson have disagreed with the widely held belief that intergovernmental aid is a significant determinant on local policy and that nonlocal revenues typically reinforce local influences.[21] The evidence (1960 to the late 1970s) in both Europe and the United States shows that intergovernmental assistance does not seem to help local governments avoid the problems associated with fiscal strain. In Europe, the cities receiving the greatest assistance experienced the most severe fiscal strain.[22]

The widely accepted view that transfer of functions mitigates fiscal strain has not been borne out in studies.[23] In fact, the transfer of functions may have the reverse effect. Moreover, the plea made by cities such as San Francisco and New York to federalize welfare programs involves many thorny issues. Does New York, with its higher welfare payments, move down to the level paid in Mississippi, or vice versa? Since it is more realistic to expect the average welfare payment to move up to the New York level, additional federal resources would be required to finance welfare.

It is generally agreed that the state debt limit on local government does not work unless the debt limit reflects local preferences, because government typically finds ways to get around the limitations.[24] Most communities never reach the debt limit for general obligation (GO) bonds, for which they must use their "full faith and credit," because they want to avoid scrutiny by the state legislature. Thus revenue bonds are floated for facilities such as water; revenues generated from the activity are earmarked to pay the debt.

STRATEGIES THAT WORK

Policies that are adopted reflect the political ideology of the governing officials (e.g., Democrats, ethnic politicians, New Deal Republicans, and new fiscal populists). The general policies of these four groups may be summarized as follows:[25]

Democrats

Typically, the Democrats are disposed toward identifying new revenue sources and increasing taxes. On the expenditure side, tough cutback decisions are delayed and capital expenditures are reduced only when difficult situations demand it. Reduction of employee compensation is viewed as an option to be followed when other alternatives have been exhausted. The most influential inputs in the decision-making process come from the mayor, city council members, employees, party leaders, relevant neighborhood groups, and service recipients.

Ethnic Politicians

While their orientation is similar to that of the Democrats, they emphasize the skill enhancement/job training of ethnic employees on the city payroll. Additionally, they advocate the provision of symbolic services, or what is sometimes called "good-will gestures," for members of the dominant ethnic group. While similar to the Democrats in their decision-making mode, they tend to defer to elected officials and employees and representatives of influential ethnic groups.

Republicans

Reduction of taxes and services, when the situation demands, is the initiating course of action for Republicans. When implementing policies, neither employees nor interest groups are given mitigating attention or special exemptions. The deepest cuts are made in programs targeted for the poor. If the situation is propitious, a policy for productivity improvement will be pursued. The decision-making process favors the individual tax paying citizen. Unlike the Democrats and the ethnic politicians, Republicans typically allow programmatic decisions to be determined by professional staff people with inputs made, in varying degrees, by relevant leaders in the community.

New Fiscal Populists

Though their tactics may appear different, their actions and results parallel those of the Republicans. They give the general appearance of responsiveness to the disadvantaged, but programs targeted toward these groups are usually cut. One of the overriding objectives of the new fiscal populists is an emphasis on productivity improvement. The populists stress input from citizens as do the Republicans. Unlike the Republicans, however, the fiscal populists give precedence to citizen input over that of the professional staff. Leaders use information such as town or open meetings or polls to assess the preferences of citizens. Finally, knowledgeable experts are consulted and ideas about improving productivity are sought.

ASSESSING FISCAL CONDITION

In a narrow accounting sense, the acceptable financial condition (known also as cash solvency) shown in Figure 19.1 may refer to a government or agency's ability to generate sufficient cash to meet obligations maturing in 30 to 60 days. It may also refer to an agency or governmental unit's ability to meet all important expenditures accruing in a budgeting period without incurring a deficit.[26] A broader perspective of financial condition views it as a government or agency's ability to meet long- and short-term costs as they come due, such

FIGURE 19.1

The Components of Financial Solvency Analysis

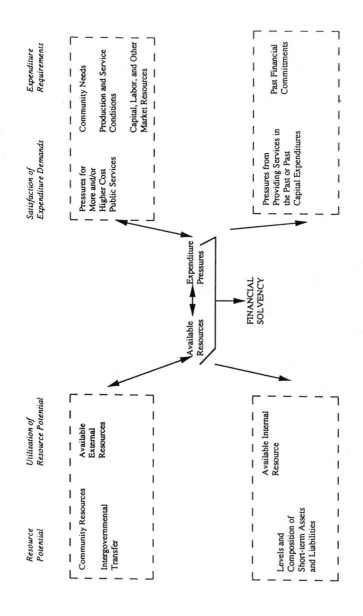

Source: Robert Berne and Richard Schramm, *The Financial Solvency of Local Governments*, in *Working Papers in Planning* (Ithaca, NY: Cornell University, January 1979), p.18.

as pension payments, accrued leaves, capital replacements, and deferred maintenance. This is referred to as long-run solvency. Ultimately, financial condition provides a reading of how well a governmental unit is capable of providing "the level and quality of services required for general health and welfare of a community as desired by its citizens."[27] Stated another way fiscal condition suggests the ability to finance existing levels of services, access to reserves and revenue base to respond to regional economic disruptions such as the closing of a major local employer, and the ability to meet growth, change, and decline.

In assessing the fiscal health environment and context, each community or organization must be carefully studied. Key features that should be considered in evaluating a government or agency's fiscal condition include the following:

- fiscal condition of local infrastructure, such as roads, bridges, and the sewer system;
- dependence on federal financial assistance, and particularly, support of regularly recurring operating expenses;
- pension liabilities, especially unfunded obligations;
- employee union demands, especially those that require contractual pay increases without offsetting productivity increases;
- militancy of local taxpayers as evidenced by tax expenditure limitations;
- inflation and its impact on fixed costs of government; and
- bond defaults and the ability to finance long-term debt repayment.[28]

The traditional approach in using bond rating as the main or sole indicator of a governmental unit's fiscal health is unwise and can be misleading, as the New York financial crisis demonstrated. The city's continued use of short-term debt to meet its chronic budget imbalance was "easily overlooked because of the city's poor accounting and reporting system and its use of long-term debt to finance current operating expenses."[29] An important point is that the possibility of a bond default is typically equated with a government's ability to pay maturing obligations. This does not say anything about the broader fiscal health of the community. Other important factors include not only an evaluation of the likelihood of default but an analysis of the government's ability to maintain current and/or acceptable levels of service. Sufficient financial resources must be available to weather economic difficulty, achieve acceptable growth in the local economy, maintain revenue stability, and generate the capacity to respond to increased demand for local services.[30]

Traditional financial statements are insufficient as a basis for evaluating the fiscal health of communities. They do provide information on how financial data conform to generally accepted accounting principles (GAAP) and other regulatory and mandated requirements. Typically, information relating to data such as reliance on outside revenue sources, uncontrollable revenues, industrial growth trends, per capita income trends, capital improvement requirements, and physical plant replacement are not found in financial statements.

Monitoring Fiscal Condition

The field of public financial management has been preoccupied with such short-term concerns as the availability of cash to meet immediate financial obligations while giving little or no attention to the long-term issues that ensure the fiscal stability of the community. Though the investment community has been concerned with debt carrying capacity, as noted earlier, it has not developed broad indicators that could be usefully employed to assess the financial condition of particular governmental units.

Many problems militate against the development of an effective monitoring system. Before the financial crises of the early 1970s, such as that in New York City, there was little interest in developing such systems. Data relating to economic and demographic activities could not be easily obtained. Data that were obtainable on governmental functions, revenue structure, and financial reports could not be reliably compared for a host of reasons. Thus it was very difficult to analyze the impact of a decline in employment or a change in the form of a major business (e.g., wholesale to retail) on revenue. No benchmark indicators were established to guide decision makers on, for example, desirable per capita expenditures, long-term and short-term amounts of debt, or levels of reserves.

Accomplishing a *Financial Trend in Monitoring System* (FTMS) is not a simple, straightforward task. (FTMS was developed by the International City Management Association during the late 1970s and early 1980s). Many elements must be considered, such as the state of the national economy, local business and economic conditions, population makeup, and employment trends. Many factors must be isolated, quantified, and evaluated. The most critical and specific pieces of data cannot always be determined until they have all been systematically brought together and meticulously evaluated. Such a process is fraught with problems, but the potential yield is likely to be worth the costs.[31]

FTMS identifies, analyzes, and measures the factors affecting the financial condition of a given community. It is a means for organizing internal data (budgeting and financial reports) and other relevant external data (demographic and economic) to produce financial indicators that may be used to monitor financial changes in a given community. FTMS does not provide a single index number to identify fiscal health, but it draws attention to potentially serious problems, suggest hints or clues to the likely causes, and gives time by which to take preventive action. By means of FTMS, the governmental unit can maintain an information system to indicate its relative financial strength and weakness. It can be used as a basis to reorder internal staff priorities, to chart or modify long-term policies, and to institutionalize strategic planning perspectives in the annual budgeting cycle routines.[32] Twelve factors (the primary impacting forces on financial condition) constitute FTMS. The financial condition factors act in concert with 36 financial indicators "to measure different aspects" of seven financial factors (see Figure 19.2).[33] The factors have been perfected and can be used to monitor the community's financial condition.

Financial condition factors are classified as environmental, financial, and organizational and are generated from the existence of the financial problems of the given community. Taken as a whole, the factors provide a basis on which the financial condition issues are evaluated. The environmental factors are both a source of demand (e.g., an increase in population brings about an increase in service needs) and a provider of resources (e.g., an increased population increases wealth and the tax base). Organizational factors indicate the ways in which governments respond to changing environmental factors. (A rational assumption is that if government officials are given adequate advance warning, they will act to avert a financial crisis.) Financial factors provide a reading of the status of internal finances which are determined by the interaction of the environmental and organizational forces (see Figure 19.2).[34]

The external or exogenous factors (community needs and resources, external economic conditions, intergovernmental constraints, natural disasters and emergencies, and political culture) are filtered through the organizational factors (legislative policies and management practices), producing the financial factors (revenues, expenditures, operating positions, debt structure, unfunded liabilities, and capital plant) which describe "the internal financial structure of the governmental unit."[35] The revenue factor informs about the growth, flexibility, elasticity, diversity, and dependability of the government. The expenditure factor provides insight about the growth, mandated cost, productivity, and effectiveness of government programs. Operating position reveals the liquidity condition.[36]

Indicators

When properly used, the indicators can be one of the strategic means for alerting government about actions that may be taken to minimize or prevent a financial situation from becoming a problem. They are quantified changes

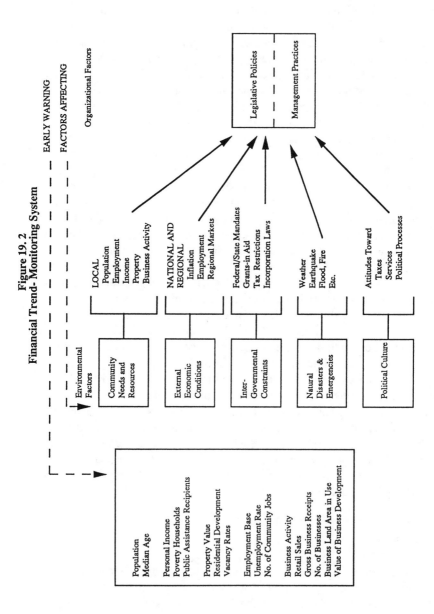

Figure 19. 2
Financial Trend- Monitoring System

EARLY WARNING
FACTORS AFFECTING
Organizational Factors

Environmental Factors

Legislative Policies

Management Practices

Community Needs and Resources

LOCAL
Population
Employment
Income
Property
Business Activity

NATIONAL AND REGIONAL
Inflation
Employment
Regional Markets

External Economic Conditions

Inter-Governmental Constraints

Federal/State Mandates
Grants-in Aid
Tax Restrictions
Incorporation Laws

Natural Disasters & Emergencies

Weather
Earthquake
Flood, Fire
Etc.

Political Culture

Attitudes Toward
Taxes
Services
Political Processes

Population
Median Age

Personal Income
Poverty Households
Public Assistance Recipients

Property Value
Residential Development
Vacancy Rates

Employment Base
Unemployment Rate
No. of Community Jobs

Business Activity
Retail Sales
Gross Business Receipts
No. of Businesses
Business Land Area in Use
Value of Business Development

Source: Sanford M. Groves, *Evaluating Local Government Financial Condition,* Handbook 2. Financial Trend Monitoring System: A Practitioner's Guide, (Washington , D.C.: International City Management Association, 1980), p.2 (reprinted with permission).

Figure 19.2 cont'd.

Source: Sanford M. Groves, *Evaluating Local Government Financial Condition , Handbook 2, Financial Trend Monitoring System: A Practitioner's Guide,* (Washington D.C.: International City Management Association, 1980). p.2 , (reprinted with permission).

455

Figure 19.3

Schema of the Financial Trend- Monitoring System Showing Financial Factors, Indicators and Formulas

Financial Factor	Financial Indicator	Formula
Revenues	1. Revenue per capita	Net operating revenues in constant dollars / Population
	2. Restricted revenues	Restricted operating revenues / Net operating revenues
	3. Intergovernmental revenues	Intergovernmental operating revenues / Gross operating revenues
	4. Elastic tax revenues	Elastic operating revenues
	5. One-time revenues	One-time operating revenues / Net operating revenues
	6. Property tax revenues	Property taxes in constant dollars
	7. Uncollected property taxes	Uncollected property taxes / Net property tax levy
	8. User charge coverage	Revenues from fees and user charges / Expenditures for related services
	9. Revenue shortfalls	Revenue shortfall / Net operating revenues
Expenditures	10. Expenditure per capita	Net operating revenues in constant dollars / Population
	11. Employees per capita	Number of employees / Population
	12. Fixed costs	Fixed costs / New operating expenditures
	13. Fringe benefits	Fringe benefit expenditures / Salaries and wages

Figure 19.3 cont'd.

Financial Factor	Financial Indicator		Formula
Operating Position	14. Operating deficits	→	General fund operating deficit / Net operating revenues
	15. Enterprise losses	→	Enterprise profits or losses in constant dollars
	16. General fund balances	→	Unrestricted fund balance of general fund / Net operating revenues
	17. Liquidity	→	Cash and short-term investments / Current liabilities
Debt Structure	18. Current liabilities	→	Current liabilities / Net operating revenues
	19. Long-term debt	→	Net direct long-term debt / Access and valuation
	20. Debt service	→	Net direct debt service / Net operating revenues
	21. Overlapping debt	→	Overlapping long-term debt / Assessed valuation
Unfunded Debt	22. Unfunded pension	→	Unfunded pension plan vested benefit / Assessed valuation
	23. Pension assets	→	Pension plan assets / Pension benefits paid
	24. Accumulated employee leave liability	→	Total days of unused vacation / Number of employees
Condition of Capital Plant	25. Maintenance effort	→	Expenditure for repair and maintenance of fixed assets / Amount of assets
	26. Level of capital outlay	→	Capital outlay from operating funds / Net operating expenditures
	27. Depreciation	→	Depreciation expense / Cost of depreciable fixed assets

Figure 19.3 cont'd.

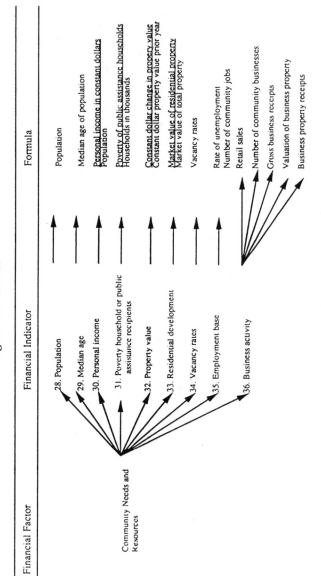

Financial Factor	Financial Indicator	Formula
Community Needs and Resources	28. Population	Population
	29. Median age	Median age of population
	30. Personal income	Personal income in constant dollars / Population
	31. Poverty household or public assistance recipients	Poverty or public assistance households / Households in thousands
	32. Property value	Constant dollar change in property value / Constant dollar property value prior year
	33. Residential development	Market value of residential property / Market value of total property
	34. Vacancy rates	Vacancy rates
	35. Employment base	Rate of unemployment / Number of community jobs
	36. Business activity	Retail sales / Number of community businesses / Gross business receipts / Valuation of business property / Business property receipts

Source: Adapted from Stanford M. Groves, *Evaluating Local Government Financial Condition, Handbook 2. Financial Trend Monitoring System. A Practitioner's Guide* (Washington, D.C.: International City Mangement Association, 1980), p.2. Reprinted with permission. See also Stanford M. Groves, "An Introduction to Evaluating Financial Condition", in John Metzer, Jr., ed., *Practical Financial Management*, (Washington, D. C.: International City Management Association, 1984), pp. 24-25.

about the environmental, organizational, and financial factors.   Thirty-six indicators are identified in Figure 19.3.

A PROPOSED TEN-POINT TEST OF FINANCIAL CONDITION ASSESSMENT FOR SMALL CITIES

Because of the large number of factors, indicators, and data that are necessary to carry out competent financial condition assessment, it can become a burdensome activity for small municipalities. This task makes it difficult for assessment to promote financial condition as "a regular part of financial management."[37]   To minimize these constraints and to facilitate financial conditions assessment in cities under 100,000 population, the GFOA proposed a "10-Point Test." It developed 10 important financial ratios that are calculated for each city and for 750 similar cities throughout the nation.   These ratio calculations allow municipal officers to make comparisons in determining where they stand vis-a-vis the financial condition of other like cities. The test was developed to satisfy the need of cities to have a quick and dependable way of assessing financial conditions and to make use of the comparative Financial Indicators Data Base which was developed and published by the Government Finance Officer's Association (GFOA) in 1992.[38]

The 10-point financial condition test is focused on four financial factors (see Table 19.1): (1) revenue ratios, 1-3; (2) expenditure ratio, 4; (3) operating position ratios, 5-7; and debt structure ratio, 8-10. The test involves a three step process: (1) based on the current financial reports, the financial ratios are calculated; (2) ratios are compared with similar size cities, and (3) the city's financial condition is graded based on calculations in step 2.

Table 19.1 is the financial condition worksheet, which can be used to calculate ratios and categorize the 750 cities by population (50,000 to 100,000; 30,000 to 50,000; and 15,000 and under). For each category, the city's score is put in one of four quartiles. Each quartile contains 25 percent of the cities in that category. Quartile one shows the ratios of the worst-ranked cities. The second quartile contains the next best ratios; and the third and fourth quartiles have progressively better ratios.   Table 19.2 shows that the cities with populations of 50,000 to 100,000 have per capita quartile revenue figures for ratio #1 as follows: the first quartile is $714 or more (the worst); the second quartile ranges from $714 to $532; the third quartile ranges from $532 to $429; and the fourth quartile is $429 or less (the best). From this information the finance officer can easily identify how his or her city compares, on financial condition, nationally in this population.[39]

Of the 10 financial condition ratios six (ratios 1, 3, 4, and 8) are viewed favorably if they have low values and four (ratios 2, 5, 6, and 7) if they have high values. The interpretation that is generally given to the ratios are as follows:

- A low #1 ratio indicates the ability to generate greater revenue
- A high #2 ratio indicates that the city is not dependent on external sources of revenue
- A low #3 ratio indicates that city is not dependent on operating transfers to maintain the operations of government from the general fund.
- A low #4 ratio indicates the adequacy of existing infrastructure.
- A high #5 ratio indicates that the city has had a greater relative rise in revenue than expenditures.
- A high #6 indicates that the city has been generating a surplus which can be sued to meet unforseen increases in expenditure or shortfalls in revenues.
- A high #7 ratio indicates the availability of cash to meet existing and maturing obligations.
- A low #8 ratio indicates the city's ability to meet short-term obligations from the regular flow of revenues.
- A low #9 ratio indicates the city's ability to meet maturing long-term obligations.
- A low #10 ratio indicates the city's ability to met debt service obligations when they become due.[40]

From Table 19.1 (the financial condition worksheet), each quartile is assigned a number from -1 for the first quartile to +2 for the highest quartile. The city that has all ratios in the first quartile will receive a score of -10, while the city that receives all scores in the second quartile will have a total score of 0. The following grading scale has been suggested:

- A score of 10 or more is identified as the best;
- A score of 5 is identified as better than most;
- A score of 1 to 4 is identified as average;
- A score of 0 to -4 is identified as worse than most; and
- A score of -5 or less is identified as among the worst.[41]

CONCLUDING OBSERVATIONS

The fiscal crises of New York, Cleveland, and many other cities focused attention on the inadequacy of traditional financial statements to effectively manage a community or agency's fiscal resources. The bond-rating

Table 19.1
FINANCIAL CONDITION WORKSHEET

(A) Ratio	(B) Your City's Ratio	(C) Points Assigned to Each Quartile				(D)
		Quartile 1 (0 to 25 percentile)	Quartile 2 (25 to 50 percentile)	Quartile 3 (50 to 75 percentile)	Quartile 4 (75 to 100 percentile)	Enter your score circled on the left
1. Total revenue / Population	1 ___	-1	0	+1	+2	—
2. Total general fund revenues from own sources	2 ___	-1	0	+1	+2	—
3. General fund sources from other funds / Total general fund sources	3 ___	-1	0	+1	+2	—
4. Operating expenditures / Total expenditures	4 ___	-1	0	+1	+2	—
5. Total revenues / Total expenditures	5 ___	-1	0	+1	+2	—
6. Unreserved general fund balance / Total general fund revenues	6 ___	-1	0	+1	+2	—
7. Total general fund cash and investments / Total general fund liabilities	7 ___	-1	0	+1	+2	—
8. Total general fund liabilities / Total general fund revenues	8 ___	-1	0	+1	+2	—
9. Direct long-term debt / Population	9 ___	-1	0	+1	+2	—
10. Debt service / Total revenues	10 ___	-1	0	+1	+2	—

Source: Ken W. Brown, "The 10-Point Test of Financial Condition: Toward an Easy-to-Use Assessment Tool for Smaller Cities" *Government Finance Review*, Vol. 9, no. 7 (December 1993): 23, (with permission of Government Finance Officers Association, 180 North Michigan, Chicago, Illinois).

Table 19.2
FY 1989 Quartile Ranges for 750 Cities
from the Financial Indicators Database

	Population 50,000-100,000 (162 Cities) Quartile				Population 30,000-50,000 (167 Cities) Quartile			
	1 25-% (worst)	2 25-50%	3 50-75%	4 75-100% (Best)	1 1-25% (Worst)	2 25-50%	3 50-75%	4 75-100% (Best)
1. Total revenues / Population	$714 or more	$714 to $532	$532 to $429	$429 or less	$631 or more	$631 to $493	$493 to $399	$399 or less
2. Total general fund revenues / Total revenues	80.2% or less	80.2% to 87.7%	87.7% to 96.8%	96.8% or more	77.5% or less	77.5% to 87.4%	87.4% to 96.4%	96.4% or more
3. General fund sources from other funds / Total general fund sources	7.285% or more	7.285% to 2.083%	2.083% to 0.003%	0.003% or less	6.598% or more	6.598% to 2.438%	2.438% to 0.001%	0.001% or less
4. Operating expenditures / Total expenditures	95.8% or more	95.8% to 89.9%	88.9% to 81.6%	81.6% or less	94.4% or more	94.4% to 86.5%	86.5% to 77.4%	77.4% or less
5. Total revenues / Total expenditures	0.878 or less	0.878 to 0.964	0.964 to 1.038	1.038 or more	0.864 or more	0.864 to 0.952	0.952 to 1.034	1.034 or more
6. Unreserved general fund balance / Total general fund revenues	0.086 or less	0.086 to 0.180	0.180 to 0.300	0.300 or more	0.133 or less	0.133 to 0.211	0.211 to 0.338	0.338 or more
7. Total general fund cash and investments / Total general fund liabilities	0.622 or less	0.622 to 1.539	1.539 to 3.372	3.372 or more	0.916 or less	0.916 to 1.909	1.909 to 3.525	3.525 or more
8. Total general fund liabilities / Total general fund revenues	0.245 or more	0.254 to 0.101	0.101 to 0.069	0.069 or less	0.193 or more	0.193 to 0.099	0.099 to 0.063	0.063 or less
9. Direct long-term debt / Population	$413 or more	$413 to $201	$201 to $21	$21 or less	$416 or more	$416 to $141	$141 to $15	$15 or less
10. Debt service / Total revenues	0.134 or more	0.134 to 0.074	0.074 to 0.041	0.041 or less	0.146 or more	0.146 to 0.080	0.080 to 0.025	0.025 or less

	Population 15,000-30,000 (213 Cities) Quartile				Population Less than 15,000 (208 Cities) Quartile			
	1 (1-25%) (Worst)	2 (25-50%)	3 (50-75%)	4 (75-100%) (Best)	1 (1-25%) (Worst)	2 (25-50%)	3 (50-75%)	4 (75-100%) (Best)
1. Total revenues / Population	$666 or more	$666 to $481	$481 to $326	$326 or less	$736 or more	$736 to $465	$465 to $368	$368 or less
2. Total general fund revenues / Total revenues	77.7% or less	77.7% to 88.6%	88.6% to 98.3%	98.3% or more	76.4% or less	76.4% to 89.2%	89.2% to 96.7%	96.7% or more
3. General fund sources from other funds / Total general fund sources	5.987 or more	5.987% to 1.157%	1.157% to 0.001%	0.001% or less	8.089% or more	8.089% to 1.270%	1.270% to 0.001%	0.001% or less
4. Operating expenditures / Total expenditures	97.9% or more	97.9% to 91.1%	91.1% to 81.9%	81.9% or less	99.0% or more	99.0% to 92.2%	92.2% to 80.3%	80.3% or less
5. Total revenues / Total expenditures	0.876 or less	0.876 to 0.954	0.954 to 1.034	1.034 or more	0.868 or more	0.868 to 0.962	0.962 to 1.038	1.038 or more
6. Unreserved general fund balance / Total general fund revenues	0.104 or less	0.104 to 0.218	0.218 to 0.386	0.386 or more	0.173 or less	0.173 to 0.278	0.278 to 0.444	0.444 or more
7. Total general fund cash and investments / Total general fund liabilities	0.819 or less	0.819 to 1.865	1.865 to 4.719	4.719 or more	1.162 or less	1.162 to 2.522	2.522 to 5.761	5.761 or more
8. Total general fund liabilities / Total general fund revenues	0.208 or more	0.208 to 0.104	0.104 to 0.061	0.061 or less	0.189 or more	0.189 to 0.102	0.102 to 0.057	0.057 or less
9. Direct long-term debt / Population	$326 or more	$326 to $133	$133 to $8	$8 or less	$329 or more	$329 to $87	$87 to $1	$1 or less
10. Debt service / Total revenues	0.133 or more	0.133 to 0.063	0.063 to 0.011	0.011 or less	0.105 or more	0.105 to 0.039	0.039 to 0.001	0.001 or less

Source: Ken W. Brown, "The 10-Point Test of Financial Condition: Toward an Easay-to-Use Assessment Tool for Smaller Cities," *Government Finance Review* Vol. 9 #7 (December 1993): 24-25. (with permission of the Government Finance Officers Association, 180 N. Michigan Ave., Chicago, Illinois).

system, while useful as a means of analyzing a governmental unit or agency's credit-worthiness, is too crude to serve as an indicator of the fiscal health or fiscal strain of a community.

Early attempts to find a single fiscal health indicator, while not successful, provided insights about the development of a series of indicators and ratios that can give early warning, permitting action to be taken before a potential problem arises.

Analysis of fiscal strain throughout the nation reveals that fiscal strain is not inevitable among older communities, especially those in the Northeast and the Midwest. It can appear in any community that fails to properly manage expenditure and debt (the equation's numerator) and private sector resources (the denominator). If a watchful eye is kept on the changes in these two critical factors, a balance can be maintained and a governmental financial crisis can be minimized or avoided. Pittsburgh and Cincinnati reduced expenditures at the appropriate time, while New York and Cleveland did not, resulting in severe fiscal stress.

NOTES

1. Terry Nichols Clark and Lorna Crowely Ferguson, *City Money* (New York: Columbia University Press, 1983), pp. 5-6.

2. See Nancy D. Suttenfield and L. Carole Wharton, "Seizing the Opportunities of Fiscal Retrenchment," *Public Budgeting and Review*, 13, no. 2 (Fall 1993): 49-62.

3. Charles H. Levine, "Organizational Decline and Cutback Management," in *Managing Fiscal Stress*, ed. Charles H. Levine (Chatham, N.J.: Chatham House Publishers, 1981), p. 15.

4. Ibid., pp. 15-16.

5. Ibid.

6. Charles H. Levine, "The New Crisis in the Public Sector," in Levine, *Managing Fiscal Stress*, p. 12.

7. Ibid.

8. Clark and Ferguson, *City Money*, p. 6; see also J. Richard Aronson, *Municipal Fiscal Indicators* (Washington, D.C.: U.S. Department of Housing and Urban Development, Office of Policy Development, 1980); Sanford M. Groves, W. Maureen Godsey, and Martha A. Schulman, "Financial Indicators for Local Government," *Public Budgeting and Finance*, 1, no. 2 (Summer 1981): 5-19; Lyman A. Glenny and Frank Bower, "Warning Signals of Distress," in *Challenges of Retrenchment*, ed. James R. Mingle et al. (San Francisco, Calif.: Jossey-Bass, 1981).

9. Nancy Humphrey, George Peterson and Peter Wilson, *The Future of Cincinnati's Capital Plant* (Washington, D.C.: Urban Institute Press, 1979), pp. 7-13.

10. Roy Bahl, *Financial State and Local Governments in the 1980s* (New York: Oxford University Press, 1984), ch. 3.

11. Ibid., pp. 4-6.

12. Clark and Ferguson, *City Money*, pp. 4-5.

13. Regarding residential choice, a person will move from a locality if the local policies diverge from his or her preferences.

14. Charles H. Levine, Irene S. Rubin and George G. Wolohojian, *The Politics of Retrenchment* (Beverly Hills, Calif.: Sage Publications, 1981), p. 31.

15. Ibid., pp. 31-32.

16. Ibid.

17. Ibid., pp. 43-44.

18. U.S. Department of Housing and Urban Development (HUD), *Local Financial Management in the 1980s: Techniques for Responding to New Fiscal Realities* (Washington, D.C.: U.S. Government Printing Office, 1979); Bahl, *Financing State and Local Governments*, pp. 71-79.

19. See Irene S. Rubin, *Running in the Red State* (Albany, N.Y.: State University of New York Press, 1982), ch. 1; Clark and Ferguson, *City Money*, ch. 1; and Levine, *Managing Fiscal Stress*, pp. 16-19.

20. Clark and Ferguson, *City Money*, p. 224; see also Jeffrey L. Pressman, *Federal Programs and City Politics* (Berkeley: University of California Press, 1975).

21. Clark and Ferguson, *City Money*, p. 227.

22. Ibid.; see also Ken Newton, *Balancing the Books* (Beverly Hills, Calif.: Sage Publications, 1980).

23. See Roy Bahl, "Estimating Equity and Budgeting Effects of Financial Assumptions," *National Tax Journal, 29* (March 1976): 54-72; Edward K. Hamilton and Francine Rabinovitz, *Whose Ox Would be Healed? Financial Effects of Federalization of Welfare* (Durham, N.C.: Institute of Policy Sciences and Public Affairs and the Ford Foundation, 1977); Bernard R. Gilford, *New York City: The Political Economy of Cosmopolitan Liberalism*, Annual Report (New York: Russell Sage Foundation, 1977).

24. See Dale Hickman, Robert Berne, and Lenna Stiefel, "Taxing over Debt Limits," *Public Administration Review*, 41 (July/August 1981): 445-53.

25. Clark and Ferguson, *City Money*, pp. 243-55.

26. Robert Berne and Richard Schramm, *Financial Solvency of Local Governments* in Working Papers in Planning (Ithaca, N.Y.: Cornell University, January 1979), pp. 3-7.

27. Sanford M. Groves, "An Introduction to Evaluating Financial Condition," in *Practical Financial Management*, ed. John Matzer, Jr. (Washington, D.C.: International City Management Association, 1984), p. 14.

28. HUD, *Local Financial Management in the 1980s*, p. 27.

29. Ibid., p. 26.

30. Ibid., pp. 26-27.

31. Groves, "Introduction to Evaluating Financial Condition," p. 17.

32. Groves, "Introduction to Evaluating Financial Condition," p. 19.

33. Ibid.

34. Ibid., p. 21.

35. Ibid., pp. 220-21.

36. Ibid.

37. Ken Brown, "The 10-Point Test of Financial Conditions: Toward an Easy-to-Use Assessment Tool for Smaller Cities," *Governmental Finance Review*, 9, no. 6 (December 1993): 21.

38. Ibid.

39. Ibid.

40. Ibid., pp. 22-23.

41. Ibid.

20

Fraud, Waste, and Abuse (FWA)

Though the problem of fraud, waste, and abuse (FWA) has always existed in varying degrees in public and other not-for-profit agencies, public attention and concern was not focused on it until the latter part of the 1970s. A number of developments helped to raise the consciousness and concern about FWA: (1) inflation kept spiraling upward; (2) the cost of conducting the business of government kept rising, causing an increase in complaints about the quality and quantity of goods and services delivered; (3) there were widespread reports of kickbacks, collusion, and corruption among public officials; (4) massive amounts of resources were being directed to the military, yet its readiness and fighting efficiency was being questioned and daily reports were uncovering the outrageous prices that the government was paying for materials from nonbid, private contractors.

The public's concern about FWA was a major factor in creating a crisis of confidence in both public and private institutions. A Daniel Yankelovich poll in 1977 registered a significant rise of public mistrust in national institutions. Trust in government declined from an 80 percent approval rating in the late 1950s to about 33 percent in 1976. In the business sector approval fell from a level of approximately 70 percent in the late 1950s to 15 percent in 1970. Three out of four people felt that too much power was concentrated in the hands of too few people, that federal officials could not generally be believed, and that far too many people were taking payoffs in exchange for favors.[1] Tax money was wasted and misappropriated, many people felt, and when it came to having a say about how things were run, "the little guy did not stand a chance."[2]

A recent poll put the number of dishonest Americans at 31 percent (rising sharply from 12 percent estimated in 1961). Forty percent are identified as situationally dishonest, suggesting those individuals in this category will be honest or dishonest depending on which situation provides the greatest payoff.[3]

Employee fraud cost American businesses approximately $200 billion yearly, compared to $11 billion by violent crime offenders. Banks estimate that 95 percent of all loses are due to employees. In contrast, bank robbery and customer fraud result in only 5 percent of the fraud.[4]

During the last 15 years, FWA acts both in the public and private sector gained national attention. In the private sector the ZZZZ Best Company of Southern California concocted a scheme that fraudulently put hundreds of millions dollars of assets on its books. Discovery led to the conviction of the owner and many of his subordinates. Management of one Denver company broke into the auditor's work papers and secretly planted evidence to inflate the financial results of the company. In Ohio, the Phar-Mor company's president and chief financial officers were indicted for stealing more than 50 percent of the company's assets. Moreover, the losses in the savings and loan debacle (the savings and loan officials misused or stole billions of dollars and lost the savings and pensions of thousands of retirees) cost the nation more than $200 billion.[5]

This chapter introduces the reader to the problem of FWA in not-for-profit organizations and discusses how it comes about and how institutional controls may be developed and/or strengthened to minimize it. Particular emphasis is given to examining internal controls and describing vulnerability assessment determination.

THE GRACE COMMISSION

Formerly known as the President's Private Sector Survey on Cost Control (PPSSCC), the Grace Commission, in the person of J. Peter Grace, has been a vocal critic of the federal government's waste and inefficiency. President Reagan charged the commission with evaluating the government's operations as if it were a private sector enterprise and the commission concluded that $424 billion in yearly savings could be realized if recommended procedures reducing waste and inefficiency were implemented. A number of outrageous examples of inefficiency and waste were circulated to the press. They include: (1) the federal General Services Administration employed 17 times as many people and needed 14 times as much space to perform essentially the same tasks as a comparable private sector enterprise; (2) the cost of building a Veterans Administration Hospital bed unit cost $61,250, or about four times more than a similar unit constructed in the private sector; and (3) a $0.03 screw cost $91.00.

While the Grace Commission did much to highlight and direct public attention to waste and inefficiency in government, it oversimplified the problems it was studying. The methods used in carrying out the study were ad hoc, unsystematic, and difficult to defend. In fact, most of the outrageous examples of waste and inefficiency that it identified could be explained away for one reason or another. Moreover, the commission's rationale that private sector production of goods and services is superior to the public sector's capability is not entirely defensible.[6]

If the charge given to the commission were applied to the J. Peter Grace's own W. R. Grace Company, its rating might be no better, and perhaps might even be worse than that of the public sector. The 1971 purchase of the Mr. Gasket Company of Brooklyn, Ohio, by the W. R. Grace Company provides a good case in point. Soon after the $17 million company was purchased, many of the experienced middle- and lower-level managers who had "grease under their nails" were dismissed and replaced by MBA degree holders steeped in the Grace management philosophy and perspective.

Ten years after the purchase of the company, the original owner, Joe Hrudka, was offered the opportunity to repurchase the Mr. Gasket Company for $4 million ($13 million less than the original selling price). Within two years after the repurchase, the company was estimated (market value) at slightly over $150 million.[7]

A number of important observations can be made here. Hrudka's reacquisition of the company brought the immediate rehiring of more than 85 employees who were let go by W. R. Grace. A Mr. Gasket official expressed the opinion that it was necessary to rehire these former employees and to dismiss Grace's MBAs because the Grace managers "simply did not know the business." The point was made that there was virtually no matching between job requirements and the experience of the people who were hired to fill them.

The major indictments of the Grace management included the following:

1. It failed to establish effective communication links with suppliers and distributors.
2. It failed to study and understand its competitors.
3. It forced out the people who knew the business when it severed its links with the original owners.
4. It suffered from decision paralysis as corporate headquarters had to be consulted for the most minute decision.
5. There was a lack of sound and creative ideas about the business. In addition, the time lag for implementation of ideas for new products continued to lengthen.
6. The MBAs, with a push from headquarters, selected a profit level and strove to realize it without understanding the means to reach it.
7. Only items with big profits were pushed. The "nickel-and-dime items" were not considered, even though this was where the profits were to be made.

8.   There was too much preoccupation with time and motion
        studies and too little with finding the right product and the
        appropriate mix at the appropriate time.

Westinghouse Electric provides another compelling example to show
that the public sector does not have a monopoly on inefficiency. During the
1980s, Westinghouse made clear to its engineering and transportation division
(as well as the others) that it had to produce a minimum profit level of 15
percent. This forced the division managers to dutifully obtain contracts with at
least 15 percent profit margin. The problem with these contracts was that they
were more paper appearance than reality when it came to meeting the agreed-
upon profit target. The engineering and transportation division head was playing
the bureaucratic game.

When hard times came to Westinghouse, it jettisoned its engineering
and transportation division. The data revealed that the division was not meeting
Westinghouse's profit target. Transformation from within was viewed as an
unacceptable option. The division was sold to AEG of Germany. Within four
years of the purchase, the number of workers had been increased from 800 to
1,200 and the division was generating robust profits.

In summary, it can be said that W. R. Grace Company was oblivious
to the business environment in which it was operating. It moved too slowly and
operated like a rigid or mature bureaucracy in an area that required a keen
understanding of its environment and the ability to act quickly. Grace's cadre
of middle-level managers was inappropriate for the time, place, and business.
At the end of 10 years, experience had not increased, and the learning curve had
not been smoothed out. Thus W. R. Grace, to forestall the possibility of the
business falling apart, was willing to resell for only the worth of the assets.
Similarly, Westinghouse could not get its engineering and transportation division
to produce targeted profits because it failed to determine the factors necessary
to motivate its workers to produce targeted expectations.

An important point that might be made here, contrary to J. Peter Grace,
Westinghouse and others, is that the private sector's supposed productive
superiority over the public sector has very little basis in fact. It is not a matter
of being public or private that determines efficiency or productivity in the
delivery of goods and services as the national report on *Creating a Government
That Works Better and Cost Less* stresses (see Chapter 2)[8]. Instead, it is more
a matter of having good managers who can motivate workers to produce
optimally.

Without question, FWA is a serious problem in the public sector and
perhaps to a lesser extent in other not-for-profit organizations. At the federal
level of government, the General Accounting Office (GAO) estimates from $5
billion to $50 billion in fraud annually, while Donald Lambro suggests that up

to $100 billion is lost due to waste and abuse.[9] As noted earlier, the Grace Commission put the figure at $424 billion. A former Inspector General at the Department of Health, Education and Welfare (now the Department of Health and Human Services) estimated that as much as $8 billion is lost yearly in that department due to FWA.

The general public feels that government officials waste a large portion of the taxpayers' money. In a 1981 Gallup Poll the public felt that 48 cents out of every federal tax dollar is wasted. Paradoxically, these same people want the government to maintain or increase major programs. A possible explanation for this is that the elimination of waste would reduce spending and make it unnecessary to disturb beneficial programs.[10]

DEFINING FWA

There is no universal definition of FWA. Sometimes the FWA concept is used interchangeably with terms such as bribery and corruption. Most observers do agree that it involves behavior that violates norms and standards. Obviously, the definition of FWA will be affected by value judgments. Thus, its application should, as far as possible, be context specific. The general attributes that might reasonably be identified with FWA have been summarized as follows:

1. It is a violation of public trust.
2. It is a conversion of public benefit to private ends.
3. It is a perversion of authority and the commission of an unacceptable act.
4. It is a failure to enforce laws, rules, and regulations or to apply sanctions to a given situation.
5. It is the intentional or unintentional misapplication or wasteful use of public resources.[11]

While the general definition and attributes discussed here are useful, greater specificity is needed to be able to apply the concept FWA consistently in specific situations.

Fraud involves trickery, cheating, and intentional deception that causes an individual or individuals to give up some lawful rights or ownership of property. There are two kinds of fraud that cause injury: actual fraud and constructive fraud. When someone relies on an individual's intentional misinterpretation of material fact, this is called actual fraud. Constructive fraud is unlike actual fraud in that it is not caused by self-interest or evil design but by the very nature of the act.[12] Fraud is, in essence, an intentional or unintentional illegal and wrongful act employed explicitly for obtaining money or benefit from public programs. The conditions that give rise to fraud have been grouped into three categories: (1) situational pressures, such as heavy losses and high debt (see Table 20.1); (2) perceived opportunities encouraging fraud, such as inadequate internal controls, poor accounting records, inadequate authorization for transaction, lack of physical security over assets, and lack of independent checks; and (3) personal characteristics, such as poor moral character, low credit rating, and rationalizing behavior.[13] The common forms and methods used to commit fraud include:

- intentional mistakes, such as arithmetical or clerical errors, for example, purposely omitting an entry or making incorrect calculations;
- purposeful misinterpretation of the facts;
- the recording of nonexistent transactions;
- intentional misallocation of contract costs;
- embezzlement and theft by means of deceit and suppression of the truth;
- the removal of varying amounts of money from cash funds and registers;
- the overcharging of clientele or service recipients while pocketing the difference;
- the placement of fictitious names on the payroll;
- advances made to nonexistent employees;
- kickbacks from suppliers for overpriced goods;
- payment for self-completed false invoices;
- the taking of agency materials, equipment, and services[14]
- pocketing money from delinquent accounts;
- overwithholding or underfunding pension benefits;
- overpaying doctors, clerics, and hospitals;
- overcharging for travel expenses;
- stealing money from one customer account to pay another (known as "lapping");
- stealing duplicate payments, especially utility payments;
- giving bogus credit memos for receipt of payment; and
- while pocketing the receipts, paying suppliers that should not be paid or paying too much.

Waste most often is comprised of unintentional acts that result in inefficient practices or misapplication of resources, causing increased public costs or reduced benefits to potential recipients.

Table 20.1

Fraud and the Purchasing Director: Alexandria, Georgia

Background

Jason Montgomery had been director of purchasing for 16 years. He bought supplies and secured various services for the city. He was an outstanding employee who had a reputation for integrity and dedication. He was married with four children. His salary combined with that of his wife, amounted to $46,000. This allowed the Montgomerys to live a comfortable life-style in a middle-class neighborhood in Alexandria. Their level of spending permitted them little opportunity to save.

The Problem

When Jason's oldest son entered college, Jason had enough money to pay the college expenses. A year later, he knew that his second son would be ready to begin college. Jason realized that he would not be in a financial position to send his other children to college. Given his position and his familiarity with suppliers, Jason approached the buyer of one of the local suppliers who had previously offered him favors and asked if he could direct a greater share of the city business to his firm. Jason sought the buyer and gave him a proposal. For a $1,000 monthly honorarium, Jason would increase the volume of city business to the supplier's firm.

Soon after the payments to Jason had begun, the supplier increased his prices and started shipping a cheaper grade of materials. When Jason sought an explanation for the changes he was told that there were no plans to return to the original prices and quality of products. Besides, there was no way that Jason could go to his supervisors and admit that he was taking kickbacks. By the time a colleague inadvertently discovered the arrangement, the city had overpaid the suppliers approximately $300,000 for paper products.

Jason was a model employee for 16 years, yet he participated in an illegal and dishonest act. He was subject to the three factors (perceived pressure, perceived opportunity to commit and conceal, and an excuse to rationalize the behavior as acceptable) that have been used to explain why people participate in fraud. Jason had fallen victim to financial pressure and the opportunity to conceal.

Source: W. Steve Albrecht, "Fraud in Government Entities: The Perpetrators and the Types of Fraud," *Government Finance Review*, 7, no. 6 (December 1991): 27.

Abuse involves the violation of agency rules, procedures, and regulations, impairing the effective and efficient implementation of an agency's programs. Acts of abuse typically involve the reduction or denial of goods or services rightfully due to eligible participants. There is an element of ambiguity about abuse because value judgment plays a bigger role here than in the case of fraud. The abusive individual may be described as being ineffective or inefficient, or as misinterpreting policies and program guidelines. Abuse is often more insidious than fraud; therefore, it is more difficult to combat.[15]

INTERNAL CONTROL SYSTEMS AND FWA

If fraud, waste, and abuse are to be minimized over the long run, the establishment of a control system that provides information about the accuracy and reliability of an agency's assets is required. The internal control system must assure that the agency's accounting transactions are accurate, complete and that procedures for detecting malfunctions are effective.[16] An internal control system is made up of a set of procedures and actions designed by the management of an agency to facilitate policy execution and to allow only a minimal amount of FWA. It was noted in Chapter 3 that internal controls have two basic elements: (1) administrative control, consisting of procedures and records to ensure the implementation of agency decisions as intended; and (2) accounting control, consisting of procedures concerned with the safeguarding of assets and the reliability of financial records. To ensure reliability, an internal control system requires the establishment of a regular internal audit program to monitor the system, evaluate its performance, and provide the agency management with the required feedback. An independent auditor audits the entire internal control system on a yearly basis.

Internal Control as a System of Action

The federal Office of Management and Budget (OMB) requires that each agency carry out an evaluation of its internal control system. An effective system of internal controls needs more than administrative and internal accounting controls. It also needs a continuous feedback of information to management indicating how well agency policies and financial information activities are being executed. The internal control system aids management in monitoring policy implementation, maintaining the accuracy of financial records, and reporting on weaknesses and corrective actions that are needed. "By frequently checking agency performance, the internal audit services to deter fraud, error, waste and abuse in government."[17] While the feedback mechanism is an important factor in minimizing FWA, each agency's overall system of internal control must be audited periodically by independent auditors. Four major components make up the internal control system: administrative controls, internal accounting, internal audits, and external controls. The most critical of these is the system of internal accounting control, which emphasizes the following:

- authorization - to ensure that transactions are executed in accordance with an agency's specified guidelines;
- recording - to ensure that transactions are recorded to permit preparation of reports in accordance with generally accepted accounting principles and to maintain accountability over assets;
- access to assets - to permit only authorized personnel to have access to assets;
- asset accountability - to compare the record for assets with existing assets from time to time, taking appropriate corrective action when relevant differences occur.[18]

"Information on assets, liabilities, revenues and expenditures must be reliable to meet legal demands and to allow investors, stockholders and the public to evaluate the organization properly."[19]

Ideally, internal accounting controls, when properly established, become a network of checks and procedures that act as an important barrier and as a deterrent to improper conduct. A breach or violation is likely to occur only when management is negligent and fails to effectively monitor and maintain the system. Internal accounting controls may be classified as preventative or detective. Most often, they are employed in combination. Preventative controls are implemented prior to the occurrence of an event and may be viewed as instruments of deterrence, while detective controls occur after the event. The former are preferable, but the typical organization should have both types in place. The point should be made that no one type or set of procedures, rules, or organizational controls is applicable to all agencies at all times. Instead, the appropriate type of internal controls will depend on the nature of each agency.[20]

Pre-audit as Preventative Check

The preaudit check is a system that determines the appropriateness of a proposed action before it takes place. For example, purchase orders and vouchers are verified and checked before the orders are sent to vendors, and vouchers are carefully reviewed before any payments are made to vendors (suppliers). Among the objectives of the preaudit are the following:

- ascertain that forms authorizing disbursement of funds are complete and accurate;
- determine that requests for payment are in accordance with administrative rules and procedures and comply with statutory requirements and contractual agreements;
- determine that appropriations are available for the request for payment; and
- determine that price and the purchase are reasonable.

In the long run, an effective system of internal controls is the most useful means for reducing FWA in government (see Figure 20.1). A strong system of internal controls will help to ensure that resources are used in accordance with legal requirements, regulations, and policies. It facilitates the generation of reliable data which are maintained and properly disclosed in reports to aid in safeguarding resources and minimizing their loss due to FWA. Several categories have been used to summarize the general requirements of an internal control system:

- competent employees who are provided with clear lines of authority, effective supervision, and technical training;
- appropriate and effective separation of duties (e.g., separating the custody of asset function from the accounting for asset activity; separating original recording of accounting transactions from posting to the general ledgers; and separating record keeping from operational responsibility);
- proper procedures for authorization (e.g., preventing the same individuals who authorize the purchase of materials from receiving them);
- adequate documents and records (requiring that forms to be used on which all transactions are summarized and entered, to include purchase orders, subsidiary ledgers, and time cards);
- physical control over assets, records, and forms to ensure protection against theft, fire, and other damage; and
- independent checks on performance by having someone not responsible for the transactions check or oversee the appropriateness and execution of performance.

Figure 20.1
OMB Process to Evaluate Internal Controls

ORGANIZE

Assign responsibilities and issue policies and
procedures for evaluating internal controls.

SEGMENT

Systematically divide the agency into
components, programs, and functions for
evaluation (called *assessable units*).

CONDUCT VULNERABILITY ASSESSMENTS

Assess susceptibility of assessable unit to
occurrence of waste, loss, unauthorized use, or
misappropriation.

DEVELOP PLANS FOR SUBSEQUENT ACTION

Develop plans and schedules for further review
or other actions based on results of
vulnerability assessment.

CONDUCT INTERNAL CONTROL REVIEWS

Make detailed reviews of internal controls to
identify necessary corrective actions.

TAKE CORRECTIVE ACTIONS

REPORT ANNUALLY ON INTERNAL CONTROLS

Source: U.S. Government Accounting Office, *Implementation of the Federal Managers'
Financial Integrity Act: First Year* (Washington, D.C.: GAO, 1984), p. 3.

Electronic Data Processing and Control (EDP)

EDP has become an increasingly important part of modern management. Financial management has been especially susceptible to EDP application. In fact, instances of computer-related fraud and abuse have been occurring far more, on the average, than fraud and abuse through conventional methods, both in the not-for-profit sector and in private organizations. In government, because of improper control, programmers and employees who have access to computers have been able to divert large sums of government money for their own use.

While EDP has not changed the purposes or objectives sought by internal controls, it has had significant impact on internal control systems, including the following:

- EDP systems significantly reduce the requirement for clerical employees, limiting the opportunities for segregated functions.
- Information is maintained internally in the machine, thereby retarding the conventional monitoring approach.
- Most transactions, documents, and record keeping-related transactions are maintained by the computer, drastically reducing or eliminating the "audit trail."[21]

At the federal level of government, Congress passed the Federal Managers Financial Integrity Act in 1982. The act requires that each agency implement a system of internal accounting and administrative controls consistent with the standards prescribed by the Comptroller General. Particularly noteworthy is the requirement that each agency evaluate its system of internal controls, indicating to what extent it is in conformity with the Comptroller general's standard, and that it submit the report to Congress and the president.

Using the Computer to Combat FWA

The EDP system can also work strategically to aid management in combatting FWA. The computer can be used to assist in detecting fraud, as shown in the following examples:

- Identify unusual activities by a purchasing agent that suggest the possibility of fraud. (In this case a number of small identical orders were placed with the same supplier. By means of the sequence of the invoice, the computer revealed that the supplier had few customers and was receiving far

more orders than might normally be expected.   These
computer indicators initiated an investigation which, in turn,
revealed fraud.)[22]

- Identify medicaid and medicare claims that show a pattern
  suggesting potential fraud.
- Match welfare and other recipients to payroll and death
  records to identify potential abuses.
- Identify taxpayers who file differing tax returns for state and
  federal governments.

ASSESSING AGENCY VULNERABILITY TO FWA

When making a fraud vulnerability assessment (FVA), an agency's
internal control system is the major focus of attention. Vulnerability assessment
is predominantly a quantitative systematic technique for measuring an agency's
exposure to FWA. In assessing exposure, an agency relies heavily on how well
its internal control system is designed to minimize FWA. Close attention to
internal controls is likely to improve the reliability of vulnerability assessment,
which may be viewed essentially as an analysis of the susceptibility of an
agency, or any component thereof, to avoidable loss (including a dissipation of
assets and unauthorized use or distribution of resources), inaccurate reports and
information, unethical or unlawful actions, and other activities that may
adversely affect the public image and standing of an organization.

By means of a survey approach, an evaluation of an agency's potential
for or vulnerability to FWA can be determined. Note that the emphasis is put
on the potential for FWA and not on how existing internal controls actually
prevent it.[23] FVA is thus an estimate of which units are susceptible to FWA -
management, program, activity, project, function, or other units. In Figure
20.2, vulnerability points for auxiliary and third-party providers are identified
from vulnerability point A to H. Each vulnerability point carries with it
particular risks associated with the program concerned.[24]

In the U.S. Department of Housing and Urban Development (HUD),
not only are existing systems evaluated for susceptibility to FWA, new and
substantially revised programs are subjected to FVA. The vulnerability
assessment not only identifies the potential for FWA, it also outlines the risks
and abuses that may occur if adequate management controls are not maintained
at the front end."[25] Known past abuse, weaknesses, or breakdown in
management controls are clearly identified. The objective is the maintenance of
a fraud vulnerability assessment system that permits programs to be managed
without fraud, waste, and inefficiency.[26] Despite the superior FWA system
that was established in HUD, widespread FWA took place during the 1980s
because effective monitoring and follow up recommendations were ignored or

Figure 20.2

Program Vulnerability Points

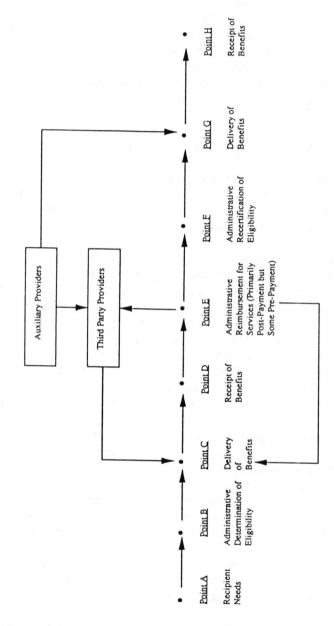

Source: Andrea G. Lange and Robert Bowers, *Fraud and Abuse in Government Benefit Programs* (Washington, D.C.: U.S Department of Justice, Law Enforcement Assistance Act, 1979), p.19.

not enforced in a timely manner. This suggests that no system is self-executing.
Its success will only be as good as the ability of the people who administer it.

The Vulnerability Process

As the first stage in FVA, the structure of the organization should be
analyzed in terms of its administrative functions. The organization should be
classified according to its various components, as follows:

- programs or functions, broken down by subprograms or
  subfunctions;
- the matrix of the organization, indicating each department's
  contribution to the operation of the program;
- the degree of independence exercised by the program function;
- allocated budget;
- relative centralization and decentralization;
- personnel assigned to each program;
- determination of goals, objectives, and the delivery system;
- management sanctions in place; and
- management incentives in place to motivate sound management
  action against FWA.

The degree of centralization and independence is an important factor in
carrying out a FVA because it tends to suggest the intensity of supervision that
may be present. When programs have multiple locations, it is usual to perform
FVA at the various different sites.[27]

In stage two, each program and/or responsibility center is evaluated for
FVA by considering the factors that lead to FWA, such as inherent riskiness in
the functions and in the organizational environment. The important objective at
this stage is the development of criteria to produce a ranking of the programs'
or functions' vulnerability to FWA.[28] The use of the ranking approach has
been gaining wide use. Among the agencies employing it are the U.S. Defense
Audit Agency, the HUD inspector general, and GAO, in its *Framework for
Assessing Job Vulnerability to Ethical Problems*.[29]

The Task Force Report (Government Accountants Association) on internal
controls has suggested a guide (see Figure 20.3) that could be used in
vulnerability assessment.

FVA has three main steps:

1. Conduct an analysis of three general control environments.
   This includes an examination of the personnel's competence

Figure 20.3

Vulnerability Assessment Grid

VULNERABILITY FACTORS	RISK VALUE
HIGHLY CONTROLLED: LITTLE VULNERABILITY	
Precise Legislative Authority Minimal Budget Authority/Outlays Complete Program Government Administration Ample Administrative Resources Provided No Commercial Value Minimal Public Involvement Extensive Written Procedures Timely and Adequate Financial Reporting	1

VULNERABILITY FACTORS	RISK VALUE
MODERATELY CONTOLLED: MODERATE VULNERABILITY	
Broad Legislative Authority Moderate Budget Authority/Outlays Joint Third-Party and Government Program Administration Adequate Administrative Resources Provided Substantial commercial Value Moderate Public Involvement Essential Areas Have Written Procedures Financial Reports Adequate but Not Timely	2

VULNERABILITY FACTORS	RISK VALUE
LITTLE CONTROL: LIMITED VULNERABILITY	
Unspecific Legislative Authority Limited Budget Authority/Outlays Mostly Third-Party Program Administration Minimal Administrative Resources Provided Limited Commercial Value Selective Public Involvement Partly Effective written Procedures Financial Reports Not Comprehensive	3

VULNERABILITY FACTORS	RISK VALUE
NO CONTROL: HIGH VULNERABILITY	
Value Legislative Authority Large Budget authority/Outlays All Third-Party Program Administration No Administrative Resources Provided High Commercial Value Widespread Public Involvement No Written Procedures Late and Incomplete Financial Reporting	4

Source: "Federal Executive Reporting on Internal Control: An AGA study, " *Government Accountants Journal* 29, no.3 (Fall 1980): 16

and integrity; effectiveness of the delegation and communication of authority; and an overview of the organizational structure, budgeting and reporting practices, and the organizational checks and balances to financial control and internal auditing.

2. Examine the inherent risks, such as outside pressures on the agency, unclear or confusing goals and objectives, budgeting constraints, decentralization, limited age and life expectancy, and potential problems suggested by prior studies.

3. Make a preliminary evaluation of the adequacy of internal controls.[30]

Once these three FVA steps are completed, a determination about the vulnerability of the program or function can be made. The results of the FVA provide the input to conduct internal control reviews on each program and administrative function. The flow process for vulnerability determination employed in the Department of Housing and Urban Development is shown in Figure 20.4.

INCENTIVE MECHANISMS TO MINIMIZE FWA

Though incentive mechanisms are an important factor in the fight against FWA, little has been said about this topic. The establishment of a conducive, accommodative, and effective organizational environment is most desirable. In such an environment, effective controls will be in place and ethical practices will be emphasized and followed at all management levels. In addition, honesty must be viewed as an indispensable asset to the organization. Among the positive practices that should be observed are:

1. Maintenance of an open line of communication with employees

2. Hiring and promoting only competent and trustworthy employees;

3. Close examination of the work of employees on a continuing basis;

4. Regular review and appropriate changes in weak control areas;

5. Unannounced inspection tours;

6. Thorough investigation of public complaints, tips, and rumors;

7. Careful review of budgetary and MIS reports, giving attention to material deviations;

8. Clear and early assignment of responsibility; and

9. Prompt issuance of agency policy.[31]

Figure 20.4
Fraud Vulnerability Determination

TRAINING PROGRAMS TO COMBAT FWA

The commitment to the fight against FWA has been given the greatest formal acceptance at the federal level of government. All departments and major agencies of the federal government have an inspector general whose major objective is to minimize or eradicate FWA. There are a number of places throughout the government where seminars and specialized training in FWA techniques and approaches can be learned. While these training programs are not yet well organized, some credible efforts have been instituted.

1. The Graduate School of Agriculture in Washington, D.C. (U.S. Department of Agriculture affiliated but an independent entity), conducts a three-day seminar throughout the year from (October to September) on (a) prevention and detection of FWA, (b) evaluation and report on internal control systems, and (c) internal control in automated systems.

2. The General Accounting Office provides a three-and-a-half-day seminar on fraud awareness for its employees involved in the FWA area.

3. The Association of Government Accountants provides, from time to time, a short seminar on financial investigation.

4. The Federal Office of Personnel Management offers a two-day seminar on evaluating, improving, and reporting on internal control in federal agencies.

5. The U.S. Defense Contract Audit Agency provides a self-study course for its auditors on the prevention and detection of fraud, waste, and abuse. Additionally, FWA prevention and detection is stressed in all audit-related training courses.

6. In the private sector, the National Association of Certified Fraud Examiners (NACFE) offers training seminars.

7. The John Jay School of Criminal Justice offers a Master's of Public Administration Inspector General Program.

CONCLUDING OBSERVATIONS

Special emphasis focusing on the comparative efficiency of public versus private agencies indicates that there is very little, or no, inherent superiority of one type over the other. The massive problems that must be faced to combat FWA require creative and innovative leadership.

Estimates of the amount of FWA in government vary depending on who is making the estimate. Irrespective of the estimates, the public feels that the degree of FWA is massive and that governmental officials cannot be trusted.

Distrust not only exists toward government but extends to other institutions, especially the business community.

The greatest efforts toward eradicating FWA have been devoted to strengthening the internal control system. This includes paying greater attention to internal auditing and to vulnerability assessments of FWA. It is my view that the long-run approach to minimization requires resocialization - a change of the internalized norms and philosophy of public officials.

NOTES

1. Reported in Seymour Lipset, "The Decline of Confidence in American Institutions," *Political Science Quarterly*, 98, no. 3 (Fall 1983): 379-98.

2. Michael Johnston, *Political Corruption and Public Policy in America* (Monterey, Calif.: Brooks/Cole Publishing Co., 1982), p. 1.

3. See Richard C. Hollinger *Dishonesty in the Work Place: A Manager's Guide to Preventing Employee Theft* (Park Ridge, Ill.: London House Press, 1989).

4. W. Steve Albrecht, "Fraud in Government Entities: The Perpetrators and Types of Fraud," *Government Finance Review*, 7 (December 1991): 27; see also Joseph T. Wells, "Six Common Myths about Fraud," *Journal of Accountancy*, 169 (February 1990): 82-88.

5. Werner Grosshaus, "Internal Assessments - Are They Really Needed in Performance Auditing?" *Government Accountant's Journal*, 40, no. 4 (Winter 1992): 41-43.

6. Steven Kelman, "The Grace Commission: How Much Waste in Government?" *Public Interest* (Winter 1985): 62-82.

7. Interview on "60 Minutes" (CBS television, July 20, 1985); author interviewed by management of Mr. Gasket Company in Brooklyn, Ohio, August 7. 1985.

8. Al Gore, *Creating a Government That Works Better and Cost Less* (Washington, D.C.: U.S. Government Printing Office, September 1993).

9. Kelman, "The Grace Commission: How Much Waste in Government?" pp. 62-66, and U.S. General Accounting Office (GAO) "Fraud in Government Programs: How Extensive? How Can It Be Controlled?" (Washington, D.C.: U.S. GAO, 1981).

10. Martin Lipset and William Schneider, *The Confidence Gap: Business, Labor and Government in the Public Mind* (New York: Free Press, 1985), chs. 1, 2; see also Mark Green and John F. Berry, *The Challenge of Hidden Profits* (New York: William Morrow, 1985), ch. 1.

11. Jerome B. McKinney and Michael Johnston, ed., *Fraud, Waste, and Abuse in Government* (Philadelphia: Institute for the Study of Human Issues, 1986).

12. See Black's Law Dictionary, rev. 4th ed., (St. Paul, Minn.: West Publishing, 1968), p. 789.

13. See W. Steven Albrecht, Marshall B. Romney, David Cherrington, I. Reed Payne, and Allan J. Roe, *How to Detect and Prevent Business Fraud* (Englewood Cliffs, NJ: Prentice-Hall, 1982), chs. 3-5.

14. See U.S. Government Accounting Office, *Fraud in Government Programs: How Extensive Is It? How Can It be Controlled?* p. 2; Martin Calpin, *Understanding Audits and Audit Reports*, 4th ed. (Ottawa: Canadian Institute of Chartered Accountants, 1984), p. 35; and Pacific Northwest Intergovernmental Audit Forum, *Auditing for Fraud* (Philadelphia: the Forum, October 1982), pp. 20-21.

15. Andrea G. Lange and Robert Bowers, *Fraud and Abuse in Government Benefit Programs* (Washington, D.C.: U.S. Department of Justice, Law Enforcement Assistance Administration, 1979), p. 16.

16. New York State Legislative Commission on Economy and Efficiency in Government, *Preventing Fraud, Waste, Abuse and Error: Internal Control Reform in New York State Government* (Albany: State of New York, June 2, 1982).

17. Ibid., p. 10.

18. Ibid., p. 11.

19. Ibid.

20. Ibid., p. 17.

21. Mark W. Dersmith and Abraham Simon, *Local Government Internal Controls: A Guide for Public Officials* (New York: Council on Municipal Performance, 1983), pt. 2, pp. 30-31; see also Thomas Whiteside, *Computercapers: Tales of Electronic Thievery, Embezzlement and Fraud* (New York: T. Y. Crowell, 1978).

22. Lawrence B. Sawyer, *The Practice of Modern Auditing* (Altamonte Springs, Fla.: Institute of Internal Auditors, 1981), p. 724.

23. Pacific Northwest Intergovernmental Audit Forum, *Auditing for Fraud*, p. 16.

24. Lange and Bowers, *Fraud and Abuse in Government Benefit Programs*; surveyed were Medicaid, Aid to Families with Dependent Children, vocational education, food stamps, summer food, service programs for children, the Comprehensive Employment and Training Act (CETA), and unemployment insurance.

25. U.S. Department of Housing and Urban Development, *Handbook: Fraud Vulnerability Assessment* (Washington, D.C.: Office of Inspector General, 1980).

26. Ibid., pp. 2-4.

27. Paul E. Weisenbach, "Vulnerability Assessment and Internal Controls," *Government Accountants Journal*, 33, no. 1 (Spring 1983): 5.

28. Ibid., p. 6.

29. U.S. Government Accounting Office (GAO), *Framework for Assessing Job Vulnerability to Ethical Problems*, FPCD-82-2 (Washington, D.C.: U.S. GAO, 1981).

30. Weisenbach, "Vulnerability Assessment," pp. 6-8.

31. Pacific Northwest Intergovernmental Audit Forum, *Auditing for Fraud*, p. 14.

21

Financial-Advising Functions: Local and Other Not-for-Profit Organizations

As the financial function has grown more complex, the need for expert financial advice has grown along with it. Over the years, a variety of sources have emerged. In the public sector the major sources have been the state, civic-minded corporations, professional associations, chambers of commerce, foundations, local universities, and paid consultants. While not-for-profit organizations have access to some of the same sources as the local government, their main sources are the United Way and paid consultants.

This chapter presents a brief overview of the advising function of local government and other not-for-profit organizations. A discussion of the three main provider groups (investment bankers, commercial banks, and independent, paid advisors) are examined.

CAPITAL FINANCING

Typically, most local governments seek financial advice when they raise funds for capital financing. The advice is sought either for a specific project or bond sale or for the preparation of a comprehensive financing strategy that involves a complement of services beyond a particular debt issue. It is generally recommended when there is a need for advising services that they be secured at the beginning of the undertaking, especially in the case of a capital investment program. "Early participation in the process permits the advisor to develop (or assist in developing) a comprehensive financing plan that articulates the government's need for capital funds, explains alternative sources and structures of those funds and examines their implications for the future fiscal health of the government."[1]

Involving the advising service early in a debt issue can often increase the financing alternatives available to the governmental unit. For example, the advisor's review of the laws may show existing practices that limit the financing options. Given enough lead time, such limits or impediments (current practices, procedures, or laws) may possibly be removed, permitting sizable cost savings to the issuer.[2]

TYPES OF ADVISORY FIRMS

There are three main types of firms from which governments can obtain advisory services: investment bankers, commercial banks, and independent consultants. Investment and commercial bankers are typically grouped together in terms of the services they provide. Both provide advisory services as part of their normal business of marketing securities and making loans. Independent advisors, on the other hand, do not sell securities, make loans, or underwrite municipal bonds; they sell only their professional services. Most advisory services to governments have been confined to a single area - bond-related financing. In the past, advice on general finance and planning or project feasibility has been more the exception than the rule. However, this situation has begun to change, and in order to cope, many firms have been expanding their capability to respond to this need.

Advisory firms that provide financial advice and underwrite municipal bonds are regulated by the Municipal Securities Rule-Making Board (MSRB). Under the MSRB Rule G-23, an underwriter may operate in a dual capacity as a financial advisor on a bond issue and a bidder for the same issue if the following conditions are satisfied: (a) the issue is competitive, and (b) the issuer interposes no objections.

The MSRB rules are applied differently to negotiated bond sales. When the underwriter is also acting as financial advisor, Rule G-23 requires that a disclosure be made in writing to the client, indicating the potential for conflict of interest between the two roles. Moreover, the advisor must resign its financial role before participating in the underwriting activities of the client. This role change has traditionally been viewed with a degree of uneasiness because of the high potential for conflict of interest. In the new role, the underwriter has two clients who have opposite interests. The governmental unit selling the bond wants the lowest interest possible, while the purchaser of the bond wants the highest. "Since the underwriter is compensated only if the deal goes through, the underwriter is under considerable pressure to make the bonds as marketable as possible to consummate the sale."[3]

DECIDING ON THE TYPE OF FIRM TO BE USED

The selection of a specific type of advisor will depend on a number of factors such as cost, reliability, experience, and confidence in the integrity of the advice. A number of arguments have been advanced for the different kinds of financial services provided.

- Independent advisors' perspectives tend to be broader in the range of services that are provided. Since advising is the independent provider's primary concern, services can be tailored and attention focused on the specific and overall needs of the client. The advisors' role is not limited to debt financing.

- The MSRB does not regulate independent advisors. This means that the governmental unit must thus rely on a firm's reputations.

- Investment bankers and commercial banks stress the fact that their size and good standing gives them a reputation that they strive to maintain.

- Investment bankers and commercial banks that participate in the underwriting are regulated by the MSRB which provides a degree of assurance that the organizations are maintain adequate levels of competency and responsibility.

- Investment banking and commercial bankers acting in dual capacities as financial advisors and underwriters create a potential for conflict of interest. In addition, since these groups typically participate in many syndicate (group underwriting) cooperative arrangements, they may not be willing to push the interest of a given client in order to maintain good working relationship with fellow bankers with whom they will be collectively involved with in future underwriting activities. It may be sometimes necessary to employ financial providers that have integrated services, that is, to permit the financial advisor to act as an underwriter and investment banker. In the case of a negotiated underwriting, the governmental unit or organization deals principally with one investment banker for selling and marketing the bond. This permits the bond counsel to provide "a multi-party advisory role by assisting the issuer, the underwriter, the trustee and the purchaser."[4]

Disadvantages of the Independent Service Advice

While there are efficiencies to be gained by using an independent advisor, there are also a number of associated disadvantages.

- Cost must be closely controlled to ensure that it does not exceed comparable in-house targets and to minimize the possibility of permitting fast-talking service providers to sell public officials unneeded services at excessive costs.
- Accountability becomes more difficult since the service provider leaves immediately after performance.
- Standards of quality must be clearly identified - an exceedingly difficult task in most public and other-not-for-profit organizations.
- Obtaining segmented independent financial advice is unwise due to the complication of some financing arrangements. To minimize cost and limit risks, it may be necessary to employ financial providers that have integrated services.
- One-time improvements and ad hoc advice are not likely to be endure, if there is no continuity to ensure that management will carry out recommendations.[5]

SELECTING THE FINANCIAL ADVISORY SERVICE

A preferred method for the selection of a financial advisory service is found through the distribution of requests for proposals (RFPs) to obtain a wide array of potential firms (see Table 21.1). This means more than a mere announcement of the RFP. A comprehensive list of advisory firms may be compiled using aids such as the *Directory of Municipal Bond Dealers of the U.S.* published by The Daily Bond Buyer. The RFP should clearly specify the type and scope of services desired, setting forth the criteria for selection and the method of compensation.

Sometime before the proposals have been reviewed, the governmental unit should clearly identify the criteria to be applied in evaluating the proposals. Among the criteria that should be used are the following: (1) past experience and familiarity of the firm with the financial services to be provided; (2) expertise and experience of staff to direct and implement the project; (3) experience with other governments within, and outside the state; and (4) estimate of the costs of carrying out the project. Once this process is completed, the top two or three applicants are invited to make presentations to provide additional input regarding the applicant's familiarity with the substantive matter of the

Table 21.1
An Action Plan and Simplified Checklist for
Obtaining and Using Professional Services

Step

1. **IDENTIFY OR CONCEPTUALIZE THE SERVICES DESIRED**
    [ ]   Somebody has an idea, an inspiration, or a problem.
    [ ]   Vendor makes a proposal.

2. **IDENTIFY INTERNAL PLAYERS AND OUTLINE THE PROCESS**
    [ ]   Who will and should participate?
    [ ]   Develop a step-by-step agenda.
    [ ]   Assign staff to specific tasks and deadlines.

3. **DEFINE THE SCOPE OF SERVICES**
    [ ]   What do we want and need? When?
    [ ]   What will be delivered?
    [ ]   What is done for other governments?
    [ ]   How will we benefit?
    [ ]   What do we do internally; what are our own capabilities?

4. **DETERMINE QUALITY STANDARDS**
    [ ]   Identify professional standards.
    [ ]   How is quality determined and described?
    [ ]   How do others define quality?
    [ ]   How will we enforce quality standards?
    [ ]   Do we need professional help to define quality?

5. **EXPLORE ALTERNATIVE PRICING METHODS**
    [ ]   Review theoretical options.
    [ ]   Which are used in this profession?
    [ ]   What is the industry standard in this market?
    [ ]   What are our fiscal goals and limitations?

6. **PREPARE A REQUEST FOR PROPOSAL (OR REQUEST FOR INFORMATION)**
    [ ]   Prepare staff assignments.
    [ ]   Review quality standards and scope of services.
    [ ]   Provide standard procurement language.
    [ ]   Will a contract be prepared using the proposal?
    [ ]   Anticipate the evaluation process and state criteria.
    [ ]   Require specific information in standard format.

7. **IDENTIFY POTENTIAL VENDORS**
    [ ]   Contact other jurisdictions.
    [ ]   Contact professional associations.
    [ ]   Consult the GFOA Directory of Financial Services.
    [ ]   Prequalify or screen if necessary.
    [ ]   Determine which vendors are inappropriate.

8. **DESIGNATE SELECTION COMMITTEE**
    [ ]   Find appropriate players.
    [ ]   Establish criteria.
    [ ]   Determine ground rules.
    [ ]   Review proposals.
    [ ]   Interview vendors/finalists if needed.

9. **FINAL SELECTION**
    [ ]   Is action by governing body required?
    [ ]   Who presents report?
    [ ]   Can rational criteria overcome political influences?
    [ ]   Is negotiation appropriate?
    [ ]   What if governing body looks for different criteria?
    [ ]   What if proposal exceeds budget?

10. **CONTRACTUAL PROVISIONS**
    [ ]   Is a control appropriate?
    [ ]   Will the RFP and the formal proposal form the basis of
           the contract?
    [ ]   Are quality standards and timetables included?
    [ ]   Is pricing/billing basis clear?

11. **IMPLEMENTATION AND ADMINISTRATION**
    [ ]   Who is the government's staff contact person?
    [ ]   Are progress payments based on performance?
    [ ]   Will performance be measured?
    [ ]   Are regular reports provided?
    [ ]   Who approves payments and maintains files?
    [ ]   How will "change orders" be controlled?

Source: Adapted from Girard Miller, *Selecting Financial Services for Government* (Chicago, Ill.: Government Finance Officers Association, 1984), pp. 39-40.

project, to obtain a reading and feel for the nature and caliber of the principals, and to clarify questions and queries that surface in the written proposals.

Negotiating for Bank Service

Because of the profitable nature of governmental unit to banks, the pressure to land the governmental entity bank account is high.[6] Competitive building has been growing as the method of choice for selecting banking services. Among the benefits that is attributed to competitive banking include the following:

- increased yield on investment;
- enhanced collection services generating greater amounts of dollars to invest;
- more economical bank services; and
- enhanced efficiency of each management operation.

Once the commitment has been made to use competitive bidding, the governmental unit makes a thorough assessment of the needs that must be met to satisfy its cash requirements. Once this is done a carefully prepared request for proposal (RFP) should be developed and sent to all banks in the (region, city, county, or state). Prior to the banks submission of their bids, the jurisdiction requesting the service holds a prebid conference. Research proposals are evaluated based on the stipulated criteria, then the award is made and the contract is signed.

Among the factors that influence which bank will be selected include:

- timing and method of notification and wire transfer;
- availability of coin counting services;
- use of a concentration/zero balance type of account;
- provision of account reconciliation services;
- availability of computer services; and
- access to check cashing services.

Compensation of Financial Advisory Service

There is no set or definable system that can be applied in determining an advisor's fee. Any of a number methods may be used, such as a bond float, an agreed-upon amount on an annual basis or an hourly rate, or a percentage of total dollar amount of the financing related to the advisor's services rendered. While there is no accepted right or wrong way to determine advisory fees, it is generally considered imprudent to tie an advisor's fee to the amount of bonds sold. This may provide the advisor with an incentive to sell bonds at rates that might be higher than otherwise. The method provides no built-in incentive to recommend alternative financing approaches or to postpone sale of the debt or the bonds in a volatile market.

The scope and content of advisory services differ so greatly that it may be hazardous to speak about comparative costs. Surveys in 1991 indicated that bond floatation advisory fees averaged from $1.50 per $1,000 on general obligation bonds of $5 - $10 million and $2.80 per $1,000 on revenue bonds. The point has been made that it is wise for an issuer to exchange informal information with other issuers or to send out RFPs to obtain some realistic ideas about the ranges of out-of-pocket costs.[7]

THE AVAILABILITY OF DIFFERENT KINDS OF FINANCIAL ADVICE

Though the most important governmental advice sought is financial, it is the least well known of all the services provided to government.[8] Attempts to obtain consistent financial answers about the criteria that governmental and other not-for-profit organizations employ in selecting financial service providers seldom meet with much success. The kinds of financial services available from the commercial marketplace, the not-for-profit interest group association, professional associations, universities, other governmental units, and civic-minded corporations are rich and diverse. In fact, it is this diversity that creates a challenge to the public finance professional. A partial list of financial providers aids in demonstrating this point.

- Accountants
- Auditors
- Bankers
- Bond counsels
- Computer services
- Financial advisors
- Leasing services
- Pension portfolio management and advisors
- Property appraisers
- Risk management consultants

Since finance is so critical, it is important that financial services be carefully chosen because the choice can have a significant impact on the financial condition of an organization. Selecting the most appropriate or best available service is a difficult task in both the public and other not-for-profit agencies. In public organizations "managers and elected officials are unfamiliar

Table 21.2
Financial Services: Contract-Pricing System

Fixed-Price Type	Upset Hybrid Fixed Price	Cost Reimbursement
Fixed fee (lump sum)	Guaranteed maximum price	Cost only
Unit price	Ceilings on overhead fee	Cost plus fixed
Percentage of total	Incentive clauses	Cost plus percentage fee
Fixed price with escalator	Penalty clauses	Loaded hourly rate
	Escalation clauses	

Source: Adapted from Girard Miller, *Selecting Financial Services for Government* (Chicago: Ill.: Government Finance Officers Association, 1984), pp. 17-18; see also Edward Weseman, *Contracting City Services* (Pittsburgh, Pa.: Innovations Press, 1981), pp. 60-61.

with varying professional standards of quality, . . ."[9] compounding the difficulty of the problem.

PRICING OF FINANCIAL ADVISORY SERVICES

Pricing methods for financial services differ among the various professional organizations. Table 21.2 shows one possibility by categorizing the different methods.

Fixed Price or Lump Sum

In this type of contract, the contractor agrees to carry out some specifically defined work in a given time period for an agreed-upon sum of money. Since there is one single price, this type of contract is viewed as the simplest of all the pricing methods. Note that this method shifts the costs risks to the contractor, because the contractor is paid the agreed-on price regardless of the cost incurred.

Unit Price

This is a variation of the fixed price contract. The contractor agrees to perform a repetitive assignment and bills the client for the unit of work completed. This approach is typically used when the quality or volume of work cannot be easily determined in advance. Unit costing facilitates marginal costing because each additional unit of output cost can be compared with the prior unit.

Percentage of Gross Fees or Revenue

This method has wide use in the financial service industry. The method allows fees to be charged as a percentage of dollar amount of the activity (e.g., a financial advisor may charge $1.65 for every $1,000 of bonds floated). This method has survived because of the imperfect nature of competition and the ability of the service provider to exact charges due to its influence and dominant position.

Fixed Price Control with Escalation

In those situations where the contract covers a long period, and especially during periods of unstable prices, contractors attempt to protect themselves and limit risk by attaching escalation clauses.

Upset Fixed Price

This pricing system has enjoyed a degree of popularity among public managers. The method allows the contractor to charge on a per-unit or per-hour basis but is limited by a maximum price that may not be exceeded. When this method is used, the operating assumption is made that the maximum price will be applied unless favorable conditions occur. In a way, it could be easily argued that the upset or maximum price is really a kind of cost reimbursement approach with the application of a ceiling or cap.

Cost-Reimbursement Type Contracts

The application of this approach to contract pricing permits the contractor to be paid for all allowable costs. The approach is premised on the view that prices are determined on the basis of variable cost which cannot be readily identified in advance. The cost reimbursement method is used when the volume and type of work cannot be easily determined. Effective operation of this pricing procedure requires considerable trust in the contractor. Additionally, there is no built-in incentive for the contractor to control cost or to meet schedule deadlines. Thus, reporting and monitoring requirements should be clearly and specifically spelled out.

Cost-only Reimbursement

This method is acceptable if the quality of the product produced can be maintained. The kind of pricing is based on direct costs and excludes overhead and profit expenses. A contractor may desire such an arrangement to enhance business relationship, keep the services of critical employees or undercut competition.

Cost-plus-fixed-fee

This permits the contractor to carry out agreed-on work within a specified period of time for an amount of money based on itemized costs plus an additional fee known as a fixed fee, which comprises the contractor's cost, overhead, and profit. This method is used in those cases when the scope of the work in question cannot be adequately defined. A number of problems may arise in this approach such as (1) the contractor's rapid completion of work to increase his or her profit ratio without due care being given to quality, and (2) the contractor obtaining unreasonable profits. To minimize these types of problems from occurring many governmental contractors have required close supervision and ceiling clauses stipulating levels that cost may not exceed.

Cost plus percentage

This is known sometimes as the "overhead" pricing system. This method requires that all cost be explicitly defined. An agreed-on percentage of these costs is calculated, generating the fee. This system has a built-in incentive for the contractor to recapture his or her overhead. Thus, it is the contractor's intent to include as much expense as possible in the total cost figure. Because of the potential for abuse, this costly approach is usually avoided and is prohibited in some jurisdictions.

Loaded Hourly Rate

This is the "cost plus percentage fee." It is commonly found in public finance agreements. Charges are determined on the basis of labor services. Worker classifications are defined for each function to be performed. A composite hourly rate (including indirect costs) is then assigned to each worker classification. Because overhead costs are built in, there is some incentive to prolong the contract. Like the other reimbursement methods, imposed deadlines and continued monitoring of work should be carried out. In cases where this method must be used, it is desirable to include ceilings.

Cost-plus-incentive-fee Contract

This has a built-in factor to reward contractors to control cost and to penalize the contractor for cost overruns. This approach typically requires that targets be set - (1) target cost, (2) target fee, (3) minimum and maximum fees, and (4) formula for fee adjustment. The target cost is the contractor's best estimate of the cost required to complete the work. When the contractor controls the hours applied or charged, an incentive is provided that increases the fees. However, if cost overruns are generated, a penalty is imposed. The operation of the minimum and maximum fees thus protects both sides from widely varying fluctuations in price.

The incentive method may be applied creatively to enhance the benefits for all concerned. Consultants may be given the incentive to find ways of reducing cost or increasing revenue. Based on the amounts involved, a percentage can then be applied to the amount to reward the consultant. Where such a system is encouraged, care should be exercised to minimize abuse. For example, a consultant should not be allowed to obtain a windfall profit from a recommendation that is general knowledge in the industry.

Hybrid Costing

Variations of the fixed and cost reimbursement types include the following. (1) The *guaranteed maximum price* establishes a price that a contractor may not exceed. It is very much like the fixed-price method (discussed earlier). This type of control is common in the public sector because legislative bodies pass appropriations that cannot be legally exceeded. (2) The *ceiling-on-overhead reimbursement* may be applied to the overhead to recapture types of contracts such as loaded hourly rates and the cost-plus-percentage fee. (3) *Incentive clauses* incorporate aspects of the fixed contract. They are an attempt to motivate contractors toward greater efficiency. Contracts that provide for specific incentives to contractors are seldom found in public and other not-for-profit agencies. (4) *Penalty clause* contracts seek to promote minimum standards of professional quality and timeliness. Typically, a fixed percentage or sum is deducted from the contract for noncompliance. Where this is designed to effect compliance, however, it may foster production of an output in which quality is impaired. (5) *Price escalators (multiyear engagements)* are used when stability in price levels is sought. Most often, indices such as the Consumer Price Index (CPI) or the gross national product (GNP) price deflator are used to avoid the possibility of contract price renegotiation. There are a number of benefits to be gained from price escalators, such as (a) technology changes that can lower cost and help the organization, (b) benefit to contractors from spiraling costs; and (c) the governmental unit can avoid start-up and retraining costs. Procurement officials feel this approach lacks certainty and thus believe that prices should be negotiated at a fixed rate at the time the contract is entered into.

PUBLIC AND OTHER NOT-FOR-PROFIT ORGANIZATIONS AS SOURCES OF FINANCIAL ADVICE

Other governmental units can often be a ready source of financial information and assistance to local governments. The type and quantity of services vary among the different governmental units. At the local level, the state is a major provider of financial advice, both to other state agencies and to the local governments. Since local governments are more often in greater need of financial advice, attention will be focused on this issue.

Advising takes several forms: (1) legally mandated or prescribed financial requirements that the state closely monitors; (2) provision of model financial management practices set forth in a series of reports, booklets, or pamphlets; (3) provision of seminars, lectures, and short courses geographically dispersed throughout the state at regular and convenient times; and (4) a combination of forms 1 through 3.

The state of Pennsylvania emphasizes forms 2 and 3. At regular times, throughout the state, seminars, lectures, and short courses are conducted for local officials. Among the written materials that have been developed for local officials are the following:

- *Fiscal Management Handbook*, containing basics on revenue sources, budgeting, bookkeeping and accounting guidelines, and municipal borrowing.
- *Purchasing Handbook for Local Government*, discussing

desired techniques and practices.

- *Auditors' Guide*, acquainting elected auditors with their duties and responsibilities; outlining the scope of an audit and suggesting programs for the audit of various funds; and explaining how to prepare various required fiscal reports.
- *Taxation Manual*, containing simplified explanations of the various kinds of local taxes permitted to be levied in the Commonwealth.
- *Tax Collectors Manual*, providing guidance and assistance to elected tax collectors.

The State of Georgia has emphasized forms 1 and 2. The Institute of Government at the University of Georgia has been a most prolific source of financial information for local officials in the state. Among the publications are the following:

- *Getting the Most From Professional Services: Fiscal Advisor*, (1979), by Charles K. Coe, containing sample contract provisions, an evaluation checklist, and a brief description of fiscal services provided by advisors, especially on bond issues.
- *Getting the Most from Professional Services Outside Auditor*, (1981), providing a brief introduction to the problem facing public officials when searching for an outsider auditor.
- *Understanding Risk Management: A Guide for Government*, (1980), by Charles K. Coe, containing a comprehensive overview of the risk management field.
- *Getting the Most from Professional Services: Computer Selection* (1979), by Charles K. Coe, indicating some basic options that should be considered in selecting a computer.
- *A Basic Budget Guide for Small Cities and Counties*, (1985), by Arthur Mahor, Jr., containing steps for preparing and adopting a budget in small governmental units.
- *Compliance Auditing in Georgia Counties and Municipalities* (1992), by Paul T. Hardy, Richard W. Campbell, and Paul E. Glick, reviewing legal requirements for conducting a compliance audit.
- *Cooperative Purchasing: A Guide for Local Governments* (1985), explaining how cooperative purchasing saves money.
- *Handbook for Collecting Delinquent Property Taxes* (1984), by J. Devereaux Weeks, describing ways of recovering unpaid taxes.
- *County and Municipal Revenue Sources* (1992), by J.

Devereaux Weeks, explaining general revenue sources available to local governments.

The North Carolina publication, *Local Government Finance in North Carolina*, has been accepted and used as an authoritative guide for local officials in that state. Colorado emphasizes form 1. It provides a comprehensive *Local Government Financial Management Manual* that is regularly updated, setting forth the legal requirements and suggested practices.

Not-for-Profit Professional Associations

This category comprises a wide spectrum of financial service providers. Only the more prominent are included here.

- *Government Finance Officer Association (GFOA)* publishes a number of handbooks, books, pamphlets, and yearly updates on current research on financial management. To foster better financial reports among local governments, the GFOA awards a Certificate of Conformance to those governmental units that meet the announced reporting criteria.
- *International City Managers Association (ICMA)* provides numerous books, pamphlets and reports. ICMA publishes books on virtually every area of financial management. Among the prominent publications are the following: *Management Information Service (MIS) Report* on timely financial topics and the *Financial Monitoring Trend System*, developed to assist governmental units in evaluating the fiscal health of their communities.
- *Association of Government Accountants (AGA)* intermittently publishes reports, books, and pamphlets. The AGA's strength lies perhaps most in the many "short, timely" seminars and lectures offered, especially to financial managers in the Washington, D.C., area.
- *Public Technology Incorporated (PTI)* is a cooperative research development and technology transfer organization providing services to American cities and counties. It assists local governments in developing and improving their financial management systems to increase efficiency, reduce costs, and improve services. It publishes books and pamphlets, conducts workshops and seminars, and offers consulting advice. It

provides technical assistance in the following areas of financial management: (1) information management/office automation; and (2) operational effectiveness, revenues and expenditure, forecasting, user charges, and fees.

Private Corporations and Foundations

The Pittsburgh corporate community, through the chamber of commerce, has been successful in providing financial advice to the city of Pittsburgh, Allegheny County, and the Pittsburgh School District in western Pennsylvania. It perhaps may serve as a useful model for other areas in the country.

The relationship established between the two large governmental units and a school district (city of Pittsburgh and Allegheny County and the Pittsburgh School District) has been most beneficial, constructive and creative. The Pittsburgh corporate community, through the chamber of commerce has provided timely and useful financial advice to Pittsburgh and Allegheny County and the Pittsburgh School Board. The business community and the governmental unit reached an operating understanding regarding the disposition that would be made of recommendations resulting from studies carried out on the governmental units' operation. "They agreed on the condition that everyone involved accepted one fundamental provision: that any recommendations made by the business and accepted by the elected officials must be implemented."[10] Among the projects that the corporate community have carried out are of the following:

- *Committee for Progress and Efficiency in Pittsburgh (COMPEP)* examined the city of Pittsburgh's purchasing process and recommended ways on how it might be streamlined to more effectively carry out its duties and responsibilities.
- *Committee for Progress in Allegheny County (COMPAC)* was aimed at improving the economy, efficiency, and effectiveness of county government. Three main objectives were sought: (1) to make immediate improvements in the operation of county government; (2) to put in place self-generating enhancements to facilitate change; and (3) to build bridges between county government professionals and business counterparts.
- *Committee for Improvements in the Courts* attempted to streamline administrative systems to enhance the efficiency and effectiveness of the courts.
- *Systems Program for Interactive Financial Forecasting (SPIFF)*

was developed for the City of Pittsburgh, Allegheny County, and the Pittsburgh Board of Public Education to provide two important capabilities: (1) maintaining and displaying historical data of up to 50 years and permitting it to be organized in tabular form; and (2) containing techniques and methods for projecting revenues and expenditure.[11]

- *Local Government Financial Forecasting Project* is a computer based in-house, long-range financial forecasting capability for the City of Pittsburgh, County of Allegheny, and Pittsburgh Board of Education.
- *Local Government Computer Capability Project (COGNET)* is an instrument to promote better management and intergovernmental cooperation among the 131 municipalities in Allegheny County. The COGNET's goal is the development of a computer network to serve the County's eight regional Councils of Government (COGs) to facilitate sharing of services, and capacity building/improving of management capability.

The COGNET project is a follow-up of earlier Pittsburgh Chamber of Commerce municipal involvement. The project is tied into the University of Pittsburgh's AT&T "Campus of the Future" and "County of the Future". A collective effort of five different organizations: (1) the Intergovernmental Cooperation Program, based in Pittsburgh, (2) the Pittsburgh Chamber of Commerce (as the main resource provider), (3) the University of Pittsburgh, and (4) Carnegie-Mellon University as the planning, research, and training arms, and (5) the County of Allegheny as the in-kind provider of administrative support. To enhance the project's capability, the Pittsburgh Foundation granted COGNET resources to develop a number of internships with students from Carnegie-Mellon University and the University of Pittsburgh. In June 1985 the Pittsburgh Chamber of Commerce received the Prudential Citation of Merit for Private Sector Initiatives for its innovative direction and accomplishments with the COGNET project.

Three main objectives were established for the project: (1) the development of a research proposal to study the organizational impact of COGNET on people; (2) using the project to study the innovation acceptance of the COGNET process; and (3) employing COGNET as an instrument for economic development of Allegheny County.

The Ford Foundation

To stimulate and share creative approaches to the operation of state and local government, the Ford Foundation initiated a program called "Innovation in State and Local Government." The objective is to provide awards to units of government that have successfully applied methods overcoming social and economic problems and improving the quality of life. A $2.5 million grant was awarded to a committee headed by former Michigan governor William J. Miller at the John F. Kennedy School of Government at Harvard University to recognize and promote innovative programs. "The goal of the Awards Program is to identify and publicize initiatives that exemplify creative inventive thinking about government, managerial climates that encourage innovations, and particular state and local innovation which are worthy of transfer and replication," with greatest attention given to innovation in such areas as families, health care, education, training jobs, housing, and community neighborhood.[12]

Municipal and Economy Leagues

These leagues are professional associations and public interest organizations that offer valuable assistance to local governments. The Maine Municipal Association (MMA) provides an example. It is made up of 495 towns and cities, and presently, 490 of the municipalities are dues-paying members. The association engages in strategic planning, as it did in 1982 when it carried out a needs analysis of local government to identify areas upon which the MMA should focus attention. A result of the 1982 strategic planning was the strong recommendation that increased financial and consulting services should be provided to member municipalities. This recommendation led to the hiring of a staff to: (1) carry out surveys; (2) collect and review member inquiries as a service to members; (3) provide consulting to members on specific financial issues for a nominal (below-market) per-hour fee; (4) develop financial workshops and publish articles in the association's monthly magazine on current financial events.

The state of Maine has facilitated the exchange of information on financial management. State agencies in Maine have developed peer-like relationships with local governments. The advantage of this approach manifests itself institutions involving state and local creative problem solving. For example, when the Reagan administration signaled its policy intent to reduce funding for waste water treatment facilities, the state of Maine, in a cooperative response, intended to minimize the financial uncertainties among local governments, enacted environmental laws tougher than those of the federal government and provided increased federal aid to this important program area.

The Economy League of Pittsburgh provides an example of civic-minded corporate leadership support for the improved delivery of public goods and services. The league gives advice and assistance to all units of government. Though it prefers to work with a collective of municipalities, it responds to individual governmental unit calls for assistance as well. For example, the **Allegheny League of Municipalities** was recently asked to evaluate the need for a regional bond bank to assist towns and cities in obtaining debt financing. The league has also developed a number of handbooks on various financial topics.

Local Universities/Colleges

Most colleges and universities, especially state-supported ones with programs in public administration, provide an array of services and publications to governmental units, often at less than cost or totally free of charge. Many of these institutions seek agencies that will provide internships for their students.

The Not-for-profit Sector

The most prolific source of financial advice comes from private professional associations and United Way-sponsored agencies. For example, in Allegheny County, the CPA association has been generous with its assistance to not-for-profit agencies. Many of the big accounting and consulting firms sit on not-for-profit agency boards. Most often the services provided are gratis or at minimal cost to the not-for-profit agencies.

Community Technical Association Center (CTAC)

This is an example of an agency that was organized to assist not-for-profit agencies. It charges fees according to ability to pay. Among the services CTAC provides are the following: (1) financial management - setting up accounting systems; and (2) computerized accounting, including cost effectiveness analysis, bookkeeping, development of financial reports, budgeting, and financial planning. These services are available to nonprofit agencies and community development corporations on a non-partisan basis in the City of Pittsburgh.

SUMMARY OBSERVATIONS

Though the financial advising function has become a most important and strategic function in government and other not-for-profit organizations, little attention has been given to it in the literature until recent efforts in the Government Finance Officer Association publications. In the past, many governmental units sought financial advice only when they needed to enter the capital markets to borrow funds. However, this situation has started to change for many reasons, among them being the many regulations and the complexity of the financial management problems faced by governmental units and other not-for-profit organizations.

Most states have developed varying ways to respond to the increasing need for financial advice as shown by the governments of Georgia, Maine, Pennsylvania, North Carolina, and Colorado. These efforts cannot, however, meet all the specific financial advising requirements of the governmental units - thus the need for financial advice from corporations, universities, foundations, and associations. As can be seen from the Pittsburgh experience, the corporate community can be a forceful and strategic source of creative financial aid to communities.

NOTES

1. West C. Hough and John E. Petersen, "Selection and Use of Financial Advisory Services," *Governmental Finance*, 13 (March 1984): 42.

2. Ibid.

3. Ibid., p. 45.

4. Girard Miller, *Selecting Financial Services for Government* (Chicago, Ill.: Government Finance Officers Association 1984), p. 9.

5. Ibid.

6. Rhett D. Harrel, "Banking Relations: Part II," in *Cash Management in Small Governments*, ed. Ivan J. Allan (Chicago, Ill.: Government Finance Officers Association, 1989), pp. 83-5.

7. Ibid., pp. 46-47.

8. Miller, *Selecting Financial Services for Government*.

9. Ibid.

10. Edward S. Kiely, "Mobilizing Business Resources for Better Government: Pittsburgh's Learned Executive Experience," *Urban Resources*, 1 (Summer 1983): 8.

11. Mellon Institute and Carnegie-Mellon University, *SPIFF User Manuel* (Pittsburgh, Pa.: Pittsburgh Chamber of Commerce, 1985), p. 1.

12. Ford Foundation and Harvard University, "Innovations in State and Local Government" (pamphlet n.d.).

Appendix 1

Decision Unit: Crime Prevention

DECISION UNIT: Crime Prevention

DECISION PACKAGE: Neighbors Watching out for Neighbors

GOALS: To establish, promote, and maintain voluntary neighborhood organizations which will be alert and report to the police suspicious, unusual activity, unfamiliar or suspicious cars, or suspicious individuals in the neighborhood.

OBJECTIVES: 1. To reduce reported crimes against persons or property by 3% through these organizations.
2. To increase arrest and conviction rates by 7% as a result of these organizations.
3. To encourage 100 percent voluntary neighborhood participation in the program on a block-by-block basis.
4. To encourage participants to notify the police of unusual activity or suspicious persons or cars in their neighborhood.
5. To raise the level of consciousness of residents to be aware of unusual happenings and/or suspicious persons or cars in their neighborhood and to report such to the police.[1]

1981 Service Level Options

	Budget ($15,000)			Positions (2)		
S/L	S/L	Cum	S/L	Cum.	Rank	Dept. Rank
1	$ 7,000	$ 7,000	1	1	4/4	4/13
2	8,000	15,000	1	2	2/4	5/13
3	16,000	31,000	1	3	1/4	7/13
4	$ 5,000	$36,000	1	4	3/4	11/13

SERVICE-LEVEL NARRATIVE

1. This level would provide the minimum level of service necessary to ensure that the goals and objectives of the program would not be jeopardized or lose their effectiveness. At this level, assistance is provided to residents in order to encourage the organization of voluntary neighborhood groups and to

report unusual or suspicious persons, cars, or activities to the police for investigation.

2. This is the current level of service, whereby assistance is provided to residents for the creation of voluntary neighborhood organizations. Police officers involved in the program are also available to speak at civic organization meetings to encourage more participation in the program and to discuss with residents possible ways of improving the program.

3. Since there is no juvenile section in the police department, this enhanced level would create an additional position to work specifically on juvenile matters and with the courts. It would also allow for an "Officer Friendly" program whereby an officer would speak before school children and answer their questions concerning police and law enforcement activities.

4. At this enhanced level the program would be expanded and would focus on training sessions for participants. Specifically, outside consultants would teach residents particular types of behavior to watch out for thereby reducing some unnecessary calls to the police for investigation.

DEMAND

Number of inquiries from residents in the program.
Increased crime rate in the jurisdiction.
Number of requests to speak before civic organizations.
Number of requests from residents to participate in the program.
Number of requests from school officials to help deter juvenile delinquency.
Number of requests from participants for additional training to increase the efficiency of the program.

WORKLOAD

Number of meetings with residents who want to establish voluntary neighborhood organizations.
Number of hours to be spent with residents in establishing these groups.
Number of calls received from participants in this program.
Number of additional neighborhood organizations to be created.
Number of appearances to be scheduled before civic groups.
Number of appearances to be made before school children.
Number of hours to be spent in court appearances.
Number of hours to be spent in informal conversations with children outside of the school environment.

Number of training sessions to be held.
Number of hours to be spent in training sessions.

Efficiency/Productivity

Number of hours worked per volunteer establishing neighborhood organizations.
Number of appearances per volunteer.
Number of training sessions held per volunteer.
Number of hours per voluntary worker in court appearances.
Number of hours per volunteer worker spent in informal conversations with children in the neighborhood.

EFFECTIVENESS

Percentage increase or decrease in requests from residents to participate in the program.
Percentage increase or decrease in suggestions implemented for improving the program.
Percentage increase or decrease in appearances before civic organizations.
Percentage increase or decrease in calls received from participants, responded to, and investigated.
Percentage increase or decrease in overall crime rate.
Percentage of residents expressing a feeling of security from crime.
Percentage increase or decrease in juveniles arrested and successfully adjudicated.
Percentage increase or decrease in speaking before school children.
Decrease in adult and juvenile crime rate.

ALTERNATIVE ANALYSIS

Several alternatives are available. The program could be: (1) entirely eliminated; (2) reduced in size; (3) maintained at its current level; (4) merged with another unit; or (5) increased in staff support personnel. Since there is a need for the program in the community, eliminating it does not seem feasible. Reducing the program is a possibility, since residents would continue to benefit from it on a limited basis. Maintaining it at its current level would provide a much needed service and allow visibility for both the program and the police within the community. Merging the program with another unit in the department would cause the program to lose its effectiveness because the amount of staff time required could no longer be given to this activity. Increasing the staff support personnel would allow for the program to be expanded in scope and provide additional services to the residents.

It would thus appear that the best alternative would be to expand the program to include one additional staff position to deal specifically with juvenile matters. The increase in juvenile crimes and the concern by residents would warrant this new position. Furthermore, the program has been well received by residents and could be enhanced with the hiring of an individual to work specifically with juvenile-related problems.

CONSEQUENCES OF NOT FUNDING

It would be detrimental to residents of the community not to fund at least the minimum level of service. As taxpayers, residents will feel that the police department is not serving or meeting their needs if the program is eliminated. Furthermore, they will feel less secure in their homes and neighborhoods if the program is not funded. In addition, the crime rate will continue to rise if residents are denied the opportunity to participate in this important program.

SUGGESTED: RANKING CRITERIA

Minimal new activities that require additional funding.
Minimal increase in personnel.
No additional special training skills required.
No new cars or major equipment purchases.
Favorable towards any outside funding (federal, state, or other) to help support the program.
Potential consequences if services are not provided.

JUSTIFICATION FOR SELECTING SERVICE LEVEL 3

It is recommended that the decision package be funded at service level 3 for several reasons. Since there is no juvenile section or juvenile officer in the police department to handle juvenile matters, it would be appropriate to include an additional position in this package. The officer would speak frequently to children at school and become better acquainted with them. This would establish rapport among the children, the school, and the community to help alleviate the recent rise in juvenile crimes.

The participants in the voluntary neighborhood program would benefit by knowing that the officer is familiar with where the children live and which ones may have problems that could eventually lead to delinquency. The residents would also feel that their needs are being served because the increase in juvenile crime is serious enough to warrant the hiring of an individual to deal specifically with this problem.

Furthermore, the officer would follow the case from arrest to adjudication for any child who became involved in the juvenile justice system. He or she would also be able to provide insight and input about the child to other police officers, social workers, and/or the court.

NOTE

Adapted from Betty Brooks, "Budgeting as Program and Policy Instrument" (course assignment, University of Pittsburgh, March 8, 1982).

Appendix 2

Present Value Factors and Future Value Factors

PRESENT VALUE FACTORS

Table A.1
Present Value of One Dollar at the End of *n* Years

Year (n)	1%	2%	3%	4%	5%	6%	7%	8%	9%	10%	12%	14%	15%	16%	18%	20%	22%	24%	25%	26%	28%	30%	35%	40%	50%
1	0.990	0.980	0.971	0.962	0.952	0.943	0.935	0.926	0.917	0.909	0.893	0.877	0.870	0.862	0.847	0.833	0.820	0.806	0.800	0.794	0.781	0.769	0.741	0.714	0.667
2	0.980	0.961	0.943	0.925	0.907	0.890	0.873	0.857	0.842	0.826	0.797	0.769	0.756	0.743	0.718	0.694	0.672	0.650	0.640	0.630	0.610	0.592	0.549	0.510	0.444
3	0.971	0.942	0.915	0.889	0.864	0.840	0.816	0.794	0.772	0.751	0.712	0.675	0.658	0.641	0.609	0.579	0.551	0.524	0.512	0.500	0.477	0.455	0.406	0.364	0.296
4	0.961	0.924	0.888	0.855	0.823	0.792	0.763	0.735	0.708	0.683	0.636	0.592	0.572	0.552	0.516	0.482	0.451	0.423	0.410	0.397	0.373	0.350	0.301	0.260	0.198
5	0.951	0.906	0.863	0.822	0.784	0.747	0.713	0.681	0.650	0.621	0.567	0.519	0.497	0.476	0.437	0.402	0.370	0.341	0.328	0.315	0.291	0.269	0.223	0.186	0.132
6	0.942	0.888	0.837	0.790	0.746	0.705	0.666	0.630	0.596	0.564	0.507	0.456	0.432	0.410	0.370	0.335	0.303	0.275	0.262	0.250	0.227	0.207	0.165	0.133	0.088
7	0.933	0.871	0.813	0.760	0.711	0.665	0.623	0.583	0.547	0.513	0.452	0.400	0.376	0.354	0.314	0.279	0.249	0.222	0.210	0.198	0.178	0.159	0.122	0.095	0.059
8	0.923	0.853	0.789	0.731	0.677	0.627	0.582	0.540	0.502	0.467	0.404	0.351	0.327	0.305	0.266	0.233	0.204	0.179	0.168	0.157	0.139	0.123	0.091	0.068	0.039
9	0.914	0.837	0.766	0.703	0.645	0.592	0.544	0.500	0.460	0.424	0.361	0.308	0.284	0.263	0.225	0.194	0.167	0.144	0.134	0.125	0.108	0.094	0.067	0.048	0.026
10	0.905	0.820	0.744	0.676	0.614	0.558	0.508	0.463	0.422	0.386	0.322	0.270	0.247	0.227	0.191	0.162	0.137	0.116	0.107	0.099	0.085	0.073	0.050	0.035	0.017
11	0.896	0.804	0.722	0.650	0.585	0.527	0.475	0.429	0.388	0.350	0.287	0.237	0.215	0.195	0.162	0.135	0.112	0.094	0.086	0.079	0.066	0.056	0.037	0.025	0.012
12	0.887	0.788	0.701	0.625	0.557	0.497	0.444	0.397	0.356	0.319	0.257	0.208	0.187	0.168	0.137	0.112	0.092	0.076	0.069	0.062	0.052	0.043	0.027	0.018	0.008
13	0.879	0.773	0.681	0.601	0.530	0.469	0.415	0.368	0.326	0.290	0.229	0.182	0.163	0.145	0.116	0.093	0.075	0.061	0.055	0.050	0.040	0.033	0.020	0.013	0.005
14	0.870	0.758	0.661	0.577	0.505	0.442	0.388	0.340	0.299	0.263	0.205	0.160	0.141	0.125	0.099	0.078	0.062	0.049	0.044	0.039	0.032	0.025	0.015	0.009	0.003
15	0.861	0.743	0.642	0.555	0.481	0.417	0.362	0.315	0.275	0.239	0.183	0.140	0.123	0.108	0.084	0.065	0.051	0.040	0.035	0.031	0.025	0.020	0.011	0.006	0.002
16	0.853	0.728	0.623	0.534	0.458	0.394	0.339	0.292	0.252	0.218	0.163	0.123	0.107	0.093	0.071	0.054	0.042	0.032	0.028	0.025	0.019	0.015	0.008	0.005	0.002
17	0.844	0.714	0.605	0.513	0.436	0.371	0.317	0.270	0.231	0.198	0.146	0.108	0.093	0.080	0.060	0.045	0.034	0.026	0.023	0.020	0.015	0.012	0.006	0.003	0.001
18	0.836	0.700	0.587	0.494	0.416	0.350	0.296	0.250	0.212	0.180	0.130	0.095	0.081	0.069	0.051	0.038	0.028	0.021	0.018	0.016	0.012	0.009	0.005	0.002	0.001
19	0.828	0.686	0.570	0.475	0.396	0.331	0.277	0.232	0.194	0.164	0.116	0.083	0.070	0.060	0.043	0.031	0.023	0.017	0.014	0.012	0.009	0.007	0.003	0.002	
20	0.820	0.673	0.554	0.456	0.377	0.312	0.258	0.215	0.178	0.149	0.104	0.073	0.061	0.051	0.037	0.026	0.019	0.014	0.012	0.010	0.007	0.005	0.002	0.001	
21	0.811	0.660	0.538	0.439	0.359	0.294	0.242	0.199	0.164	0.135	0.093	0.064	0.053	0.044	0.031	0.022	0.015	0.011	0.009	0.008	0.006	0.004	0.002	0.001	
22	0.803	0.647	0.522	0.422	0.342	0.278	0.226	0.184	0.150	0.123	0.083	0.056	0.046	0.038	0.026	0.018	0.013	0.009	0.007	0.006	0.004	0.003	0.001	0.001	
23	0.795	0.634	0.507	0.406	0.326	0.262	0.211	0.170	0.138	0.112	0.074	0.049	0.040	0.033	0.022	0.015	0.010	0.007	0.006	0.005	0.003	0.002	0.001		
24	0.788	0.622	0.492	0.390	0.310	0.247	0.197	0.158	0.126	0.102	0.066	0.043	0.035	0.028	0.019	0.013	0.008	0.006	0.005	0.004	0.003	0.002	0.001		
25	0.780	0.610	0.478	0.375	0.295	0.233	0.184	0.146	0.116	0.092	0.059	0.038	0.030	0.024	0.016	0.010	0.007	0.005	0.004	0.003	0.002	0.001	0.001		

Table A.2
Present Value of One Dollar Per Year for *n* Years

Year (n)	1%	2%	3%	4%	5%	6%	7%	8%	9%	10%	12%	14%	15%	16%	18%	20%	22%	24%	25%	26%	28%	30%	35%	40%	50%
1	0.990	0.980	0.971	0.962	0.952	0.943	0.935	0.926	0.917	0.909	0.893	0.877	0.870	0.862	0.847	0.833	0.820	0.806	0.800	0.794	0.781	0.769	0.741	0.714	0.667
2	1.970	1.942	1.913	1.886	1.859	1.833	1.808	1.783	1.759	1.736	1.690	1.647	1.626	1.605	1.566	1.528	1.492	1.457	1.440	1.424	1.392	1.361	1.289	1.224	1.111
3	2.941	2.884	2.829	2.775	2.723	2.673	2.624	2.577	2.531	2.487	2.402	2.322	2.283	2.246	2.174	2.106	2.042	1.981	1.952	1.923	1.868	1.816	1.696	1.589	1.407
4	3.902	3.808	3.717	3.630	3.546	3.465	3.387	3.312	3.240	3.170	3.037	2.914	2.855	2.798	2.690	2.589	2.494	2.404	2.362	2.320	2.241	2.166	1.997	1.849	1.605
5	4.853	4.713	4.580	4.452	4.329	4.212	4.100	3.993	3.890	3.791	3.605	3.433	3.352	3.274	3.127	2.991	2.864	2.745	2.689	2.635	2.532	2.436	2.220	2.035	1.737
6	5.795	5.601	5.417	5.242	5.076	4.917	4.767	4.623	4.486	4.355	4.111	3.889	3.784	3.685	3.498	3.326	3.167	3.020	2.951	2.885	2.759	2.643	2.385	2.168	1.824
7	6.728	6.472	6.230	6.002	5.786	5.582	5.389	5.206	5.033	4.868	4.564	4.288	4.160	4.039	3.812	3.605	3.416	3.242	3.161	3.083	2.937	2.802	2.508	2.263	1.883
8	7.652	7.325	7.020	6.733	6.463	6.210	5.971	5.747	5.535	5.335	4.968	4.639	4.487	4.344	4.078	3.837	3.619	3.421	3.329	3.241	3.076	2.925	2.598	2.331	1.922
9	8.566	8.162	7.786	7.435	7.108	6.802	6.515	6.247	5.995	5.759	5.328	4.946	4.772	4.607	4.303	4.031	3.786	3.566	3.463	3.366	3.184	3.019	2.665	2.379	1.948
10	9.471	8.983	8.530	8.111	7.722	7.360	7.024	6.710	6.418	6.145	5.650	5.216	5.019	4.833	4.494	4.192	3.923	3.682	3.571	3.465	3.269	3.092	2.715	2.414	1.965
11	10.368	9.787	9.253	8.760	8.306	7.887	7.499	7.139	6.805	6.495	5.938	5.453	5.234	5.029	4.656	4.327	4.035	3.776	3.656	3.543	3.335	3.147	2.752	2.438	1.977
12	11.255	10.575	9.954	9.385	8.863	8.384	7.943	7.536	7.161	6.814	6.194	5.660	5.421	5.197	4.793	4.439	4.127	3.851	3.725	3.606	3.387	3.190	2.779	2.456	1.985
13	12.134	11.348	10.635	9.986	9.394	8.853	8.358	7.904	7.487	7.103	6.424	5.842	5.583	5.342	4.910	4.533	4.203	3.912	3.780	3.656	3.427	3.223	2.799	2.469	1.990
14	13.004	12.106	11.296	10.563	9.899	9.295	8.745	8.244	7.786	7.367	6.628	6.002	5.724	5.468	5.008	4.611	4.265	3.962	3.824	3.695	3.459	3.249	2.814	2.478	1.993
15	13.865	12.849	11.938	11.118	10.380	9.712	9.108	8.559	8.061	7.606	6.811	6.142	5.847	5.575	5.092	4.675	4.315	4.001	3.859	3.726	3.483	3.268	2.825	2.484	1.995
16	14.718	13.578	12.561	11.652	10.838	10.106	9.447	8.851	8.313	7.824	6.974	6.265	5.954	5.668	5.162	4.730	4.357	4.033	3.887	3.751	3.503	3.283	2.834	2.489	1.997
17	15.562	14.292	13.166	12.166	11.274	10.477	9.763	9.122	8.544	8.022	7.120	6.373	6.047	5.749	5.222	4.775	4.391	4.059	3.910	3.771	3.518	3.295	2.840	2.492	1.998
18	16.398	14.992	13.754	12.659	11.690	10.828	10.059	9.372	8.756	8.201	7.250	6.467	6.128	5.818	5.273	4.812	4.419	4.080	3.928	3.786	3.529	3.304	2.844	2.494	1.999
19	17.226	15.678	14.324	13.134	12.085	11.158	10.336	9.604	8.950	8.365	7.366	6.550	6.198	5.877	5.316	4.843	4.442	4.097	3.942	3.799	3.539	3.311	2.848	2.496	1.999
20	18.046	16.351	14.877	13.590	12.462	11.470	10.594	9.818	9.129	8.514	7.469	6.623	6.259	5.929	5.353	4.870	4.460	4.110	3.954	3.808	3.546	3.316	2.850	2.497	1.999
21	18.857	17.011	15.415	14.029	12.821	11.764	10.836	10.017	9.292	8.649	7.562	6.687	6.312	5.973	5.384	4.891	4.476	4.121	3.963	3.816	3.551	3.320	2.852	2.498	2.000
22	19.660	17.658	15.937	14.451	13.163	12.042	11.061	10.201	9.442	8.772	7.645	6.743	6.359	6.011	5.410	4.909	4.488	4.130	3.970	3.822	3.556	3.323	2.853	2.498	2.000
23	20.456	18.292	16.444	14.857	13.489	12.303	11.272	10.371	9.580	8.883	7.718	6.792	6.399	6.044	5.432	4.925	4.499	4.137	3.976	3.827	3.559	3.325	2.854	2.498	2.000
24	21.243	18.914	16.936	15.247	13.799	12.550	11.469	10.529	9.707	8.985	7.784	6.835	6.434	6.073	5.451	4.937	4.507	4.143	3.981	3.831	3.562	3.327	2.855	2.499	2.000
25	22.023	19.523	17.413	15.622	14.094	12.783	11.654	10.675	9.823	9.077	7.843	6.873	6.464	6.097	5.467	4.948	4.514	4.147	3.985	3.834	3.564	3.329	2.856	2.499	2.000

FUTURE VALUE FACTORS

Table A.3
Future Value of One Dollar at the End of *n* Years

Periods	0.5%	1.0%	1.5%	2.0%	3.0%	4.0%	5.0%	6.0%	7.0%	8.0%	9.0%	10.0%	12.0%	14.0%	16.0%	18.0%	20.0%
1	1.005	1.010	1.015	1.020	1.030	1.040	1.050	1.060	1.070	1.080	1.090	1.100	1.120	1.140	1.160	1.180	1.200
2	1.010	1.020	1.030	1.040	1.061	1.082	1.103	1.125	1.145	1.166	1.188	1.210	1.254	1.300	1.346	1.392	1.440
3	1.015	1.030	1.046	1.061	1.093	1.125	1.158	1.191	1.225	1.260	1.295	1.331	1.405	1.482	1.561	1.643	1.728
4	1.020	1.041	1.061	1.082	1.126	1.170	1.216	1.262	1.311	1.360	1.412	1.464	1.574	1.689	1.811	1.939	2.074
5	1.025	1.051	1.077	1.104	1.159	1.217	1.276	1.338	1.403	1.469	1.539	1.611	1.762	1.925	2.100	2.288	2.488
6	1.030	1.062	1.093	1.126	1.194	1.265	1.340	1.419	1.501	1.587	1.677	1.772	1.974	2.195	2.436	2.700	2.986
7	1.036	1.072	1.110	1.149	1.230	1.316	1.407	1.504	1.606	1.714	1.828	1.949	2.211	2.502	2.826	3.185	3.583
8	1.041	1.083	1.126	1.172	1.267	1.369	1.477	1.594	1.718	1.851	1.993	2.144	2.476	2.853	3.278	3.759	4.300
9	1.046	1.094	1.143	1.195	1.305	1.423	1.551	1.689	1.838	1.999	2.172	2.358	2.773	3.252	3.803	4.435	5.160
10	1.051	1.105	1.161	1.219	1.344	1.480	1.629	1.791	1.967	2.159	2.367	2.594	3.106	3.707	4.411	5.234	6.192
11	1.056	1.116	1.178	1.243	1.384	1.539	1.710	1.898	2.105	2.332	2.580	2.853	3.479	4.226	5.117	6.176	7.430
12	1.062	1.127	1.196	1.268	1.426	1.601	1.796	2.012	2.252	2.512	2.813	3.138	3.896	4.818	5.936	7.288	8.916
13	1.067	1.138	1.214	1.294	1.469	1.665	1.886	2.133	2.410	2.720	3.066	3.452	4.363	5.492	6.886	8.599	10.699
14	1.072	1.149	1.232	1.319	1.513	1.732	1.980	2.261	2.579	2.937	3.342	3.797	4.887	6.261	7.988	10.147	12.839
15	1.078	1.161	1.250	1.346	1.558	1.801	2.079	2.397	2.759	3.172	3.642	4.177	5.474	7.138	9.266	11.974	15.407
16	1.083	1.173	1.269	1.373	1.605	1.873	2.183	2.540	2.952	3.426	3.970	4.595	6.130	8.137	10.748	14.129	18.488
18	1.094	1.196	1.307	1.428	1.702	2.026	2.407	2.854	3.380	3.996	4.717	5.560	7.690	10.575	14.463	19.673	26.623
20	1.105	1.220	1.347	1.486	1.806	2.191	2.653	3.207	3.870	4.661	5.604	6.727	9.646	13.743	19.461	27.393	38.338
22	1.116	1.245	1.388	1.546	1.916	2.370	2.925	3.604	4.430	5.437	6.659	8.140	12.100	17.861	26.186	38.142	55.206
24	1.127	1.270	1.430	1.608	2.033	2.563	3.225	4.049	5.072	6.341	7.911	9.850	15.179	23.212	35.236	53.109	79.497
26	1.138	1.295	1.473	1.673	2.157	2.772	3.556	4.549	5.807	7.396	9.399	11.918	19.040	30.167	47.414	73.949	114.475
28	1.145	1.321	1.517	1.741	2.288	2.999	3.920	5.112	6.649	8.627	11.167	14.421	23.884	39.204	63.800	102.967	164.845
30	1.161	1.348	1.563	1.811	2.427	3.243	4.322	5.743	7.612	10.063	13.268	17.449	29.960	50.950	85.850	143.371	237.376
32	1.173	1.375	1.610	1.885	2.575	3.508	4.760	6.453	8.715	11.737	15.763	21.114	37.582	66.215	115.520	199.629	341.822
34	1.185	1.403	1.659	1.961	2.732	3.794	5.253	7.251	9.978	13.690	18.728	25.548	47.143	86.053	155.443	277.964	492.224
36	1.197	1.431	1.709	2.040	2.898	4.104	5.792	8.147	11.242	15.968	22.251	30.913	59.136	11.834	209.164	387.037	708.802
40	1.221	1.488	1.814	2.208	3.262	4.801	7.040	10.286	14.974	21.725	31.409	45.259	93.051	188.884	378.721	750.378	1463.722
44	1.245	1.549	1.925	2.390	3.671	5.617	8.557	12.985	19.628	29.556	44.337	66.264	146.418	319.017	685.727	1454.817	3047.718
48	1.270	1.621	2.043	2.587	4.132	6.571	10.401	16.394	25.729	40.211	62.585	97.017	230.391	538.807	1241.605	2820.567	6319.749

Table A.4
Future Value of One Dollar Per Year for *n* Years

Periods	0.5%	1.0%	1.5%	2.0%	3.0%	4.0%	5.0%	6.0%	7.0%	8.0%	9.0%	10.0%	12.0%	14.0%	16.0%	18.0%	20.0%
1	1.000	1.000	1.000	1.000	1.000	1.000	1.000	1.000	1.000	1.000	1.000	1.000	1.000	1.000	1.000	1.000	1.000
2	2.005	2.010	2.015	2.020	2.030	2.040	2.050	2.060	2.070	2.080	2.090	2.100	2.120	2.140	2.160	2.180	2.200
3	3.015	3.030	3.045	3.060	3.091	3.122	3.152	3.184	3.215	3.246	3.278	3.310	3.374	3.440	3.506	3.572	3.640
4	4.030	4.060	4.091	4.122	4.184	4.246	4.310	4.375	4.440	4.506	4.573	4.641	4.779	4.921	5.066	5.215	5.368
5	5.050	5.101	5.152	5.204	5.309	5.416	5.526	5.637	5.751	5.867	5.985	6.105	6.353	6.610	6.877	7.154	7.442
6	6.076	6.152	6.230	6.308	6.468	6.633	6.802	6.975	7.153	7.336	7.523	7.716	8.115	8.536	8.977	9.442	9.930
7	7.106	7.214	7.323	7.434	7.662	7.898	8.142	8.394	8.654	8.923	9.200	9.487	10.089	10.730	11.414	12.142	12.916
8	8.141	8.286	8.433	8.583	8.892	9.214	9.549	9.897	10.260	10.637	11.028	11.436	12.300	13.233	14.240	15.327	16.499
9	9.182	9.369	9.559	9.755	10.159	10.583	11.027	11.491	11.978	12.488	13.021	13.579	14.776	16.085	17.519	19.086	20.799
10	10.228	10.462	10.703	10.950	11.464	12.006	12.578	13.181	13.816	14.487	15.193	15.937	17.549	19.337	21.321	23.521	25.959
11	11.279	11.567	11.863	12.169	12.808	13.486	14.207	14.972	15.784	16.645	17.560	18.531	20.655	23.045	25.733	28.755	32.150
12	12.336	12.683	13.041	13.412	14.192	15.026	15.917	16.870	17.888	18.977	20.141	21.384	24.133	27.271	30.850	34.931	39.581
13	13.397	13.809	14.237	14.680	15.618	16.627	17.713	18.882	20.141	21.495	22.953	24.523	28.029	32.089	36.786	42.219	48.497
14	14.464	14.947	15.450	15.974	17.086	18.292	19.599	21.015	22.550	24.215	26.019	27.975	32.393	37.581	43.672	50.818	59.196
15	15.537	16.097	16.682	17.293	18.599	20.024	21.579	23.276	25.129	27.152	29.361	31.772	37.280	43.842	51.660	60.965	72.035
16	16.614	17.258	17.932	18.639	20.157	21.825	23.657	25.673	27.888	30.324	33.003	35.950	42.753	50.980	60.925	72.939	87.442
18	18.786	19.615	20.489	21.412	23.414	25.645	28.132	30.906	33.999	37.450	41.301	45.599	55.750	68.394	84.141	103.740	128.117
20	20.979	22.019	23.124	24.297	26.870	29.778	33.066	36.786	40.995	45.762	51.160	57.275	72.052	91.025	115.380	146.628	186.688
22	23.194	24.472	25.838	27.299	30.537	34.248	38.505	43.392	49.006	55.457	62.873	71.403	92.503	120.436	157.415	206.345	271.031
24	25.432	26.973	28.634	30.422	34.426	39.083	44.502	50.816	58.177	66.765	76.790	88.497	118.155	158.659	213.978	289.494	392.484
26	27.692	29.526	31.514	33.671	38.553	44.312	51.113	59.156	68.676	79.954	93.324	109.182	150.334	208.333	290.088	405.272	567.377
28	29.975	32.129	34.481	37.051	42.931	49.968	58.403	68.528	80.698	95.339	112.968	134.210	190.699	272.889	392.503	566.481	819.223
30	32.280	34.785	37.539	40.568	47.575	56.085	66.439	79.058	94.461	113.283	136.308	164.494	241.333	356.787	530.312	790.948	1181.882
32	34.609	37.494	40.688	44.227	52.503	62.701	75.299	90.890	110.218	134.214	164.037	201.138	304.848	465.820	715.747	1103.496	1704.109
34	36.961	40.258	43.933	48.034	57.730	69.858	85.067	104.184	128.259	158.627	196.982	245.477	384.521	607.520	965.270	1538.688	2456.118
36	39.336	43.077	47.276	51.994	63.276	77.598	95.836	119.121	148.913	187.102	236.125	299.127	484.463	791.673	1301.027	2144.649	3539.009
40	44.159	48.886	54.268	60.402	75.401	95.026	120.800	154.762	199.635	259.057	337.882	442.593	767.091	1342.025	2360.757	4163.213	7343.858
44	49.079	54.932	61.689	69.503	89.048	115.413	151.143	199.758	266.121	356.950	481.522	652.641	1211.813	2271.548	4279.546	8076.760	15233.592
48	54.098	61.223	69.565	79.354	104.408	139.263	188.025	256.565	353.270	490.132	684.280	960.172	1911.590	3841.475	7753.782	15664.259	31593.744

Selected Bibliography

Albrecht, W. Steve. "Fraud in Government Entities: The Perpetrators and the Type of Fraud." *Government Finance Review*, 7, no. 6 (December 1991): 27-32.

Albrecht, Steven W., Marshall J. Romney, David S. Cherrington, I Reed Payne, and Allan J. Roe. *How to Detect and Prevent Business Fraud*. Englewood Cliffs, N.J.: Prentice-Hall, 1982.

Albrecht, W. Steve, Keith Howe, Kevin Stock, and Dennis Schuler. *Evaluating the Effectiveness of Internal Control*. Department of Altamonte Springs; Fl.: Institute of Internal Auditors, 1988.

Allan, Ian J., ed. *Cash Management for Small Governments*. Chicago, Ill.: Government Finance Officers Association, 1989.

Allcorn, Seth. *Internal Auditing for Hospitals*. Germantown, Md.: Aspen Systems Corporation, 1979.

American Public Works Association. *Revenue Shortfall*. Chicago, Ill.: American Public Works Association, 1981.

Anthony, Robert N., and David W. Young. *Management Control in Nonprofit Organizations*. Homewood, Ill.: Richard D. Irwin, 1984.

Anton, Thomas. *The Politics of State Expenditures in Illinois*. Champaign, Ill.: University of Illinois Press, 1966.

Bahl, Roy. "Estimating Equity and Budgeting Effects of Financial Assumptions." *National Tax Journal*, 29 (March 1976): 54-72.

———. *Financing State and Local Government in the 1980s*. New York: Oxford University Press, 1984.

Biggs, Charles L., Evan G. Birks, and William Atkins. *Managing the System Development Process*. Englewood Cliffs, N.J.: Prentice-Hall, 1980.

Bland, Robert L. *A Revenue Guide for Local Government*. Washington, D.C.: International City Management Association, 1989.

Boskin, Michael J., and Aaron Wildavsky, eds. *The Federal Budget: Economics and Politics*. New Brunswick, N.J.: Transaction Books, 1982.

Brinkerhoff, Roberto, and Dennis Dressler. *Productivity Measurement: A Guide for Managers*. Newbury Park, Calif.: Sage Publications, 1990.

Brown, Richard E., Thomas Gallagher, and Meredith C. Williams. *Auditing Performance in Government: Concepts and Cases*. New York: Wiley, 1982.

Canada. Ontario. Ministry of Intergovernmental Affairs. *Managing Purchasing*. Toronto: Ontario Government Book Store, 1981.

Carr, David K., and Ian Litterman. *Excellence in Government: Total Quality Management in the 1990s*. 2nd ed. Arlington, Va.: Coopers and Lybrand, 1993.

Clark, Terry Nichols, G. Edward DeSeve, and J. Chester Johnson. *Financial Handbook for Mayors and City Managers*. New York: Van Nostrand Reinhold Co., 1985.

Clark, Terry Nichols, and Lorna Crowley Ferguson. *City Money*. New York: Columbia University Press, 1983.

Clynn, John J. *Value for Money Auditing in the Public Sector*. Englewood Cliffs, N.J.: Prentice-Hall, 1985.

Coe, Charles K. *Understanding Risk Management*. Athens, Ga.: Institute of Local Government, 1980.

Connors, Tracy D., and Christopher T. Callaghan, eds. *Financial Management in Non-Profit Organizations*. New York: American Management Association, 1982.

Council of State Governments. *State and Local Government Purchasing*. 3rd ed. Lexington, Ky.: Council of State Governments, 1988.

Cramer, Robert M. "Local Government Expenditure Forecasting." *Governmental Finance*, 7, no. 4 (November 1978): 4.

Dotsey, Michael. "An Investigation of Cash Management Practices and Their Effects on the Demand for Money." *Economic Review*, 70, no. 5 (September/October 1984): 3.

Douglas, Patricia. *Government and Non-Profit Accounting: Theory and Practice*. San Diego, Calif.: Harcourt Brace Jovanovich, 1991.

Drebin, Allan R. "Criteria for Performance Measurement in State and Local Government." *Governmental Finance* 10 (December 1980): 4.

Drebin, Allan R., James L. Chan, and Lorna Ferguson. *Objectives of Accounting and Financial Reporting for Governmental Units: A Research Study*. Vol. 1. Chicago, Ill.: National Council on Governmental Accounting, 1981.

Garner, C. William. *Accounting and Budgeting in Public and Non-Profit Organizations*. San Francisco, Calif.: Jossey-Bass Publishers, 1991.

Gore, Al. *Creating a Government That Works Better and Costs Less*. Washington, D.C.: U.S. Government Printing Office, 1993.

Green, Mark, and John F. Berry. *The Challenge of Hidden Profits*. New York: William Morrow, 1985.

Hall, John R. *Factors Related to Local Government Use of Performance Measurement*. Washington, D.C.: Urban Institute, April 1978.

Hall, Robert W. *Attaining Manufacturing Excellence*. Homewood, Ill.: Dow Jones-Irwin, 1987.

Haller, Leon, *Financial Resource Management for Non-Profit Organizations*. Englewood Cliffs, N.J.: Prentice-Hall, 1982.

Harper, Charles, Curtis P. McLaughlin, and John W. Bartley. *Financial Systems for Community Health Organizations*. Belmont, Calif.: Life Learning Publications, 1981.

Harrell, Rhett D. *Developing a Financial Management Information System for Local Government: The Key Issues*. Washington, D.C.: Government Finance Research, Municipal Finance Officers Association, 1980.

Hatry, Harry P., and John F. Cotton. *Program Planning for Country and City*. Washington, D.C.: George Washington University, January 1967.

Hayes, Frederick O'R., David A. Grossman, Jerry E. Mechiling, John S. Thomas, and Steven S. Rosenbloom. *Linkages: Improving Financial Management in Local Government*. Washington, D.C.: Urban Institute Press, 1982.

Herbert, Leo, Larry N. Killough, and Alan Walter Steiss. *Governmental Accounting and Control*. Monterey, Calif.: Brooks/Cole Publishing, 1984.

Herzlinger, Regina E. and Denese Nitterhouse. *Financial Accounting and Managerial Control for Non-Profit Organizations*. Cincinnati, Ohio: South-Western Publishing, 1994.

Hickam, Dale, Robert Berne, and Leanna Stiefel. "Taxing over Debt Limits." *Public Administration Review*, 41 (July/August 1981): 445-53.

Hough, West C., and John E. Petersen. "Selection and Use of Financial Advisory Services." *Governmental Finance*, 13 (March 1984): 42.

Housley, Charles E., ed. *Hospital Purchasing*. Rockville, Md.: Aspen Systems Corporation, 1983.

Huber, Peter W. and Robert E. Litan, eds. *The Liability Maze*. Washington, D.C.: Brookings Institution, 1991.

Humphrey, Nancy, George Peterson, and Peter Wilson. *The Future of Cincinnati's Capital Plant*. Washington, D.C.: Urban Institute Press, 1979.

Institute for Local Self-Government. *Public Agency Liability: The Law and the Risks; Management, Avoidance and Transfer.* Berkeley, Calif.: Institute for Local Government, 1978.

International City Management Association (ICMA). "Planning for Capital Improvements." *Management Information Service Report*, 16, no. 18 (August 1984): 5-8.

Jamison, Conny M. "Collecting Deliquent Revenues: No Stone Unturned in the City of San Diego." *Governmental Finance Review*, 7, no. 1 (February 1991): 25-32.

Kamensky, John M. "Budgeting for State and Local Infrastructure: Developing a Strategy." *Public Budgeting and Finance*, 4, no. 3 (Autumn 1984): 3-17.

Kane, Thomas J., Jr. "Budget Directors View Budget Control." *Public Budgeting and Finance,* 2, no. 2 (Summer 1982): 44-47.

Kelman, Steven. "The Grace Commission: How Much Waste in Government?" *Public Interest*, Winter 1985, pp. 62-82.

Kettinger, William J. *Information Resource Management and the Use of Information in Local Government: A Policy Guide.* Columbia: University of South Carolina Press, 1980.

Knezevich, Stephen. *Program Budgeting (PPBS): A Resource Allocation Decision System for Education.* Berkeley, Calif.: McCutchan Publishing, 1973.

Knight, Henry C. *Zero-Based Budgeting Process: A Practical Guide to Evaluation, Implementation and Use.* Hamilton, Ontario: Society of Management Accounts of Canada, 1979.

Knighton, Lennis M. "Four Keys of Effectiveness Auditing." *Governmental Finance*, 8, no. 2 (September 1979): pp. 3-12.

Lange, Andrea G., and Robert Bowers. *Fraud and Abuse in Government Benefit Programs.* Washington, D.C.: U.S. Department of Justice, Law Enforcement Assistance Administration, 1979.

Levine, Charles H., ed. *Managing Fiscal Stress.* Chatham, N.J.: Chatham House Publishers, 1981.

Levine, Charles H., Irene S. Rubin, and George Wolohojian. *The Politics of Retrenchment: How Local Governemnts Manage Fiscal Stress.* Beverly Hills, Calif.: Sage Publications, 1981.

Light, Paul C. *Monitoring Government: Inspectors General and the Search for Accountability.* Washington, D.C.: Brookings Institution, 1993.

Liner, Charles D. "Projecting Local Government Revenues." *Popular Government*, 43 (Spring 1978): 33-37.

Lipset, Martin, and William Schneider. *The Confidence Gap: Business, Labor and Government in the Public Mind.* New York: Free Press, 1985.

Litechy, Charles R., and Earl R. Wilson. "Systems Development for Small Governments." *Governmental Finance*, 10, no. 3 (September 1981): 11-18.

Luksus, Edward J. "Strategic Budgeting: How to Turn Financial Records into Strategic Assets." *Management Review*, 70 (March 1981): 44-47.

McCabe, Raymond L. "Electronic Funds Transfer as a Cash Management Tool." *Governmental Finance*, 10, no. 4 (December 1981): 9-14.

McKinney, Jerome B. *Understanding ZBB: Promise and Reality*. Chicago, Ill.: Public Policy Press, 1979.

McKinney, Jerome B., and Lawrence C. Howard. *Public Administration: Balancing Power and Accountability*. Oak Park, Ill.: Moore Publishing, 1979.

MacSherry, Cathy Daicuff. "Infrastructure and S & P Credit Rating." *Public Budgeting and Finance*, 4, no. 3 (Autumn 1984): 41-45.

Matzer, John, Jr., ed. *Practical Financial Management*. Washington, D.C.: International City Management Assocation, 1984.

Mendonsa, Arthur. *Financial Management in Local Government*. Athens: Institute of Local Government, University of Georgia, 1969.

Mikesell, John L. *Fiscal Administration*. Homewood, Ill.: Dorsey Press, 1982.

Miller, Girard. *Selecting Financial Services for Government*. Chicago, Ill.: Government Finance Officers Association, 1984.

Moak, Lennox L., and Albert M. Hillhouse. *Local Government Finance*. Chicago, Ill.: Municipal Finance Officers Association, 1975.

Moak, Lennox L., and Kathryn W. Killian. *A Manual of Techniques for the Preparation, Consideration, Adoption, and Administration of Operating Budgets*. Chicago, Ill.: Municipal Finance Officers Association, 1963.

Mundt, Barry M., Raymond T. Olsen, and Harold Steinberg. *Managing Public Resources*. Stamford, Conn.: Peat Marwick International, 1982.

Municipal Finance Officers Association, *Governmental Accounting, Auditing and Financial Reporting*. Chicago, Ill.: Municipal Finance Officers Association, 1980.

National Committee on Governmental Accounting (NCGA). *Statement #1, Governmental Accounting and Financial Reporting Principles*. Chicago: NCGA, 1979.

Neuber, Keith A., et al. *Needs Assessment: A Model for Community Planning*. Beverly Hills, Calif.: Sage Publications, 1975.

Newton, Ken. *Balancing the Books*. Beverly Hills, Calif.: Sage Publications, 1980.

Omachonu, Vincent K. *Total Quality and Productivity Management in Health Care Organizations*. Norcross, Ga.: Industrial Engineering and Management Press, 1991.

Patitucci, Frank M., and Michael H. Lichtenstein. *Improving Cash Management in Local Government: A Comprehensive Approach.* Chicago, Ill.: Municipal Finance Officers Association, 1977.

Peger, Hal, and Gerald Lonergner. "Popular Financial Reporting in the Public Sector(?)" *Governmental Finance,* 5, no. 2 (May 1976): 33-38.

Peterson, Johne, and Pat Ulatt, eds. *The Price of Advice.* Chicago, Ill.: Government Finance Officers Association, 1986.

Premchand, A., ed. *Government Financial Management: Issues and Country Studies.* Washington, D.C.: International Monetary Fund, 1991.

Public Securities Association. *Fundamentals of Municipal Bonds.* Rev. ed. New York: Public Securities Association, 1982.

Rivlin, Alice M. "Budgeting for Performance." *Intergovernmental Perspective,* 20, no. 1 (Fall 1993-Winter 1994): 11-15.

Rosenberg, Philip, and C. Wayne Stallings. *An Operating Handbook for Small Cities and Other Government Units.* Chicago, Ill.: Municipal Finance Officers Association, 1978.

Rubin, Irene S. *Running in the Red State.* Albany: State University of New York Press, 1982.

_____. *The Politics of Public Budgeting.* Chatham, N.J.: Chatham House Publishers, 1990.

Schick, Allen. *Budget Innovations in the States.* Washington, D.C.: Brookings Institution, 1971.

Sherman, Phyllis. *Basic Risk Management Handbook for Local Government.* Darien, Conn.: Public Risk Management Association, 1983.

Sneider, Richard M. *Management Guide to Health Care Information Systems.* Rockville, Md.: Aspen Systems, 1987.

Solomon, Ezra, and John J. Pringle. *An Introduction to Financial Management.* 2nd ed. Santa Monica, Calif.: Good Year Publishing Co., 1980.

Steiss, Alan Walter. *Local Government Finance.* Lexington, Mass.: Lexington Books, 1975.

_____. *Management Control in Government.* Lexington, Mass.: Lexington Books, 1982.

Tenner, Arthur R., and Irving J. Detoro. *Total Quality Management.* Reading, Mass.: Addison-Wesley, 1992.

United States. Comptroller General. *Standards for Audit of Governmental Organizations.* Washington, D.C.: U.S. General Accounting Organization, 1981.

United States. General Accounting Office (GAO). *Study of Selected Local Procurement Systems Part I.* Washington, D.C.: GAO, 1978.

_____. *Federal Capital Budgeting: A Collection of Haphazard Practices.* Washington, D.C.: U.S. GAO, 1981.

_____. *Framework for Assessing Job Vulnerability to Ethical*

Problems. Washington, D.C.: U.S. GAO, 1981.

_____. *The Cost of Government*. Vol. 1. Washington, D.C.: U.S. GAO, 1985.

_____. *Program Performance Measures*. Washington, D.C.: U.S. GAO, 1992.

_____. *Government Auditing Standards*. Exposure draft. Washington, D.C.: U.S. GAO, 1993.

United States Government Accounting Service Board (GSAB), *Service Efforts and Accomplishments Reporting*. (Draft). September 15, 1993.

United Way. *A "PPBS" Approach to Budgeting Human Service Programs for United Ways*. Alexandria, Va.: United Way of America, 1974.

_____. *Budgeting: A Guide for United Way and Not-for-Profit Service Organizations*. Alexandria, Va.: United Way of America, 1975.

Vinter, Robert D., and Rhea K. Kish. *Budgeting for Not-for-Profit Organizations*. New York: Free Press, 1984.

Wacht, Richard F. *Financial Management in Non-profit Organizations*. 2nd ed. Atlanta: Georgia State University Press, 1991.

Wantuck, Kenneth A. *Just-in-Time for America*. Milwaukee, Wisc.: Forum Ltd., 1989.

Wasserman, Natalie, and Dean G. Phelus, eds. *Risk Management Today*. Washington, D.C.: International City Management Association, 1985.

Weisenbach, Paul E. "Vulnerability Assessment and Internal Controls." *Government Accountants Journal*, 33, no. 1 (Spring 1983): 5-10.

Wildavsky, Aaron. *The Politics of the Budgetary Process*. Boston, Mass.: Little Brown, 1984.

_____. *The New Politic of the Budgetary Process*. 2nd ed. New York: Harper Collins, 1992.

Wold, Geoffrey H. "The System Selection Process." *Government Finance Review*, 9, no. 3 (June 1993): 25-28.

Ziebell, Mary T. *Management Control Systems in Non-Profit Organizations*. San Diego, Calif.: Harcourt Brace Jovanovich, 1991.

Index

About the Author

JEROME B. McKINNEY is Professor of Public Management and Policy at the University of Pittsburgh.